'A most welcome revision and updating
– **Anna Clark**, *University of Minnesota*

'An excellent and comprehensive revision
become again a leading *tour de force* in t.   .... ~~~ ᴍorgan, *University of Chichester*

Sexual attitudes and behaviour have changed radically in Britain between the Victorian era and the twenty-first century. However, Lesley A. Hall reveals how slow and halting the processes of change have been, and how many continuities have persisted under a façade of modernity.

Thoroughly revised, updated and expanded, the second edition of this established text:

- explores a wide range of relevant topics including marriage, homosexuality, commercial sex, media representations, censorship, sexually transmitted diseases and sex education
- features an entirely new last chapter which brings the narrative right up to the present day
- provides fresh insights by bringing together further original research and recent scholarship in the area.

Lively and authoritative, this is an essential volume for anyone studying the history of sexual culture in Britain during a period of rapid social change.

Lesley A. Hall is Senior Archivist at the Wellcome Library, London, and Honorary Lecturer in History of Medicine at University College London. She has published extensively on issues of gender and sexuality and maintains a website at www.lesleyahall.net.

Gender and History

Series editors: Amanda Capern and Louella McCarthy

Published

Gender and History Series
Series Standing Order ISBN 978–14039–9374–8 hardback
ISBN 978–14039–9375–5 paperback
(*outside North America only*)

You can receive future titles in this series as they are published by placing a standing order. Please contact your bookseller or, in case of difficulty, write to us at the address below with your name and address, the title of the series and one of the ISBNs quoted above.

Customer Services Department, Macmillan Distribution Ltd
Houndmills, Basingstoke, Hampshire RG21 6XS, England

Sex, Gender and Social Change in Britain since 1880

Second Edition

Lesley A. Hall

First edition published 2000
Second edition published 2013 by
PALGRAVE MACMILLAN

Palgrave Macmillan in the UK is an imprint of Macmillan Publishers Limited, registered in England, company number 785998, of Houndmills, Basingstoke, Hampshire RG21 6XS.

Palgrave Macmillan in the US is a division of St Martin's Press LLC, 175 Fifth Avenue, New York, NY 10010.

Palgrave Macmillan is the global academic imprint of the above companies and has companies and representatives throughout the world.

Palgrave® and Macmillan® are registered trademarks in the United States, the United Kingdom, Europe and other countries.

ISBN: 978–0–230–29780–7 hardback
ISBN: 978–0–230–29781–4 paperback

This book is printed on paper suitable for recycling and made from fully managed and sustained forest sources. Logging, pulping and manufacturing processes are expected to conform to the environmental regulations of the country of origin.

A catalogue record for this book is available from the British Library.

A catalog record for this book is available from the Library of Congress.

10 9 8 7 6 5 4 3 2 1
22 21 20 19 18 17 16 15 14 13

Printed and bound in China

This is once more for Ray McNamee, who, yet again, has had to endure a state of more than usual domestic chaos during the writing of this book, which he has borne with a truly remarkable degree of equanimity.

Praise for the book when it was first published:

'A super text which draws together a number of themes previously neglected – a good addition to any social history course.' – **Yvonne Brown**, *Glasgow Caledonian University*

'...one of a few rare books which can be enjoyed by the general reader, used as an undergraduate text, offer fresh insights to social historians and indicate further lines of enquiry for future researchers...This is history written with transparent warmth and humanity – it will undoubtedly give pleasure to all who are fortunate enough to read it.' – **Paula Bartley**, *Reviews in History*

'Hall's credentials for marshalling great quantities of information on her topic are impeccable.' – *Times Literary Supplement*

'This is an excellent book; superbly well informed but not weighted down with detail...It is also lively and entertaining.' – **Chris Nottingham**, *Glasgow Caledonian University*

'Wide-ranging and accurate coverage of complex and sensitive issues regarding sexuality, gender and social change.' – **Melinda Barone**, *University College Salford*

'There are few better people better placed to give an overview of the histories of sexuality since the late nineteenth century than Lesley Hall. As a senior medical archivist at the Wellcome Trust Library and author, she has been at the forefront of new historical work on sexuality over the last ten years. The value of this book is that it displays the breadth of recent historical research into fields of enquiry that can still sometimes seem almost impossible to illuminate. *Sex, Gender and Social Change since 1880* demonstrates an accumulation of knowledge of British sexuality that would have amazed an observer only a decade ago.' – **Sam Pryke**, *Sexualities*

'...*Sex, Gender and Social Change in Britain since 1880* is an ideal textbook for students. It offers the best overview of the development of sexuality in twentieth-century Britain, and promises to become essential reading for anyone interested in the topic, or to anyone hoping to teach a course on the topic. There is enough primary material to make important contributions to the field of the history of sexuality, and the synthesis of previous historical writing, which was long overdue, is both thought-provoking and convincing.' – **Ivan Dalley Crozier**, *Journal of the History of Sexuality*

'This is an excellent overview which fills a gap in the market.' – **C. Collette**, *Edge Hill University College*

Contents

Acknowledgements

As always, I am exceedingly grateful to my colleagues at the Wellcome Library (and to the shade of Sir Henry Wellcome). My particular thanks are due to Melanie Brocklehurst and Louise Stemp of the Information Service for dealing with numerous interlibrary loan requests, to the Reader Services team, and to Simon Jones and all in Library Services for photocopying and production of books and archives (1998) and to Ed Bishop and Rebecca Parrott for servicing my plethora of ILL requests in 2011.

For the opportunity to pursue research in North America, useful in writing this book although this was not its main purpose, I should like to thank my employers, the Wellcome Trust, for periods of research leave and travel support; the Harry Ransom Humanities Research Center, University of Texas at Austin, which provided me in 1992 with a short-term research fellowship to undertake research in their wonderful collections; and to the British Academy for a Small Research Grant in 1996.

I am truly privileged to be part of a wider community of scholars working in this area, without whom this book would never have come into existence. For published works and access to work in progress, conference and seminar papers, personal communications in the flesh and via the Internet, friendship and inspiration, I should like to express my deep appreciation in particular to Peter Bartlett, Paula Bartley, Virginia Berridge, Lucy Bland (for far more than the cuttings about herpes and cervical cancer in the 1980s), Sean Brady, Barbara Brookes, Anne Caron-Delion, Hera Cook, Matt Cook, Heather Creaton, Ivan Crozier, Roger Davidson, Gayle Davis, Shani d'Cruze, Joanne de Groot, Laura Doan, Ralf Dose, David Doughan, Carol Dyhouse, Kate Fisher, Ginger Frost, Antony Grey, Daniel Grey, Jenny Haynes, Katherine Holden, Matt Houlbrook, Louise Jackson, Emma Jones, Julia Laite, Philippa Levine, Angus McLaren, Lara Marks, Sue Morgan, Frank Mort, Chris Nottingham, Alison Oram, Naomi Pfeffer, Dorothy Porter (after all this time the 'pox-box' is still being useful!), Sam Pryke, George Robb, Katharine Rogers, Gail Savage, Chandak Sengoopta, Lisa Z. Sigel, Carol Smart, the late Richard Soloway, Liz Stanley, Julie-Marie Strange, Lutz Sauerteig, Penny Summerfield, Anne Summers, Simon Szreter, Mary Thomas, Martha Vicinus, Chris Waters, Jeff Weeks, Susan Williams: a list by no means exhaustive.

While I was able to do much of the necessary reading and research for this book at the Wellcome, I also used material in the Fawcett Library at London Guildhall University (now the Women's Library, London Metropolitan University); the Tom Harrisson-Mass Observation archives at the University of Sussex (material copyright the Trustees of the Mass Observation Archives at the University of Sussex, reproduced by permission of Curtis Brown Group Ltd, London); the British Library Department of Manuscripts; Sheffield

City Archives; the Modern Records Centre, King's College Cambridge; the Bodleian Library; the archives of the Royal College of Obstetricians and Gynaecologists; the archives department of the Library of the London School of Economics; The National Archives; the International Institute for Social History, Amsterdam; the Harry Ransom Humanities Research Center, University of Texas at Austin; the Library of Congress, Washington DC; the Sophia Smith Collection at Smith College; the Ready Division of Archives and Research Collections, Mills Memorial Library, McMaster University, Hamilton, Ontario; the Manuscripts Department, Woodson Research Centre, Fondren Library, Rice University, Houston, Texas; the Countway Library, Boston; and the Rare Books and Manuscripts Department, Fisher Library, University of Sydney; the Centre for Crime and Justice Studies, Kings College London; the Modern Records Centre, University of Warwick; and Cambridge University Library. To all the librarians, archivists and curators of these collections I extend very hearty thanks. I would also like to record my gratitude to the members of the two classes I taught on the themes of this book: the University of North Carolina Honors Program in London, autumn 1997, and the participants in the Masters course in Medicine, Science and Society, Birkbeck College, University of London, spring term 1998. I am also grateful to members of the Critsex listserv, in particular Jad Adams, Catherine Aicken, Eric Anderson, Y. Gavriel Ansara, Clare Bale, Mark Carrigan, Brian Dempsey, Makeda Gerressu, Clare Hemmings, Sharron Hinchliff, Jennie Kermode, Amy M. Russell, Margaret Simmonds, although constraints of space meant that I have not been able to follow up all their valuable suggestions in detail.

I am particularly grateful to my editor at Palgrave Macmillan, Sonya Barker, for suggesting this new edition and being so accommodating over its expansion beyond the original imaginings; also the Gender and History series editors, Amanda Capern and Louella McCarthy, and the anonymous readers of my initial draft.

As always, I have been sustained by the companionship of Ray McNamee while working on both editions.

Introduction

Then and now

Historians of the nineteenth century have perceived a definite change in sexual attitudes, and in ways of talking about and dealing with sexual issues, around 1880, the beginnings of certain 'modern' ways of thinking about sex. Michael Mason has suggested that much early twentieth-century reaction against Victorianism was aimed specifically at those decades, during which leading anti-Victorians had grown up, while Simon Szreter has made a persuasive case for the persistence of a 'long Victorian era' in Britain, which only dissolved in the 1960s, rather than at the death of the Queen in 1901.[1]

The period since 1880 has seen apparently enormous changes in sexual attitudes, behaviour, and gender relations, and indeed in society as a whole. Sex and reproduction have become separated: not only does effective contraception mean that intercourse need have no reproductive consequences, but conception can now occur without intercourse. The legal, social, and economic status of women has changed in ways which would astound late Victorian campaigners for women's rights to education, employment, the ownership of property, and involvement in the political process. No longer is heterosexual marriage the only acceptable form of sexual relationship with all others stigmatized and marginalized. Family structure and size have undergone considerable mutation. Marriages were then terminated (except in a very small proportion of cases) only by death or desertion, sometimes followed by remarriage, in the first case, or bigamy, in the second. Now there may be one or more sequential unions, either remarriage or cohabitation, and the maintenance of amicable relationships with former spouses.[2]

However, continuities remain. For a few decades in the mid-twentieth century, it seemed that the centuries-old fear of lethal or debilitating sexually transmitted diseases had been lifted by the advances of science: a halcyon era ended chiefly with the advent of AIDS/HIV in the early 1980s, but also by a recognition of the spread of a number of other unpleasant, though less fatal, conditions. Convictions for rape remain at a depressingly low rate and the mindset of victim culpability persists, with preventive campaigns geared towards modifying female, rather than male, behaviour. While the penitential regimes and social exclusion awaiting the Victorian fallen woman no longer exist, a woman's sexual reputation is still something about which she can seldom be as cavalier as a man – imputations of promiscuity can still harm – while single mothers remain a stigmatized group. Homophobia is far from extinct.

While the number of single-person households continues to rise, still the majority of people live in some kind of familial situation, or have done for at least part of their lives. The meaning of 'family values' in an era of divorce, cohabitation, reformation of couples in sequentially monogamous relationships, and the increasing establishment of gay households with children, may be very different to what it was a hundred or even fifty years ago, yet the family remains not only a potent icon but a very real presence and continues to be invoked by politicians. Sexual scandal can still adversely affect the careers of those in public life – in fact, given the aggressiveness of the press in pursuing such cases, not to mention the extent to which news can proliferate via the internet in the twenty-first century, this may be even more of a problem than it was in an age when influence could keep scandals at bay, even when transgressive behaviour was an open secret among those in the know. Changes are not the same as triumphant progression towards sexual liberation.

Uncovering the past

How can we ascertain what a complex society like Britain thought and felt, and did, about sex from the nineteenth to the beginning of the twenty-first century? What meanings did it assign to particular phenomena: what phenomena, indeed, were defined as falling within the realm of the sexual? We can look at the laws which overtly regulated a range of behaviours, and the ways these actually operated in practice.

Medicine had an increasing say on the relationship between sexuality and health: however, unlike the law, most medical practice takes place in the private and confidential space of the doctor's surgery or consulting room, and what goes on there can be hard to recover. While doctors might have been considered to be appropriate authorities on sexuality, for much of the period under discussion, it was regarded as a subject on which they should communicate only to other doctors rather than to the general public. Courts, however, are open to the public (though, when dealing with cases of 'immorality', they might be cleared) and their proceedings were and are reported in the media.

New specialisms in the twentieth century – psychology, sociology, pedagogy – claimed intellectual rights over this area. Religious and moral ideologies – not always clearly distinguished from issues of health and hygiene – have been expressed in advice on conduct in a range of forms, from sermons to the 'agony pages' in women's magazines. From the later nineteenth century, an eclectic science of sexology, drawing on a variety of other disciplines, laid claims to rational investigation of the complex phenomena of sexuality. From the 1930s, there were attempts to use social survey methods to enquire into people's attitudes and beliefs about sex, and even their behaviour, though early investigators were aware of the problems: how truthful would respondents be on such a touchy subject – indeed, would they respond at all? – and several encountered the belief that there was a 'correct' answer to the questions. The media has played an increasingly important role in generating and disseminating sexual discourse, with the increase of literacy, the rise of new forms such as film and television, and new technologies of creation and distribution.

The relation between regulatory codes, societal beliefs more generally, and practice is by no means simple: because certain acts or relationships were tabooed does not mean that they did not occur – proscription or deprecation indicates that a possibility, if no more, might exist. What does appear from historical analysis is some degree of fit – by no means absolute – between a society's ideologies about sex and behaviour. For example, a taboo on sexual intercourse outside marriage may lead to a relatively low, but seldom non-existent, illegitimacy rate. Male same-sex activities may be the subject of stringent legal penalties, but since these were actually enforced, some men must have been engaging in such practices. The pressures against forbidden activities may not entirely prevent them, but may lead to extreme means of concealment (e.g. infanticide of illegitimate children) or internalization of guilt (as in the case of masturbation, pervasively condemned as a menace to health and morality throughout the nineteenth and early twentieth centuries, although the practise was almost universal among men).

The polyphony of ideas

As Michel Foucault famously wrote in *The History of Sexuality*, sexuality is constituted by discourse:[3] however, at any given moment in history several discourses may be operating at both the social and the individual level. 'Orthodox' discourses, such as religion, law, and medicine, were not internally monolithic nor always in agreement among themselves. In Victorian England sex outside marriage was a sin and chastity part of a Christian life, and the middle-class male was defined by his ability to control his baser urges; but it was also widely believed that it was unhealthy for a mature man to go without sex, which could lead to conflicts and compromises in both behaviour and social arrangements. In the early to mid-twentieth century, British law defined the homosexual as a criminal, while medical and psychological opinion considered homosexuality a disorder. Within the medical model, there were further differences of opinion: homosexuality might be seen as an inborn defect analogous to colour-blindness about which nothing could be done, or amenable to the latest developments of science. Thus there are always several discourses in play, contradicting or undermining one another. Not only is 'discourse' not monolithic, discourses are not impermeable sets of ideas with distinct boundaries.

People (and indeed societies) are capable of simultaneously holding ideas inconsistent with one another: a prime example of this would be the belief that women were by nature maternal and destined for monogamous marriage, alongside fears that given the slightest encouragement – education, employment opportunities, the granting of political rights, the accessibility of birth control – they would immediately renege on their duty to marry and keep the world populated. Similarly, homosexuality has been conceived of as unnatural, disgusting, and horrible, and yet one experience in adolescence, or even maturity, was supposed to be seductive enough to 'corrupt' a male. Most examples are not so extreme, but this lack of consistency is (perhaps) particularly strong in the area of ideas about sex, since these are less likely than other ideas to be consciously analysed and interrogated.

Entering the Twilight Zone

Although the creation of knowledge has been studied for many years, agnotology, dealing with the creation of ignorance, has only just begun to be explored. It may involve deliberate obsfuscation by interested parties with an agenda of deception, but can also be the product of the inability to see various things and their connections at particular historical moments, or even a refusal of knowledge.[4] Recent oral history work by Kate Fisher and Simon Szreter has demonstrated that the demands of female sexual respectability in the early twentieth century required avoidance of knowledge of sexual matters before marriage, a mindset which continued after marriage and affected, for example, women's attitudes towards birth control.[5] This concept clearly has interesting implications for thinking about sexuality in the past.

There is much that cannot be retrieved about sexual lives in the past, but this area is not so blank as might be imagined. Some of the kinds of texts generated by the orthodox authorities – evidence given in court, case histories presented to doctors – contain embedded accounts or hints of other ways of looking at things. Courts of law sat on, and medical journals reported, cases of sexual assault on children in the belief that this would cure venereal diseases. This was also mentioned in evidence to government commissions, as was the belief among prostitutes that when they got old and sick and went into hospital, they would be smothered.[6] Private communications between individuals may speak of matters deemed inappropriate for public discussion. Letters to birth-control pioneer Marie Stopes mentioned the belief that, by government edict, there was always one dud in a box of contraceptives (conflating the perceived unreliability of these products with establishment pronatalism),[7] and also the very widespread idea that it was not illegal to terminate pregnancy in its early stages.[8] The pronouncements of figures representing the establishment, judges, doctors, and politicians, illuminate their own unexamined beliefs about class, gender, and sexuality, including such mythologies as the enormous prevalence of false accusations of rape and designing girls preying on innocent upper-class youths, and that only a doctor could possibly ask women about birth-control practices.

There has been a strong tradition of discretion – or nervous evasiveness – about sex in Britain. Governments have been persistently reluctant to venture too far in statutory regulation of this area, drawing a definite (if in practice sometimes fuzzy) line between private conduct and public manifestations. Thus, prostitution is not illegal, but there have been continuing measures to keep it out of the public eye, from the routine policing of street soliciting, to concerns about the proliferation of 'tartcards' in phone boxes advertising sexual services. The general legislative story has been one of delaying action, in spite of significant instances of governments being pushed into hasty and often ill-drafted legislative action by specific immediate pressures. This has been almost inevitably in the direction of punishing or controlling sexual problems (and usually punishing and controlling the bodies of groups, such as prostitutes, perceived as embodying these problems), never of the liberalization of laws known to be causing suffering to large numbers.

In fact, once a law, any law, has been passed it can take decades to change it, even in the face of persistent demands. Time after time concerns were expressed over, for example, divorce, venereal diseases, obscenity, abortion, to which governments responded by the appointment of an official investigatory body, thus demonstrating recognition of the seriousness of the issue, while relieving them of the need for immediate action that was likely to prove politically contentious. An alternative strategy was to handle the issue through administrative extension of existing legislation. Private Members of Parliament were always at liberty to introduce reforming measures, though the fate of these, lacking government support, was hazardous.[9] Although official attitudes at the top level may have been hands-off, a good deal of policing of moral behaviour went on at local levels, however, by agencies of central and local government, and by voluntary bodies, often in alliance with local authorities or police forces.

Anna Clark has recently adumbrated the useful concept of 'twilight moments' as a way to discuss 'those sexual activities or desires which people are not supposed to engage in, but they do.... acts which people committed, or desires they felt, which could be temporary; they returned to their everyday lives, and evaded a stigmatized identity as deviant'. All sorts of acts might occur at such moments but never be openly acknowledged or named.[10] This formulation could apply across a range of activities ranging from the merely shameful (the married man buying condoms from a distant shop) to the deeply illegal (homosexual activities). Lost in this twilight are the many couples throughout the period who, legally unable to marry, nevertheless presented themselves as married, and the children whose illegitimacy was concealed through familial stratagems such as pretending that their mother was their sister or their aunt.[11] This concept has interesting resonances with what David Nash and Anne-Marie Kilday have argued was an enduring culture of shame and shaming practices.[12]

'Twilight moments' can also describe the ways in which sexual activities were controlled and regulated, in subtle and not always articulated ways. A wide-ranging system for the provision of free, voluntary, and confidential treatment of venereal diseases (which might well have proved controversial) was introduced in 1917 via the extension of existing powers of public health administration rather than being contested in Parliamentary debates.[13] Policing of prostitution under the solicitation laws technically required the woman to have been behaving riotously and indecently, or soliciting to the annoyance of the public: however, contemporary observers and historians have pointed out that once a woman had been designated as a 'common prostitute', actual annoyance or indecent behaviour was seldom involved: she could be arrested for being in a public place even when not seeking business.[14] Sean Brady has drawn attention to Home Office secrecy in the late nineteenth century over establishing sentencing policies for cases involving sex between men or men and boys,[15] and Alan Travis has revealed its secret blacklist of banned books and magazines of the 1950s.[16] A number of studies have adumbrated complex relationships between governmental authorities (national and local) and voluntary organizations over issues to do with sexuality: Pamela Cox has illuminated the labyrinthine networks of public and private bodies dealing with 'delinquent girls' in the early twentieth century.[17] All of these were about keeping sexual matters and their surveillance and control in the realm of the hidden or the inexplicit.

David Vincent, in *The Culture of Secrecy, Britain 1832–1998*, dealt mainly with government secrecy and concealment, but also touched on how this reflected wider cultural attitudes about rights to privacy and accepted class-based codes of conduct. He pointed out the different strategies deployed towards the 'civilized' and 'the great unwashed'. Both public and voluntary initiatives in the later nineteenth century increased surveillance of the urban poor, and the lesser right of the lower classes to personal privacy has been a persisting theme. Their private lives have been more likely to have a public dimension, as they sought charitable aid or state assistance, often administered according to concepts of 'the deserving poor' who conformed to middle-class defined standards of respectability.[18]

Sexual transgressions were much more visible at the lower social end of their much wider spectrum: as the traditional song, 'She Was Poor But She Was Honest' argued, 'It's the rich wot gets the pleasure, it's the poor wot gets the blame.'[19] Emma Jones has demonstrated that via court cases and newspaper reports, it is possible to discover a good deal about the practice of illegal 'back-street' abortion and the mechanisms by which individuals located practitioners, but it remains less easy to reconstruct the discreet world of the 'Harley Street' abortionist and his clientele.[20] Recent local studies of prostitution provide us with a nuanced picture of the lives of women who became street prostitutes,[21] but there were other forms of sex work less readily reconstructed. The 1916 survey *Downward Paths* pointed out that it was far less easy to research the more discreet manifestations.[22] While clear connections between street prostitution, poverty, and expedients for survival can be made, there was a whole range of other possibilities between that and the highest class of renowned courtesans, such as 'Skittles' (Catherine Walters) and Laura Bell, who mingled with the social elite and now grace the pages of the *Oxford Dictionary of National Biography*.

It is thus not surprising that most early British surveys relating to sexual activities focused on the working classes: the Royal College of Obstetricians and Gynaecologists 1940s' survey into birth control use for the Royal Commission on Population drew its sample from patients in publicly funded or voluntary hospitals, not private nursing homes, and Eliot Slater and Moya Woodside's almost contemporary *Patterns of Marriage* was confined to the urban working class, although the Mass Observation 'Little Kinsey' was an exception, both questioning a wide range of members of the general population and seeking information from its largely middle-class 'Panel'.[23] Breaching sexual secrecy, however, also had repercussions for the upper and ruling classes. Once codes of confidentiality and discretion had been violated, they were not exempt: if their marriages reached the stage of the divorce court, their matrimonial difficulties were extensively rehearsed in the press. Sexual scandals about the eminent, famous, and wealthy continue to flourish.[24]

Official ideas about secrecy drew strength from assumptions about what was and was not acceptable to the public, and also, perhaps, a reluctance to consider that the public's opinions might differ. Cases of obscenity tried before magistrates showed rather different results to those tried before juries, as in the famous 1960 case of Penguin Books for publishing D. H. Lawrence's *Lady Chatterley's Lover*. Governments and establishment bodies have been nervous about undertaking surveys into the sexual habits of the nation, but Mass Observation in 1949 was agreeably startled at the almost unanimously positive public response to its 'Little Kinsey' investigation. It has been suggested that Margaret Thatcher's alleged personal intervention to forbid governmental funding for a survey of sexual attitudes and behaviour in Britain came from fear that it might disclose how great the mismatch was between the 'family values' promoted by her government, and the actual conduct of the governed.

Slicing up the story

There are a number of ways in which the story of sex, gender and social change during this period could be presented. It could be sliced thematically (marriage, reproductive questions, sexually transmitted diseases, same-sex relations, censorship, etc.), but all these issues were strongly intertwined, or had mutual repercussions, and to discuss them in isolation down plays important connections, as well as presenting perhaps rather too coherent narratives – many of these stories were stop-start affairs, incidents emerging out of silence or obscurity and followed once more by silence. Traditional periodizations, such as from the death of Victoria to the Great War, the War, the interwar period, the Second World War, tend to overemphasize monarchs' reigns and situate war as a major source of disruption and agent of change when it often brought into prominence and visibility themes already present, and even halted processes of change. The period is therefore divided up by decades, an artificial arrangement which, nonetheless, enables the juxtaposition of contemporaneous phenomena and the indication of the ebb and flow of the importance given to particular elements in the complexity of British sexual culture. It also reveals the constant interplay of 'reactionary', 'progressive', and apathetic forces in the creation of policy and the dissemination of knowledge.

The particular areas discussed are: marriage, divorce, and heterosexual relations more generally; the changing status of women; birth control, abortion, and other reproductive issues; prostitution and the sex-trade; same-sex relations; censorship and perceptions of obscenity; sexually transmitted diseases; state of sexual knowledge and sexual ignorance; and ways in which sex was analysed and understood with the rise of new intellectual disciplines. Attention is given to the role of pressure-groups. Sexual violence and abuse is also touched on. Where it is possible to do so, mention is made of changes in ideas about manhood and masculinity: 'being a man' was always a precarious endeavour and fraught with complications. What is beginning to emerge is the extent to which large numbers of men behaved decently and responsibly, whether this was in providing support for women to whom they were not married and their offspring, or taking contraceptive precautions within marriage.

Much of the material in this study is implicitly or explicitly about England, and many of the concerns discussed had a specifically metropolitan bias (London being seen as the place where 'vice' particularly flourished, as well as the base of many investigators). Because the history of sexual attitudes and behaviour is still a relatively new and somewhat controversial area, there tends to be a lack of locally based studies, although this is beginning to change. Roger Davidson's work on the control of venereal diseases in Scotland has indicated the extent to which not merely the different legal system, but specifically Scottish moral and civic traditions put a decisively variant twist on the 'English system' implemented in 1917.[25] His more recent work with Gayle Davis on wider issues of the governance of sexuality in late twentieth-century Scotland illuminates these issues still further.[26] Kate Fisher's work on attitudes around reproduction and birth control in Wales suggests community values contrary to the models birth-control campaigners tended to promote;[27] her more recent joint work with Simon Szreter is a valuable analysis of oral history testimonies from communities in the north and south of England.[28] Russell Davies has also considered sexuality in the Welsh context, specifically Carmarthenshire, in *Secret Sins*, while a number of articles have looked at the introduction of birth control clinics into several Welsh areas.[29] Jeffrey Weeks, considering *The World We Have Won* in 2007, locates his wider narrative against his own background in the Rhondda at a specific historical moment.[30] In Ireland before independence, attitudes towards sexuality (strongly influenced by religion) played an important part in defining national identity, an argument borne out by Maria Luddy's recent important work on prostitution in Ireland and Diarmaid Ferriter's study of sex and society in modern Ireland, which also demonstrate how this continued after the establishment of the Republic. Leanne McCormick illuminates the related, yet also distinctive, pressures in play in Northern Ireland.[31] Even within England itself considerable variations by region, occupation, and class were reflected in differing demographic patterns.[32] So far, work on homosexuality has tended to concentrate on London, although Harry Cocks has illuminated the Bolton Whitmanite circle of the late nineteenth century and Sheila Rowbotham's magisterial biography of Edward Carpenter indicates his provincial networks. Work on Manchester's subcultures of men having sex with men is in progress.[33]

Historiographical developments

Scholarship has proliferated since the first edition of *Sex, Gender and Social Change in 1880*. While Jeff Weeks's *Sex, Politics and Society* (1981) remains an important pioneering text,[34] numerous studies since then, and since 1999, have illuminated the field or provided nuance to his arguments. Even so, a great deal of work still remains to be done and there are significant gaps in our knowledge and understanding. There has been outstanding work on cultures of male homosexuality, although this has been, as already mentioned, predominantly London-centred.[35] Exciting work on female same-sex relationships has emerged in spite of the difficulty of researching these hidden histories.[36] Outstanding studies on marital sexuality and questions about reproduction and its control have appeared.[37] New work on prostitution is both closely analysing policy debates on regulation and looking beyond them to consider routine police management, the role of rescue organizations, and the ways in which women sex workers were agents rather than victims.[38] Foundational and nuanced work on the role of the popular press in making sexual knowledge and creating understandings of gender has appeared.[39]

An increasing amount of work is being done on the role of race and ethnicity and the Empire in the creation of national sexual identities and attitudes: much of this has specifically addressed the colonial and imperial context, although there were implications for the home country and notions of appropriate British sexuality as avoiding, on the one hand, the promiscuous brutality of the primitive and, on the other, the sensual excess of the decadent and over-refined. Particularly following the Second World War and mass immigration from the 'New Commonwealth', Britain has become a multicultural society: some of the complex issues around the role of race, gender, and sexuality in constructing new ideas of nationhood in the postwar era are addressed in Wendy Webster's *Imagining Home*.[40]

Recent work has manifested a 'spatial turn', looking at specific sites of sexual interaction, their definition, their usage, and their contestation, whether this was the 'monkey-walk' of adolescents in Northern cities, nude displays in the Windmill Theatre on the boundary between Soho and the West End of the legitimate theatre, 'cottaging' by men in public urinals, or, indeed, the juxtaposition of serious sexological studies and frankly pornographic works in the stockrooms and catalogues of mail-order booksellers.[41] The significance of religion and spirituality in changing attitudes around sexuality is beginning to be investigated and to demonstrate their so far rather undervalued importance. A number of studies suggest that class and economic status remain a useful category of analysis and interpretation.

Constraints of space continue, as they did in the first edition, to operate as to how much detail could have been gone into and how deeply certain areas could have been covered.

1
The Victorian Background

Defining the Victorians

'The Victorians' and their sex lives remain endlessly fascinating in the popular mind. Several memorable but erroneous ideas are constantly recirculated by journalists and the media.[1] In spite of numerous scholarly works deconstructing any idea of a monolithic Victorian morality, there is a continuing stereotypical picture of the Victorians as sexually repressed hypocrites; while every few years for the past forty or so somebody publishes a popular book promising to overturn all these received ideas about the Victorians (usually by focusing on particular individuals, groups, or subcultures behaving in ways counter to the stereotype).[2]

The changes and developments during the final decades of Victoria's reign, continuing into the new century, were the outcome of trends and possibilities already present. On the other hand, many 'Victorian values' persisted well into the twentieth century: a plausible case can be made for 'a long Victorian era' in Britain which did not finally dissipate until around 1960.

How far is it realistic or useful to bracket sexual attitudes and behaviour between 1837 and 1901 as having something unique and specific in common? To what extent did the several generations who lived through that era, as members of a complex culture spread widely across the globe, undergoing radical change as a result of technological and economic developments, during a period of over sixty years, have enough in common to be lumped together as they so often are? The roots of many facets of 'Victorianism' lay well back during the reaches of the long eighteenth century.

Ideas about sexuality were embedded in an intricate nexus of not always clearly articulated ideas about gender, race, and class, even as the Victorian era saw the rise of scientific analyses of race and gender and sociological investigations of the lower classes – which, however, did not necessarily represent entirely new ways of thinking rather than revised encodings of well-established prejudices. Racialized imagery pervaded perceptions of sex. On the one hand there was the notion of the primitive, the out-of-control (primarily associated with Africa), on the other the effetely decadent (tending to be associated with 'The Orient'), which were to be avoided, even while they returned as recurrent features in, for example, Victorian pornography and even high art. Complex hierarchies and categories were constructed and phenomena which might blur those boundaries perceived as highly threatening.[3]

There were significant changes in the Victorian era as well as persisting beliefs and attitudes. Significant pieces of legislation dealing with aspects of sexual conduct were passed, partly the result of attempts to tidy up and consolidate the inherited mass of criminal legislation, but also reflecting growing secularization of the regulation of moral conduct, formerly the purlieu of the church and ecclesiastical courts: in 1837, for example, civil registration of marriage was introduced.

Wholly matrimony

In 1857 a Matrimonial Causes Act made divorce more widely accessible (it also covered separations and annulments), as part of the shift of non-doctrinal jurisdiction from ecclesiastical to secular courts to simplify an entangled system of probate jurisdiction, although the intent was simply procedural, not to make divorce more widely accessible. Previously, only a small elite had been able to pursue the complicated and expensive private Parliamentary divorce, which required the plaintiff first to obtain an ecclesiastical separation and fight a successful civil case ('crim. con.': 'criminal conversation') for damages against his wife's seducer. A Divorce Court was established in London. The law enshrined an adversarial process between guilty and innocent parties, with the innocent rewarded with a decree. Two equally guilty spouses, or an innocent party who had condoned their partner's transgression (e.g. George Henry Lewes, the consort of the novelist George Eliot) or colluded with them to dissolve the union, were to be punished by making them stay together.

Ideas about the different sexual natures of men and women, and the relative weight of their respective transgressions of the moral code, were clearly inscribed into this Act. Adultery by a woman was so horrendous that a single act permitted her husband to sue for divorce. In a man, however, the offence was sufficiently trivial that even when persistent, it was not regarded as reason for a woman to terminate her marriage, unless added to cruelty, desertion, bigamy, or incest. The traditional reason given was fear of a wife introducing a spurious child into the family, whereas the man's promiscuity had no such deleterious effects.[4]

This Act, compromised though it might be, did represent a blow against the ecclesiastical doctrine of the indissolubility of marriage (Church law had permitted separation but not remarriage). It did grant some rights to women in intolerable unions. Of the 253 petitions heard in the first year of the Court's existence, 97 (well over a third) were from women. While judges and lawyers could not change the law itself, case-law – for example two cases in 1865 and 1866 establishing the knowing and reckless communication of venereal disease by the husband as cruelty – influenced its practical operation.[5] Numbers of divorces in Britain remained low by comparison with other European countries and North America: although the percentage of cases appeared to demonstrate a massive increase (100 per cent over 40 years), the absolute numbers were relatively small.[6] Gail Savage has revealed a social range of petitioners much broader than once supposed: even the extremely poor were sometimes able to obtain release from bad marriages. Press attention, however, focused on not necessarily typical cases among the upper classes or entertainment professions (the relatively advantaged financial status of women in these groups enabled them to initiate cases, a recourse less available to most women).[7] Olive Anderson has drawn attention to the continuing significance of private contracts of separation enabling couples to live apart amicably, but this solution did not permit remarriage.[8] Although technically divorce was easier to obtain in Scotland and the law more egalitarian, social disapproval (and possibly expense) kept numbers low.[9]

It was a very limited concession to the rights of women, however. A more or less simultaneous attempt to pass a Married Women's Property Bill failed, although the Divorce Act gave divorced and judicially separated women the status 'feme sole', able to own property and make contracts. Under common law, a married woman's independent identity was totally subsumed in that of her husband's under the doctrine of 'coverture'. She was unable to enter into legal contracts and had no rights in her own property, all she had (earned or inherited) being deemed to belong to her husband. This was not merely degrading, but actively oppressive and hurtful to women's interests, as in the cases of men who kept mistresses on, or drank away, or gambled their wives' earnings. An alternative system, equity, regulated through the Court of Chancery, enabled the trust settlement of property on a woman, protecting it from her husband's common-law rights, but did not usually grant full rights (e.g. she could not usually alienate it). This option was only open to the privileged property-owning elite.

An inadequate Married Women's Property Act was passed in 1870 after several years of active campaigning. Parliament conceded the righteousness of preventing the exploitation of working-class women, but qualms about any wholesale alteration of the economic relations of husband and wife produced a 'legislative abortion' with a dangerous lack of clarity, inconsistencies, and unnecessary complications, although it did guarantee to women income earned in occupations carried on separately from their husbands. The Act also made women liable for support of their husbands and children, which, given their disadvantageous position, was invidious. But it did grant, in however restricted a way, the principle that in certain circumstances, married women could and should have ownership and control over their property.[10]

Women were not even entitled to the custody of their own children born in wedlock (ironically, unmarried mothers were more favourably placed, though at the cost of serious restrictions on suing for affiliation orders under the bastardy clauses of the New Poor Law of 1834[11]). The father was regarded as the 'natural' guardian of his children whatever his faults, without even right of maternal access. A Custody of Infants Act had been passed in 1839 following the notorious case of Caroline Norton, a writer well-connected with influential political and literary circles, whose brutal husband removed and concealed her children. The Act permitted a mother to petition in the equity courts for custody of her children up to the age of seven and access to older ones. She had, however, to be wealthy enough to undertake a Chancery action, innocent of sexual misconduct, and legally separated: serious limitations. The 1857 Divorce Act gave some leeway to the judge's discretion in awarding custody, even to a guilty spouse, but again divorce was only available to a relatively limited group of women. A further Infant Custody Act in 1873 allowed mothers in exceptional circumstances to petition for custody of or access to children under the age of 16 rather than seven, and permitted husbands to relinquish custody of their children as part of the terms of separation. It also removed the absolute bar to custody of a wife's sexual misconduct. However, it failed to recognize equal parental rights, thus disappointing feminist supporters.[12]

There was considerable concern about male violence within marriage. Official investigations and some MPs advocated flogging as a punishment for domestic brutality and other crimes of violence. Legislation passed in 1878, however, concentrated not on punishing the miscreant but helping his victim. Largely at the instigation of Victorian feminist Frances Power Cobbe, who in that year published an influential essay, 'Wife-torture in England', the Matrimonial Causes Act enabled brutalized wives to obtain a Protection Order with the force of a judicial separation in the Magistrates' Court, to receive custody of their children, and to be awarded maintenance. This did not constitute divorce and the woman could not remarry. Like much other Victorian legislation affecting women, it was aimed largely at the working-class woman, perceived as a deserving victim, and protecting her from the wrong kind of man. In practice, magistrates might give credence to husbands' promises of reform and refuse the order. But this law did overturn the notion that husbands were permitted physical chastisement of their wives.[13] Gail Savage has recently demonstrated that, although rape within marriage was not considered a crime (a belief founded in common law rather than statute and occasionally the subject of judicial debate[14]), judges in the matrimonial court often took husbands' abusive sexual behaviour into consideration in cases of divorce or separation, and such behaviour could constitute grounds for refusal by wives to comply with orders for restitution of conjugal rights.[15] Martin Wiener suggests that these increasingly hardening attitudes of legislature and judiciary towards male domestic violence, in the context of changing paradigms of manliness, did not necessarily accrue popular support, adducing the case of George Hall, who had murdered his faithless wife. Popular feeling against the capital verdict forced the grant of a reprieve.[16] Nash and Kilday, however, in an intriguing study, argue that popular media revived older community practices of public shame both for excessively abusive husbands and for such traditional behaviours.[17]

Another matrimonial issue agitated for by the Marriage Law Reform Association, to heated opposition, was the desire to legalize marriages with a deceased wife's sister (the first bill was introduced in 1841). In many households the wife's sister took over the functions of mother to orphaned nieces and nephews and housekeeper to her widowed brother-in-law, and often, for either convenience or out of developing mutual affection, a sexual relationship resulted. As the law stood, the potential partners were within 'forbidden degrees' of kinship and could not marry as the union was technically incestuous. This apparently humane piece of legislation, likely to affect only a minority of the population, generated enormous moral panic, not only among ecclesiastics who cited Biblical authority, but also among others who felt that this might be the beginning of a slippery slope into moral anarchy, although women campaigners for matrimonial law reform pointed out that the Bill's sponsors refused to contemplate extending an equal right to marry deceased husbands' brothers.[18]

Given the deleterious position of women within wedlock, it is hardly surprising that some Victorian women not only protested verbally against the denigration of married women implicit in coverture ('a species of legal prostitution' according to feminist campaigner Josephine Butler), but rejected overt marks of marital servitude, such as wearing a wedding ring or taking the husband's surname, and chose a registry office ceremony, in which the woman was not required to promise to obey. Leading male feminist John Stuart Mill (author of *The Subjection of Women*, 1869, who, as independent MP for Westminster, supported numerous women's causes in Parliament), while he did marry his longtime companion Harriet Taylor in 1851 after her husband's death, openly renounced the rights over her granted him in law.

Some refused to enter marriage at all. Alice Vickery, one of the first women to qualify in medicine, apparently never married her consort Charles Robert Drysdale, doctor and Malthusian campaigner, while Elizabeth Wolstenholme, agitator for women's rights in many fields, initially entered an 'informal marriage' with silk manufacturer Ben Elmy, rejecting the interference of church or state in a private matter and opposing the patriarchal values inscribed in matrimony. Principle was one thing, however, and practice another. Vickery and Drysdale were always assumed to be married and their children were born abroad, obviating the need to register their births in the United Kingdom. Their medical careers (especially Vickery's) and their work in promoting contraception were both at risk from any whisper of 'immorality'. For similar reasons, Wolstenholme was under pressure from fellow feminists to regularize her union, especially once she became pregnant, and she finally submitted in 1875. Perhaps the most famous Victorian free union was that of George Eliot and G. H. Lewes, who were unable to marry: had he been able to get a divorce they presumably would have married, and she certainly acted as a benevolent stepmother to his sons.[19]

Ginger Frost has demonstrated that conscientious objectors to marriage were a distinct minority among those 'living in sin' in Victorian England. Apart from members of the unrespectable poor and criminal classes, to whom the legalities of marriage were a matter of indifference, many couples of a more respectable station were unable to marry either because one or other partner was unable to dissolve a previous union, or because they were within forbidden degrees of kinship (usually brother- and sister-in-law). Those who could afford to sometimes married abroad where the laws were more lenient, even though such marriages were not legally valid in England: others formalized the union bigamously. Frost also indicates that some men set up quasi-matrimonial menages with women of a lower class who would not have been acceptable wives for their social position.[20]

Heterosexual marriage, as the only legitimate place in which sexual activity could take place, had a large degree of privilege within Victorian society – reflected in the reluctance to make any alteration in its terms and conditions. Yet small, significant changes were being made: the shrill anti-feminist and misogynistic tone of much Victorian writing on the 'Woman Question' has to be seen in the context of altering expectations of women and their changing status.

The Woman Question

Very gradually, women (apart from those of the lower classes, who had always had to engage in paid work) were entering the economic marketplace and claiming the right to careers other than that of governess, although initially this was envisaged as only applying to women who failed to marry. That marriage did not obviate the necessity for earning money was apparent in the cases of, for example, several successful women writers who resorted to authorship in order to maintain invalid or incompetent husbands and other male relatives. A handful of women (several of whom married) engaged in the ultimately successful struggle to become doctors, Florence Nightingale and other reformers were claiming a role for nurses as skilled professionals rather than subservient handmaidens to male doctors, and women's voices were raised in the cause of sanitary reform. The Post Office, the Civil Service, and some businesses, notably the Prudential Insurance Company, began to recruit 'young ladies' to undertake routine clerical tasks. Women were also actively campaigning for rights to political representation and to improved educational opportunities, and improvements in women's status, both economically (through the Married Women's Property Acts) and as mothers of children. In 1869 the Municipal Franchise Act allowed women to vote in municipal elections on exactly the same terms as men. By 1879, 70 women had themselves been elected to Local School Boards.[21]

The vision of Victorian households as monolithically patriarchal and accruing unmarried female relatives as dependents has been subjected to critique, and Gordon and Nair's analysis of household composition in a suburb of Victorian Glasgow suggests that a significant proportion of middle-class establishments were headed by (widowed or single) women. They add further evidence to contest the idea of the Victorian (middle-class) woman as enmeshed in the private sphere, reclining on a sofa in a state of real or hysterical ill-health, arguing that the public and private were far from readily separable. The home itself was a permeable space, with sociability playing an important role, rather than a secluded haven of nuclear family privacy. Women were also advancing their rights to be heard in, and to have influence in, the public world, in some cases deploying the very doctrine of 'separate spheres' as a rhetorical tool for arguing that the values of 'women's sphere' ought to be brought to bear on the world outside the home. The ways in which women were literally active outside the home, for example in various forms of voluntary work, as well as becoming increasingly part of the urban landscape with the development of department stores and public amenities, and even engaging in business activities, are still sometimes overlooked.[22] The importance of female reputation, however, should not be underestimated. 'Respectability' remained an important asset, among the lower as well as the middle classes.

Chastity was regarded as the pre-eminent female virtue: however, the absolute dichotomy often posited between the chaste, sexless, 'good' woman and the promiscuous, sexual, 'bad' woman was rather more nuanced. Plenty of writers and authorities either implicitly or explicitly put the case for the desirability of the sexually responsive wife. The opinion of William Acton, the much-cited mid-Victorian medical authority on sex, that decent women seldom desired sexual gratification on their own account, but only submitted to please their husbands and achieve maternity was never universally accepted (and was a mere passing comment in Acton's analysis of the functions and disorders of the male). On the other hand, some historians suggest that far from being sexless, under the crinoline the Victorian female was a hot little number. While many Victorian women probably did manage to enjoy sex at least occasionally, the lack of effective contraception and the consequent frequency of (or fear of) pregnancy, the long-term effects of obstetric incompetence, the sexual fears, and probable ineptness as lovers of many Victorian middle-class males (and the brutality of males in all classes of which only the worst examples came to the attention of the courts) must have militated against any universality of sexual enjoyment.

There was something of a sliding scale between the 'good' and the 'fallen' woman: a strong case can be made for a concept of the retrievable fall. A woman who had once become the mother of an illegitimate child did not thereby lose all hope of returning to decent society, at least in the lower echelons. In some communities bearing a child might not even adversely affect chances of marriage, and society as a whole regarded the unfortunate once-fallen as a different case to the habitually promiscuous. As discussed in more detail below, women seduced under promise of marriage and subsequently jilted found courts sympathetic, as did unfortunates driven to infanticide. The Foundling Hospital specifically provided for the (first) children of unwed mothers, raped or seduced under promise of marriage, who found themselves unable to support themselves and a child.[23] Even William Acton, not usually regarded as particularly sympathetic to the plights of women, differentiated the 'young-housemaid or pretty parlour-maid' who 'with shame or horror bears a child to the butler, or the policeman, or her master's son' from 'streetwalkers and professional prostitutes', and advocated the employment of these unfortunates as wet-nurses to enable them to earn an honest living.[24] Much of the moral impetus behind the prostitute rescue movement came from a sense that many were unwilling recruits forced into the life by the severity of society towards a first slip.[25]

Victorian manhood

The Victorian male has been far less studied than the Victorian woman, but a number of recent studies have begun to explore nineteenth-century paradigms of masculinity. These were shaped not only by the basic division of gender – a man should eschew effeminacy – but by class and race. The middle-class Victorian man was supposed to be able to exercise control, not merely over others, but over himself, and to avoid falling into excess of any kind. Men were expected to have an appropriate degree of assertion and even aggression, but this was ideally to be kept in rational check (although assumptions about working-class masculinity tended to assume that they were less capable of this and thus more likely to be violent). Nash and Kilday suggest that press accounts of divorce and other aristocratic scandals drew on older shaming models as a middle-class critique of aristocratic and even royal manhood.[26]

John Tosh has depicted the rise of a domestic ideal. Marriage was already central to adult male status, but greater stress was being laid on the importance of home life for men working under increasingly alienated professional and business conditions. Tosh also suggests, however, that this ideal was in practice a source of significant tensions, and that by the 1870s the long interim between maturity and achieving a position to marry created a bachelor culture that some men were reluctant to eschew. Working-class men formed their identity around being good providers for their families and heads of households: this was, however, not only under constant threat from economic conditions but from increasing interventions by the state and voluntary bodies (such as the National Society for the Prevention of Cruelty to Children) into working-class homes and infringing upon their paternal rights.[27] 'Manliness' was an inherently unstable category.

There were still libertine subcultures with values counter to the above constructions of respectable masculinity. The Cannibal Club epitomized elite male privilege: it was 'defined by wealth, education and social standing'. The members were able to travel widely, collect, consume, and catalogue rare and expensive volumes of pornography, even indulge perverse whims for books bound in human skin. Whatever their anthropological and scientific credibility, the members were aware of the potential to fall foul of the obscenity laws despite their status, so published anonymously or under pseudonyms in limited editions. Unlike a previous generation of pornographers, they had no wider agenda of political subversion. The Club embodied the privileged white male turning his scientifically classificatory (and possibly also lustful) gaze upon women and other races.[28] At a very different level, young men who desired to be 'men about town' consumed aspirational 'sporting guides', purporting to provide insider knowledge of the urban jungle and the sexual pleasures that might be found there.[29]

Sexual crimes

In 1861 The Offences Against the Person Act incorporated various existing sexual crimes: 'Rape, Abduction and Defilement of Women', 'Bigamy', 'Attempts to Procure Abortion', 'Concealing the Birth of a Child', and 'Unnatural Offences'. Rape was defined as a felony and severely penalized, and might incur life imprisonment (though the court had discretion to impose a lower sentence). However, the actual definition of 'genuine' rape was problematic.

Alfred Swaine Taylor's *The Principles and Practice of Medical Jurisprudence*, 1865 (first edition following the 1861 Act), mentioned 'false accusation' in the second paragraph of the relevant chapter, with the anecdotal claim that 'for one real rape tried in the circuits, there were on the average twelve pretended cases!' The medical witness was advised to note various phenomena extraneous to the medical examination in order to testify to the truthfulness or otherwise of the woman's tale. Even in the case of assaults on children with actual injury, a caveat was registered about the purposeful production of such signs 'for false charges...with a view of extorting money'. As for adult women, 'it does not appear probable that intercourse could be accomplished against the consent of a healthy adult', unless the woman were drunk, drugged, unconscious or hypnotized, set upon by more than one man, or terrorized by threat or duress or possibly 'if she falls into a state of syncope or is rendered powerless by terror and exhaustion'. Taylor did counter the belief that pregnancy could not result from genuine rape.[30]

Studies based on local juridical sources relating to rape and violence against women indicate that the kinds of evidence available and the ways in which sources were generated cannot answer questions about actual incidence or policing policy. There are problems of what women identified as rape, whether it was regarded as appropriate to take it into the legal system, and where sexual violence stood in the broader spectrum of male-female brutality. Above all, conflicting interpretations of the same act were generated by men and women. Given the degree of determination and courage needed for a woman to take a case to court, it seems improbable that this would be done with spurious charges as often as Swaine Taylor and his legal colleagues assumed. There were major problems of communication in the courtroom, with a substantial misfit between women's accounts and the demands and formulas of the legal structure. Both women and their assailants were judged on the basis of adventitious indications of 'respectability' or the reverse, and this had significant implications for whose account was believed.[31] Louise Jackson has meticulously documented the extent to which even children were believed to be mendacious about sexual assaults.[32]

Another legal theatre in which women's sexual lives were foregrounded was the civil action for breach of promise, in which women could sue men for reneging on a commitment to marry. While this action was regarded with some hostility by middle-class advocates of sexual equality, it provided a degree of protection for a vulnerable subgroup of women. Ginger Frost discovered that courts and juries were usually sympathetic to women of meagre economic resources who might have been kept waiting for years (losing the opportunity for other offers), been at the expense of a trousseau, had sometimes lent or given money to their supposed fiancé, and occasionally been seduced in anticipation of marriage. Issues of respectability were certainly at stake, but having succumbed to the advances of a cad in the belief that his ultimate intentions were honourable did not inevitably compromise claims to respectability. Why women gained sympathy in this context but not in that of rape is an interesting question. It may have been because the woman was not trying to put the man in prison, but wanted compensation for deprivation of what was regarded as a woman's major asset, an appropriate marriage, and her wasted hopes. There was also a class aspect: the women who undertook these suits were mainly of a similar background and with the same value system as the men on the jury, and likely to arouse the protective and chivalrous instincts of the judge. Rape, however, was much more of a risk for lower-class women, who were less likely to share assumptions with the court.[33]

Legal and jury sympathy for pathetic disadvantaged women was also found in cases of infanticide. Very few of these ever resulted in a murder verdict, lawyers, judges, and juries equivocating with the exact terms of the relevant statute and the contested state of medical evidence, to bring in the lesser charge of concealment of pregnancy. As with the sympathy for jilted fiancées, there was a sense that these women were (largely) sad victims of irresponsible male seducers (against whom, under the 1834 Poor Law, they could not even claim affiliation orders[34]). Medical reformers, however, were inclined to view the problem as a sanitary question of preventable infant mortality and were thus hostile to this 'sentimental' attitude. Medical coroners were noticeably harsher in such cases.[35] While desperate women who murdered their illegitimate infants did receive significant leniency from the courts, men who murdered their illegitimate offspring out of fear of exposure or resentment against the mothers' demands for support were regarded with great severity by judges: issues of appropriate masculinity, that is, control of emotions, and taking responsibility, were at stake.[36]

'Unnatural' Offences

Offences against the Person included 'Unnatural Offences' (rape, along with bigamy, carnally knowing young girls, procuring defilement of young girls, forcible abduction of women, etc., not to mention murder and assaults, presumably being 'natural'). Principal was the 'abominable Crime of Buggery, committed either with Mankind or with any Animal' (described in the margin as 'Sodomy and Bestiality'). It was assumed that everyone knew what exactly this consisted of, as it was not more specifically defined. The penalty was reduced from death to imprisonment for from ten years to life. Attempts to commit buggery, or assault with intent to commit same, or 'any indecent assault upon any male person' counted as misdemeanours with a maximum sentence of ten years (it is sometimes incorrectly stated that prior to the 1885 Criminal Law Amendment Act only buggery, i.e., anal intercourse, was actually penalized).[37] Swaine Taylor, after nearly thirty closely printed pages on rape, devoted two paragraphs, less than a page, to 'Sodomy, Bestiality'. These are surprisingly coy, never actually mentioning anal intercourse, following detailed accounts of lacerations, contusions, and discharges of the female genitalia and the significance of semen traces and how to look for them. 'This crime is defined, the unnatural connection of a man with mankind or with an animal...penetration alone [i.e., emission was not necessary] is sufficient to constitute it', and further on he remarks obliquely, 'the act must be in the part where it is usually committed...if done elsewhere it is not sodomy'. Lack of consent was not an issue (a consenting partner was equally guilty) and it was possible to commit 'this offence with a woman' and the same penalties applied. He claimed that, like rape, it generated a large number of false charges for the purposes of extortion: 'frequently made by soldiers and a bad class of policemen!'[38]

There has relatively recently been a significant amount of investigation of homosexuality in Victorian Britain, moving beyond the well-known cases of Boulton and Park, the Cleveland Street affair, and Oscar Wilde. Upchurch, for example, has illuminated the ways that legal changes affected the policing of homosexuality before 1861 or 1885, uncovering the reporting of hundreds of routine cases in newspapers. 'Routine' was a particularly significant element, with a shift from exemplary punishments in occasional cases to less severe penalties applied with greater consistency, as modern policing practices developed. Upchurch, like Cocks in *Nameless Offences*, discovered that regulatory attention was less about raiding private gathering places than surveillance of encounters in public or semi-public venues such as streets and parks. Brady presents a persuasive case that the possibility of same-sex desire was perceived as dangerously destabilizing to existing paradigms of British manliness, and generated massive agnotological attempts to invisiblize it. Class dynamics were significantly imbricated in the policing and prosecution of male same-sex activity: prosecutions for 'attempted sodomy' tended to be directed up the social scale, while those for extortion and blackmail went the other way. Laws on blackmail in the United Kingdom had initially come into existence to protect well-off men from accusations of 'infamous offenses', designed to extort money.[39]

There is some evidence about the lives of individual homosexuals, largely from the upper reaches of society, and usually in a context of scandal. Even in the privacy of diaries Victorian homosexual men were usually discreet: Edward Leeves's diary covers the period of this middle-class gentleman's love affair with a trooper of the Horse Guards, who died of cholera in December 1849. The passages relating to their meetings were erased though decipherable, and three-months' worth of pages completely torn out, although Leeves movingly recorded his mourning for 'My poor boy'.[40] Among the classically educated upper classes, a rhetoric of 'Greek Love', conceptualized as an idealized manly passion between social equals, was diametrically opposed to carnal lust, at least in theory, but even this could arouse suspicions. The relationship between William Johnson (later Cory), who suddenly resigned his post as a master at Eton in 1872, and his former pupil 'Regy' Brett (Lord Esher) and his circles provides a fascinating window into a world of romantic male attachments persisting long into adult life and beyond marriage.[41] Oscar Browning, a housemaster at Eton, was dismissed in 1875 for his obvious (though, he claimed, entirely platonic) devotion to the latest in a series of good-looking favourites, combined with a philosophy of aestheticism, out of step with the increasing emphasis on athleticism in public schools (and possibly also for his friendship with the homosexual Pre-Raphaelite painter Simeon Solomon, imprisoned for sodomy in 1873). But Browning found a comfortable niche as a Fellow of King's College Cambridge.[42] There were further scandals at Eton and other public schools, where homoerotic relationships were very prevalent: a notorious case was that of Charles Vaughan, headmaster of Harrow, induced to resign in 1859 when a former pupil, John Addington Symonds, told his father about Vaughan's improper relationship with his pupils (Symonds later described Harrow as 'rotten to the core').[43]

One of the most famous mid-Victorian homosexual scandals was that of Boulton and Park, who were arrested, dressed in female clothing, outside the Strand theatre in 1870, on a charge of 'public indecency', and subsequently charged with 'conspiracy to commit buggery'. In spite of all the efforts of the police (who had been observing them for some time), the prosecution, and their (rather dubiously) expert witnesses, it proved impossible to establish that Boulton and Park were doing anything but masquerading in travesty (transvestism as a sexual perversion still waited to be defined). Morris Kaplan has shown how the case reveals a relatively developed subculture with its own argot (such as 'drag').[44]

Much less is known about female same-sex relationships in Victorian Britain. The life of Anne Lister and her copious diaries revealing her sapphic desires and activities undercuts the notion that any such relationships at the period must have been confined to effusive romantic friendships, but evidence is sparse, since sexual activity between women was not a criminal offence and thus did not generate either legal proceedings or forensic medical discussions. Chiara Beccalossi indicates that British medical discussions of female same-sex activity were rare, muted, and evasive, even when there was some awareness of continental ideas on sexual inversion. Rather than being seen as a thing in itself, it tended to be associated with other forms of female deviancy and excess, such as nymphomania, prostitution, and masturbation.[45] While lesbianism featured in Victorian pornography as one more manifestation of its pansexuality, how extensively this circulated is extremely dubious, much surviving written pornography having been produced in limited editions for a wealthy specialized market.

The intense emotional devotions between Victorian women of the middle and upper classes, for which there is evidence, were not defined as sexual in their nature: whether they may in some cases have included physical expression remains in most instances a matter of conjecture. Sharon Marcus has shed a good deal of light on to the prevalence and acceptability of intense emotions and physical appreciation between Victorian women, and the extent to which there were accepted 'female marriages' between devoted same-sex couples. The very lack of definitions and categories arguably provided a space for a range of female responses to their own sex.

Martha Vicinus has done much to illuminate this particularly twilit area. She argues that the evasions and silences around feminist Emily Faithfull's unfortunate youthful embroilment in the scandalous aristocratic Codrington divorce case of 1864 were understood, at least by the sophisticated, in a 'knowing without telling', to have involved a lesbian relationship beyond romantic friendship with the racy and adulterous older woman, Helen Codrington.[46] She has also examined a range of relationships between women, from the wealthy Anglo-American elite able to live independently in like-minded expatriate colonies in Italy and elsewhere, to Mary Benson, wife of the Archbishop of Canterbury, who do appear to have perceived their desires towards other women as erotic in nature rather than purely emotional or spiritual. Women who were increasingly able to earn their own living, or who were financially independent, set up households with other women: some of these may have been sexual partnerships rather than simple mutual convenience.[47]

Sex and disease

Perhaps the most contentious legislation concerning Victorian sexual conduct was the Contagious Diseases (CD) Acts of 1864, 1866, and 1869, addressing the overwhelming problem of venereal diseases in the Armed Forces by using police measures against prostitutes in designated port and garrison towns. Prostitution was already an issue of considerable public concern, openly debated in the leading newspapers of the day, with *The Times* itself publishing a letter from 'One more unfortunate' and resulting correspondence in 1858. It was not illegal in British law for a woman to sell sexual services and there was no system of licensing, or approved brothels, or defined red-light districts such as pertained in other European nations and parts of North America. In fact, it would seem that most prostitutes in Britain were individual, independent operators rather than brothel inmates, a lack of institutional organization rendering the profession somewhat harder to regulate. There was also a good deal of casual prostitution by women augmenting a scanty income or tiding themselves over during seasonal unemployment.

There were various angles to the concern over prostitutes, not necessarily distinct. There was a long-standing religious attitude towards the prostitute as fallen – but redeemable – sinner, manifested in Midnight Prayer Meetings, and the provision of magdalene homes and asylums for the repentant.[48] Policing measures claiming to be in the interests of public order, the presence of prostitutes on the street being deemed contrary to decency, were already in place. Prostitutes were subject to Vagrancy Acts and local by-laws making it an offence for them to create a nuisance: soliciting was defined as a nuisance, and indeed being a prostitute looking for business was quite often deemed to be a nuisance in itself. The major impact of such laws was clearly on the lower echelons of prostitutes who walked the streets rather than on those having less public means of encountering prospective clients. Studies such as Maria Luddy's on Ireland and Catherine Lee's on Kent provide nuanced and detailed accounts of this sector, demonstrating that careful linkage across policing, social welfare, and voluntary organization records can reveal much about individual careers and lifecycles. It is, however, less easy to uncover details of sex-workers above the level seeking customers on the street as part of a strategy of survival in poverty which might include seasonal work, petty theft, and occasional resort to the workhouse.[49]

There was also a public-health angle. Venereal diseases were a considerable problem in mid-Victorian Britain, although the extent of their prevalence could not be determined. The medical state of knowledge was not particularly developed, in particular the relationship of syphilis to its late manifestations in debility, paralysis, and insanity was not established, and there was no easy means of distinguishing gonorrhoea from syphilis, or the local affliction of soft chancre from a primary syphilitic sore. Treatments were largely ineffectual, often severely debilitating (e.g. mercurial treatment for syphilis), and sometimes punitive (cauterization and the application of caustic substances). British medical knowledge and practice was well behind that of France, for example, and William Acton, in fact, went to Paris to pursue his studies under the leading French specialist, Philippe Ricord. These diseases were understood as the result of vice and promiscuity, and thus largely located within the bodies of prostitutes (men being defined as victims of the diseases rather than instrumental in their circulation). Progressive medical approaches looked to France, where medical understanding was not only more advanced, there was also an active health policing strategy based on licensing prostitutes. However a powerful strand of British opinion was articulated by Sir Samuel Solly, President of the Royal Medical and Chirurgical Society: syphilis 'was intended as a punishment for our sins and we should not interfere in the matter'.[50]

Other approaches did not look to continental Europe. Philip Howell has revealed the care taken in Cambridge, a town with a large transient population of young unattached males, to contain and regulate the concomitant population of prostitutes. Although the system included medical inspections, it was less a modernizing development than based on longstanding practices of the University authorities.[51] Philippa Levine in her magisterial study of *Prostitution, Race and Politics* within the British Empire has pointed out that measures for regulation of prostitution in the colonies to protect the health of Imperial forces dated back at least to the late eighteenth century and influenced policies in the metropole.[52]

As a result of the Crimean War, a Royal Commission was set up to investigate the health of the Army. In 1860, 394 per 1000 other ranks were hospitalized for venereal diseases, equal to the sum total for tuberculosis, respiratory infections, and fevers. This compared very unfavourably with other European nations.[53] It was clearly an enormous and, it was believed, avoidable drain on manpower. The CD Acts, aimed at reducing this epidemic, targeted the prostitute population to whom soldiers, themselves a stigmatized group perceived as dangerous to public order, resorted. These women were to be treated with a severity more appropriate to martial law than to civil legislation, subjected to compulsory physical examination if suspected of disease, and incarcerated in Lock Hospitals until 'cured', if they were.

This assumed that the diseases were reliably diagnosable, and that they were 'curable'. Certainly, if a woman was incarcerated while in the most active stage of gonorrhoea, or virulent secondary syphilis, she might well have become less infectious by the time of release. However, the job of examining surgeon under the Acts did not appeal to the most ambitious and competent of medical men, and the conditions under which examination took place, and the time allowed, were far from optimal. It was also, of course, somewhat otiose to treat infected women and then discharge them to take up once more servicing men who had not undergone examination or treatment.

As the trial period was extended and additional areas were designated, the Acts appear to have been welcomed and to have been working; organizations lobbied for their further extension, even to the civilian population. However, both the ideology behind the Acts and their actual benefits were far from uncontested. As a piece of public health legislation, they were condemned by John Simon, Medical Officer to the Privy Council, perhaps the leading sanitarian of the day. They were also morally and politically offensive to a wide range of interests. Religious opinion, in general, could hardly approve 'making vice safe' (though some clergymen supported the Acts). The compulsory incarceration of prostitutes for medical purposes was seen as a dangerous violation of civil liberties. Working-class activists objected to a measure bearing exclusively upon working-class women and open to abuses such as false accusation and blackmail. And it horrified the middle-class women who had already been protesting against the iniquities of women's status. The idea of women being forcibly examined and incarcerated, to preserve the health of men, while protecting male rights to enjoy promiscuous intercourse with impunity, led to the Acts becoming an anathematized symbol of female oppression. Led by the charismatic Josephine Butler, women attacked the Acts, while also establishing claims to make wider moral reforms within society, arguing for a single rather than a double moral standard. A Royal Commission on the working of the Acts claimed in 1870 that they were working well and effectively, and that the public health benefits outweighed any objections. However, the campaign against the Acts swelled, and the force of the moral crusade was such as to draw into it many who had previously supported the Acts (though often bringing with them attitudes which did not harmonize with those of the initiators of the protest).[54]

The fight against filth

Other areas of sexual conduct were also being increasingly legislated for and policed. The Society for the Suppression of Vice had been campaigning against obscenity for many decades, for example by bringing private prosecutions and obtaining legislation against 'obscene displays' (e.g. in shop windows) through the 1824 Vagrancy Act. Even after the founding of modern police forces (1829), the Society continued to be active, employing spies and *agents provocateurs*, although police cooperation was by no means guaranteed.[55]

In 1857 a couple of cases of the selling of obscene literature came before the then Lord Chancellor, Lord Campbell, who was particularly shocked at the availability of these publications, sold in the streets for a few pence to the lower classes. A letter from the secretary of the Society for the Suppression of Vice, George Prichard, to Campbell claimed that it had undertaken 159 prosecutions in the previous 55 years, with only five acquittals: however only one in six, maybe in ten, of the cases brought to the Society's attention ever proceeded to prosecution. It had failed to eradicate all shops selling such material, though their numbers were reduced. Travelling purveyors of smut visited fairs, races, and markets in the country to 'circulate these abominations', and one regularly visited Oxford and Cambridge with a stock of 'highly finished French prints'. Much of the material objected to was visual (prints, copperplates, and lithographic stones confiscated far outnumbered books, and one case featured 'indecent pipe-heads'), suggesting a market among the non- or barely literate.

The influence of technological developments was seen in the early appearance of pornographic photographs and stereoscopic slides.[56] The Society's concerns appeared to be the dangers of stirring up the lusts of the lower classes (or depleting their vital forces through self-abuse) rather than restraining the sale of expensive, privately printed volumes of erotica and curiosa to members of the elite classes, though there was also concern over protecting the morals of middle- and lower-middle-class youths.

Campbell pushed an Obscene Publications Act, largely instigated by the Society, through Parliament in 1857, in spite of criticism over the powers it gave the police. It enabled search warrants to be issued by magistrates on the receipt of sworn information about suspect operations, and defendants had to show cause why their merchandise should not be destroyed. Campbell gave assurances in the House of Lords that the measure would not affect serious works of art. However, Lord Justice Cockburn's judgement in Regina v. Hicklin, 1868, made the test of obscenity 'whether the tendency of the matter charged is to deprave and corrupt those whose minds are open to such immoral influences and into whose hands a publication of this sort might fall', a ruling which greatly widened the opportunities for interested parties to pursue vigorous censorship campaigns.

Much censorship during the Victorian era was self-censorship: writers who wished to reach a mass market had to satisfy the moral standards not only of publishers, but of what was acceptable to the (predominantly middle-class) subscribers of the circulating libraries, such as Mudie's, which provided the main source of revenue for authors.[57] So significant was the idea of suitable family reading that even the Bible was not exempt: while, unlike Shakespeare, the text was too sacrosanct to be bowdlerized or expurgated, Mary Wilson Carpenter has drawn attention to the extensive publication of 'Family Bibles', with problematic passages printed in very small type or marked 'Not Suitable for Family Reading'. She also hints that the Bible as source of sexual knowledge in the Victorian era has perhaps been overlooked.[58]

Beyond the law

The various legal enactments described above indicate the parameters of what Victorian society, operating through its Parliamentary institutions, thought was acceptable or unacceptable sexual conduct. How the law operated in court differed somewhat from what statutes laid down. Interpretations by judges could make important modifications, as in the increasing definition of marital cruelty in terms beyond crude and brutal physical assault, and Cockburn's gloss on Campbell's Obscene Publications Act.

There was a wide range of conduct which did not fall within the purlieu of the law (quite apart from illegal acts which evaded the law's attention). The sexual culture of Victorian Britain was far from monolithic and manifested a good deal of variety, to which Michael Mason's two volumes, *The Making of Victorian Sexuality* and *The Making of Victorian Sexual Attitudes* remain particularly thorough guides.[59] However, there were behaviours which were subject to considerable social and moral policing.

Widely reprobated almost universally throughout Victorian society were the most private of sexual activities, masturbation, and the most involuntary, nocturnal emissions. Although this paranoia has often been described as directed against children, there was as much, if not more, concern about the effects of the practice in adolescence and early adulthood. This was possibly related to the increasingly late age of marriage among middle-class men and anxieties about the consequences of the various sexual expedients to which they might be driven (which also doubtless stimulated much of the anxiety over prostitution). So numerous and overbearing are the voices which spoke against self-abuse that only very fleetingly can the faint flicker of counter-discourses – for example that it was appropriate behaviour for adolescent boys, to 'make a man of them' – be discerned. Yet the very prevalence of the trade in pornography suggests that the practice must have been more widespread than the climate of terror generated at all social levels might suggest.[60]

Few authorities were prepared to concede that the habit might be anything but wholly deleterious, and medics who disagreed about nearly everything else (such as William Acton and George Drysdale) concurred that spermatorrhoea (pathological loss of semen through nocturnal or involuntary daytime emissions) was a dangerous and debilitating ailment, even while positing entirely different remedies; Acton an austere attempt at physical and mental chastity, Drysdale early marriage and the use of contraception. Those who might never come into contact with texts written by these respected professionals would encounter small advertisements at the back of newspapers, quack leaflets thrust into their hands in the street or stuck up on walls, the cures proffered after the salacious lure of the exhibits in an 'anatomical museum' had been concluded with horror-mongering displays on the dire consequences of onanism, and an almost folk-culture belief that it was better to have sex with a prostitute than to become addicted to self-abuse.[61]

Even more feared, perhaps because not under conscious control, were nocturnal emissions. These were believed to be symptomatic of a pathological wasting away of the semen (spermatorrhoea) which might have devastating results. While the idea was a gift to commercial quacks (given the multitudinous and often vague symptoms), spermatorrhoea was a reputable medical diagnosis, with articles appearing in the leading medical journal, *The Lancet*, and books on the subject respectfully reviewed. Stringent remedies, from cauterization of the penis to the application of devices to wake the sufferer up should erection occur (toothed rings, electrical alarms), were applied not merely by fiendish doctors to unconsenting victims, but to themselves by panicked men.[62]

These anxieties applied almost exclusively to men, who were also cautioned against too great a drain on the 'spermatic economy' through intercourse, even in marriage. There was no comparable medical literature on female masturbation and no trade in spurious remedies (those targeted at women were purported abortifacients). Laurie Garrison has pointed out that it was largely marginalized, or else intensely pathologized, and concerns were negligible compared to the outpouring of anxieties about male self-abuse.[63] Much has been made of the furore caused by Dr Isaac Baker Brown, who believed that many female maladies were caused by self-abuse, for which he advocated clitoridectomy, performed at his London Surgical Home. There is little evidence that this ever became a routine prescription of Victorian medical men for 'female disorders' such as hysteria. In fact, given the lack of attention paid to the clitoris in medical textbooks, probably few doctors could reliably have located it.

The protests within the medical profession about Baker Brown arose from a variety of causes, including his inappropriate direct advertisement to lay audiences rather than seeking referrals from other doctors. While Victorian doctors have often been assumed to have been rigorously defining and policing the female body as an object of medical authority and intervention, attitudes to women and female sexuality expressed in the medical press, and during the meeting of the London Obstetrical Society which led to Baker Brown's expulsion, were extremely complex and far from monolithic. Some considered it a foul insult to British womanhood to claim that they practised self-abuse at all, others registered horror at 'mutilating operations' with serious implications for future married life. But the whole case was an isolated outburst rather than the pervasive climate of terror concerning male solitary vice and emissions.[64]

Also not illegal, but hardly approved of, was birth control. There was no law against practising contraception, or manufacturing and selling devices, but public propaganda and advertising were likely to fall foul of anti-vice campaigners and obscenity laws, and the subject was strongly associated with radical politics and free-thought.[65] In 1854 George Drysdale published *Physical, Sexual and Natural Religion* anonymously as 'by a Student of Medicine', making a detailed case for contraception, but giving minimal practical information. As *Elements of Social Science* the book was repeatedly republished well into the twentieth century, but seldom noticed except in free-thought and secularist publications, and even there not universally approved. Tentative attempts to discuss family limitation aroused furious objections from the press and public opinion. Viscount Amberley suggested to the London Dialectical Society in 1868 that small families were desirable and means of limitation should be discussed. He was viciously attacked in both the medical and lay press, and lost a Parliamentary election amid the display of obscene cartoons 'representing his lordship selling certain quack mixtures to prevent large families' and scenes of riot.

In 1877 Charles Bradlaugh and his colleague Annie Besant produced a cheap edition of the American birth-control tract, Charles Knowlton's *Fruits of Philosophy*, as a test case. They were tried for publishing 'a dirty, filthy book', although the verdict finally achieved was ambiguous (the book was obscene, but their intentions were good). In the same year, 1877, the Malthusian League was founded with C. R. Drysdale (George Drysdale's brother) as President and Annie Besant as secretary, producing a monthly journal from 1879. The League's arguments consciously appealed to archetypal 'Victorian values' of prudence, foresight, and self-help. However, the prevalent view at that time was that sex was not an area in which prudence and foresight were appropriate – except from the point of view of avoiding temptation and maintaining continence, that is, not doing it – or at least, this could not be publicly admitted. Malthusian doctrines were violently attacked, on both medical and moral grounds, by C. H. F. Routh in a paper to the Obstetrical section of the British Medical Association in 1878: 'On the Moral and Physical Evils likely to follow if practices intended to act as Checks to Population be not strongly discouraged and condemned'. The British medical profession tried extremely hard to ignore Malthusianism (and other manifestations of sexuality which could not be subsumed to procreative matrimony), but burst forth in condemnatory diatribes when provoked by events such as the Amberley affair and the Bradlaugh-Besant trial. There was no sustained medical debate on the subject.[66]

However, from 1870 the British birthrate began to decline, for reasons which are still subject to debate. It is clear that there was a growing desire to have smaller families for complex economic and social reasons, and also a developing trade in contraceptive devices, but the exact relationship between the two is not as clear-cut as this chronological synchronicity might suggest. Decades later there was still both enormous ignorance about methods and dissatisfaction with those available. A range of strategies were deployed, with greater or lesser success, by different groups in order to achieve an apparently similar outcome.[67]

A climate of ideas in which female sexual excitation outside the paradigm of (prudent amounts of) potentially reproductive intercourse within the marriage bed was seen as potentially leading to a range of consequences deleterious to women's health and moral character, as evidenced in both the Baker Brown case and Routh's diatribe about contraception, inclines towards a certain scepticism about claims that Victorian doctors in the United Kingdom were routinely treating hysteria by genital massage.[68] Policed by the General Medical Council, doctors were becoming intensely fearful of accusations of sexual impropriety: indeed, they were advised when administering chloroform always to ensure that a third person was present in case the patient hallucinated sexual molestation.[69] While there was certainly a brisk trade in all kinds of electro-therapeutic quackery, many of the devices invoked the magical powers of electricity rather than doing anything specific.[70] It is not impossible that there were certain niche practitioners who engaged in such ministrations but numerous factors suggest that this was not widespread[71] (any more than doctors recommending clean brothels to victims of masturbation was likely to have been a mainstream practice[72]).

2

Social Purity and Evolving Sex in the 1880s

The 1880s saw a new development: an increasingly conscious interest in, and attention to, the phenomena of sexuality. The social purity movement, stimulated by the injustices of the Contagious Diseases (CD) Acts, had developed an articulate attack on what it saw as the evils of the existing sexual system, embodied in the double moral standard which permitted sexual peccadilloes to men, while punishing the slightest deviation from chastity in women. Sex was becoming a topic of discussion: contested and censored, but moving from the realm of silent assumptions into the forum of debate. It was also, though rather more slowly in Britain than on the continent, becoming a subject for scientific analysis.

Silences and speaking out

Michael Mason, in *The Making of Victorian Sexual Attitudes*, adumbrated the useful concept of 'classic moralism', a set of conventional moral attitudes towards sexual matters (strongly rooted in ideas of 'the natural') scarcely ever explicitly formulated. It operated, he suggests, in 'private precept' among a somewhat amorphous middle- to upper-class male social group, rather than being expounded in prescriptive texts. Perhaps typically English in its assumption of no-nonsense, down-to-earth, common sense untroubled by theorizing or 'systematic and speculative enquiry', it was based on uninterrogated 'inherited beliefs' and did not bother about consistency. Sex was not a matter for serious enquiry and thought, and was thus not for discussion, though there were certain recreational (and exclusively masculine) modes of talking about it. While this viewpoint might sympathize with the medical attitudes behind the CD Acts (seeing prostitution as a necessary outlet for male urges), it was remote from religious modes of perceiving the sexual as either sinful or sacred, though conceding a certain conventional respect to 'Christian morality' and rejecting free thought and secularism.[1] Some attacks on 'Victorian hypocrisy' have conflated the moral pronouncements of Evangelical religion and the rising social purity movement with the attitudes and behaviour of the rather different sector of the population influenced by the conventional assumptions embodied in this 'classic moralism'. It did not disappear in the 1880s. Although, by its very nature, it did not produce thought-out manifestos or statements of position, or engage in the campaigns for reform undertaken by the social purity lobby and the emergent voices of sexology, it remained influential. It was strongly represented, it is probably true to say, in the major institutions of established power, and emerged in, for example, Parliamentary debates over the raising of the age of consent.

The new articulateness about sexual morality may be attributed to some extent to the entry into the public political domain of hitherto excluded or marginal groups. In some cases (in particular, of course, women) they were operating in extra-Parliamentary channels through voluntary action. With the extension of the franchise, and the introduction of competitive examinations for the civil service, non-members of the traditional ruling elite, such as provincial Nonconformists, were gaining access to formal political power. These groups tended to take accepted codes of sexual morality seriously. The governing classes (in Parliament, the civil service, the judiciary, and other focuses of social power) had, on the whole, substantially cleaned up their act to conform to Victorian standards of public propriety, though traditional aristocratic mores had certainly not vanished, and were to be observed, in particular, in the rather louche circles around the Prince of Wales, later Edward VII. The traditional ruling elite operated very largely on assumptions that public declarations about moral behaviour were one thing (and public order and decency were desirable), but private conduct was another, to which a certain laissez-faire tolerance should be extended (within understood, but seldom explicitly defined limits).

The social purity movement had already, by 1880, moved well beyond its initial focus on repealing the CD Acts, even before this was achieved. Symptomatic of a pernicious male-dominated moral ethos pervasive throughout society and its institutions, these had to be abolished, but the movement aimed at the complete moral transformation of society, replacing the corrupt and inequitable double standard with a higher, single, moral standard. However, while there was a general consensus among adherents of this movement that this was desirable, diverse means by which it might be achieved were offered by different groups and individuals, and the movement was by no means monolithic.

One strategy was that of intervention at an early stage for the prevention of immorality and the inculcation of right attitudes, by the conscious sex education of children. Some moral reformers who worked with children were already apparently undertaking this: around 1880 or 1881, Agnes Cotton, founder of the first Moral Welfare Home for Children, wrote to L. M. Hubbard about the 'plain talks' she gave 'to my children', telling them that 'Every little bit of our bodies is given to us by God our Father, and to be used for the work he made it for – and for nothing else'.[2] She referred to a book which she found helpful, possibly pioneering woman doctor Elizabeth Blackwell's *Counsel to Parents on the Moral Education of their Children* (1878): but little literature was available for the intending sex educator.

The *British Medical Journal* (*BMJ*) conceded, in an 1881 leader on 'A Grave Social Problem', that it might be beneficial to warn children 'against certain forms of vice, to the temptation of which it seems almost inevitable that many of them should be exposed'. Children, here, apparently equalled boys, and public schoolboys at that, endangered by 'the parasite which has so deeply eaten its insidious way into the heart of their system'; the never overtly named practice of masturbation. While arguing for 'moral as well as physical ventilation', the *BMJ* deprecated both physiological instruction (inappropriate knowledge), or appeal to religious feeling (undesirable emotionalism), advocating instead 'commonsense principles' of treating 'these faults as disgusting rather than sinful … a disgrace to the school … rather than as a defilement', combined with 'hard physical exertion'.[3]

From time to time, articles in leading medical journals exhorted the profession to deal with 'venereal and sexual hypochondriasis' rather than abandoning the sufferers to 'advertising quacks'. However, such patients were usually regarded as dupes, imagining themselves 'suffering from that disease [syphilis], of which, thanks to advertising quacks, [they have] heard so much', and refusing to be reassured by orthodox medical authority. As for the 'sexual hypochondriacs', their appearance was 'so characteristic, that one diagnoses them almost intuitively. … too frequently … the victims of previous excessive sexual intercourse or self-abuse'. While 'patience and kindness' were recommended, the tone was not sympathetic.[4] The furtive, but commercially rewarding, subculture of quacks purveying remedies for venereal diseases and 'sexual debility' continued to flourish, with 17 major establishments in central London, as well as those 'carrying on their nefarious trade in a small way' by distributing handbills in the streets. Small ads appeared in relatively respectable newspapers, as well as the risqué journal, *The Sporting Times: Otherwise known as the 'Pink 'Un'* (price tuppence), for remedies for 'diseases of the urinary organs, debility, derangements of the generative organs, nervousness, loss of energy, and vital power'.[5] Quack practice was supported not only by the pervasiveness of male sexual anxieties, but by the reluctance of doctors to deal with these ailments, or presumed ailments; or, at least, to deal with them sympathetically. One outcome of medical hostility towards 'advertising quacks' was an alliance with the forces of social purity to pass an Indecent Advertisements Act in 1889. This cleared the streets of quack posters and handbills, although leaving several loopholes through which they continued to operate.[6]

Improving the position of women

In 1883 the Married Women's Property Act (1882) finally established the reform that the Married Women's Property Committee had for so long been struggling for, a measure which *The Times* declared 'revolutionizes the law' and described by the *Woman's Suffrage Journal* as 'the Magna Carta' of women's liberties. To some extent it had benefited from other attempts to tidy up conflicts between common law and equity. Under the Act, every woman without a marriage settlement could hold her own separate property as if unmarried, without trustees. The Act precisely defined what sort of property was covered, and women's rights to its disposal as well as their responsibilities, and the provisions protecting wives' separate property. There were a number of limitations: married women still did not have quite the same rights as unmarried or widowed women. And, of course, few women were the economic equals of men.[7]

Another slight improvement in women's position within marriage took place in the following year. Previously, a woman who left a husband who had not committed a matrimonial offence – thus who had no grounds for divorce or judicial separation – could have a writ issued against her for return to the matrimonial bed and board, and be imprisoned for non-compliance. Thus a woman who found her husband sexually repulsive or even sexually abusive (though in such cases, Gail Savage indicates, this might become valid grounds for non-compliance), or merely incompatible, could be forced to return to him under threat of gaol. Parliament abolished the penalty for non-compliance, although the action remained on the books and non-compliance with a writ became evidence of wilful desertion.[8]

There was still much criticism of marriage and of women's position within it. In 1888, feminist novelist Mona Caird published in the *Westminster Review* one of several essays on why and how contemporary marriage was a failure, and how this might be remedied. This generated a more popular article 'Is Marriage a Failure' in the *Daily Telegraph*, during August (the journalistic 'silly season'). There was an overwhelming response: 27,000 readers' letters, the vast majority expressing negative feelings. These were not conscious critics or reformers, but conventional middle-class readers of the *Telegraph*, most of whom saw their problem as individual and due to incompatibility with their spouse, even while complaining of the inadequacy of the legal recourse open to them.[9]

Reforming the modern Babylon

In 1883 the CD Acts were suspended, though not repealed until 1886. But the forces of social purity, already active in the rescue and reclamation of prostitutes, in preventive work with girls in moral danger, in youth organizations for adolescents of both sexes, and in holding mass meetings to promote the cause, increasingly believed that legislation was necessary and state intervention desirable. There were, however, differences within the movement. On one side was a belief in making the nation 'moral by Act of Parliament', and compulsion as a tactic was not ruled out. Control over prostitution was sought by measures bearing upon the women themselves. On the other side was the group which, while believing that the law should intervene to protect the young and vulnerable, also considered that morality was an individual choice and could not be compelled, and that respect for individual rights took precedence over eradicating vice. This latter group included some of the most distinguished leaders of the campaign against the CD Acts, including Josephine Butler. Butler had a sophisticated analysis of prostitution as the outcome of a sexual system based on violating the rights of women and of the poor, but believed that the prostitute herself was entitled not to be harassed and, if an adult, had a right to choose to engage in prostitution. Along with others in the Vigilance Association for the Defence of Personal Rights, Butler was opposed to any measures which increased the powers of the police, and rejected several Criminal Law Amendment Bills which seemed to be reintroducing legalized harassment of an unfortunate group of women.[10]

The social purity movement wanted to raise the age of consent (increased from 12, originally established in the thirteenth century, to 13 in 1875), a measure related to other late-Victorian legislation defining and regulating childhood and adolescence. The issue initially surfaced from agitation against the traffic in English girls to regulated brothels on the continent. Investigations in Belgium indicated that English women had been induced by fraud to enter brothels there, and once in brothels were virtual prisoners. The allegations of social purity reformer Alfred Dyer were corroborated by a Home Office report indicating the various legal loopholes (such as the low age of consent) enabling this traffic.

It also seemed desirable to protect young women from sexual predation by older males and, by protecting them from early seduction, lessen the chance of their becoming prostitutes. There was also a wish to extend to the vulnerable daughters of the working classes the protection enjoyed by the sheltered girls of the middle classes, without always considering whether this was appropriate for girls in very different circumstances. While much social purity rhetoric positioned these girls as vulnerable, those who worked to 'rescue' lower-class girls often perceived them as wild and out of control, addicted to cheap flashy finery and dangerously independent in their ways (and any girl who had had sexual intercourse, whatever the circumstances, was defined as 'corrupted' and fallen). There was thus also an agenda of controlling this unruly group. Some social purity campaigners advocated an age of consent as high as 21.

This should be seen in the context of opinions expressed, for example in Parliamentary debates, by opponents of raising the age. Lower-class girls were regarded as a traditional sexual perquisite by men in higher social stations, and on one level the opposition to raising the age of consent could be seen as simply a refusal to accept restrictions on this right. There was in addition a belief that these girls were already 'corrupt' by the age of 14 as a result of deleterious environment and upbringing, and, in fact, posed a sexual danger to the far more innocent (even if older) males of higher social class. As remarked in an 1884 debate in the House of Lords, most of their Lordships had 'when young men, been guilty of immorality'. Would they pass an Act which might penalize their sons? This is one of the points at which the voice of 'classic moralism' can be heard, being 'realistic' about a state of affairs presumed to be 'natural' (middle- and upper-class young men may sexually exploit lower-class women, but are 'innocent' compared to these vicious temptresses: compare this with attitudes towards male and female adultery embodied in the divorce law).

It might thus seem improbable that legislation raising the age of consent would ever reach the law books, given not only the lack of any common ground between the cases for and against, but also the caution of the 'personal rights' wing of the social purity movement, sensitive to issues of class and economics, and the tendency of existing laws and the mechanisms of their enforcement to penalize women to the exclusion of men. Nevertheless, in 1885 a 'moral panic' roused the country and swept in a Criminal Law Amendment Act. Investigators had become aware that child prostitution was not merely a foreign phenomenon, but something also occurring in London. The journalist and editor of the *Pall Mall Gazette*, W. T. Stead, was persuaded by Bramwell Booth of the Salvation Army to undertake an exposé.[11]

Stead's series of articles, 'The Maiden Tribute of Modern Babylon', have a prime place in the annals of sensationalist journalism: sentimental, salacious, and rampant with moral indignation, they had something for everybody. Judith Walkowitz has drawn attention to Stead's deployment of tropes and narrative strategies from pornographic literature, although he did tell, as Deborah Gorham argues, 'an irrefutable story of sexual exploitation'. His narrative of the exploitation of helpless young girls (the characters are all either innocent young victims, corrupt debauchees, sinister bawds or callous mothers) reached its apogee in his own exploitation of Eliza Armstrong, whom he purchased from her parents, had certified as a virgin, and took to Belgium to prove that this was possible. He was subsequently tried and imprisoned for abduction, as were his associates, including the reformed prostitute Rebecca Jarrett to whom he had been introduced by Josephine Butler.[12] While Stead was constructing this gothic narrative of the organized sexual exploitation of young girls for the benefit of members of high society, cases were routinely reported of assaults on often even younger girls, as a result of the persistent belief, attributed to lower-class superstition, that venereal disease could be cured by intercourse with a virgin or young child.[13]

The 1885 Criminal Law Amendment Act raised the age of consent to 16, and introduced new measures against disorderly houses, procuration, and abduction, which, just as Butler and her cohorts had feared, tended to be applied by the police in ways oppressive to women and girls rather than restraining the conduct of men (except male procurers and brothel-keepers). Quite shortly after the passage of the Act, the police began to be even more severe in endeavouring to control prostitution, and there were a number of cases of the arrest (or threatened arrest, as with novelist Olive Schreiner) for streetwalking of respectable women out at night on legitimate business. These aroused sufficient protest that curbs were instituted on arrests without preceding complaint of solicitation.[14]

Grossly indecent

The 1885 Act is perhaps most notorious, however, for the infamous 'Labouchère' Amendment. Why Labouchère introduced this and what his intentions were remain obscure. Introducing the clause during the Committee stage of the Bill, he alleged that the Government were willing to accept it. It has been suggested either that the clause was a wrecking measure aimed at halting the progress of the Act, or that Labouchère intended to extend to boys the same protection against sexual assault as was being provided for girls, on the model of the French law protecting minors of both sexes from seduction (Louise Jackson makes an extremely plausible case for this in the light of contemporary concerns about adolescent male prostitution in London, and the fit between such concern and the focus of the Act as a whole[15]). If so, the clause was appallingly badly drafted:

> Any male person who, in public or in private, commits, or is the party to the commission of, or procures or attempts to procure the commission by any male person of, any act of gross indecency with another male person, shall be guilty of a misdemeanour, and, being convicted thereof, shall be liable, at the discretion of the court, to be imprisoned for any term not exceeding one year with or without hard labour.

No age limit was mentioned. 'Gross indecency' was a vague term capable of far more flexible interpretation than 'indecent assault'. Neither consent nor commission of the act in private (thus without 'outrage to public decency') were to mitigate this new crime. Apart from an amendment of the maximum penalty to two years, the clause was hardly debated during a thinly attended late-night sitting, shortly before a General Election. It may be assumed that the general consensus among MPs was that homosexual activity was appalling and should be penalized if not eradicated, without engaging in distasteful discussions of the subject. No objections were raised even to the dangerous precedent introduced of creating a class of offences defined as 'public outrages' even though they occurred in private.

Whatever the intention of the Amendment, it provided a lesser offence, analogous to the verdict of concealment of pregnancy in cases of possible infanticide, which was more likely to result in conviction. It did not require contestable medical evidence, whereas the Offences against the Person Act 1861 focused specifically on anal intercourse (buggery), proving which was problematic, although lesser charges of attempting sodomy were more usually brought. Taylor's *Medical Jurisprudence* (1883) invoked the parallel with infanticide in discussing medical 'examination of an accused person', which could only be made, as in the case of women accused of this crime, with the consent of the accused, who 'was not bound to furnish evidence against himself'. The Amendment has been characterized as a 'Blackmailer's Charter', but Upchurch and Cocks have drawn attention to the prevalence of extortion and blackmail in previous decades. Their recent analyses of the policing of homosexual activity before 1885, and Sean Brady's painstaking analysis of this legislation, tend to suggest that the Act was much less of a significant moment than earlier historians have suggested. It was not linked to the rise of medical models of the homosexual as a distinctive type, and Brady indeed suggests that it was a brief 'leak' during a lengthy administrative regime of secrecy intended to keep discussion of sex between men out of the public domain.[16]

The first serious British work on homosexuality had emerged neither from medicine, which in Britain largely ignored deviations of desire except in their forensic aspects or as manifestations of insanity, nor from legal authorities. In 1883 the poet and critic John Addington Symonds (1840–1893) published, privately in a limited edition, *A Problem in Greek Ethics.* Although aware of his own homosexual desires from an early age, Symonds was repelled by the excesses he encountered at Harrow and by the hypocrisy of the headmaster,

Dr Vaughan. Following medical advice he married, but this did not eradicate his desires for working-class men and peasants. He found inspiration in the works of the American poet Walt Whitman glorifying the body and presenting a vision of manly comradeship. His own inclinations were not along the Greek model of a pedagogic/pederastic relationship between an older and a younger man, but he drew on the pervasive Classical ideal to present 'a great and highly developed race not only tolerating homosexual passions but deeming them of spiritual value'. This presented a counter to claims that homosexuality was decadent, corrupt, and a destructive force in society.[17]

In contrast to Symonds's elevated and idealistic vision of erotic comradeship, Taylor's *Principles and Practice of Medical Jurisprudence* continued to discuss same-sex relationships as 'unnatural offences', while expanding its treatment in revised editions. The topic acquired its own chapter, possibly because trials were 'not unfrequent', although 'reports of evidence are not made public'. The case of Boulton and Park, which 'drew public attention to this subject' was cited, along with that of 'Eliza Adams' in 1833, found after death to be a man 'for many years addicted to unnatural habits'. Slightly more detail was given as to the examination of the 'parts' involved to determine both the 'recent or acute form' and the 'chronic state' induced by 'these practices'. The work of Continental sexologists such as Tardieu and Casper was alluded to, as well as the fact that 'the medical jurists of Germany have taken a great interest in cases of sodomy and bestiality' (one may possibly detect a certain tone of disapproval).[18]

There is an apocryphal story that the Amendment originally included 'gross indecency' between women, but that this was either struck out by Queen Victoria herself, who refused to believe it possible, or officials quailed at the thought of explaining it to her. The Queen surely stands as a metonym for the reluctance of the Victorian age to conceive of sexual autonomy in women. There was no existing offence analogous to buggery, relating to lesbianism. Female same-sex activity did not count as a 'matrimonial offence' for the purposes of divorce. Women were not conceived of as capable of rape or the seduction of minors, and equality before the law on such charges was never argued. The torrent of warnings against self-abuse in the male had no female equivalent. Immediately prior to the introduction of Labouchère's amendment, the House of Commons strongly rejected as cruel and unjust the suggestion that a girl under 15 who consented to unlawful intercourse with a boy of the same age (for which the boy was liable to imprisonment) ought to be sent to a reformatory.[19]

Curiously and rather counter-intuitively, during the 1880s the Home Office was giving some thought to bestiality, civil servants and successive Home Secretaries considering the minimum sentence of ten years to be excessive. Pending any actual change in the law, directions were given to review all cases after a year as a result of which many offenders, most of them very young, were paroled. It is not clear whether this was at all inflected by the wider context of concerns around sexuality during this period (or indeed rising agitation around cruelty to animals), or based in perceptions that it was a crime of agrarian adolescent males, ignorant if not 'imbecile' or 'lunatic'.[20]

Let's talk about sex

The publicity given to sexual issues as a result of the campaign against the CD Acts, and by Stead's revelations and the furore they caused, led among certain groups in society to a more radical querying of the nature of the sexual system. Just talking about sex was, of course, a radical and rather dangerous act, especially if undertaken in mixed-sex gatherings (this was so even in respect of the social purity movement, though it tended to believe that it already knew what the problems were and what the means of dealing with them might be, in spite of dissensions over strategy).

The most well-known group deliberately setting out to think about sex was the Men and Women's Club, founded by barrister, mathematician, socialist, and disciple of Darwin, Karl Pearson, in 1885, which has been extensively written about as a result of the survival of substantial records. This fascinating entity brought together a handful of men of the professional middle classes (doctors, lawyers, university lecturers) and women, married and unmarried, of similar social background with some degree of economic independence and a shared interest in feminist causes, along with a penumbra of guests and associates. It was rather staid in its attitudes to sexual nonconformity, and a little fearful of being connected to scandal. Both Lucy Bland and Judith Walkowitz have pointed out the problems that the women experienced as the terms of debate were set by Pearson and his male friends, who commanded a medical and scientific vocabulary alien to even the university-educated women among the membership. The religious and moral modes which came more easily to the women were dismissed as 'emotional' compared to male rationality. The women felt less like equal partners in exploring sensitive and ill-understood subjects than specimens for analysis.

The Club was a visible and highly formalized manifestation of a much more pervasive desire to discuss sexual matters in an open-ended and exploratory way. Walkowitz alludes to the 'bohemian, radical circle of the British Museum Reading Room' including Olive Schreiner, a Club member. There were also connections to the recently founded Fabian Society, and its precursor the Fellowship of the New Life, of which Havelock Ellis, already preparing to produce his great work on sex, was part.[21] Eleanor Marx (a close friend of Schreiner) and her consort, Edward Aveling, of the Marxist Social Democratic Federation, wrote a pamphlet on *The Woman Question* (1887): even this less lifestyle-orientated edge of the left was interested in these issues.[22] The rather obscure Pioneer Club, aimed at 'providing with a common medium of intercourse and expression...the large and increasing number of men and women, interested in, and anxious to promote, the serious discussion of Social, Philosophical and Literary questions generally', also appears part of this phenomenon.[23]

There was a significant overlap between the concerns raised during the campaign against the Contagious Diseases Acts and the interests of these groups anxious to explore problems of sex. Both were resisting the pressures of 'classic moralism' and convention to treat sex as a never-openly discussed twilight activity of the privileged male. Both were inclined to critique accepted assumptions about what was 'natural' about the given sexual mores of society.[24]

Promoting purity

As a result of Stead's campaign, the National Vigilance Association was founded under the leadership of William Coote, taking over the assets of the Society for the Suppression of Vice, supported by many feminists who had fought to repeal the CD Acts. It took on a very broad remit of campaigns under the general aegis of social purity, forming such a mixed bag that it is easy to understand how different historians have characterized it as both regressive and progressive. It simply does not fit readily into standard conservative versus liberal moral categories. Among issues considered by the executive committee during 1886 were: local resistance to the repeal of the CD Acts; the problem of men (unclear whether this meant men soliciting women or male prostitutes, but probably the former); preventive work, including a conference for school teachers and managers and the preparation of a paper for schoolgirls; dissemination of information about local refuges; Italian organ-grinders; rowdyism in the streets; immorality in parks; theatre children (no cruelty alleged, but their demoralization deplorable); the continuing problem of the plea of 'reasonable belief' that a girl was 16 in cases of underage seduction. A number of individual cases of rape, assault, and affiliation were taken up, as well as the tracing of missing girls. Various further legislative action was mooted: the punishment of incest (not passed for over 20 years) and the extension of laws on parental abuse of children generally; the provision for women to have friends of their own sex in court with them, given the overwhelmingly male legal system and the intimidation of female witnesses; and the introduction of flogging for rape and offences against girls under 13.[25] Many of these measures met with a positive response from local authorities.

The issues noted above paid little attention to obscene publications. Lisa Sigel persuasively argues that access to pornography remained the purlieu of the relatively well-off and educated until very late in the century. To obtain pornographic works required money and the ability to locate the dealers, while to consume them demanded not just literacy but often sophisticated reading skills. She notes, however, that from around 1880 pornography was becoming increasingly formulaic and its sexual acts detached from any wider social context, while an increasing array of perversions aimed at specialized tastes in a consumerist market was supplied by dealers developing a slick professionalism.[26] She has also suggested that the elaborate vocabulary of eighteenth-century erotica had become degraded in Victorian pornography to 'filthy' language (once merely vulgar, but now subject to stringent taboos on use) to invoke arousal, with increasing associations of sex and dirt.[27]

Besides the NVA, other bodies, such as the Alliance of Honour, the Moral Reform Union, the White Cross League, actively pursued preventive measures of enlightening the public and, especially, the young. Again, the appropriate means was subject to debate. The *BMJ*, in a leader on 'Sexual Ignorance' inspired by the Stead furore, came out in favour of teaching children basic sexual anatomy and physiology, though ended on the unanswered question: 'how then is the girl... to be made acquainted with the solemn facts of creative act, and guarded against associating them with the base impulses of passion?'

The *Lancet*, however, argued that these were 'essentially moral and religious questions' and should be dealt with on that basis, though also agreeing: 'Let our streets and literature be purged...of the filth that now disgraces them.'[28] How to enlighten girls was always a problem given the enduring belief that too much theoretical knowledge about sex was itself subtly contaminating. It was perhaps easier to warn boys, as it was accepted that they were likely to acquire some knowledge from 'corrupt companions' (and the more overtly sexual manifestations of puberty in the adolescent boy, although this was seldom explicitly mentioned). They could be advised not to abuse themselves and against interpreting nocturnal emissions as evidence of spermatorrhoea on the basis of quack literature, and exhorted to a chivalrous respect for womanhood.[29]

Medical matters

During the 1880s, the issue of male responsibility for circulating venereal diseases was beginning to emerge above the horizon. A long-drawn-out, high-profile, and scandalous matrimonial dispute turning upon the husband's syphilis was first a topic of gossip within society and then broke in the newspapers. In 1883 Lady Colin Campbell sought a separation from her husband on the grounds that he had forcibly exacted conjugal rights when knowingly suffering from syphilis, and had infected her. In 1886 their divorce case – her husband cross-petitioning on the grounds of her adultery with several co-respondents – dragged on for three weeks, longer than any previous case, generated huge amounts of press reportage, and finally concluded with the anticlimactic failure to find either of them guilty as charged and therefore no decree granted, leaving this ill-assorted and bitterly hostile couple still legally married.[30] Arguably, given the wider context of changes in legislation and the success of social purity, this was a significant moment in revealing a topic previously obscured in silence and not infrequently by medical obfuscation of the causes of wives' persistent ill-health.

Worboys has argued that discursive changes turning a spotlight onto male immorality and the Double Moral Standard played an important part in bringing about the recognition of male responsibility for disseminating gonorrhoea, and the hitherto hidden ill-effects of this disease on the infected women. Previously it had been considered an almost exclusively male affliction, spread to them by healthy female carriers of 'gonorrhoeal poisons'. Neisser's discovery of the causative gonococcus was a significant stride forward in establishing it as an infectious disease, but Worboys plausibly suggests that this discovery was embedded in wider social and professional medical developments which meant that within a couple of decades, gonorrhoea had been 'unsexed', and, moreover, from being merely a trivial localized male genital problem, was understood as the cause of serious pelvic disease and infertility in women.[31]

It is sometimes assumed that social purity and the late nineteenth-century medical profession remained antagonistic, underestimating the reshuffling of alliances during the 1880s and assuming that the anti-medical rhetoric of the campaign against the CD Acts continued unmodified. Not only was there sympathy among certain doctors for the sexual education arguments of the social purity movement, the movement deployed medical arguments for chastity and against masturbation. Pamphlets issued by the White Cross League (aimed at inculcating chastity and chivalry in men) included *True Manliness*, advising those struggling against onanism to consult a properly qualified doctor (as opposed to a quack) for assistance with measures of prevention, and *The Testimony of Medical Men*, which cited eminent authorities for the healthfulness of chastity in the male. As mentioned earlier, social purity and the medical profession were both concerned to pass legislation to curb the promotional activities of quacks, though for somewhat different reasons.

Their convergence of interests is apparent in the case of Henry Arthur Allbutt, a radical Leeds medical practitioner who issued a cheap pamphlet (subsidized by the inclusion of advertisements), *The Wife's Handbook*, advising poor women on health maintenance, including information about contraception when pregnancy was contraindicated. The Leeds Vigilance Association brought it to the attention of the General Medical Council. In 1887 Allbutt was struck off the Medical Register and deprived of his membership of the Royal College of Physicians of Edinburgh. The *BMJ* piously applauded these actions, suggesting that Allbutt might legitimately have 'ventilated his views...to medical men instead of to the public' rather than 'publishing in a cheap and popular form information which...may be used for the worst purposes'.[32]

Scandals and crimes

Curiously, there was no specific mention of contraceptive devices in the Indecent Advertisements Act of 1889. However, the opprobrium with which birth control was regarded (and its persisting connection with illicit and promiscuous sex) was manifested in a couple of causes célèbres of the late 1880s. The very name 'French letters' for condoms attributed them to the nation the British most associated with rampant sexual vice. In 1886 the radical Liberal MP, Sir Charles Dilke (a considerable friend to women's rights and shortly to marry feminist and socialist Emilia Pattison), was named as co-respondent in the Crawford v. Crawford divorce. Dilke and the Crawfords were connected by numerous familial, political, and social ties, within which a number of less than conventional relationships were already common knowledge. Virginia Crawford claimed that Dilke had 'taught me every French vice', involved her in a threesome with one of the maids, and employed 'French letters' during their intercourse. Crawford was granted a divorce on the grounds of his wife's adultery, but the judge found no evidence that this had occurred with Dilke. W. T. Stead, however, instigated a vigorous press campaign against Dilke, claiming that his name had not been definitively cleared and that such a man ought not to be in Parliament. Dilke suffered a fate more usually associated with women who had 'fallen' and was subjected to widespread social exclusion, becoming anathema to many in women's rights and social purity organizations – in 1889 the National Vigilance Association organized opposition to his election as an alderman. The case became a site of complex and conflicting meanings about class, sex, gender, public and private life, exacerbated by the lack of certainty at the centre of the story: was Dilke lying, or was Virginia Crawford?[33]

Adelaide Bartlett, whose prosperous grocer husband was poisoned with chloroform in 1886, also had the disadvantage of a French education. The case attracted a good deal of attention, like several others involving middle-class women and rumours of unconventionality or impropriety within their marriages. Current fads – hydropathy, hypnosis – also figured. Women were more often than not found guilty in cases of poisoning, but Bartlett, in spite of her apparent disadvantages, went free, partly because the prosecution could not make a convincing case for how the chloroform had been administered, but also partly because, as Mary Hartman suggests, 'she was able to convince a prepared audience that she had been victimized by a perverted husband' rather than ridding herself of one she found sexually repugnant.

According to her testimony the marriage had been extremely peculiar. 'French letters' were found in the pocket of the deceased, although the widow claimed that their marriage had been platonic, apart from one act of intercourse for the purpose of begetting a child, and that Bartlett had encouraged her association with a young Nonconformist clergyman. She also claimed that she had acquired the chloroform to deter her husband's suddenly aroused sexual interest in her. *Esoteric Anthropology*, a manual on the conduct of married life, featured: though it recommended a stringent standard of sexual continence, with intercourse for procreation only, the very fact of possessing a volume dealing explicitly with this topic drew condemnation from the judge.[34]

Another case in which the imputed salacity of the French played a significant role was the prosecution in 1888 of the elderly publisher Henry Vizetelly for his English editions of the novels of Zola, which initiated the trend of using obscenity laws to prosecute serious literature. At the instigation of the NVA, the government proceeded against Vizetelly, who pleaded guilty and was fined; a few months later he was imprisoned after a further prosecution involving works by other French writers such as Maupassant and Bourget. The prosecution argued that the edition was not intended for a 'select literary class', but was being promoted to 'the common market' (even though Vizetelly had himself censored the most objectionable passages).[35]

A major moral panic of the later 1880s owed much of its impact both to the role of the press in bringing it to public attention and keeping it there, and to the lack of closure of the story itself. In 1888 five prostitutes were horribly murdered in Whitechapel, in the East End of London. This area was already, in popular imagination, a symbol for the dark underside of the metropolis, the physical location of 'Darkest England', as barbaric and alien as any outpost of Empire. The murders were not only horrible (and unsolved), they had a strong sexual element. Figures already perceived as sexually suspect – debauched aristocrats, depraved vivisecting doctors, religious fanatics, aliens such as the Jews (then immigrating to that area in unprecedented numbers) – were among those identified as 'Jack the Ripper'. The victims were sometimes depicted as drawing this fate upon themselves (and even somehow generating the sexual madness of their killer) simply by being prostitutes, furthering social purity arguments for 'cleaning up the streets'. However, the women's vulnerability owed a good deal to the previous intensive campaign to close down 'bad houses', forcing them to conduct their business on the streets.[36]

*   *   *

While both the eminent Viennese psychiatrist Richard von Krafft-Ebing, and American doctors, discussed the Ripper 'lust murders' as part of the range of perversions being analysed and named by the emerging speciality of sexology, British voices were silent on the subject. One of the earliest works of British sexology dealt not with the abnormal and the 'perverse', but with 'normal' sexuality envisioned from a Darwinian perspective. Scottish biologists Patrick Geddes and J. Arthur Thomson published *The Evolution of Sex* in 1889, the first volume in the Contemporary Science Series under the editorship of medical man and literary figure, Havelock Ellis. They emphasized the 'fundamental unity underlying the protean phenomena of sex and reproduction'. Human sexuality reflected the evolution of sexual reproduction in animals, manifested in the 'anabolic' or constructive and conservative energies of the female, and the 'katabolic' or disruptive and destructive energies of the male. The authors carefully ascended the evolutionary ladder, finding the cochineal insect and the flatworm illustrative of the passivity of the female and the activity of the male, and deducing the greater liability to exhaustion in the male following reproductive activity from spiders, rotifers, and mayflies. Although even this detached view of sexual phenomena (dealing only with the human in the last chapter) was not viewed as entirely acceptable, it supplied a new and (on the whole) non-emotive way of discussing the subject. Geddes and Thomson surely stimulated the pervasive prevalence of the 'birds and bees' in purveying sexual enlightenment.[37]

3

Scientific Sex, Unspeakable Oscar, and Insurgent Women in the 'Naughty Nineties'

Revelations and concealments

The 1890s opened with a cause célèbre focusing on an 'unmentionable crime' that became a recurrent theme of the decade: homosexuality. The 'Cleveland Street Scandal' initially broke during 1889. In the course of an enquiry into thefts at the General Post Office, Charles Swinscow, a messenger boy, revealed that the suspicious amount of money in his possession had been given to him 'for going to bed with gentlemen' at a house in Cleveland Street in central London, owned by a Mr Charles Hammond. Henry Newlove, a third-class clerk, was indulging in 'indecent' behaviour with the messengers in an underground lavatory in the Post Office building, then procuring them for male prostitution (the telegraph-boy had become a fetishized erotic object for upper- and upper-middle-class Victorian homosexuals).

The police switched their attention to this at once, and Inspector Frederick G. Abberline, a leading detective, was assigned to the case. Warrants of arrest were hastily sought but, none the less, Hammond, warned, took off at once for the Continent. Newlove, cautioned by Hammond to deny everything, perhaps resentful at becoming the fall-guy, remarked to the constable taking him to the police station that it was 'very hard that I should get into trouble while men in high position are allowed to walk about free' and named Lord Arthur Somerset, a member of the royal entourage, and the Earl of Euston as habitués of the Cleveland Street house. Lord Arthur's brother, Lord Henry Somerset, had been divorced by his wife some ten years previously after finding him in bed with his valet (a course of action causing her, rather than him, to be scorned by society: similar opprobrium was heaped on Lady Russell over her accusations concerning her husband's homosexual activities[1]) but Lord Arthur ('Podge'), a cavalry officer, had been assumed to be 'manly' in all particulars. The police placed the house under surveillance. However, prosecution hung fire, until finally Newlove, and Hammond's confederate, fake clergyman George Daniel Veck, were indicted on charges of procuration, conspiracy to solicit for sodomy, and gross indecency. Veck pleaded guilty to gross indecency, and Newlove to all charges except attempted buggery. They both received light sentences, probably paid off (via the solicitor Arthur Newton) to plead guilty and take a moderate prison term, to avoid embarrassing courtroom revelations.

There were press outcries that a cover-up was protecting socially eminent guilty parties, though only the *North London Press* named Lord Arthur Somerset and Lord Euston. Somerset had fled the country, never to return. Euston, however, sued Parke, the editor, for libel, claiming to have been lured to the Cleveland Street house by the promise of 'poses plastique', an erotic exhibition involving scantily dressed women. While judgement went against Parke, who was imprisoned, there was a good deal of press criticism of the government's actions. In February 1890, Henry Labouchère suggested during a House of Commons debate that 'certain official persons...have conspired together to defeat the course of justice'. Some later accounts of this case have advanced conspiracy theories, even alleging that Prince 'Eddy' – Albert Victor, Duke of Clarence, eldest son of the Prince of Wales (also identified as 'Jack the Ripper') – was being protected. A legal historian, however, suggests disagreements between different government officers about whether pursuing a case against Somerset would be in the public interest. The case remains a rich site of issues to do with gender, class, and perceptions of deviant sexuality, revealing a hidden world of Victorian homosexuality, the casual route of young working men into homosexual prostitution, and the social disaster of identification as homosexual in the higher social classes. Government shilly-shallying over prosecution appears partially motivated by fears of the undesirable effects of publicizing the existence of homosexuality, especially among the upper classes.[2] But the ill-effects of the Government's inept attempts to play down the entire situation were to have repercussions on decisions taken in a later more celebrated case.

The advocacy of other forms of non-procreative sex, even within matrimony, was also liable to be penalized. In 1891 Henry Young, a barrister, was tried at Bow Street for 'having unlawfully sent a postal packet, which enclosed a certain indecent and obscene printed book or pamphlet entitled "Some Reasons for the Prudential Limitation of Families"', and also mailing 'a certain obscene article' (presumably a contraceptive). His sealed packets had been intercepted and opened by the Post Office. The prosecution, on behalf of the Home Office, aimed at enforcing the Post Office Act of 1884 to 'prevent a public department being used for the dissemination by private means of matter which was objectionable and calculated to deprave the public morals'. The defendant claimed that he sent circulars only to fathers of families at addresses given in newspaper birth announcements – although a few had reached ladies by mistake. He argued that he was a serious adherent of neo-Malthusianism, and while sending out a large number of appliances at a guinea a time, also provided information gratuitously to the poor. The prosecution declared 'it was contrary to the highest interests of morality that the natural consequences of cohabitation should be interfered with'. The judge, while finding the pamphlets 'written in very careful language, and not intended at all to be offensive...could not for a moment doubt that they were obscene', having been 'sent out broadcast, and...obviously intended to promote illicit intercourse'.[3]

Young complained that 'it was impossible to get Malthusian questions discussed in the Press, or to engage any large hall to discuss them in.' Beyond the house-organ of the Malthusian League, *The Malthusian*, few journals were prepared to admit the subject. However, *Shafts: Light comes to those who dare to think* (later *A journal for women and the working classes*), founded 1892, did open its pages to advocacy of 'scientific checks to undue and immoral reproduction', as well as counterclaims that these 'enable the husband to indulge himself without restraint', in the context of free debate on issues of the day. The editor herself (Margaret Shurmer Sibthorp) considered that 'Women must themselves be the controlling power' and that 'there is no justifiable remedy for overpopulation but self-restraint', but, none the less, published an article by veteran Malthusian Jane Clapperton, on 'Reform in Domestic Life'.[4]

Shafts can be seen as one continuation of that desire to discuss questions around sexuality tentatively started in the previous decade. Other issues debated in its pages included sex education, problem novels, the marriage issue, social purity, prostitution, rational dress, and whether female chastity was innate or achieved through meritorious moral struggle. *Shafts's* pages reveal a background of meetings and classes on similar topics. A group of young Fabians in the provinces circulated a notebook recording thoughts on free love and the woman question, as well as the prospects of socialist revolution.[5] There were presumably many unrecorded and less formal discussions of these matters going on among those who considered themselves progressive and anti-conventional, as suggested in Chris Nottingham's work on Havelock Ellis's political and social milieu and his cultural impact.[6]

On and off the city streets

Prostitution was an issue which did not, for all the efforts of the social purity movement, go away, although the social purity movement became increasingly less sanguine about the possibility of reclaiming the 'hardened prostitute' and thus shifted its focus towards early intervention with young girls and the partially fallen.[7] Societal attitudes continued deeply hostile and stigmatizing. In 1892, Canadian doctor Thomas Neill Cream was found guilty of poisoning prostitutes with strychnine pills, apparently claiming that these were abortifacients or cures for venereal disease. In his masterly analysis of the case, Angus McLaren suggested that far from being an asocial beast, Cream was 'over-socialized', internalizing prevalent beliefs about prostitutes, and carrying out in practice 'the sentences that society at large had levelled against rebellious females'. The court, sentencing him to hang, none the less condemned his victims as 'unfortunates', the 'legion of the lost', 'degraded women'.[8]

Cream's victims had been streetwalkers, the most visible and despised of prostitutes. The 'massage scandal' of 1894 revealed a new, at least, previously concealed, form of clandestine prostitution, among several emerging in response to the new laws. The *British Medical Journal* (*BMJ*) broke the story as an issue of medical policing, since massage was becoming a recognized legitimate adjunct to medical practice. An increasing number of sumptuous West

End establishments were offering massage for non-therapeutic purposes. The proprietor would hire a number of attractive young women,

> for whom the remuneration is nominal, but they are at liberty to accept presents from the customers .... If the young lady is willing to make herself 'agreeable' she is retained on the staff.

Even more horrible to relate, 'it has become a fashionable fad for certain ladies of position to frequent the rooms of a young and good-looking masseur.' This was the upper end of the prostitution market, and most reports explicitly harped on the 'aristocratic vice' theme. *Astounding Revelations concerning supposed Massage houses or Pandemoniums of Vice frequented by both sexes* remarked that 'The horrible scandal of Cleveland Street' – that, too, an aristocratic scandal – 'still fouls the air'. *Reynold's Weekly* fulminated that 'the profession of massage has been largely made a cloak for unbridled sexual intercourse on the part of the rich and aristocratic classes.' Some accounts implied worse than mere 'unbridled sexual intercourse': Thomas Maltby, a serious and reputable practitioner, alleged: 'immoralities as bad, if not worse, in their nature than are reported as occurring in houses of ill-fame are daily, aye hourly, resorted to ... too degrading, too infamous, to detail.' There were recurrent stories of young girls innocently responding to advertisements offering training as masseuses. In fact proprietors, rather than employing 'masseuses', seem to have charged prostitutes, who then negotiated individually with clients, to use the premises. Under the pressure of public, or at least media, outcry, the Home Office ordered an enquiry: the establishments could not be closed under existing laws on bawdy houses. Labouchère, in his journal *Truth* the following year, argued that the publicity had greatly increased the establishments' trade. *Today* considered the phenomenon 'the natural result of unconsidered attempts to abolish the unabolishable'.[9]

This scandal has not had the enduring fascination of the Cleveland Street case, possibly because, in spite of the hints of upper-class debauchery, no specific names figured. Yet it does reflect themes of its time: the hints of sexual perversity, as well as the problems of the labour market for women. In how many jobs – and not just those, such as barmaid, for which Peter Bailey has persuasively argued that an aura of 'parasexuality', or promise rather than performance, was a requisite[10] – did the young woman, only desirous of doing well at the task she was hired for and earning a decent day's wage, find that there was an unspoken contract that she should be good-looking and 'willing to make herself "agreeable"'?

A better-known case of more overt prostitution and protest against it was the affair of the Empire Promenade, a resort for high-class prostitutes able to pay the admission fee; thus a haunt of 'upper-class vice' and those who wished to imitate it. The National Vigilance Association was concerned about music halls and places of public entertainment from its inception, and had put pressure on the newly created London County Council to incorporate moral criteria in its licensing system. The LCC, controlled by a 'Progressive Party' of 'Municipal Puritans' was sympathetic to this agenda. Mrs Laura Ormiston Chant, a stalwart of social purity and editor of *The Vigilance Record*, was informed about the Empire Promenade by two (male) American friends, shocked by what they had encountered. She visited it herself and then formally opposed renewal of the Empire's licence. In spite of the strong defence by George Edwardes, the proprietor, the LCC insisted on several conditions for renewal, including abolition of the Promenade and a ban on selling drinks in the auditorium. There was a press outcry, headed by the *Daily Telegraph*, which published a tide of letters of protest. Mrs Chant acutely pointed out that 'successful vice' was being championed by those who would have hounded common streetwalkers from the Empire's elegant portals. It closed for alterations, reopening with a reduced promenade area, and a flimsy screen separating the bar from the auditorium. In a riotous incident this was torn down by Sandhurst cadets, including the young Winston Churchill. The partitions were rebuilt in more solid materials following this 'triumph of freedom'. However, a year later the Empire's licence was restored on an unconditional basis. Lucy Bland has cogently argued that while, on the one hand, Chant and her cohorts were unsympathetic to the women frequenting the Promenade, and careless of the consequences of driving them on to the streets and putting performers and other Empire staff out of work, she was also part of the movement to make public spaces available and safe for 'respectable' women.[11]

This was still far from the case. The risqué journal *The Pelican*, which one would not suppose a champion of women's rights, wrote in 1890:

> Any number of aged scoundrels…religiously spend their afternoons in tottering up and down Regent Street, not only addressing the various ladies they may meet, but insulting them in many and various ways…. A woman has no sort of protection either, from these scoundrels, and even if she had the pluck to call a policeman, it would, in the first place, be difficult to prove or substantiate any charge…the attendant bothers and notoriety of a police court, would frighten off most ordinarily constructed women.

The pests were characterized – in a carefully distancing strategy – as old enough to know better and under no illusions about their own attractions. This was a rather unexpected intervention in the debate about women and street harassment in the West End, extensively analysed by Judith Walkowitz, in which most male voices tended to be hostile to female complaints of persistent annoyance and to argue that mutual interest was involved.[12]

At this period the city, and in particular London, was generally being depicted as a space of sexual opportunity and danger, and as the place where vice flourished. Matt Cook has argued that the gradually increasing press reporting of homosexual cases identified these with urban debauchery and aristocratic decadence.[13] It was largely in cities that working-class 'monkey-walks' were visible to shocked observers.[14] However, this idea of the city as corrupt and the country as a rural haven of pure morals is undercut by Russell Davies's account of the extent of illegitimacy in South West Wales. This region was positioned as a land of pure morals uncorrupted by the English or creeping industrialization. In fact, rural, Welsh-speaking Cardiganshire had an illegitimacy rate twice that of

Anglicized and industrial Glamorganshire. Attempts to obtain affiliation orders were frequently met with attempts to blacken the woman's character, and cases of sexual assault trivialized and dismissed.[15]

Policing masculinity

Not all males were pestiferous roués, harassing brutes, or chivalrous defenders of womanhood: some were weak and vulnerable. The *BMJ* preached on the evils of quack literature exploiting 'adolescents and nervous or dyspeptic or hypochondriac young men' by identifying 'ordinary and frequent' symptoms as serious maladies, creating 'despondency and erroneous fears'. At the inquest at Westminster on a young butcher who had cut his throat, 'a varied selection of the sort of pamphlets sent to the unwary' were produced in court, and the divisional surgeon remarked, 'Suicides had occurred before under similar circumstances.' The *BMJ* extrapolated 'countless cases of protracted misery, alarm and depression from mental anxiety among young men of the less educated and wealthy classes'. This attribution of the misery, despondency, and fears to pernicious horror-mongering by quacks reflects the retreat of medical opinion from the position that masturbation itself caused insanity to emphasize the dangers of worrying about it unduly.[16]

While suggesting that lower-class young men were weak-minded creatures particularly susceptible to quack horror-mongering, the *BMJ* did extend a degree of sympathy. Less fortunate were the clients of the World's Great Marriage Association, whose owners were charged with conspiracy to defraud in November 1895. Lower-class males milked of fees and subscriptions were derided in court for their pathetic aspirations. Unrealistic and presumptuous in their expectations of young, pretty, and above all, well-off, brides, they had not got anywhere near meeting their doom at Trinity Church ('told me she was five and twenty, cash in the bank of course she'd plenty...I was an M-U-G'), since such women allegedly on the Association's books did not exist. These men failed to match society's expectations of manliness in courtship.[17] Even less fortunate were men who 'stood by' women they had got pregnant out of wedlock and assisted in obtaining an abortion, an act perceived as the acme of caddishness rather than chivalry. John Hindson was sentenced to death for murder (later commuted) in 1896 for organizing an abortion for his pregnant girlfriend, from which she died while he was miles away. He was depicted as a cad and a bounder, less deserving of mercy than the female abortionist, deemed to have been helping out a fellow-woman.[18]

Policing the borders of masculinity took in various transgressions against the ideal, usually defined by the middle-class male. There were many ways in which a man could fall away from this ideal, not all subsumable to homosexuality, indeed appropriate manliness was a precariously balanced state at the presumed summit of hierarchies of gender, class, and race. Oscar Wilde and his three trials (the failed libel case against the Marquess of Queensberry, the father of his lover Lord Alfred 'Bosie' Douglas; a subsequent inconclusive trial under the Labouchère Amendment of the Criminal Law Amendment Act 1885; and a final trial ending in conviction) are a well-known story which continues to be rehearsed. Contemporary reportage of the trials was euphemistic and evasive about what it was that Wilde was accused of doing/being, the text of the Marquess's semi-legible scrawled libel being censored or omitted and the actual crimes in question remaining unspecified: as Alan Sinfield has suggested, 'not only did this love not dare to speak its name, it hardly had a name'. The Wilde debacle collapsed a number of transgressive male possibilities (effeminacy, decadence, aestheticism, bohemianism, dandyism, self-indulgence, and excess), in practice pertaining equally to heterosexual men, into one monstrous cautionary figure. When Maurice, in E. M. Forster's posthumously published homosexual novel, described himself as 'an unspeakable of the Oscar Wilde sort', he did not mean he was witty, politically radical, intellectually subversive, or a dandified aesthete: he meant he desired other men.[19]

The Wilde case was therefore a significant moment in the construction of British notions of 'the homosexual' and 'homosexual identity'. Without his 1895 martyrdom, would there have been alternatives – an unspeakable of the 'Podge' Somerset type?, a Cleveland-streeter? The authorities, fearful of another furore over the protection of vice in high life, did not dare hold back from a high-profile prosecution of Wilde and his associates.[20] Although Wilde's famous peroration in court on 'the love that dares not speak its name' (a phrase initially coined in one of 'Bosie's' poems) represented it as an ennobling and beneficent relationship between an older and a younger man, this perspective was badly undercut by revelations about young lower-class 'renters' and allusions to stained sheets. Meanwhile, London clubs were allegedly decimated by the flight abroad of socially prominent homosexuals. According to reclusive diarist, penologist, humanitarian, and homosexual rights advocate, George Ives, perhaps uniquely placed in both upper-class and homosexual networks, the Prime Minister, Lord Rosebery, had wanted to release Wilde, but was told it would lose him the election: he did, however, assist him financially. According to Ives, Rosebery was 'said by almost everybody to have been a homosexual ... . Hyde Park Police had orders never to arrest Lord R. on the principle that too big a fish often breaks the line.'[21]

Homophilia

Even before the Wilde trials, however, there had been attempts to construct a more positive vision of same sex love. There were some literary representations, for example the poems of the 'Uranian' coterie praising the love of lads.[22] J. Addington Symonds completed *A Problem in Modern Ethics* in 1890, and the following year had 50 copies printed for private circulation, with wide margins for comment. As well as introducing terms such as 'urning' and 'inversion' from European sexology, he argued, citing Continental experts, that the existing law was unjust and caused unnecessary suffering.[23] At some point preceding the Wilde trial, George Ives, who was acquainted with him, founded 'The Order of Chaeronea', a secret and high-minded homophile organization, named in memory of the Theban Sacred Band and involving, as far as one can gather from the rather sparse records (not only was the society itself clandestine, Ives was pathologically secretive), quasi-masonic rituals and insignia (Wilde, however, did not join).[24]

In 1894 the utopian socialist reformer Edward Carpenter (a colleague of Ives, but not a member of his Order) published an essay on 'Homogenic Love in a Free Society' with the Manchester Labour Press, in a series on sex and gender relations in a free society. Carpenter's plan to publish an extended version in *Love's Coming of Age* in 1895 led to the publisher T. Fisher Unwin's withdrawal – the volume later appeared (from the Labour Press) temporarily shorn of the controversial chapter, which resurfaced in later editions.[25] The degree to which societal taboos against sexual indulgence and excess had been internalized by those who recognized themselves in works such as Carpenter's and Symonds's, is suggested by a letter from Laurence Housman to Carpenter, arguing, 'An emotional embrace, so long as it permits of physical continence, seems to me quite natural whatever the sex.... But I strongly regard the ultra-physical side of it as a thing to be kept in the severest restraint.'[26] An attempt to spiritualize intense homoerotic bonds between men can also be seen in a provincial setting with the group of 'Bolton Whitmanites', influenced by the poet and by Carpenter's works.[27]

A further major work on the subject appeared from Havelock Ellis, not himself homosexual, although a close friend of several male homosexuals and married to Edith Lees, who came out as lesbian subsequent to their marriage. Ellis had determined over a decade previously to devote his life to the scientific study of sex and its elucidation for the general benefit. He had trained as a doctor, but practised very briefly before devoting himself to literary work and his great project. A proem, the volume *Man and Woman* (1894), had synthesized existing data on sexual differences. In 1892 Symonds approached Ellis, via an intermediary, to lend his medical authority to a collaborative study.[28] Ellis was undoubtedly predisposed in favour of the project. He wrote to Edward Carpenter that he was 'independently attracted to it' and hoped to obtain 'sympathetic recognition', while clearing away 'many vulgar errors', preparing the way for a change in the law.[29]

Symonds, however, died from tuberculosis in the following year. Ellis had access to his notes and materials, and a German edition appeared in 1896. It was harder to find a UK publisher, and Ellis eventually arranged for it to be published by the Watford University Press, established by a rather dubious character going under the name de Villiers. Horatio Brown, Symonds's literary executor, bought up the entire first edition and persuaded Ellis to remove Symonds's name and all material attributed to him, for the sake of the family. After this massive task of revision and rewriting, a new edition appeared in 1897 under Ellis's sole name.[30] Ellis commented that the existing literature was exceedingly sparse, especially in Britain, where experienced medical men claimed never to have encountered a case, and no case had ever been recorded 'unconnected with the asylum or the prison'. Yet in Britain inversion was subjected to 'heavy penal burden' and 'severe social stigma'. The authorities he relied on (apart from Symonds and Carpenter) were either European or American.[31]

Watford University Press also published *The Adult*, the journal of the Legitimation League. Initially established in 1893 to fight for the removal of the legal disabilities on the illegitimate, in 1897 it broadened its remit to take in free love, marriage reform, and other radical sexual causes. The police had it under surveillance for suspected anarchist associations, and in May 1898 purchased a copy of *Sexual Inversion* from George Bedborough, editor of *The Adult*. In order to prevent the alleged flooding of the nation with 'books of the "psychology" type' (this was the third copy of *Sexual Inversion* to be sold) and to strike a blow against 'free love and anarchism', Bedborough was charged with selling and uttering 'a certain lewd bawdy scandalous and obscene libel'. A Free Press Defence Committee was formed, including literary figures and socialists, but no medical men or scientists. Bedborough struck a deal with the police, laying the blame on the elusive and shady de Villiers, and claiming that he himself had sold *Sexual Inversion* in all innocence. There was never any chance to defend the book's bona fides: the trial in 1898, proceeding on assumptions of its obscenity, considered only who was responsible for publishing it. Ellis was devastated. Even so, he permitted Volume II of the studies to be published in Watford the following year (although it appeared under the imprint of the University Press, Leipzig). Subsequent volumes and later editions of the first two were published in Philadelphia; Ellis's *Studies in the Psychology of Sex* have never been published in their entirety in Britain.[32]

After the prosecution, both the *BMJ* and *The Lancet* demonstrated professional solidarity by arguing that Ellis, as a medical man, had a legitimate claim to discuss 'unpleasant matters with which the medical profession should have some acquaintance'. *Sexual Inversion*, though dealing with a subject 'odious in itself ', could not be included 'under the head of indecent literature'. The subject had 'proper claims for discussion' among 'persons of particular attainments': but issuing it through a non-specialist publisher ran the risk of exposing the distasteful matter to the man in the street, even, perhaps, 'the boy and girl in the street'. The arguments echo those in the Allbutt case ten years previously.[33]

The works of Ellis and Carpenter, though consoling, and even inspiring to individuals, had no influence on legislation. The laws relating to homosexuality were tightened up still further by the Vagrancy Act of 1898, aimed both at those living on the earnings of prostitutes ('bullies' or 'souteneurs', themselves categorized as deviant and unmanly, often 'alien'), and at soliciting or importuning for immoral purposes in public places. It applied not only to female prostitutes but to males importuning other males.[34]

Destabilizing matrimony?

Gender was a major preoccupation of the 1890s. While many were rendered deeply anxious by the changing status and demands of women, the new public visibility of male homosexuality, and other signs that previously clear-cut boundaries of masculinity and femininity were becoming blurred and destabilized, for others the changes were still pathetically slow. None the less, women struggling for some recognition of equal rights could find cause for optimism over quite small gains in strategic or symbolically important areas. Thus the decision in the 'Clitheroe case' in 1891 gained perhaps unwonted significance. Edward Jackson married in 1887 and almost immediately left his wife Emily (aged 42 and apparently rather better-off than he) in England, while he went to New Zealand to set up a business, anticipating that she would join him. She did not and, when he returned to England, refused to cohabit or even see him. Jackson then commenced proceedings for restitution of conjugal rights, but Emily Jackson refused to comply with the court order. Conjugal rights, though technically only enjoining co-residence in the matrimonial home, were interpreted by feminist reformers as a licence for marital rape. Normally, failure to comply with an order for restitution of conjugal rights counted as desertion and grounds for an order of separation (application for restitution in the expectation of failure to comply was becoming a procedure of choice for women wishing to divorce adulterous husbands). Jackson, however, took the law into his own hands, and kidnapped his wife on her way home from church with her sister, incarcerating her in his house under medical surveillance. Emily was fortunate in having supportive relatives, who picketed the house, while her sisters applied for a writ of habeas corpus. The Court of Queen's Bench initially refused, on the grounds that the unique relationship between husband and wife granted him custody over her (except in cases of cruelty or misconduct), but the Court of Appeal reversed this decision and issued the writ, ordering Jackson to release his wife, since no English subject had the right to imprison another English subject, even if she were his wife.

The anti-feminist journalist Eliza Lynn Linton fulminated that marriage had been 'suddenly abolished one fine morning!' and claimed that the judgement would encourage women to leave their husbands for 'mere caprice', while it advanced the dangerous designs of 'free lovers' and 'women's rights women'. Free-lover and veteran women's rights campaigner Elizabeth Wolstenholme Elmy, however, greeted the decision as a great victory – ' "coverture" is dead and buried' – replacing 'the old and worn-out code of master and slave' with 'the ethics of justice and equality'. It certainly registered how far legal views of the rights of the wife had come in the course of the half-century. But it was far from being the radical hiatus in attitudes towards marriage and the relations of the sexes within matrimony envisaged by either Lynn Linton or Wolstenholme Elmy.[35] The latter indeed saw it as only one further step towards full recognition of a wife's bodily autonomy, including the right to refuse unwanted intercourse. In spite of repeated attempts, she found no MP, among 40 or 50 approached, willing to introduce a Bill removing the presumption that a husband could not rape his wife. She was also unsuccessful in attempts to equalize the gender inequality in the divorce law and introduce desertion as one of the grounds.[36]

While 'free love' was represented by sensationalist conservative journalists, such as Lynn Linton, as the spectre of dangerous promiscuity haunting established society, the reality, for those engaged in its discussion and practice, was rather different, strongly inflected by existing critiques of the inegalitarian position of the sexes within marriage and antipathy to control of unions between the sexes by church and state. It was intended to be a serious and lifelong commitment: few were as radical as Edith Lees Ellis (wife of Havelock Ellis) who in an 1892 article, 'A Novitiate for Marriage', suggested trial cohabitation to test compatibility and capacity for domestic cooperation.[37] 'Free love' was debated within the Marxist Social Democratic Federation, and some SDF couples did choose free unions, rejecting bourgeois marriage and the interference of church or state. Promiscuity was reprehended and male and female sexuality were still envisaged as respectively active and passive.[38] The Legitimation League, a mixed organization with a strong representation of women, became explicitly connected with free relationships in 1897, much debated in its journal, *The Adult.* The practical problems particularly affecting women were recognized, and some doubts expressed as to whether men would surrender ownership in women's bodies, or indeed honour the commitment without external sanctions.[39]

Women in the Malthusian League deployed the long neo-Malthusian tradition of sex as a natural pleasure good for women's health within the context of overtly feminist concerns of the 1890s, even suggesting that contraceptive information might be taught to working girls who 'might easily get into trouble': more to prevent illegitimate pregnancy in a context of harassment or exploitation, than to enable experimentation. They still located licit sexuality within monogamous commitment, arguing that 'preventive checks' conduced to better health in both sexes and a better standard of living for the family, and that, by enabling early marriages, they would eradicate prostitution, male promiscuity, and female ill-health due to prolonged celibacy.[40]

'Free love' as an open commitment of principle could not be undertaken with impunity. A cause célèbre in 1895 was that of Edith Lanchester, a science graduate of London University, one-time secretary to Eleanor Marx and active in the Social Democratic Federation, kidnapped and incarcerated in a lunatic asylum by her middle-class family when she proposed to live in free union with fellow-socialist James Sullivan, a railway clerk. As with Emily Jackson, she was fortunate in having friends and allies – Sullivan applied for a writ of habeas corpus, while members of the SDF stood outside the Priory, the private asylum in Roehampton where she was incarcerated, singing 'The People's Flag'. Two Commissioners in Lunacy deemed her perfectly sane on examination, and ordered her discharge – expedited by the intervention of John Burns, MP for Battersea, a former SDF member. Lanchester severed all ties with her family and went to live with Sullivan. The case, also taken up by the Legitimation League, incited considerable debate in socialist circles, with widespread concerns about associating socialism with sexual unconventionality.[41]

While legal changes were of necessity important in reforming existing sexual relations, they were perceived as one strand among several strategies. One of these was to re-vision marriage to emphasize woman's bodily ownership of herself and downplay the importance of sexuality, stress being laid instead on 'psychic love'. This has been discussed by a number of historians.[42] As Bland, in particular, has noted, while women played an important part in voicing these concerns, men were not absent, and one of the central texts, the polemical poem *Woman Free*, 1893, by 'Ellis Ethelmer', with its citations to contemporary scientists, sometimes attributed to Elizabeth Wolstenholme Elmy, was in fact by her husband Ben, who further complicated the whole issue of 'psychic love' by affiliation to the Malthusian League.[43]

The genre of 'New Woman' novels dramatized crucial questions about marriage and sexuality, making explicit connections between various forms of women's exploitation. As novels and as serious representations of pressing problems their quality varies widely. One of the most notorious, Grant Allen's *The Woman Who Did*, 1895, is a sentimentalized and ultimately conventional novel about an idealistic girl who enters a free union and bears a child out of wedlock. Others, however, if they did not evade melodrama, sentimentality, and dubiously tacked-on happy endings, tackled not merely questions such as women's right to a fulfilling occupation, but the problem of marital communication of venereal disease and congenital syphilis, and made both symbolic and explicit connections between marriage and prostitution.[44]

Prudential restraints

Feminist debates on marital continence, while influenced by social purity and contemporary debates on women's position in marriage, should not be seen in isolation from more general notions of the appropriate place for sex within marriage. Simon Szreter makes a strong case for the importance of male choice and agency, manifested in sexual restraint rather than use of artificial contraceptives, in the reduction of family size, especially among the middle classes, in the final decades of the nineteenth century,[45] though perhaps underestimates the significance of a pervasive ideology of marital continence in reducing incidence of intercourse below optimum frequency for conception.[46] Medical texts, commercially produced advice manuals, alternative health sources, all decreed sex licitly pleasurable, while cautioning against excessive indulgence and (male) selfishness, and this view seems to have been extensively internalized.[47]

There were other expedients for controlling the size of families, none entirely satisfactory. The trade in contraceptives was largely subterranean and sleazy, and lacking in quality control, though some convinced Malthusians went into the business. Some men successfully practised withdrawal. The 'safe period', allegedly consistent with the laws of Nature, was calculated on the basis of the prohibitions on sex during menstruation in the Mosaic Law and placed the 'safe period' at possibly the most risky point of the cycle: Janet Farrell Brodie, however, has demonstrated how this might at least retard further conception.[48] Prolonged breast-feeding was practised by some women. And then there was abortion.

Many women, as a first recourse, thought about 'bringing on the period'. Many patent medicines euphemistically promised to produce menstruation and relieve female minds from worry. Most of these were ineffective, though often named after traditional herbal (and efficacious, if dangerous) preparations such as pennyroyal, tansy, and apiol, no longer readily accessible to a largely urbanized population. Some manufacturers, not content to exploit women with sugar pills, then blackmailed them for attempting to procure abortion: sensational trials took place in 1899 of the Chrimes Brothers and William Brown and Associates, distributors of 'Madame Frain's' preparations. When pills failed, women might resort to douches, hot baths and gin, attempts physically to induce miscarriage (such as throwing themselves downstairs), or the insertion of slippery elm bark or an instrument such as a knitting needle or crochet hook. Much, probably most, abortion was self-abortion, but there was also a twilight world of abortionists, male and female, illegal and semi-legal, with no guarantees of competence. Certain qualified medical specialists were known to undertake the operation but this area remains obscure to historical interrogation.[49]

Purifying the nation

Although the clinical understanding of syphilis was presenting an ever-gloomier picture, not only of its responsibility for congenital defects, but also for long-delayed tertiary manifestations in physical, nervous, and mental debility, while measures for reliable earlier diagnosis, treatment, cure or prevention still remained to be discovered, the British Government, still shaken by the furore over the Contagious Diseases Acts, was disinclined to take any action, at least in Britain itself. In 1897 there was considerable feminist concern over the proposed reintroduction of the Acts (or similar legislation) in India, promoted by Lady Henry Somerset, an active figure in the social purity and temperance movements.[50] Informal contacts between concerned medical professionals and philanthropic workers led in 1897 to a memorial requesting the appointment of a Royal Commission to investigate the prevalence and effects of venereal diseases in the United Kingdom, believed to be more extensive than commonly thought (though other authorities believed them in decline). The next year, a meeting passed a resolution in favour of the memorial and, signed by representatives of rescue associations, social workers, medical men, and others, it was presented to Lord Salisbury, the Prime Minister. He shelved it, even though it called initially merely for the collection of evidence about the extent of 'the evil' and arrangements for dealing with it, and in spite of strong resolutions backed by the British Medical Association passed at the Brussels International Medical Congress of that year.[51]

Intervention at an early stage, by influencing the hearts and minds of the young, seemed the most appropriate long-term strategy towards improved sexual mores. The heavily pathologized and disciplinary warnings to the pubertal male about masturbation continued, in the usual pedagogical context as well as from emerging youth organizations, with a renewed edge of Imperial anxiety: perhaps the most influential texts were the American imports by Sylvanus Stall, *What a Young Boy/Young Man Ought to Know*.[52] Feminists and social purity advocates were concerned about preparing girls for the dangers that lay in wait for them, and some went so far as to contest the complete sexual ignorance inculcated in young women. There was a new vision of early sex education of both girls and boys, undertaken by the mother within the home (fathers being noticeably absent from such recommendations until the point where it was deemed appropriate for him to warn the adolescent boy against self-abuse), foregrounding Nature and the natural, the healthy and reproductive, and also the sacred character of motherhood. 'Pure' and 'clean' were keywords, applied to physiological information about the human reproductive process as well as to flowers and birds: flowers often had to bear a somewhat strained burden of symbolism:

> important flower-like organs...are already developing in you...be most daintily cautious that no playing or meddling with them ever takes place. For, till you are fully grown up, these parts are as a delicate bud to the coming flower.[53]

Some mothers did indeed undertake instruction of their young precisely in terms of 'Nature's ... beautiful schemes for the fertilization of flowers.'[54]

Countercultures and carnivalesque

The 1890s thus appear a decade of diverse anxieties about sex and gender, a period of discontent, a time of somewhat po-faced but eminently high-minded recommendations for improvements. However, pornographic representations were becoming much more widely accessible as developments in photographs and their reproduction led to the evolution of the pornographic postcard. These were cheap to produce, easy to distribute, within reach of all but the poorest, and often found alongside postcards on more innocuous themes. While some cards harked back to early nineteenth-century radical subversive pornography with obscene satire on the upper classes, most tended to circulate already standardized visual tropes and constructions of sexuality to a new audience. Exotic representations of 'natives' and 'Oriental' subjects were common. Women were exposed as objects of the gaze, often with backdrops of 'nature', flowers or animals. The audience to whom these representations were now available did not seem troubled by them, but this accessibility of such materials to 'the wrong people' was found enormously threatening by the police, the National Vigilance Association and other social purity bodies.[55]

Similarly, something of a counter- or resistant culture was to be found in the extremely popular music halls. These were subject to municipal licensing, a process in many localities strongly influenced by the social purity movement, concerned not only about the presence of prostitutes and the potential dangers of the mixing of classes, sexes, and the respectable and unrespectable, but also with the content of the performances. During the 1890s emphasis on 'family' entertainment led to management-imposed bans on indecency in language and dress. However, while there was little explicitly bawdy, shared codes of 'know-ingness' between performer and audience enabled a discourse extremely hard to police, being not in the actual words, sometimes not even in gesture, body language, or intonation, but in mutually understood encoding.[56] Carina Reed of the British Women's Temperance Association spoke against renewal of the licence of the Oxford with specific objections to Marie Lloyd's popular 'Johnny Jones', sung in the character of a brattish young girl, with the chorus:

> What's that for, eh? Oh tell me, Ma
> If you don't tell me, I'll ask Pa
> But Ma said 'Oh it's nothing, shut your row'
> Well, I've asked Johnny Jones, see! So, I know now.

but came out looking ridiculous. While managements responded by tightening up procedures for the selection of songs, Lloyd commissioned her team of writers to produce 'You Can't Stop a Girl from Thinking'.[57]

4

Degenerating Nation? Anxieties and Protests in a New Century

The first decade of the twentieth century in Britain has been characterized in contradictory ways. Samuel Hynes, in his influential study *The Edwardian Turn of Mind* (1968), contrasted the nostalgic image of Edwardian England as a 'golden afternoon', a 'long garden-party', with the contemporaneous 'Labour Party World' (the Labour Party actually became a Parliamentary political force during this decade) and characteristically modern developments technological (aircraft, radiotelegraphy, cinema) and cultural (psychoanalysis, literary modernism, 'modern art').[1] Yet 1900 was neither the dawn of a hopeful new era, casting off the outworn shackles of Victorianism (symbolized in the death of the old Queen herself in 1901), or the continuation of Victorian Imperial glories. Simple dualisms hardly begin to define this time of ferment.

Population anxieties

All was not happy even in the Garden Party World. Britain was increasingly looking over one shoulder at competitors. In South Africa, Imperial forces had been humiliated by Boer farmers (and the number of recruits rejected revealed the poor physical condition of much of the nation), there were demands for greater degrees of self-determination not just from colonial populations in Canada or the Antipodes, but from ethnic groups usually considered by nature subordinate and incapable of self-rule. Within Britain itself the traditional scheme of things was menaced by the demands of the Irish, the Labour movement, and increasingly militant women. The birth rate had noticeably declined over the preceding 30 years, most markedly among the professional and administrative classes, while maternal and infant mortality rates did not figure favourably in international comparisons or even over time. While epidemic diseases had declined enormously as a result of the achievements of Victorian sanitation, this only made more visible the continued persistence of less tractable menaces to public and national health such as tuberculosis, cancer, and syphilis.

Not only the decline in absolute numbers caused concern over population: there was also a perceived differential birth rate, with the most 'desirable' classes failing to keep up their strength, while the 'residuum' proliferated recklessly. Eugenics was thus a pervasive theme of the 1900s, although neither hegemonic or uncontested. Throughout the period there were increasing interventions in matters of health and welfare on the local and national level, and numerous bodies advocating the possibilities of personal self-, and wider environmental, improvements.[2]

The term eugenics, 'that science which deals with all influences which improve the inborn qualities of a race; also with those which develop them to the utmost advantage', had been coined by Sir Francis Galton, polymath scientist and cousin of Charles Darwin, in his 1883 *Inquiries into Human Faculty*. Galton had a pre-Mendelian view of heredity, as straightforward like-begets-like (the rediscovery of Mendel's researches did not greatly affect eugenic debates until the 1920s). Most early eugenic arguments and proposals were based on the assumption that desirable and undesirable characteristics, physical, mental, and even moral, were unproblematically transmitted.

As embodied in the British Eugenics Education Society (f.1907, with the extremely elderly Galton as President), eugenics appeared the creed of an established (male) meritocracy, and indeed to be a symbolic system for dealing with its fears of weakening gender and class virility. There were two facets: 'positive' and 'negative'. The 'fit' had a duty to reproduce themselves at replacement rates (at least) and policies should be directed towards encouraging them in this. On the other hand, means ought to be devised to discourage, if not actively prevent, the 'unfit' from perpetuating themselves. Some hardliners argued that public health and social welfare encouraged the survival of individuals deleterious to the national stock: but few argued for dismantling existing provisions. Orthodox mainline eugenics wanted nothing to do with contraception, partly from the belief that it was already perniciously affecting the middle-class birth rate, while the lower classes lacked sufficient forethought to employ it, and partly from a general distaste for this unrespectable subject. The Society, indeed, seemed to want to keep breeding as remote from actual sex as it could.[3]

Eugenics, however, was far from a monolithic doctrine supportive of a conservative status quo, and could be deployed to much more radical ends. Quite apart from the pervasive confusion in many minds concerning acquired versus innate characteristics (which the existence of congenital, but not hereditary, conditions like syphilis did little to clarify), the idea of eugenics was capable of being used critically and subversively to assert 'nature' versus 'culture' and attack existing economic and social arrangements. George Robb has drawn attention to a vibrant 'counter-paradigm in which degeneration was actually attributed to traditional morality'. Figures such as George Bernard Shaw and H. G. Wells saw rigid and unadaptable ideas of morality stifling sexual passion and thus endangering the procreative urge. Even a relatively (in comparison, and by the 1900s) conservative figure such as Karl Pearson considered that natural sexual selection in the human species had been dangerously eroded by the demands of advanced civilization. Marriage as conventionally accepted was about property, class, religion, and inegalitarian power relations between the sexes rather than the facilitation of matings good for 'the race'. Thus free love became not only a principled rejection of church and state interference in a private matter: it became the channel of evolution. Passion itself was 'Nature' selecting the best mate, irrespective of worldly considerations.[4]

This agenda could, as Robb acutely points out, verge on naive male fantasy, ignoring the realities of rearing splendid children of Nature once born. However, there was also a feminist version, or rather versions, of eugenics. Even the most conservative eugenics envisaged motherhood as of central importance, while many women, from militant feminists to outright anti-feminists, believed in revitalizing the nation through improving the conditions and status of motherhood (Carolyn Burdett and Ann Allen have drawn attention to underlying racial and ethnocentric assumptions[5]). In so far as eugenics was in harmony with this, women were inclined to be sympathetic, even if they did not regard hereditary factors as the only issue. Nor were many likely to listen with much sympathy to the arguments eugenicists advanced against the higher education of and careers for women as hindering the early and fecund marriage of 'desirable types'. Nearly 50 per cent of the early membership of the Eugenics Education Society were women. Many were unmarried professionals – teachers, social workers, civil servants, doctors – who might, however, have defined themselves as 'social mothers', extending the essential qualities of maternity into the wider community. Although so far no detailed study of this interesting group of women has been undertaken, many were involved in reforming activities which had obvious overlaps of interest with eugenics, for example mental welfare and social purity, which presumably drove their interest in the Eugenics Education Society (rather than the quest for a mate more concerned about sound hereditary qualities than superficial attractions).

More radically, women already vigorously critiquing the iniquities of the marriage system suggested that genuinely free female mate-choice, liberated from conventional social and economic pressures, would improve a race degenerating under existing patriarchal arrangements. In particular, the primacy of a woman's decision when to bear a child, as well as to whom, was emphasized. This vision of free motherhood had distinctive differences from the male version of free love and progressive eugenics: it was unsympathetic to its utopian vision of joyous procreative sexuality, emerging instead from social purity discourses on sexuality and motherhood, and endowing eugenics with a moral dimension of selecting the ethically fittest. Lust was seen as deleterious and a cause of, rather than a remedy for, degeneration and strongly associated with the male.[6]

Perhaps the most well-known spokeswoman for this school of thought was Mrs Frances Swiney, an active suffragist who combined theosophical beliefs with a wide knowledge of contemporary developments in biological science. She believed that women's sexual subjugation to men caused not merely social ills, but also debilitation through excessive and deleterious childbearing, and infection with poisons such as syphilis via semen, in fact, she regarded sperm itself as toxic. In the ideal state of society women would be the arbiters of sexual activity, having intercourse only for the purposes of reproduction, never during gestation or lactation, at intervals of four to five years. Male desire, in Swiney's scheme of things, was a pathological excrescence, not a natural impulse. Swiney promoted her views in a number of books and eventually set up her own 'League of Isis' along theosophical lines. She was involved in both the Malthusian League (which one might assume the diametrical opposite to her beliefs) and the Eugenics Education Society.[7]

What is false within

It is extremely hard to tease out eugenic concerns over hereditary unfitness from other concerns, both the deteriorating effect of modern urban life, and congenital diseases, of which syphilis was the most obvious. The relationship between syphilis in the father and an incalculable number of miscarriages, stillbirths, deaths in early infancy, and the birth of wizened puny babies, and longer-term effects of prenatal infection, had been identified. By the end of the nineteenth century syphilis was already perceived as 'an imitator' mimicking many other diseases, and the great physician Sir William Osler claimed that knowing syphilis was at the heart of clinical expertise. The pervasiveness and insidiousness of syphilis was confirmed and extended when Schaudinn and Hoffman finally identified the spirochaete, and demonstrated its presence in late manifestations, in 1905. In the following year, the 'Wasserman test' for serum diagnosis of syphilis revealed the extent of latent asymptomatic syphilis among the population, and in cases which had undergone thorough mercurial treatment.

There was in Britain, however, still governmental resistance to doing anything about the problem, although the medical profession and voluntary organizations kept up the pressure. The problem was increasingly seen as being about protecting women and children (i.e., the source of contamination was perceived to be men). The Interdepartmental Committee on Physical Deterioration, 1904, resulting from concerns over the high rejection rate of recruits for the Boer War, recommended a Commission of Enquiry into the prevalence and effects of syphilis. An attempt to present a memorial to the Prime Minister in 1905 foundered as the Government was defeated. In 1908 under the auspices of the National Union of Women's Suffrage Societies, Dr Louisa Martindale published *Under the Surface*, arguing that when women had the vote and economic independence, prostitution (and thus venereal diseases) would radically decline. Horror was expressed in Parliament at the dissemination of such information by the NUWSS, giving Martindale's work useful free publicity. The inadequacy of existing provisions for diagnosis and treatment was touched on in the Select Committee Report on Metropolitan Hospitals and the 1909 Report of the Royal Commission on the Poor Law. There was concern over the deleterious consequences for public health of the still-thriving trade in spurious remedies both to the diseased and those merely fearful that they were infected. Successive governments hesitated to take action since in the existing state of clinical knowledge, there was little they could do without offending someone.[8]

Although some advances had been made in treating syphilis, mainly in the military context, even in these relatively ideal conditions the actual results were 'heartbreaking': the treatment was lengthy, involved toxic doses of mercury, and a large proportion of patients relapsed or still showed positive Wasserman results. Then the situation was transformed. In 1909 German bacteriologist Paul Ehrlich discovered his 'magic bullet' – 'Compound 606' – the arsenical drug Salvarsan. Colonel L. W. Harrison, of the military teaching hospital in Rochester Row, obtained some for testing. Harrison's awed excitement at the results resonates in an account written nearly 50 years later:

> The almost miraculous disappearance of T[reponema] pallidum from the juice of the early lesions, as also the effect on the serum reactions....[It] would change the prospects out of recognition for every patient with early syphilis.

The 'problem of syphilis was solved', he concluded: it was all down to details of administration and dosage.[9] A new therapeutic optimism was born, but it took some years for this epoch-making discovery to influence government policy. There were less grounds for optimism in the case of gonorrhoea, increasingly recognized as a cause of female infertility and implicated in neonatal blindness.[10]

There were continued anxieties around prostitution and the new problem of delinquent girls. Paula Bartley has analysed the increasing deployment of eugenic discourse to categorize prostitutes as 'feeble-minded' and impose care and control on young women perceived to be at risk or already fallen. Pamela Cox has documented, following the Children's Act of 1908, a tendency to consider girls who came within the purlieu of the new juvenile justice system to be either 'wayward' and in need of control, or victims in need of care, and also control, and to absorb them into a complex institutional network of public and private bodies. Whatever the actual nature of their offence, the issues were perceived as being sexual.[11]

Whom God Hath Joined

Besides concerns about breeding and disease, there were wider dissatisfactions around marriage during the 1900s, largely focusing on the specific issue of divorce. Women had already criticized the gender inequity at the heart of English law (Scottish law was more even-handed), and the centrality of sexual misconduct, but by the 1900s men too were increasingly finding the divorce law inadequate. Even a wealthy, aristocratic, and privileged man might find release from an unsatisfactory marriage difficult, as the case of John Francis Stanley, second Earl Russell (son of Lord Amberley who lost an election for advocating birth control) proved. He married Mabel Edith Scott in 1890: five months later Mabel returned to her mother and filed a petition for separation on the grounds of cruelty. Russell was exonerated, but the couple, still at odds, remained married though apart through a series of suits and counter-suits. In 1900 Russell obtained a divorce in Nevada, USA (invalid under British law) and married Mollie Somerville. Mabel now had grounds for divorce (adultery plus bigamy), and was encouraged to proceed by a gift of £5000 from Russell. A decree nisi was granted in 1901 and Russell promptly married Mollie again in Britain. He was then tried for bigamy in the House of Lords, and sentenced to three months in prison.

In prison Russell wrote *Lay Sermons*, including a discussion of marriage. His arguments for divorce law reform picked up themes already in the air: the influence of economics and social status on partner choice, pervasive sexual ignorance and negative attitudes towards sex, the failure of marriage to reflect inner reality rather than social conventions. As a peer of the realm, he had unusual access to lawmaking: soon after his release he introduced a bill in the House of Lords aimed at thoroughly reforming divorce law. His reasoned case, however, did not stimulate debate: the Lord Chancellor called upon the Lords to reject the bill utterly, as tantamount to 'the abolition of marriage'. Russell made several more failed efforts to introduce bills. Initially fighting almost a lone cause, somewhat suspect due to his own murky matrimonial history, he did found (1903) a Society for Promoting Reform in the Marriage and Divorce Laws of England.[12]

In 1906, divorce became much higher profile. Sir John Gorell Barnes, President of the Divorce Court (widely known as a 'woman's judge'), made a speech in court concerning his ruling (denial of the wife's justified petition for divorce on technical grounds) in the case of Dodd v. Dodd. He described the law as 'full of inconsistencies, anomalies and inequities, amounting almost to absurdities'. Dissatisfied with existing grounds, the gender inequity of the law, and costs prohibitive for the vast majority of the population, as well as the enormous and complicating inconsistencies between separation and divorce jurisdiction, he wanted a Royal Commission to investigate the whole question thoroughly.[13]

This gave a needed fillip to the cause of reform. E. S. P. Haynes's formerly struggling Divorce Law Reform Association (f.1903) took on a new lease of life, merging with Russell's society to form the Divorce Law Reform Union under the presidency of Sir Arthur Conan Doyle. In the same year best-selling novelist Arnold Bennett published *Whom God Hath Joined*, a novel concerning divorce cases among two provincial middle-class couples causing suffering to innocent and guilty alike. This initiated a genre of novels and plays about divorce (pro and con), as well as more general writing concerning the state of marriage and the law. Eugenic and national fitness arguments were, not surprisingly, deployed by both sides: either divorce would free unhappy spouses to enter new and fecund unions, or, by destabilizing the institution of marriage, would erode the basis of the nation.[14]

Members of Parliament began to ask questions in the Commons as Russell continued his lonely campaign in the Lords, and in 1909 a Royal Commission was finally appointed. Gorell Barnes, now Lord Gorell, was chairman, and at his insistence, two women were included, although the King himself considered that it was 'not a subject upon which women's opinions could be conveniently expressed'. Lady Frances Balfour, suffragist and social activist, and May Edith Tennant, first woman Inspector of Factories, belonged to established political elite kinship networks. Other Commissioners brought legal expertise, the authority of the Church, political experience, press representation, and advocacy for (if not actual membership of) the working class and the poor. From early in 1910 the Commission took evidence from police court magistrates and court missionaries, probation officers, lawyers, doctors, representatives of women's groups, and 'miscellaneous witnesses'. It also received resolutions from citizen's groups and letters from individuals.[15]

Janice Hubbard Harris, in *Edwardian Stories of Divorce*, draws attention to the way in which this body provided a potent forum for 'counter-stories' of divorce by or on behalf of excluded groups, predominantly women and the working classes. These aimed at 'creating sympathy for the suffering outsider and a vivid sense of the social disorder created by current policies', focusing on specific individual tribulations rather than generalized statements of principle. In particular, the evidence of Margaret Llewelyn Davies, for the Women's Cooperative Guild, based on a survey of opinions of Guild members, gave working-class women voice and agency within the debates rather than positioning them as passive victims to be benefited or harmed by decisions made by their 'betters'. Davies recounted compelling tales of brutality, humiliation, squalor, and poverty. Guild members had a sophisticated understanding of cruelty within marriage as being about far more than physical violence; which women might have difficulty in getting judged sufficient to warrant separation, rather than framed by classist preconceptions concerning working-class matrimony.[16]

Protecting the child

This was not the first or only intervention into previously private spaces. Working-class homes and mothers, in particular, were the increasing object of sometimes intrusive surveillance by official and voluntary agencies in the interests of mother and child, especially child, welfare. While many of the middle-class women involved in these initiatives, as social workers for charities or health visitors, were intensely aware of the economic and structural reasons for the difficulties of the working-class wife (poor housing, inadequate income, etc.), the system as set up was inclined to place responsibility for every facet of her children's well-being on the already overburdened mother rather than facilitating her efforts to carry them out.[17] One expedient hardly ever mentioned was birth control, though there is one known instance of a middle-class settlement worker organizing instruction. Anna Martin, suffragist and social worker, who resided among the poor of Rotherhithe, arranged for Dr Alice Vickery of the Malthusian League to lecture on birth control and give private practical instruction at her house.[18] Szreter has plausibly argued that intervention in hitherto unthinkingly accepted motherhood, as well as the perceived greater cost of children, inclined working-class women to think about restricting their families, although he has also drawn attention to the underestimated part played by husbands in concern over and the control of marital fertility.[19]

It was not just the mother who was the recipient of this intensified gaze. Voluntary bodies concerned with child protection and social purity organizations were aware of the problem of incest, almost exclusively a crime of fathers or other male relatives, which remained an ecclesiastical rather than criminal offence much later than most other sexual offences. There was thus no effective legal means of dealing with cases of incest – felt to be taboo, probably rare, and an issue of morality with which the criminal law was ill-fitted to deal. Housing reformers of the late nineteenth century persistently alluded to it as an outcome of overcrowding in sordid surroundings. Both the NVA and the NSPCC came across numerous instances in their casework, and were already using the Criminal Law Amendment Act of 1885 to prosecute incest with girls under 16, although time limitations and the need for parental consent to medical examination restricted its usefulness. Bills were put before Parliament during 1899–1900, 1903, and 1907. An Act was finally passed in 1908. The Home Office, whose support was crucial, had been convinced of the prevalence of the problem and of the need to do something. Eugenic arguments were surprisingly sparse, though deployed as a supporting consideration. There was considerable opposition, largely along the grounds that introducing legislation would only undesirably publicize a horrible subject, and that 'offences against morality' were not crimes. There was also some anxiety about destabilizing family life by promoting distrust and even blackmail within the domestic circle. Bailey and Blackburn suggest that the Act's passage was a major symbolic triumph for the social purity movement, but express reservations about its actual effect. Carol Smart has delineated the continuing problems of dealing with child sexual abuse within a rigid legal system.[20]

Sexual science

As these various issues became topics of public debate and calls for legislation, the development of a 'sexual science' was quietly proceeding. Ellis was steadily producing his *Studies in the Psychology of Sex* (published in Philadelphia), and his works were gaining increasing approval among the medical profession (though possibly in order to position him as a sound British authority against the 'turbid continental outpourings' of foreign sexologists[21]). As early as 1901 he was praised for writing in a 'proper manner, saying clearly what must be said', and treating delicate subjects with 'thoroughness and decency'.[22]

'Turbid continental outpourings' were having some impact on the British scene, though often issued for the use of the medical profession, lawyers, and others who might be supposed to have a licit professional interest in such a sordid subject. The translation of Iwan Bloch's *The Sexual Life of Our Times* was condemned to be destroyed in 1907, but Ellis wrote to Carpenter: 'I expect a compromise will be arranged and that the publisher will agree to limit the sale to doctors.'[23] In 1908 the *British Medical Journal* published a leader concerning the 'particularly interesting and lively controversy' over Professor Freud of Vienna's views on hysteria. While conceding that Freud's 'psychopathological researches place him in the ranks of the most eminent', the *BMJ* felt that the resurrection of recollections of 'the most intimate kind', was 'very undesirable' and potentially hazardous. Dean Rapp has usefully demonstrated that at this date, Freud and psychoanalysis, though discussed among a progressive vanguard of the lay public, made little impact on the medical profession. Doctors taking an interest in this subject were often marginalized in the profession, for example by their gender (a number of women doctors trained in analysis and were involved in setting up the first clinic in the United Kingdom).[24]

The Viennese thinker on sex and gender probably most well-known in Britain at this date was Otto Weininger, who published *Geschlect und Charakter* (Sex and Character) in 1903 at the age of 23, and shot himself a few months after publication. The English translation was published in 1906 and widely read and discussed. Judy Greenway suggests that 'Misogynist, anti-semitic, anti-sexual, the book's themes highlight the anxieties of the age.'[25] Chandak Sengoopta has helpfully illuminated the 'polyphony' of contemporary ideas and anxieties in Weininger's pages.[26] Many who dissented from the despairing misogyny of Weininger's conclusions none the less found the book useful, if only as a dire example, as Frances Swiney did when she referred to it as:

> the cry from the abyss of human suffering, misery, and despair … man is confronted by the perverted sex-principle in human depravity through abnormal sensuality and sex-abuse.[27]

Edward Carpenter wrote to Ellis that he found

> His general estimate of woman is good – provided of course you apply it as representing the extreme type – what he calls the Absolute Female. (It is a pity he did not balance the book by shewing the absurdities of the Absolute Male.)[28]

Many, while dissenting from Weininger's conclusions, found his theory that all individuals were made up of differing proportions of male and female qualities (M or W), an extremely useful way of thinking about sexuality and gender as a spectrum, particularly in conceptualizing 'intermediacy'.[29]

Carpenter continued to promote his vision of the healthiness of the same-sex bond in *Iolaus: An anthology of friendship* (1902), in 1906 *Love's Coming of Age* finally included a chapter on the 'Intermediate Sex', and in 1908 *The Intermediate Sex* appeared. He was increasingly becoming something of a guru for 'inverts', 'Urnings', and 'Uranians', who sought his advice and made pilgrimages to Millthorpe.[30] Carpenter's status among a broad constituency of intermediates, socialists, feminists, and other progressive thinkers was not echoed by acceptance in medical circles. Without the professional qualifications which gained sympathy for Ellis's works, *The Intermediate Sex* was dismissed as 'of no scientific or literary merit, advocating the culture of unnatural and criminal practices', available to 'anyone who likes to pay 3s. 6d'.[31]

Issues of censorship and appropriate audience continued to dog discussion of sexual matters in Britain. *The Lancet*, in a favourable review of Volume II of Ellis's *Studies in the Psychology of Sex*, cautioned:

> But his book must not be sold to the public, for the reading and discussion of such topics are dangerous. The young and the weak would not be fortified in their purity by the knowledge that they would gain from these studies, while they certainly might be more open to temptation after the perusal.[32]

While Ellis's volumes were available in specialist libraries (including the International Women's Suffrage Club), the average lay person had some diffi-culties in obtaining them. D. A. Thomas, later Lord Rhondda, mine-owner, politician, and eventual Cabinet Minister, was informed that 'one had to produce some kind of signed certificate from a doctor or lawyer to the effect that one was a suitable person to read it.'[33] This was presumably self-policing by publishers and booksellers.

In 1909 the Home Office considered whether Carpenter's works contained grounds for prosecution, and if action should be taken. Attention had been drawn to them by Irish anti-socialist and social purity adherent, M. D. O'Brien, who had conducted a single-handed local campaign against Carpenter, as a result of which, according to the Chief Constable of Derbyshire, Carpenter and his companion George Merrill were under observation. O'Brien was admitted to be 'a crank', but none the less officials read and wrote extensive minutes on Carpenter's work. They were of the opinion that the books did 'a good deal of harm', even though (or perhaps because) 'the grosser side of the subject is kept discreetly in the background', but there was a general consen-sus as to

> the unwisdom of calling public attention to Mr Carpenter and his works...any public discussion of this subject greatly exceeds any mischief which is possible to the readers of books, who would not buy them unless they were in search of what they contain, and who would not read them unless they had already become followers of what they affect to teach. [34]

This decision not to intervene suggests not tolerance, but the peculiar horror associated with any public discussion of homosexuality and the desire to render this an area of silence which Sean Brady has delineated in detail.[35] Curiously, and perhaps contradictorily, a significant theme in Edwardian literature was 'bromance' – intense romantic friendship between two males (implicitly platonic). This was a common motif in the popular genre of school stories, depicted as having an elevating and moral effect on the participants.[36]

Alison Oram has drawn attention to recurrent reports in the early twenti-eth-century popular press of women who passed as men and lived as husbands to other women, only to be discovered as the result of some accident. Rather than being pathologized, they were depicted as daring pranksters who had got away with deceiving their workmates and neighbours by their effective perfor-mance of masculinity. The issue tended to be framed as narratives of gender-crossing masquerade, rather than about sexuality: the 'wives' might praise their 'husbands', but this was in terms of their conformity to the accepted masculine role of responsible provider and head of household in working- or lower middle-class communities. Couples' affection was largely read within the conventions of devoted female friendship. In a rather more titillating mode, male impersonators were also among the most popular music-hall acts of the period, mocking and satirizing male pretensions rather than 'passing', and had substantial followings of adoring female fans.[37]

Keeping it clean

Such manifestations fell below the horizon of Home Office and Post Office attempts to hinder if not entirely stop trade (mostly with the Continent by this period) in 'indecent and obscene articles, books and pictures' (including 'Indecent Mechanical Devices' made in Switzerland). Raffish journals, such as *The Pelican*, consistently included small ads for 'Scarce Books, Photographs etc. – Catalogue, with samples', 'New and Old English Books (Facetiae, Literary Curiosities &C)' from dealers in Paris, as well as 'Photos for collectors. Continental Studies from Life' available from Battersea but presumably imported. The Postmaster General was anxious to obtain warrants to intercept not only mail from, but also to known Continental dealers. While admitting that there might be 'awkward questions', no difficulties had arisen in an earlier use of this ploy, 'probably because the senders did not wish to advertise the fact that they were purchasing indecent literature'.[38]

This was business as usual about material defined at the outset as pornographic which no-one, even its producers and purchasers, was going to defend. However, the Post Office does not seem to have interfered with the posting of saucy postcards, such as those of Donald McGill, sold in seaside and other resorts.[39] A Postcard Traders' Association filled up the censorship gap, setting up pre-censorship committees of stationers and dealers in all major resorts with the power to reject designs deemed unsuitable.[40]

One aspect of the reaction against 'Victorianism' was the desire to explore pressing issues of the day in serious literature. The theatre was still under the authority of the Lord Chamberlain (an official of the Royal Household not responsible to Parliament): every play accepted for performance by a London manager had to be approved by an Examiner of Plays, who could refuse a licence or ask for alterations. The criteria applied were mysterious and arbitrary, and strongly influenced by the individual opinions and prejudices of the Examiner, at this date, G. A. Redford, a former bank manager whose qualifications for the post were almost totally negative. He had a 'hangman's power' over the English stage during this period of considerable dramatic vibrancy. Following the refusal of licences to plays by Edward Garnett and Harley Granville Barker, a group of dramatists petitioned the Prime Minister for a meeting to discuss stage censorship (a copy of their letter was published in *The Times*). Serious playwrights were particularly annoyed that farcical and comic treatments of sexual matters were seldom refused a licence. Theatre managers urged the extension of the Lord Chamberlain's powers: anxious to preserve commercial receipts, without licensing they feared objections from local authorities, and pressures from, and even prosecution by, social purity organizations. In 1909 Robert Harcourt MP, himself something of a dramatist, introduced a Theatres and Music Halls Bill to abolish censorship, and harried the Commons with questions until the Prime Minister appointed a Joint Committee to investigate the question. In spite of evidence from leading writers of the day, the Committee ultimately recommended the continuation of censorship, although making licensing optional. Although no legislation resulted, this Committee recommended clarifying the conditions for refusal of a licence, and their suggestions were adopted by the

Lord Chamberlain's Office in 1910. An Advisory Board for doubtful cases was also established.[41]

At least a defined official was responsible for stage censorship and licensing. As there was no court of appeal for books, publishers were particularly vulnerable to social purity crusades against 'pernicious literature'. The National Vigilance Association prosecuted publisher John Long over Hubert Wales's *The Yoke*, a novel about a transient sexual liaison between a middle-aged woman and her young male ward, depicted as good for both of them, for which neither was punished. The book had been out for some while when prosecution occurred: probably the issue of a cheap paperbound edition precipitated the action. The NVA and allied bodies, however, did not want to pick off obscene novels one by one. They next approached circulating libraries, a major mode of distribution and a significant market for fiction. Many already had systems of self-censorship, and were highly sensitive to complaints.

In 1909 the major libraries formed the Circulating Libraries Association, which informed publishers of their criteria for selection and the classification of books as satisfactory, doubtful, and objectionable, instituting a secret pre-censorship. There were attacks from the literary world, but various bodies concerned with public morality were anxious to extend similar censorship to other organs of distribution such as public libraries (presumably already heavily policed by local authorities) and railway bookstalls.[42] The effect of this climate on publishers (and writers) is less easy to determine than public statements, but it doubtless made them cautious about what they risked publishing or writing, that is, created an internalized self-censorship. It also had consequences perhaps not envisaged by the forces of purification:

> The booksellers of the middle, or publishing, section of the Charing Cross Road ... have hit upon a brilliant scheme for extending the guardianship of public morals, lately instituted by public libraries, to doubtful tomes already in stock. It consists of grouping all the naughty novels on a separate shelf beneath a glaring notice: 'BANNED BY THE CENSOR' – and if youth and innocence insists on buying those volumes then it's youth and innocence's own fault, that's all.[43]

Circulating libraries were largely patronized by the middle classes and thus their censorship may be seen as about not offending the susceptibilities of paying subscribers rather than concern about disseminating inappropriate materials to the 'wrong' classes. New technologies, however, posed new problems. Mutascope ('What the Butler Saw') machines and the cinema were available to the lower classes at a low price and often in vulgar venues – music halls, 'penny gaffs' and fairgrounds – although by the 1900s purpose-built picture palaces were proliferating. The National Vigilance Association was involved in prosecutions of mutascopes, sometimes contested on the grounds that what was being shown was 'art',[44] but although there were concerns about the potentially deleterious effects of the actual films, there do not seem to have been any prosecutions for indecency or obscenity involving cinema exhibitions. In 1909 a Cinematograph Act granted county councils (or bodies to whom they delegated authority) the power of issuing cinematograph licences. While the Act itself, and related Home Office Regulations, dealt only with building safety, some local authorities soon extended the conditions under which they would grant licences, firstly to prohibit Sunday performances, and within a few years to insist that films exhibited should not be immoral or indecent.[45]

While there were these various efforts to censor what the public saw and read, divorce court proceedings continued to be extensively published in the press, combining voyeurism, sensationalism, comedy (pervasive use of punning and wordplay), and sometimes pathos. While there were protests at the pernicious effects of these accounts of matrimonial misconduct, it was also argued that the openness of judicial actions was an essential of English law, and that fear of publicity had a useful deterrent effect (a mass-media version of tradition community charivaris). What this meant in practice was that things which could not be said on stage or written in a novel were available in a far cheaper and more accessible form.[46]

*   *   *

With all this anxiety about censorship, it might be imagined that Britain was an immoral society pullulating with sexual vice. In fact, the number of divorces was very low given the size of the married population, partly due to the state of the law, and partly to social stigma. Illegitimate births had declined since the mid-nineteenth century, for reasons which are debated. Cook and Szreter both argue that this was due to a culture of sexual restraint in tandem with ideas of respectability.[47] Within marriage (at least among the middle/respectable classes) it is likely that sex was relatively infrequent, either due to the persistence of the ideology of marital continence discussed in Chapter 3, or for purposes of attempted family restriction.[48] The visibility of prostitution had declined to the point at which social purity campaigner William Coote could claim: 'London today...is an open-air cathedral.' Streetwalkers conducted themselves 'unobtrusively, communicating furtively with passers-by', and a good deal of clandestine prostitution was concealed under advertisements for manicure, massage or chiropody, schools of foreign languages, and 'nurses' offering 'rheumatism cures' and 'electrical treatment for all muscular ailments'. Ferris suggests that the nurse figure in early twentieth-century British prostitution hints at the therapeutic role it played: it may equally relate to fetishization of one of the few female figures licensed to have physical contact with the opposite sex.[49] It seems that the British of the 1900s were allergically sensitive to sexual hints, reacting to levels of innuendo imperceptible to other nations.

5

Divorce, Disease, and War

In 1920 a Committee considering the question of the state and sexual morality remarked:

> In the years immediately preceding the outbreak of war in August 1914, British people had been increasingly concerned about the question of sexual morality, its effects upon the status of women, on the birth-rate and general health, as well as the existence (and some thought the increase) of commercialized vice.[1]

Concern for these issues thus pre-dated what is often considered a precipitating event for anxieties and action.

Matters matrimonial

Havelock Ellis regarded the appearance of Volume 6 of *Studies in the Psychology of Sex, Sex in Relation to Society*, in 1910, as the culmination of his endeavours (although an afterthought volume appeared in 1927), writing to Edward Carpenter: 'It is certainly a deep joy and relief to me to see the work safely completed.'[2] *The Lancet* remarked that in his 'peculiar field' Ellis had 'given the dignity of scholarship to a very delicate and difficult subject'. However, it expressed reservations about his chapter on 'The Art of Love'.[3] While marriage was much under discussion at the time, few were as explicit in their advocacy of the need to cultivate the art of mutual conjugal pleasure. Carpenter, arguing for a more equal and comradely relationship between the sexes, and retrieving sex and the body from their degraded status, was chary of making specific recommendations.[4] Various popular writings indicated that occasional sexual connection within marriage was healthy and should be pleasurable for both sexes, and cautioned men against selfish disregard for wives (especially on the wedding night) but only Ellis suggested not merely that sexual pleasure was not a given, but in addition the means by which it might be achieved.[5]

Meanwhile, the Royal Commission on Marriage and Divorce continued to hear evidence: it became painfully clear that no consensus would result. A powerful minority of Commissioners strongly identified with the Church of England opposed any extension of grounds, although prepared to concede that existing grounds should be gender-equal, that costs should be lowered, and that publicity should be restricted (Gail Savage acutely suggests that mass-media reporting of the sexual peccadilloes of the privileged classes was a factor in anxieties over this specific issue[6]). But there they stuck: the Minority Report was widely circulated through Church channels and published in its entirety in *The Times.*

The Majority (including both women commissioners) Report recommended decentralizing facilities for divorce and other matrimonial cases so that persons of limited means could have their cases heard locally, along with abolishing existing provision for separations to be dealt with in the Courts of Summary Jurisdiction. It wanted gender equality, and to add desertion of over three years, cruelty, incurable insanity, habitual drunkenness, and imprisonment under commuted death sentence as grounds. Various other tidying-up measures were recommended. The rights of Anglican clergy to refuse marriage and holy communion to divorced persons with living spouses were protected.[7]

Fiery young journalist Rebecca West, whilst acclaiming the 'feminist revolu-tion' it embodied, also, prophetically, described it as 'A Report that Will Not Become Law'.[8] The Divorce Law Reform Union turned its efforts to getting the Royal Commission recommendations embodied in law: the advent of the war stymied a bill that merely introduced those measures on which Majority and Minority Reports concurred, and the whole subject went on hold for the duration.[9] Samuel Hynes suggests that the Liberal Government seemed to feel that 'the mere appointment of a committee could be taken as a favourable gesture by the morally concerned, but that changes in the status quo would surely offend someone', and Petrow, in *Policing Morals*, concurs that 'legislat-ing for morality was a politically dangerous practice' unless public support was overwhelming, a phenomenon which can be traced throughout much of the twentieth century.[10]

Janice Hubbard Harris argues that none the less, the Report 'heighten[ed] awareness and refine[d] understanding'. The changes recommended by the Majority Commissioners 'asserted a new view of English marriage'. The minor-ity Commissioners' alternative position did imply that action to improve failing marriages needed to take place at an earlier stage.[11] The issues raised formed the groundwork upon which thinking about and legislating for marriage would be founded for several decades. 'A dramatic increase in divorce' occurred between 1910 and 1920: usually attributed to the upheavals of the First World War, it may also owe something to the concern over the question manifested in the Royal Commission and the increasing thinkability of divorce as a solution to a bad marriage.[12]

Other narratives about marriage and its problems emerged in the context of high-profile murder cases. In 1910 the papers were full of the Crippen case, 'a love-triangle gone disastrously wrong'. Julie English Early's work reveals the various facets that made it so compelling. It was a murder of the suburbs, a location regarded as suspect in terms of both class and gender, which could not be adequately placed on existing social or geographical maps. The suburban

male was constructed as unmanly and unfit, and the suburban woman as a slat-
ternly housekeeper of vulgar tastes who spent her days in trashy consumerism.
However, in the course of the case, Crippen became the 'little man' provoked
into the murder of a coarse and domineering wife. As a music-hall performer of
Eastern European origin, her morals were suspect even lacking any substantiat-
ing evidence. Ethel Le Neve, Crippen's mistress, was also a working woman, a
shorthand typist who had worked in mixed offices, lived in lodgings, and had
been having an affair with him for some years, but was presented as a 'ladylike'
young women forced into the perilous world of employment by family financial
problems.[13]

   While the ill-effects of the existing matrimonial system were extensively
rehearsed, few argued for completely abolishing marriage. Divorce, after all, was
deemed desirable so that individuals could make new and healthier marriages.
Writers such as Ellis and Carpenter prophesied transformed unions. There
was thus an optimistic side to the 'marriage question' which did not assume
complete lack of common interests between male and female, but looked to a
joyous reconciliation of their complementary qualities in an improved state of
society.

Disorderly women

This may have looked utopian given the heating up of the wars of gender. As
the suffrage campaign was thwarted, some organizations, most notably the
Women's Social and Political Union (WSPU), became increasingly militant in
expressing their demands. Militancy was met with brutal policing even before
the extensive imprisonment of suffragettes. The forcible feeding of hunger
strikers had powerful overtones of symbolic rape, while Rebecca West described
her own assault by a 'policeman in a state of hysteria with quivering eyelids and
twitching Adam's apple', and elderly respectable women with a lifetime of social
service to their credit 'kicked and shaken and flung downstairs' at the Houses
of Parliament.[14] While suffrage campaigners tended to emphasize their own
respectability, and to eschew any association with demands for risqué causes
such as birth control or divorce law reform (or with individuals such as Edward
Carpenter), their behaviour was widely perceived as dangerously transgressive.
It resonated with the terms of legislation controlling prostitutes: 'loitering or
being in any thoroughfare or public place … to the annoyance of inhabitants
or passengers' (though suffragists were demanding votes rather than soliciting
sex); 'wandering the public streets or highways, or in any place of public resort,
and behaving in a riotous and indecent manner'.[15]

   A significant number of male writers, artists, lawyers, academics, scientists,
clergymen, doctors and politicians, as well as socialists and other less privileged
males, actively supported the struggle for women's suffrage. Though attempting
to redefine 'manliness', few took the critical stance towards entrenched gender
attitudes advanced by Laurence Housman. Some new images of progressive,
'modern' masculinity were advanced, but pervasive ideals of chivalry remained
deeply imbued with assumptions about men as champions and protectors. How
men participated was also problematic. Some undertook women's traditional

auxiliary and support roles. Others deployed their privilege and authority to advance the cause. Some themselves engaged in militant action, a dubious tactic conveying very different messages from women's often purely symbolic violence.[16]

Opponents offered not only overt violence, but assertions that advocates of suffrage were abnormal, mentally or physically. Sir Almroth Wright, a distinguished bacteriologist (whose marriage to an advocate of women's rights was breaking down), produced a statement so extreme in its attribution of mental and physiological abnormality to the 'militant suffragist' (and its implications about the role played by sex starvation in 'excess women') that it was repudiated by other doctors, one describing the diatribe as 'pornographic', and other anti-suffragists.[17] However, insult to the other sex was not uniquely male: apart from the continuing publications of Mrs Frances Swiney on the toxicity of semen and male biological inferiority, in 1913 Christabel Pankhurst of the WSPU published a series of articles, later published as *The Great Scourge and How to End It*, which claimed that the vast majority of men were riddled with venereal disease, 75–80 per cent with gonorrhoea and 'a considerable percentage' with syphilis.[18]

Tackling the 'great scourge'

Pankhurst was neither the first nor the only voice raised in concern about the issues of venereal disease at this period. Louisa Martindale's *Under the Surface* was mentioned in the previous chapter, while Cicely Hamilton's 1909 *Marriage as a Trade* also drew attention to this unspoken occupational hazard. The medical press occasionally alluded to the question of 'fitness for marriage' and the dangers of marital communication of venereal disease.[19] The subject was touched on by several Government investigations. The *Report as to the Practice of Medicine and Surgery by Unqualified Persons*, 1910, complained of the prevalence of resort by sufferers to 'Chemists, qualified and (more frequently) unqualified, and herbalists' and 'so-called specialists…entirely ignorant of medicine'.[20] The Departmental Committee on Sickness Benefit Claims under the National Insurance Act, 1914, drew attention to miscertification of venereal diseases so that sufferers might claim benefit, and the Select Committee on Patent Medicines of the same year reiterated concerns about quack remedies. The Royal Commission on the Poor Laws, 1911, recommended that powers of detention should be extended to the venereally infectious. While the President of the Local Government Board sympathetically received a memorial urging more widespread action, this was pigeonholed, although the Board did institute an official inquiry – by Dr R. W. Johnstone, amidst other duties.

Without waiting for this report, Sir Malcolm Morris and others, feeling strongly about the subject and, from past experience, considering that approaching politicians and Government departments was futile, and since an International Medical Congress was due to meet in London in 1913, decided to 'startle and impress the "man in the street" in order that public pressure should be brought to bear on the Government'. Many well-known names as well as nearly every doctor holding an official position subscribed to a manifesto, laying out a 'plain unvarnished statement of the facts', published in the *Morning Post*: tactics which 'succeeded to perfection'. The matter was openly discussed by the general press, and even former opponents agitated for an inquiry. The International Congress passed strong resolutions, and when Parliament next rose, the Prime Minister announced the appointment of a Royal Commission under Lord Sydenham.[21]

Three women were among the Commissioners: Mary Scharlieb, one of the first British women to qualify in medicine, by this date a very eminent practitioner, Mrs E. M. Burgwin, an Inspector of the Feebleminded, and Louise Creighton, of the National Vigilance Association. A significant number of women gave evidence. The Commission spent several years hearing copious evidence on the existing prevalence of the 'terrible peril to our Imperial race', and provisions for its diagnosis and treatment, as well as recommendations as to what should be done to combat it.[22] While years of agitation by concerned individuals (who formalized their campaign by setting up the National Council for Combating Venereal Diseases in November 1914[23]) played its part in the setting up of a Royal Commission, the advent of both reliable diagnosis and effective curative treatment for syphilis were clearly an important stimulus to official action.

Moral crusades

While venereal disease remained one sexual danger, 'White Slavery' was another. Though sometimes used as a general synonym for prostitution, by the early twentieth century it generally meant girls and women being deceived or forced into brothels, especially abroad. Many women, already prostitutes or on the borderline, were tempted abroad, into disadvantageous conditions, by spurious employment offers. But the image of 'white slavery' in the media and popular perception was of the helpless innocent victim decoyed by procurers. A mythology arose of 'drugged handkerchiefs, sweets and flowers', of surreptitiously chloroformed girls abducted from public places by apparently helpful strangers, sometimes dressed as nurses or nuns.[24] Petrow comments that white slavery was a 'displacement of anxieties about Britain's industrial and imperial position, mass immigration, the aggressive campaign for political rights by women, alleged racial deterioration and definitely declining birth rate'.[25] It was surely also a displacement of women's own anxieties about urban spaces and increasing freedoms – and also, perhaps, the problem of retaining 'respectability' – on to a melodramatic narrative of lurking menace, of vicious and dangerous (and racially-othered) men (and sinister older women) bringing about a fall that could happen to anyone, without volition. In spite of radical debunking by feminist journalist Theresa Billington-Greig, these myths persisted for decades.[26]

The suffrage movement, in alliance with social purity organizations, was anxious to take action against this supposed menace. The Government at first gave no assistance to successive Criminal Law Amendment Bills. In 1912 Unionist MP Arthur Lee introduced a private member's bill: W. T. Stead died in the *Titanic* and feminists and social purity advocates looked on this bill as a memorial to his work. The Government wished to placate the Women's Liberal Federation over the omission of women's suffrage from their Reform Bill. Sensational narratives – including strongly racist perceptions of the procurer as 'Other', Jewish, or 'Oriental' – as in 1885, propelled this Act to success. It made procuration a much more serious offence with heavier penalties, introduced arrest without warrant of suspected procurers (and made it necessary for them to prove that they were not living on immoral earnings), and flogging for procurers following a second conviction. Landlords were required to evict tenants using the premises for prostitution. As with previous measures, this new law made life harder for the prostitute. But the demonized figure was the transgressive male 'bully', the alien criminal living on a woman having sex with other men.[27]

The campaign against White Slavery was part of a more general moral crusade. In 1911 the National Council on Public Morals held its inaugural conference, producing a 'Manifesto on Public Morals'. It accrued very diverse support from church leaders, medical professionals, eugenicists, social purity advocates, Fabian socialists, and assorted believers in national efficiency and moral improvement, for an agenda allying commitment to regenerating morals to belief in modern medicine and science. Under the leadership of the Reverend James Marchant, within the discourse of 'social hygiene' the medical and moral were thoroughly interpenetrated. The Manifesto – published in *The Times* – expressed alarm at current 'low and degrading views of the racial instinct', not merely on moral and religious grounds but because they imperilled 'the very life of the nation'. The obligations of parenthood were being evaded and marriage degraded, the declining birth rate evidenced. Pernicious literature threatened corruption of the young, who should be taught that the 'racial instinct' was not for individual pleasure, but for the 'wholesome perpetuation of the human family'. 'Physiological knowledge' would protect youth against 'those who would seduce their innocence or trade upon their ignorance'. Measures to counteract the proliferation of 'degeneracy' were called for.[28]

The NCPM initiated 'the issue of a series of Tracts on the Regeneration of the Race...at the nominal price of 6d. for the purpose of educating public opinion.'[29] Marchant was keen to get the most up-to-date authors: the first title in the 'New Tracts for the Times' series was, astonishingly, *The Problem of Race Regeneration* by Havelock Ellis (which manifested all Ellis's characteristic scepticism about moral compulsion and his belief in 'freedom' and 'joy'), while the second was *Problems of Sex* by Scottish biologists Patrick Geddes and J. Arthur Thomson.[30] Geddes's approach seems to have suited Marchant, who later solicited two further volumes on sex education for children (using botany, 'on scientific lines' to 'lift these subjects out of the sentimental rut') and sex within marriage.[31]

While the great and good who subscribed to social hygiene believed the enlightenment of children in the ways of 'racial health' was essential, this was not uncontested by communities to whom this was introduced, as Frank Mort indicates in his account of the 1913 case of Miss Outram, headmistress of Dronfield Elementary School. Local resistance to her dissemination of 'race hygiene' caused press furore and the case was investigated by the Board of Education.[32]

Theodora Bonwick, however, in her work with the National Federation of Woman Teachers and at the Enfield Road Elementary School, Hackney, stressed involving parents and explaining what was intended, and achieved considerable success, but her enterprise was unique. The London County Council's 1914 Commission of Inquiry on the Teaching of Sex Hygiene found most teachers 'averse' from discussing the subject and concluded that it should not be taught in class.[33] The feminist NFWT did not differ essentially from the NCPM in the literature and teaching it advocated: 'a mixture of homily, religion, science, botany, and soap and water cleanliness'. The emphasis was heavily on sex as reproduction, and the biological analogies – plants, birds' eggs, salmon spawning – safely distinct from humanity: 'the natural world...was moralized to carry the significations of goodness, health, and social harmony.'[34]

This was rhetoric deemed suitable for girls, and the basic instruction of younger boys. Adolescent boys continued the focus of more specific warnings about the evils of self-abuse, though Alan Hunt claims that the 'purity hawks' had considerably modified their messages by 1914.[35] None the less, one of the most enduringly influential manuals, Baden-Powell's *Scouting for Boys* (1908), had no truck with the slightly more benign views some authorities were advancing, but bluntly claimed self-abuse 'brings weakness of head and heart, and, if persisted in, idiocy and lunacy'.[36] While more enlightened educators might caution against the fearsome warnings of earlier generations (and panic-mongering quacks), and emphasize mental attitude rather than physical measures, the need for control and the struggle to achieve it still predominated, even in the works of writers influenced, at least tangentially, by Freud or Ellis.[37]

In order to reduce ambient levels of stimulus to erotic susceptibilities, the NCPM and allied organizations persisted with campaigns of censorship. They were aided by self-regulating organizations. As mentioned in the previous chapter, circulating libraries had produced a code of conduct and in 1912 publishers asked for more severe book censorship. West-End theatre managers petitioned for the retention of pre-censorship of plays. The nascent British film industry, threatened by local authorities deploying their licensing powers to censor the actual content of films, feared that this might lead to a central government system of film censorship. In 1913, therefore, the industry approached the Home Secretary, who approved their establishment of a British Board of Film Censors. This had no legal status but simply classified as A (adult) or U (universal), or cut, or rejected films submitted, to provide standardized guidelines for local authorities. Occasionally local authorities, most notably the London County Council, overrode the BBFC decision and permitted the showing of uncertificated films, while others felt the BBFC too lenient. Issues bearing upon the grant of a certificate were not exclusively sexual (religion and politics were also contentious), but questions of sexual morality and what might be shown remained debated issues for several decades. The first president of the BBFC was G. A. Redford, previously Reader of Plays for the Lord Chamberlain's Office in its work of theatrical censorship, and the two bodies initially showed marked resemblances. Meanwhile, the Postcard Traders' Association rejected a quarter of the 7000 designs submitted.[38]

This campaign to clean up society was not uncontested, nor were successes guaranteed. Circulating libraries no longer maintained their monopoly on the dissemination of literature: public libraries were spreading (though might be subjected to censorship by local authorities, an area which still remains to be explored) and book purchase became more widespread with the issue of cheap editions. In 1913 three books banned by the circulating libraries none the less became bestsellers. Writers kept up their protest against systematic censorship. However, in 1915 D. H. Lawrence's *The Rainbow* was prosecuted for obscenity.[39]

Talking about sex

In 1913 the National Council on Public Morals established a National Birthrate Commission to investigate the declining birth rate and its causes, and related problems, including the preparation of the young for healthy parenthood. It had no official status, although there was a Parliamentary announcement that its report would be awaited with interest (an expression of goodwill which cost nothing), and Drs Stevenson of the General Register Office and Newsholme of the Local Government Board sat on it. It spent the next ten years acquiring expert opinion, or at least the opinions of those who felt qualified to pronounce on the subject or had strong feelings about it. The NCPM instigated a similar enquiry into the effects on morality of the cinema. Mere propaganda for social and moral hygiene was no longer enough: investigation and the production of evidence were also requisite and underlined the NCPM's commitment to the 'scientific' line.[40]

The desire to discuss sexual questions in a rather more radical fashion continued. In 1911 Dora Marsden, a former Women's Social and Political Union activist, founded *The Freewoman*, a fortnightly journal. Its greatest service, suggested Rebecca West, was 'unblushingness.... [It] mentioned sex loudly and clearly and repeatedly, and in the worst possible taste.' It provided a forum in which women could vent their dissatisfactions as 'vexed human beings'.[41] Among the topics ventilated in its columns were contraception, marriage and divorce law reform, prostitution, venereal diseases, illegitimacy, and homosexuality. It aroused considerable hostility and antipathy among suffrage stalwarts ('objectionable and mischievous') as well as anti-suffragists ('the dark and dangerous side of the women's movement').[42] There were constant problems with newsagents and publishers.

The Freewoman saw a heated debate early in 1912 about female chastity. Were women less lustful than men by nature, and therefore their moral superiors? Or, a new voice, that of 'A New Subscriber' (later revealed to be socialist feminist sex radical Stella Browne) enquired, were women actually suffering, physically and mentally, from the constraints society placed on their sexual expression? This debate has received considerable attention from feminist historians, to the exclusion of consideration of other sexual questions being discussed in *The Freewoman*.[43] And not just in its pages: 'Freewoman Discussion circles', inaugurated in London, sprang up around the country. Topics on which talks were given included 'Sex Oppression', 'The Problems of

Celibacy', 'Neo-Malthusianism', and divorce law reform, as well as the abolition of domestic drudgery. Smaller meetings continued discussion of subjects raised in the larger assemblies, such as 'Sex Oppression and the Way Out'.[44]

The life-span of *The Freewoman* was short; in 1913 it mutated into *The New Freewoman* and subsequently, as *The Egoist*, became a literary modernist journal, but it had been a significant moment. In 1913 playwright, male suffragist, and homosexual rights advocate Laurence Housman wrote to his friend Janet Ashbee: 'I was bidden to a conference on an intimate and painful sex-problem: and rejoiced greatly to find women there also, taking part in it and not embarrassing by their presence.' Later the same year he wrote: 'It is wonderful how open to a free discussion of everything I now find women – suffragist women I mean…even in the last two years the advance has been immense.'[45] The 'conference' was probably the meeting at the Hotel Cecil during the International Medical Congress, chaired by Magnus Hirschfeld, eminent German sexologist and campaigner for homosexual rights, on homosexual law reform. As a result an ad hoc committee was set up, founding what became the British Society for the Study of Sex Psychology. Although its initial members were mainly male 'inverts', and it has been described as a crypto-homosexual organization, its interests were far wider and not mere camouflage for a covert agenda. It embodied the sex reform movement based on the works of Ellis and Carpenter, but its aims do not look entirely antithetical to those of the social purity movement (adherents of which were invited to join): problems for discussion and investigation included the evils of prostitution, sexual ignorance, and disease, as well as inversion and aberrations, and the suggested reading list compiled by the committee included a number of standard social purity texts. The approaches might be different, but there was a considerable overlap in defining the problems.

The importance of both sexes being represented was recognized at an early stage, not surprisingly considering the strong representation of male suffragists such as Housman, Carpenter, and E. B. Lloyd on the committee. Cicely Hamilton was the first woman to join and 'Lady Doctors' were especially solicited: several connected with the Brunswick Square Clinic became members. A wide range of individuals – Malthusians, progressive educators, anti-censorship literary figures, nudists, clergyman, psychoanalysts, anthropologists – joined, representing also a wide range of personal sexual interests (from celibacy, via idealistic free love, to the occasional lecher).[46]

Khaki fevers

The impact of the First World War on sexual mores and gender roles has been much debated. Many characteristics of the postwar era had manifested well before 1914, and arguably the war hindered, rather than facilitated, a number of trends. In 1916 Stella Browne complained to Havelock Ellis that war conditions deleteriously affected 'various admirable movements, highly needed just now', such as the Divorce Law Reform Union.[47] In a 1917 letter to Bertrand Russell she commented that 'the newer manifestations of sexual liberty are very far from encouraging or attractive', but attributed this to 'the hateful war atmosphere & conditions' as well as the continuing disadvantaged position of women.[48]

For many, the War seemed a cauterizing and cleansing agent, fighting back the inroads of national degeneration, 'advanced thought', Modernism, changes in traditional gender roles, 'infecting' 'true' English national character lolling in an 'opium dream of comfort': Sir Edmund Gosse called it the 'sovereign disinfectant'. Rupert Brooke's image of 'swimmers into cleanness leaping' from a 'world grown old and cold and weary' full of 'sick hearts that honour could not move, and half-men' had a deep resonance, although his contrast of war with 'all the little emptiness of love' could well be read in the light of his previous history of bisexual emotional complications.[49] The mixed response of the suffrage movement has been extensively described: from Emmeline and her daughter Christabel Pankhurst flinging themselves behind the war effort and renaming *The Suffragette*, the WSPU journal, *The Britannia* to the pacifist and socialist activism of her other daughter Sylvia Pankhurst.[50]

However, while war might be regenerating the national character, it has also been claimed – as it was at the time – that normal sexual morality was overthrown. Laurence Housman wrote to Janet Ashbee:

> A friend of mine in the police tells me ... that in his district absolutely 'respectable' and 'virtuous' woman have given themselves day after day to different soldiers as if it were a sort of religious duty.[51]

Reversing gender expectations, men in uniform allegedly fled from young women maddened by 'khaki fever'. Angela Woollacott has demonstrated the complex anxieties about gender, class, and age this moral panic revealed. The focus was on young adolescent girls (some even said with horror to be of 'the respectable class'), not professional prostitutes, (allegedly), 'blatant, aggressive and overt' in harassing soldiers. Boys under military age and noncombatant males also hung around troop bases, admiring the soldiers, treating them to drinks and so forth, but women, caught up by similar patriotic fervour and the hypnotic glamour of uniform, were uniquely stigmatized. Woollacott suggests that this was a transient stage, fading when girls and women began taking over jobs to release men for the front, serving as nurses and VADs, in the Land Army, and eventually in the women's auxiliary forces.[52]

However, anxiety over unruly women persisted throughout the War. Feminists and the social purity movement had long been arguing for more women to be involved in the policing process. Women police in the First World War, however, seem to have been affected by the moral 'Forward Movement' with its desire to control immoral manifestations, as well as by class-biased attitudes and assumptions: they undertook much-resented surveillance activities (including of soldiers' wives, liable to have their separation allowances stopped for 'immoral conduct') and were often punitive in their response to disorderly young girls.[53] Concerns over 'war babies' were more ambivalent in an atmosphere of intense pronatalism, seeing reproduction as an essential national resource. Allowances were granted to the dependants of servicemen even if no formal marriage existed, based on the special claims of soldiers' offspring. But the rather different case of pregnancy resulting from transient liaisons aroused even more conflicting responses of both extreme punitiveness and almost complete excusing of the offence.[54] The atmosphere was sufficiently benign towards the unmarried mother to facilitate the establishment of the National Council for the Unmarried Mother and her Child in 1918, aiming to support this discriminated against group in keeping their children, lobbying to improve the status of illegitimate offspring, and ensuring that fathers acknowledged and supported their children.[55]

Soldiers' diseases

The idea of war as a morally regenerating cataclysm was further undermined by the problem of venereal diseases, especially given the earlier breach of the long-standing conspiracy of silence. Four hundred thousand cases of venereal disease, about a quarter syphilis, were treated during the War. Although rates actually declined between 1911 and 1916, as the incidence of venereal diseases tended to be higher in the military than the civil population, and absolutely larger numbers of men were involved, the question was sensitive, especially after the introduction of conscription.[56] 'Careful enquiry in some thousands of cases' showed that 'over 60 per cent of the infections' amongst British troops 'resulted from intercourse with women who were not prostitutes in the ordinary sense of the word', unlike Dominion soldiers (who had much higher venereal rates).[57]

Means of reducing the prevalence of venereal diseases varied, from exhortations to sexual continence, the training of special lecturers, the traditional provision, especially in France, of inspected brothels (in 1918 public opinion finally closed these), ablution stations for early treatment, and prophylactic packs (usually containing disinfectant ointment rather than condoms), though these were felt by many to be encouraging fornication. Methods of control increasingly focused on the man rather than, or as well as, his potential partners. Public education remained a problematic area: the BBFC refused a licence to a cautionary film about VD in 1915, but the NCCVD pressured the Lord Chamberlain's Office to lift the existing ban on Brieux's propaganda/morality play, *Damaged Goods*, in the interest of public enlightenment: achieved through the personal intervention of George V. It had a successful West End production and also toured the provinces. A film version, 1919, although already subjected to alterations in the story to render it more acceptable, was refused a licence in spite of interventions by concerned clergymen and MPs, the peacetime context being less favourable. In March 1918, Regulation under the Defence of the Realm Act (DORA) 40D provided for the forcible removal for treatment of any woman known to be a source of infection. It evoked a considerable amount of feminist and social purity opposition as reinstating the Contagious Diseases Acts under the guise of wartime necessity.[58]

DORA 40D was particularly egregious in the light of the legislation introduced, as a result of the Royal Commission's Report, through Local Government Board Regulations under existing Public Health legislation in 1916 and the Public Health (Venereal Diseases) Act of 1917, which emphatically did not discriminate between the sexes and aimed to eradicate the aura of guilt and shame which exacerbated the venereal disease problem. A free, voluntary, and confidential nationwide system aimed to bring sufferers and adequate expert treatment together. Administration of Salvarsan was restricted to authorized trained doctors, and the purveying of purported remedies by any but qualified doctors criminalized. Attempts to make communicating venereal disease a crime failed.[59]

Further degrees of moral panic were added to the issue of unruly women and the problem of venereal disease control by the presence of soldiers from the Colonies, introducing a visible element of racial difference (and fears of virulent tropical sexually-transmitted diseases). Systems of control eschewed the invocation of personal responsibility accorded to British and Dominions soldiers and relied on the imposition of disinfection on return to camp or restriction of mobility. Ferocious measures were taken to ensure that British nurses did not tend wounded Indian soldiers returned to the United Kingdom for treatment, and they were confined to the hospital grounds when convalescent. [60]

Destabilizations

The sexual and gender messages sent and received during the war were complex indeed. Initially it was felt to re-establish traditional relationships between the sexes, but also raised troubling questions about manhood and womanhood. If the soldier epitomized masculinity, what was the situation of the non-combatant – the essential worker, those too old or too young to enlist, or with some minor but disqualifying ailment (quite apart from shirkers, profiteers, and pacifists)? And, as the War drew on, what of the damaged males it produced, wounded in body and (as there was increasing awareness) in mind, and what indeed of the warriors of attested gallantry who declared against militarism? The generational conflict between the Old Men at home and the New Men at the Front was perhaps as, or more, acute than any war of gender. Women were at first confined to traditional roles – symbolizing the values being fought for, the recreation of the warrior, and the nurse – but soon took over men's work, including hard physical labour (and some skills thought beyond them), tending the sick within earshot of the battlefront, and even wearing uniforms (even, in some cases, breeches). And the 'khaki fever' panic inverted the usual image of a soldier's wooing.

For some the war was a painful hiatus: apart from the danger and physical privations, not all men enjoyed barrack room camaraderie or found male bonding in the face of adversity a recompense for loss of domestic comforts.[61] Not all women were liberated into a new world of exciting and remunerative labour: those in the workforce experienced long hours and disagreeable, even lethal conditions, while many women had to keep a home together in spite of the privations of a wartime economy, with their husbands not only absent but in danger. (Though some were 'blooming glad the old Kayser went potty', as one woman told Leonora Eyles in 1923.[62]) For some it offered opportunities impossible during peacetime. But the febrile carnival of entertainment available in London was probably pursued very much by a minority.

The idea of inner dangers associated with sexual immorality and deviance remained prominent in the media and popular assumptions. Several leading pacifists were homosexual, and though there were probably even more homosexuals among the serving troops, these were relatively speaking invisible, except in the infrequent cases when matters reached a court-martial. In December 1915 Edward Carpenter wrote to Havelock Ellis that

> an Inspector from Scotland Yard called at George Allen's, my publisher, to speak about my Intermediate Sex, characterised it as 'indecent and unfit for publication' – and asked if we were prepared to withdraw it! Our answer was 'No!'[63]

Stella Browne surmised to Ellis: 'Is it feared that it might endanger the innocence and virtue of the British barrack-rooms...??'[64] Early in 1918 Noel Pemberton-Billing alleged in his paper, *The Vigilante*, that the Germans had names of 47,000 British men and women vulnerable to blackmail on account of 'sexual perversions', seen as innately un-English and leading to treachery. A subsequent article entitled 'The Cult of the Clitoris' and referring to Maud Allan's performance in Oscar Wilde's *Salome*, led her to sue him for libel. As with Wilde, this was ill-judged, the case becoming the trial of Allan rather than her libeller. Her knowledge of the word 'clitoris' was seen as suspect in itself. How far the implication of lesbianism was understood is unclear (one Lord claimed: 'I've never heard of this Greek chap Clitoris'), but a general miasma of 'vice' and 'degeneracy' was attached to Allan and her associates, who included a number of socially prominent women.[65]

Female homosexuality was becoming somewhat more visible. Some women were identifying themselves as 'inverted' or 'uranian' in letters to Edward Carpenter.[66] Stella Browne gave a paper on the subject at the BSSSP, though she requested that no visitors be admitted (probably because the Allan furore was raging).[67] Rose Allatini's novel *Despised and Rejected*, published as by 'A. T. Fitzroy', contained sympathetic portrayals of female and male homosexuals, but was banned for pacifist content.[68]

If sexual alternatives to conventional models were gaining more prominence, the benefit was ambiguous, given the atmosphere of stigmatization within which much of the debate took place. None the less, the existence of alternatives was being registered. And, while heterosexuality might be 'normal', most sexual activity was shrouded in dark clouds of condemnation, fear, and ignorance.

A new solution?

To lift this cloud was the mission of *Married Love*, published by Marie Stopes, a distinguished woman scientist, in the early months of 1918. She had married a Canadian fellow botanist in 1911: the marriage soon became a disaster. The couple were childless and Stopes alleged that she had discovered, from research in the restricted 'Cupboard' collection of sexological texts at the British Museum, that the union had never been consummated. She obtained an annulment. A court-certified virgin, she then produced the definitive founding text of an entirely new genre of marriage manual.

Sex, declared Stopes, was beautiful, and the ideal sexual relationship approached mystical experience. 'Normal, healthy, mating creatures' (her audience) desired mutually enjoyable conjugal relationships, but in a terrible number of cases this did not happen. Stopes had a remedy. Women were capable of profound sexual responsiveness, but centuries of masculine misunderstanding (Stopes was a second-generation suffragist) meant that neither men nor women appreciated this, and were uninstructed how to achieve it. After introductory chapters in idealistic and somewhat purple inspirational prose, she provided clear and remarkably explicit details about the physiology of the sexual act, stressing the importance of the woman being aroused before penetration took place, and achieving a satisfying orgasm. The work was a runaway bestseller, greeted as a stunning revelation of the potential of marriage by both male and female readers: their copious correspondence praised the beauty, cleanness, and informativeness of her writing and requested further information.

Stopes is usually remembered as an advocate of birth control, but *Married Love* merely indicated its possibility. Later in 1918, *Wise Parenthood* remedied this deficiency, advocating the female cervical cap as the ideal method. Stopes was aware of women for whom her instruction, 'insert while dressing for dinner', was inappropriate, and in 1919 produced *A Letter to Working Mothers on How to Have Healthy Children and Avoid Weakening Pregnancies*, written in simple language and sensitive to the living conditions of poorer women. Stopes's tone was radically different from the instructional leaflet the Malthusian League had rather belatedly introduced in 1913. Her vision of birth control was not about 'preventive restraint', but a gateway into a new world of healthy wanted babies and erotic joy.[69]

One still occasionally hears claims that Stopes did more for women than the vote. A cap in the hand may have seemed to some more immediately empowering than access to the ballot box, although a little-known clause of the 1912 Maternity Act had already allowed the establishment of birth control clinics in hospitals: not taken advantage of until well after the war.[70] Not that the vote was available to the bulk of the female population when the Government finally granted the limited suffrage in June 1918 (women over 30 with certain qualifications), necessitating the continuation for another ten years, though in less militant form, of the struggle for electoral equality. The Sex Disqualification (Removal) Act 1919 lifted various restrictions on women's access to professions and education. The first women magistrates were appointed. How far these reforms actually went in redressing the inequality of the sexes was a question which would continue to be askable for several decades.

In the aftermath

Issues of sex and race exploded in the aftermath of the War. Race riots in UK port towns in 1919 were very much framed in terms of the threat to, or rivalry for, white women: the women who chose non-white partners were depicted in a very stigmatized and degraded way (women from port areas already being under default suspicion of being prostitutes). Members of the heterogeneous racial groups who had settled in UK port areas from the late nineteenth century had reason to suppose that service for the nation in wartime conferred certain rights as Imperial citizens which, however, local populations and government were reluctant to concede. The masculinity of white working men was under threat, with declining employment opportunities and increasing competition in the job market, and the increasing freedom of women as a result of the social upheavals of the War. The situation was thus highly volatile and riots occurred throughout the winter, spring, and summer of 1919 in nine major ports, with several deaths, much injury and significant damage to property.[71]

Celebrating an Armistice rather than outright victory; trying to retreat into normality; devastated by the 'forgotten epidemic' of Spanish flu in 1918–19, which killed more than all the war dead together but could not be subsumed to heroic, or at least dramatic, myths; shaken by the war, and desirous that nothing like it should happen again; hostile to the 'Old Men' and their conventions which had made the war; endeavouring to restore those secure conventions after years of upheaval – there was no one reaction to the end of hostilities and the end of the decade.

6

Roars of Rebellion, Roars of Reaction: The Ambivalences of the Twenties

Women of the transition

Writer Douglas Goldring looked back nostalgically at 'the little girls in the 1917 Club who used to run about talking about libidos and orgasms',[1] but while claiming that the twenties saw 'a new freedom of discussion among the advanced of both sexes', also considered that for the majority of women, 'marriage, motherhood, professional activity or hard physical labour continued to absorb creative energy' and kept them on the paths of 'virtue'. Temporarily during the twenties, he claimed, fashion-setting society and the intelligentsia touched and even overlapped. This Bohemian ferment's 'stream of new and iconoclastic ideas' was widely disseminated through the writings of members of the group (and probably also through media versions, not necessarily approving). The effect of all this 'on the sex behaviour of the average young person' was conjectural.[2]

Studies drawing on oral history evidence suggest that such behaviour was limited to a very small vanguard, and that for most couples, sexual ignorance or misinformation was rife and courtship heavily constrained by canons of respectability and reputation. Ignorance and constraint often continued well into marriage.[3] Recurrent flurries of moral panic over young women who had met a dire fate (whether murder or white slavery) through responding to personal advertisements, reveal continuing concerns over the transgressive behaviours of the modern girl. We know much less about how extensively these means of widening one's social circle or meeting eligible partners were used and who was doing so.[4]

Only women over 30 could vote, and not all fulfilled the necessary qualifications, while some electoral registration officers obstructed even entitled women. The 'flapper vote', granting the franchise on the same terms as men, was only finally achieved in 1928, following a decade of continuing agitation.[5] Opportunities opened up for women by the war were largely closed down, from the dismissal of 'munitionettes' to the relegation of female civil servants to routine work to open up positions for returning servicemen, to the closure to women of several London medical schools which had thrown open their doors during the wartime demand for doctors. Eligibility for unemployment benefit depended on having paid contributions before the war: and women who refused posts in domestic service were denied payment. The media excoriated women both for holding on to jobs, and 'idling on the dole'. Weeding out of women persisted until the general slump of 1920, which affected even traditionally female industries. Domestic service – in spite of women's persistent reluctance to return – continued the largest female occupation. The Ministry of Labour ceased reporting female unemployment separately, and many women simply stopped registering.[6]

Marriage bars affected women in civil service and local government posts and the professions. Dr Isabel Hutton, refused consideration for the post of Commissioner in Lunacy on the grounds that she was married, retorted 'that it was a pity I had disclosed this heinous crime of marriage...better...would it have been to live in sin and then all posts would have been open':[7] strictly speaking, not true, since women still had to maintain respectability, the appearance (if not the actuality) of chastity. While some single women did engage in sexual activity, this was fraught with pressures and risk. Radical socialist feminist Stella Browne commented as early as 1917 that women who rejected marriage, but wanted a sexual relationship, had to struggle against 'the whole social order', given 'ceaseless, grinding, social pressure' against free unions. Dora Russell, her younger colleague in the birth control movement, remarked that 'dread of the scandal that will end the work Aspasia loves' and 'fear of starvation' compelled 'outward acceptance of old codes and conventions', thus increased 'freedom in action' was unmatched with 'boldness in speech' (except, of course, among the relatively privileged bohemian intelligentsia).[8]

Marie Stopes argued in *Radiant Motherhood* (1921) that pursuing a meaningful career both benefited individual women and made them better wives and mothers, but this was a utopian vision.[9] Women writers, doctors in private practice, and scientific researchers might combine marriage with work, but many occupations were dependent on employers' rulings. As always, antipathy to married women working outside the home did not extend to extra-domestic labour by women of the working class. No feminist revolution followed the restricted grant of suffrage and the very equivocal removal of certain sex disqualifications: due less to the ideological effects of sexology, as argued by Sheila Jeffreys and Margaret Jackson,[10] than to persisting economic and social disadvantage and continuing pressures of convention and tradition.

Sexual offences

Very soon after the grant of the suffrage a Criminal Law Amendment Bill was under discussion, aiming at a number of reforms for which women and social purity organizations had long been agitating. Concurrently with the Parliamentary Joint Committee on this CLA Bill, the Association of Moral and Social Hygiene, perhaps the most feminist and libertarian of the social purity organizations, instigated, with the support of other groups, a Committee to survey 'The State and Sexual Morality'. The Committee's liberalism should not be overestimated: they still promoted a high moral standard along conventional lines, arguing that 'promiscuous intercourse is in itself essentially unhygienic'. However, they did believe that

> it is not the function of the State to attempt to interfere in the case of adult persons with their sexual relations, which should be a matter of individual conscience, and with which the community is not concerned, unless their conduct involves some act of public indecency.[11]

The Committee was adamantly against the continuing stigmatization of prostitutes and found it most undesirable to 'subject women to any special regulations not applicable to men'.[12] They were critical both of the law as it existed and the way it was administered (even apparently gender-neutral laws being enforced more stringently upon women).[13]

The Criminal Law Amendment Bill of 1921 was thrown off course late in its progress, when opponents called for the insertion of a contentious new clause applying the Labouchère Amendment to 'Acts of Indecency by Females'. Alleged by Davenport-Hines to manifest 'fear of female encroachment upon the male domain, a desire to preserve feminine submission and phallocentric power',[14] this is perhaps more plausibly interpreted as a 'wrecking measure', though influenced by concerns over lesbianism recently brought to public attention by the 'Cult of the Clitoris' case discussed in the previous chapter, and pervasive societal anxieties around gender generated by the upheavals of the War, and the entry, however compromised, of women into the national political process and, increasingly, into employment and public life. The issue had been raised, in the context of protecting minors from sexual assaults by women, during the proceedings of the Joint Select Committee, by Cecil Chapman, a magistrate of impeccable feminist credentials, who had denounced 'the sense-lessness and cruelty of the sentences passed on inverts' to the British Society for the Study of Sex Psychology.[15] As with Labouchère's amendment, apparently aimed at protecting vulnerable male adolescents, it was entirely misunderstood. No such clause figured in the bill before Parliament, but these deliberations may have inspired the wreckers. They deployed expressions such as 'cannot in a public assembly go into details', 'an undercurrent of dreadful degradation', and explicitly stated the subject to be 'disgusting'. While some opponents of the clause were influenced by theories of innate inversion as not amenable to legal regulation, or liberal disdain for enforcing morality by Act of Parliament, others felt that to publicize lesbianism by inscribing it within the law was itself undesirable, drawing practices of 'an extremely small minority' to the attention of the innumerable women of Britain 'who have never heard of this at all', to deleterious effect. The bill did not become law.[16]

Alison Oram has observed that the narratives about gender-crossing women in the early part of the 1920s retained much of the same tone of adventurous tricksters as before the war, though there was also increasing anxiety about the erosion of gender distinctions in the light of general social changes. In a series of articles in the popular Sunday paper *The People* in 1924, about 'decadent' people of both sexes given to 'perversion', this coded the 'vice' as prevalent among 'artists, theatrical and society people', echoing the Maud Allan case, rather than having anything to do with solid lower-class female husbands.[17]

The Criminal Law Amendment Act which finally passed into law in 1922 made some improvements to the law respecting assaults on minors, and placed restrictions on the much abused loophole 'reason to believe' that a girl was over the age of consent. Severer penalties were imposed for brothel-keeping. While it did not criminalize transmission of venereal disease or impose further penalties on the prostitute herself, it failed to incorporate any penalization of male solicitation and left the unique legal status of 'prostitute' in place. Continued pressures from groups, largely feminist, concerned with the issues embodied in the Act, led to the appointment of two committees, which testify to continued and intense concern over these matters in spite of the failure to obtain relevant legislation.

Carol Smart depicts the policy recommendations of the Committee on Sexual Offences Against Young People, 1924–25, as 'too radical and too child-centred' to achieve implementation. Some of the evidence indicates growing awareness that 'sexual precocity' in girls might be the result of sexual abuse rather than an innate moral defect, but this was still a minority view. Resistance to the construction of girls as victims and men as dangerous and culpable, and any acceptance that there was harm done, was manifested in enraged opinions from male MPs in debates on the Criminal Law Amendment Act and their desire to punish sexually molested underage young women as well as the man involved (class was another factor). Changes in law criminalizing sexual abuse of children simply channelled them into an unsympathetic criminal justice system ill-equipped to deal with such cases.[18] Pamela Cox has delineated similar attitudes in the punitive and controlling ways in which the juvenile justice system handled 'delinquent girls', constructed as dangerous beings even when perceived as being victims in need of care.[19] Angus McLaren has drawn attention to contemporary fears that designing lower-class women were targeting men of higher social status (mostly professional men, for whom reputation was particularly crucial) for blackmail, and that laws against underage sex were being cynically exploited for this purpose.[20]

The Street Offences Committee, reporting in 1928, recommended replacing the multitude of general and local enactments on soliciting with a new, gender-neutral, statutory offence of 'molestation by offensive words or behaviour', omitting invocation of 'common prostitutes', and making it necessary for aggrieved victims to give evidence (rather than relying on unsupported police testimony). A Minority Memorandum also recommended doing away with the deprivation of the right to jury trial of men accused of homosexual importuning. None of the recommendations became law.[21]

Attitudes to male homosexuality were in something of a state of flux. The paradigm of romantic friendship that had flourished at least up to the time of the Great War had apparently had its day. An attempt to produce a 'journal of friendship', *The Quorum*, in 1920 failed after a single issue, and the forces ranged against it included veteran homophile campaigner George Ives.[22] This was possibly prescient: in December that year the editor of the contact magazine *Link* was arrested as a result of homosexuals using its columns to make contact, in advertisements invoking same-sex friendship alongside certain well-understood code words.[23] Matt Houlbrook has demonstrated that the extent to which the law bore upon men engaging in same-sex acts was significantly inflected by class and economic and social privilege. Policing focused on public spaces (increasingly urinals/'cottages') and upon bodies which they suspected to be those of homosexuals, indicated by the use of cosmetics and the carrying of associated paraphernalia such as powder-puffs. Yet there was further development of significant homosexual subcultures and spaces in London (and probably in other large cities), both in terms of private clubs and certain pubs and other public venues such as cinemas.[24]

From combating VD to social hygiene

In the new climate of concern over venereal diseases created by the Royal Commission and the War, there were demands for even more aggressive public action. Debates about prevention versus provision of early treatment, already occurring in the military context during the War, became more general, with heated exchanges in medical and even lay journals in 1920. A Society for the Prevention of Venereal Disease seceded from the National Council for Combating Venereal Diseases, arguing that it should face medical realities instead of adhering to moral aspirations, and promote preventive methods rather than simply treatment after exposure. 'Preventionists' argued for wider dissemination of information about the prophylactic use of calomel ointment (rather than condoms[25]), and for chemists to be allowed to sell this (illegal under the 1917 Venereal Diseases Act). Some historians have regarded the SPVD as a force of modernity battling the forces of obscurantism, but while Stella Browne praised prevention as 'perfectly free from the hideous barefaced sex-injustice involved in "regulation"',[26] Dr Hugh Wansey Bayly, the Secretary of the SPVD was an anti-feminist and proto-fascist with a strong adherence to the sexual double standard,[27] who admitted that SPVD 'Directions to Women' were aimed at prostitutes.[28]

The Trevethin Committee appointed to investigate the question reported in 1923 that individuals could not be obstructed from obtaining means of disinfection and that chemists might be permitted to sell disinfectants in 'a form approved and with instructions for use approved by some competent authority', as they were already allowed to sell condoms, but that advertising, or providing more general facilities for disinfection, was not advisable. They also considered that prevention might suitably be mentioned by doctors to (male) patients in VD clinics. However, they placed greater reliance on extension of the existing provisions for treatment, increased public knowledge, and improved attention to diagnosing and treating pregnant women and babies, basically advocating a continuation of the status quo. This enabled the Government to leave the situation as it was.[29]

Venereal diseases were responding to the measures resulting from the Royal Commission: and, although many more men had been exposed to infection during the War: 'Never was there a period…when those infected received treatment as satisfactory and complete.'[30] Nearly 200 clinics throughout the country catered for increasing numbers of patients, but although attendances increased (1,488,514 to 1,605,617 between 1920 and 1923), numbers of actual cases declined significantly: syphilis by nearly a half and gonorrhoea by nearly a quarter,[31] although improvements in recognition and recording would have tended to show an increase. By 1924 deaths registered as due to syphilis revealed a dramatic reduction since 1918.[32] While the medical and official picture of the efficacy of the fight against syphilis was rosy, the increased amount of propaganda may have created unprecedented anxieties among the general population: presumably the growing attendance at clinics reflected a rise in the 'worried well' as well as the diseased. While the system was founded on the principle of voluntary treatment based on free, accessible and private clinics, there were certain classes for whom compulsion was still an issue: men in certain occupations, principally the forces, were subjected to regular medical inspection, while Pamela Cox has demonstrated that for 'problem groups' of women – prostitutes, delinquent girls, the 'feeble-minded' – compulsory inspection, or at least inspections that they did not realize they could refuse, and even incarceration for treatment, remained the order of the day.[33] Another problem group was merchant seamen: there had been a long struggle to ensure that they were not obliged to pay for treatment, and to provide continuity of treatment for this mobile population. A leading figure in this campaign was Sybil Neville-Rolfe of the National Council for Combatting Venereal Diseases, whose social position provided informal opportunities to tackle shipowners at dinner-parties (probably not the most popular guest).[34]

Given the success of official provisions for treatment, the National Council for Combating Venereal Diseases began to focus its attention upon educative measures to protect the next generation. They undertook various propaganda campaigns – including deploying the potential of film – and initiatives to educate teachers, as well as health professionals, and promoted the teaching of biology in schools. Endeavours in the Scottish context have been discussed by Roger Davidson, and Leanne McCormick has shown its rather contested activities in Northern Ireland, but less investigation so far has been made into its activities in England and Wales. In 1926, to reflect this more broadly based agenda to produce a VD-free society, the NCCVD changed its name to the British Social Hygiene Council. It continued to work closely with the Ministry of Health and to receive a block grant to undertake educational and propaganda work.[35]

Matrimonial causes

Another burning issue of the prewar era, shelved during hostilities, was divorce law reform. As a result of the War, and the effects of either hasty wartime marriage or the strains placed on unions of longer duration, petitions for divorce rose slightly, 1911–15 (55 per cent sought by the woman, in spite of the legal difficulties), then nearly tripled during the years 1916–20 (67 per cent at male initiative), and remained at a similar level during 1921–25 (with a swing back towards female instigation in 59 per cent of cases).[36] The number of decrees absolute granted in 1920 was nearly four and a half times that of 1910, leading one member of the Royal Commission to remark sourly that had their recommendations passed into law, they would be blamed for this vast increase.[37]

The Lord Chancellor complained of congestion in the Divorce Courts.[38] The Divorce Law Reform Union stepped up campaigning, while Lord Buckmaster, former Lord Chancellor and a passionate advocate of reform, took advantage of his position in the House of Lords to introduce several bills. However, there continued to be significant opposition to implementing the terms of the Majority Report, although the Archbishop of Canterbury was prepared to support equalization of grounds and more access for the less well-off, to forestall more radical reforms. The time was propitious for the National Union of Societies for Equal Citizenship (formerly the 'constitutionalist' National Union of Women's Suffrage Societies) to sponsor a single-issue divorce bill, making adultery of either spouse the sole ground and thus merely equalizing existing grounds. This absolute minimum (much less than the Majority Report of the Royal Commission had called for) was relatively non-contentious except to those who abhorred all divorce; even so, it was introduced as a Private Member's bill rather than Government legislation (though the Government was 'friendly'), by the Liberal MP Major Cyril Entwhistle, and supported in the Lords by Lord Buckmaster. It received wide-ranging support – the Archbishop of Canterbury spoke in favour and persuaded the influential morally conservative Mother's Union not to protest – and only 26 MPs voted against the Third Reading. The Matrimonial Causes Act (1923) received the Royal Assent on 10 July. It reflected changes in the status of women in and out of marriage since 1857, and also the increasing emphasis on the role of male sexual licence in the spread of 'social diseases'. However, this concession, though symbolically of great significance for granting women's right to 'the same law and the same justice that man enjoys', slowed down the progress of any wider reforms.[39]

Numbers of petitions increased, and although condonement and collusion continued to be legal bars, the convention arose, for couples mutually desirous of ending their marriage, that the husband would supply (sometimes spurious) evidence of adultery. The extension in 1920 of divorce jurisdiction to assize courts in cases involving poor persons and undefended actions, and the Poor Persons' Rules, 1925, enabled greater access for a wider social range.[40] The stigma – to a great extent due to the central position of sexual misconduct – remained. In 1924 journalist Charlotte Burghes left her husband for controversial Cambridge scientist J. B. S. Haldane. Her husband refused to enable her to divorce him and instead divorced her, citing Haldane as co-respondent, although both denied adultery. Haldane was accused of 'habitual immorality' by the University administration and threatened with the loss of his Readership, though reinstated following appeal.[41]

Controlling conception

A new issue which characterized the twenties was the rise in discussability of birth control, even if the extent of the actual employment of artificial birth control, rather than abstention or withdrawal, remains a matter of considerable debate among demographers and social historians.[42] There was certainly a contemporary perception, voiced in the medical journal *The Practitioner*, that the subject had 'become a commonplace of conversation at women's clubs and mixed tea-tables'.[43] Almost single-handed, Marie Stopes had achieved this radical change in the climate of discussion. While her *New Gospel to All Peoples* (1920), claiming divine revelation on the desirability of contraception, was ignored by the Lambeth Conference of Anglican bishops to whom she addressed it, her manual, *Wise Parenthood* (1918), had sold well, though ignored in the press, even (or especially) medical journals. In the spring of 1921 she set up in Holloway, a North London slum district, a 'Mothers' Clinic', the name underlining her vision of happy and fulfilled maternity. A few months later the Malthusian League established its own Women's Welfare Centre in Walworth in South London: again, the title carefully avoided mentioning birth control. Stopes went public with a mass meeting at the Queen's Hall in central London in July, featuring distinguished speakers, inaugurating her Society for Constructive Birth Control, envisaged as a modern, up-to-date campaigning body putting a positive, rather than a negative, case for the use of birth control.

Throughout the 1920s the campaign for birth control proceeded on several fronts. Stopes and other reformers believed that contraception ought to be available via existing publicly funded maternal welfare centres. Early clinics were intended partly as models, as well as providing information unavailable through other channels. Contraception on the rates received a setback in 1922 when Elizabeth Daniels, a nurse and health visitor, was dismissed from her post in Edmonton for giving birth control advice. For the birth control struggle, 1923 was a year of causes célèbres. In January libertarian communists Guy Aldred and Rose Witcop were prosecuted for publishing and selling American birth control pioneer Margaret Sanger's pamphlet *Family Limitation* at their Bakunin Press, which they had been doing since 1920, but illustrations and vague allusions to abortion in the new edition caused concern. Distinguished names rallied to their defence, but the magistrate found the work obscene. Marie Stopes refused support, and shortly afterwards made birth control newsworthy and a topic of polite conversation, to a far greater degree than yet achieved, through her highly publicized libel suit against Dr Halliday Sutherland. In an anti-birth control tract Sutherland, a Roman Catholic, had described a woman clearly identifiable as Stopes as experimenting on slum women. The case, which went through various stages of appeal, ran for several years and accrued considerable newspaper coverage.[44]

Meanwhile, other campaigners established clinics in different parts of the country. There have recently been studies of several local initiatives, which shed a significant light on the motivations of the individuals and groups who were promoting clinics, the kinds of opposition they met, and the factors that led to some degree of success. However, they all tend to support claims made by Szreter and Fisher that only a very small group of the population even attended clinics, while persistence with recommended methods was discontinued in a significant percentage of instances. While eugenics was a recurrent motivation for supporters of clinics, Deborah Cohen's work on Marie Stopes's Mothers'

Clinic, where actual practice is well documented, suggests that this did not play much part in day-to-day operations, and Greta Jones has suggested, *vis-à-vis* the Mother's Clinic in Belfast, that 'the Malthusian attitude to poverty and the philosophy of eugenics were marginalized by the practical day to day demands of providing birth control advice to the women who requested it'. Clare Debenham has pointed out that volunteers and staff in clinics set up by the Society for the Promotion of Birth Control Clinics were often working-class themselves, usually with a background in the Women's Cooperative Guild or Labour Party.[45]

The female barrier methods favoured by clinics were found problematic by many users, for reasons both practical (e.g. lack of bathroom or safe place to store the necessaries) and psychological (women's deep resistance to 'preparing themselves' for sex – a feeling evinced even by the radical and emancipated Naomi Mitchison[46]). Whilst Fisher and Szreter have made a compelling case for the significant involvement of husbands in limiting family size through withdrawal, condom use, or abstinence,[47] female contraceptive products requiring less to-do of medical fitting and constant checking were available, but so far have been historiographically invisible. Rendell's 'Wife's Friend' Pessaries were widely advertised in women's magazines and available from chemists.[48]

Women in the Labour Party set up the Workers' Birth Control Group to persuade the Ministry of Health to permit birth control in local authority welfare centres, but in spite of repeated overwhelming votes in support at conferences of Labour women, the Party hierarchy was exceedingly timid, fearing both Catholic and Nonconformist antagonism. Various attempts were made to debate the issue in Parliament.[49] The medical profession did its best to ignore the entire manifestation, rousing only to produce *The Practitioner*'s Contraception issue in the summer of 1923. Most articles (including two by women medics) were implacably hostile and there were a number of veiled digs at Stopes ('non-medical "doctors" who write erotic treatises on birth control'), even in the pro-birth control article by Norman Haire, consultant at the Walworth Clinic.[50] Women doctors tended to be more open-minded. If the older generation still adhered to a social-purity feminist view that contraception licensed male indulgence, a new generation, eager to have it all, aware of the desirability of reliable contraceptive methods not only for their patients but in managing their own careers and families, were prepared not only to discuss the subject among themselves, but to seek expert instruction at Stopes's clinic.[51]

Making marriage modern?

Paradigms of marriage were changing though the extent of changes is still very debatable. Marriage continued popular, and the fears (and the continuing image) of vast hordes of women left husbandless by the war are not supported by the statistics, though Katherine Holden has made a persuasive argument for the influence of this belief on attitudes towards single women as 'imaginary widows' during the interwar period.[52] Emigration, always mostly male, had been checked by the War. The rate of marriage in the 1920s was only slightly reduced from that prewar, and among the younger age groups was, in fact, higher. More men were marrying and doing so at younger ages. If the flight from domestic service created a 'servant problem' for the middle classes, the introduction of domestic appliances made housekeeping a less gruelling undertaking, though for many their possession remained a dream. New ideas of the roles of husband and wife and new forms of relationship were being found beyond the 'chattering classes' of Bloomsbury and Bohemia. Drinking declined, and tended to take place on joint marital excursions rather than in male-only spit-and-sawdust dens, or else couples went together to one of the many picture palaces. Standards of living were rising and the home was increasingly a pleasanter place to be, with its own attractions and entertainments, such as the radio. Moving away from traditional communities also tended to throw husband and wife on to each other's company more, without the old homosocial and kinship networks.[53]

The idea of spouses as companions and 'chums', and sex as something for both partners to enjoy, was voiced in the new, Stopes-founded, genre of marital literature, in novels at all literary levels and in women's magazines, especially those which promoted 'modern' womanhood (within the boundaries of marriage and maternity). This new discourse was far from monolithic: while Marcus Collins's differentiation of 'Christian mutualists' from 'sex radicals' is too binary a categorization for a complicated spectrum, distinctions did manifest, as Hera Cook has shown, along lines of gender and medical qualification.[54]

That the general idea struck a chord in many hearts can be deduced from the sales of Stopes's books (*Married Love* sold half a million copies by 1925, putting it in the 'bestseller' category) and the overwhelming response of her readers, both women and men, from all social classes, thousands of whose letters survive. Almost all were passionately enthusiastic and grateful, few were hostile, and they revealed a stunning level of sexual ignorance and timidity in both sexes. Women often married in complete ignorance of the physical facts, but men also found their knowledge very inadequate[55] – Naomi Mitchison, daughter of Oxford physiologist J. S. Haldane and sister of biologist J. B. S. Haldane, wrote what a revelation she and her husband found *Married Love* in the light of disappointing early sexual attempts.[56] The level of sexual ignorance and the culture of silence around sexuality, even among the relatively middle class, is corroborated by oral historians.[57]

For many, however, especially among the poorer classes, sex was, at least for the woman, an ordeal constantly overshadowed with the fear of pregnancy. Several women informed Leonora Eyles that 'I shouldn't mind married life so much if it wasn't for bedtime', conveying complete revulsion from the sexual act.[58] The lack of knowledge of birth control, or of access to reliable methods, was vividly recounted in the letters Marie Stopes published as *Mother England*.[59]

Science and sexology

'Modern' ideas about sex were becoming more widely disseminated, but were often a melding of strands now thought of as distinct (e.g. 'monkey-glands' vs. Freudianism). Intelligent people who had given considerable thought to the subject did not necessarily differentiate psychoanalytic discourse on sexuality (and Freud was by no means the unique authority) from the 'new science' of glands and endocrine secretions. Stella Browne, a radical feminist theorist of sexuality widely read in the relevant literature, considered that 'individual psychology, including psychoanalysis, and the study of the endocrine glands' were the two most important influences on reconsideration of questions of sex.[60] Following Jungian analysis, physiologist Vernon Mottram attributed his own homosexual phase to 'a deep-seated Oedipus complex', yet described a colleague as 'a feminine soul in a masculine body'.[61]

This spirit of intellectual eclecticism was embodied in the British Society for the Study of Sex Psychology, which survived the War years and continued to exist, if not exactly flourish, during the twenties in a state of chronic financial insecurity. There was allegedly a 'decrease in the study of homosexuality and abnormal facts of sex', and the age-limit for membership was reduced to 21. While psychoanalytic subjects continued to be discussed, the failure of Freudian Ernest Jones's 1919 attempt to incorporate the society into the 'British Psychological Society' led to a withdrawal of several psychoanalytically inclined members. The anthropological approach seems to have been at least as popular, and talks were also given on new glandular theories and biological intersexuality. Birth control, sex education, censorship, and legal issues relating to sexuality were also discussed. Membership was never more than a few hundred, although non-member guests did attend meetings.[62] There were, of course, less formal discussions of sexual matters, from Goldring's girls at the 1917 Club 'talking about libidos and orgasms',[63] to the deliberations (and actions) of the Bloomsbury Group, so extensively recorded.

These ideas percolated to more popular levels: some were taken up as press 'stunts'. After reading about monkey glands in *The Daily Mail*, a doctor wrote to Professor Julian Huxley in 1920 asking for further information and details of where he might obtain 'the genuine article', one of several letters Huxley received on the subject.[64] After lecturing on 'Reversing the Sexes' in 1922, Huxley was besought to interest himself in 'a friend of mine who has been pronounced a hermaphrodite' and wanted to be made 'more pronounced for a male'.[65] Freudian terminology seeped into the problem pages of the more up-to-date women's magazines: Leonora Eyles, agony aunt of *Modern Woman*, wrote of men's 'various little complexes'.[66]

Meanwhile, the social purity movement was increasingly using the languages of sexology; the assumed distinction between social purity and sexual reform remained, as ever, rather fuzzy. Popular preacher and writer on religious matters Maude Royden drew heavily on modern sexological and psychological discourses;[67] Freudian Ernest Jones helped revise the White Cross League's literature;[68] Reverend A. Herbert Gray included an approving citation to Havelock Ellis in his doctor brother's Appendix to *Men, Women and God* published by the Student Christian Movement.[69] Julian Huxley, J. A. Thomson, and Kenneth Walker (all with strong connections to sexology and sex reform) worked with the British Social Hygiene Council.[70] Elderly social purity stalwart (and pioneer woman doctor) Dame Mary Scharlieb supported Radclyffe Hall during the trial of *The Well of Loneliness*.[71]

Protecting the public

The continuing degree of censorship meant that this filtered-down version of major intellectual developments of the day was for many the sole means of access: Ellis's *Studies in the Psychology of Sex*, for example, was still not readily available in Britain. Even readers at the British Museum were protected from volumes deemed potentially corrupting, excluded from the main catalogue, and assigned to the 'Cupboard', with a separate catalogue for the eyes of the librarians only. The British Society for the Study of Sex Psychology attempted to obtain access to this catalogue, and declassification for wider availability of recent sexological works. While the Society's members were recognized as fit and proper persons to be allowed access,[72] the resistance to declassification was manifested by the presence of the BSSSP's own publications in the 'Cupboard' in the 1990s.

Bookshops also policed their readers, for fear of prosecution for purveying obscene materials. Many took seriously title-page provisos that certain works were for the medical and allied professions only. Walter Gallichan, a widely published non-medical writer on 'sexual psychology', alleged that he was prevented from purchasing the work of German psychoanalyst Wilhelm Stekel on frigidity in women, and Denny's in the Strand informed a would-be purchaser that production of a medical or law degree certificate was a precondition for buying Marie Stopes's *Contraception* (1923). It is not surprising that Stopes's publishers, Fifield, reported an unusually large number of direct mail orders for *Married Love*.[73] Some booksellers went even further: in 1926 Galloway and Porter, of Cambridge, informed the Chief Constable, who informed the Home Office, when young don F. R. Leavis ordered a copy of James Joyce's *Ulysses* (published in Paris, 1922). Following the confiscation of a copy at Croydon Aerodrome in 1922, the book had been ruled obscene by Sir Archibald Bodkin, Director of Public Prosecutions. Bodkin himself took up the Leavis case, corresponding with the Vice-Chancellor of the University, who defended Leavis from accusations of corrupting the morals of undergraduates. A reader who requested a copy via Stepney Public Library was also subjected to police inquiries.[74]

This arbitrary operation of censorship was more worrying than definite rules. Dr Isabel Hutton believed her *The Hygiene of Marriage* was 'simple, realistic and contains essential information that is not instinctive'. In spite of advice from colleagues not to publish ('you will wear a crown of thorns'), discouragement by solicitors, and ambivalent reactions from publishers, she eventually concluded a contract with Heinemann's Medical Publications. Notwithstanding, she 'had many a spasm of apprehension in the watches of the night' for 'there was a real risk of its being suppressed with ignominy.' It received no press publicity, and Hutton was informed by the editor of a popular daily, 'we never touch sex stuff'.[75] Stopes, though her books received much calumny during her action against Sutherland, was never subjected to bans or censorship. She was adept at knowing exactly how to convey 'the maximum amount of sex education possible' and when to have recourse to 'reticence and inexplicitness',[76] going rather further in replies to correspondents than she was prepared to risk in published form, in particular occasionally recommending abortion, although in public she presented contraception as the remedy for induced abortion.[77]

Adrian Bingham has done important work delineating the extent to which the popular press was a player in the development of sexual knowledge and concerns around gender during this period. Popular newspapers were increasingly endeavouring to attract women readers, by the introduction of women's pages and a general move towards 'softer' news items. This also appealed to male readers, and the importance of sex as a selling point was becoming ever greater: the use of photographs of attractive young women, if possible in bathing suits, among the letterpress was becoming common. Bingham points out that the day-to-day demand for topics of interest and stirring up of sales-gathering controversy led to these papers representing a plurality of positions and voices on matters of sex and gender. However, certain matters were not mentioned, or only seldom, with implicit assumptions of conventional heterosexuality and appropriate standards of masculinity and femininity, however much the audience relished tales of scandalous highlife antics or freakish masquerades. Care not to offend readers' existing sensibilities was a persistent necessity, and there was a pervasive use of euphemisms requiring some degree of knowingness to decode.[78]

Abortion remained taboo, in spite of Stella Browne's single-handed campaign for legalization as part of an integrated approach to birth control[79] and although, as Emma Jones has shown, resort to backstreet abortion was pervasive.[80] In the highly publicized Thompson/Bywaters murder case (Bywaters had stabbed his lover's husband), the fact that Edith Thompson had endeavoured to administer herself an abortifacient, which her husband inadvertently consumed, was considered too horrendous to introduce in evidence, even though the unexplained incident gave credence to the case that she had been endeavouring to poison him.[81]

Ambivalence over the repurposing of admonitory texts about the outcome of sexual misconduct into salacious entertainment for the masses was evident in the reaction of the British Board of Film Censors to the propaganda films promoted by the National Council for Combating Venereal Disease. The NCCVD imported from the United States, and sponsored the production in the United Kingdom of, a number of films deploying conventions of cinematic melodrama to convey the perils of sexually loose behaviour. The BBFC instituted a policy of declining to certificate any 'propaganda' films, as inappropriate for an entertainment medium, and the Home Office held similar views, based on assumptions about the class and age composition of cinema audiences. Sometimes special private screenings were arranged by social purity groups. Some local authorities did permit showings in cinemas, others banned them entirely and others imposed special conditions. Special arrangements – age restrictions on admissions, men- and women-only showings – 'must undoubtedly have suggested an element of the forbidden to the film-going public' and destabilized the propagandists' good intentions. Much of the social purity movement continued to regard cinema itself as morally contaminating.[82]

Sex in the courtroom

As Lucy Bland has shown, the Bywaters/Thompson case provided a site where many anxieties about class and gender and the modern women proliferated. As with the Crippen case, it drew on negative constructions of the suburban, with Edith Thompson positioned as a disruptive woman who continued her successful business career after marriage, refused to have children, actively pursued pleasure, and engaged in an adulterous relationship with a younger man, to whom she wrote torrid love-letters while he was away at sea. Her conviction for the murder of her husband by Freddie Bywaters, which she did not commit, did not incite, and was horrified to witness, forms a startling contrast with the case of Madame Fahmy, also analysed by Bland. There was no doubt that Madame Fahmy had emptied a pistol into her husband, but by constructing her as a white woman (even though she was a Frenchwoman of significantly dubious antecedents: Stefan Slater has documented police concern over foreign, i.e., Continental European, prostitutes being brought to London[83]) provoked to the point of panic by a cruel and sexually perverse Egyptian husband, the defence achieved her acquittal.[84] Another case of the period which raised conflicting interconnections of race and gender was that of 'Mr A' (Sir Hari Singh, nephew of the Maharajah of Jammu and Kashmir), targeted by a group of blackmailers. On the one hand he was a 'black' man who had had sex with a white woman, on the other hand the woman had been party to a criminal scheme of entrapment which had extorted vast sums of money.[85]

The public, protected from the works of Havelock Ellis and major works of modernist literature, was able to enjoy titillating details of murder trials and blackmail cases, and salacious proceedings in the divorce courts, in the newspapers (including those which 'never touched sex stuff' such as Hutton's advice manual). Bingham suggests that though divorce cases were the most controversial matter in court reporting, they were particularly attractive since they offered readers 'a convenient opportunity to satisfy some of their curiosity about sexual indulgence and moral transgression while maintaining their attachment to conventional values'.[86] King George V himself expressed disgust, via a letter from his private secretary to the Lord Chancellor, over the reporting of Russell v. Russell, 1922. The husband had petitioned for divorce on the grounds of his wife's adultery resulting in a child, alleging that he had never consummated the marriage. She, however, claimed that he had subjected her to 'Hunnish practices' resulting in conception. The Lord Chancellor's office was cautious about introducing secrecy into legal proceedings, contrary to established principles of English justice (although Sir Archibald Bodkin, the Director of Public Prosecutions and counsel to the National Vigilance Association, favoured the measure). When Sir Evelyn Cecil introduced a private member's bill to regulate reporting of divorce proceedings, the standard delaying (while appearing to do something) tactic of appointing a Select Committee was suggested. The question was reopened in 1925 by another vice-in-high-society case, Dennistoun v. Dennistoun, in which a wife sued her divorced husband for failure to pay support, revealing that she had granted favours to a high-ranking military officer to advance her husband's career. George V was again appalled. A bill, based on Cecil's, was given Government support and passed into law in 1926, ending the long tradition, going back to pre-1857 crim. con. proceedings, of revelations of sexual misconduct in high life being served up for the delectation of the general public.[87]

Love between women

The most famous censorship case of the 1920s was probably that of Radclyffe Hall's novel *The Well of Loneliness*, 1928. Hall, herself an 'invert', was a literary novelist of some reputation, who felt it her mission to produce a serious work pleading for tolerance. Her theories owed more to turn of the century sexology than more recent developments such as psychoanalysis, and she regarded Havelock Ellis (whom she did not know personally prior to writing the book) as a major inspiration. The publisher, Jonathan Cape, was a well-respected firm and eschewed sensationalism in promoting *The Well*, issuing it in a plain jacket, at a rather high price, and sending review copies only to serious dailies and periodicals. Reviews were mostly favourable and the book went into a second printing within a month or so of publication. Shortly afterwards, during the journalistic 'silly season', sensationalist journalist James Douglas launched an attack in the *Sunday Express*, 'A Book that must be Suppressed' (claiming that he would rather 'give a healthy boy or a healthy girl a vial of prussic acid'). One of Douglas's previous campaigns had been to demand Lord Dawson's resignation as Royal Physician ('LORD DAWSON MUST GO!'[88]) following his public advocacy of birth control. By 1928 birth control was less marginalized: the connection between decoupling sex from babies and heterosexuality altogether may well have been present, as some level, in this 'moral panic'. Sales and requests at lending libraries immediately soared.

Cape offered to submit the book for approval to the Home Secretary, Sir William Joynson-Hicks ('Jix'), notorious for extremely conservative moral attitudes. He did not approve: Cape voluntarily withdrew the book and cancelled a third printing, had a new edition printed in Paris and imported these for sale. Cape and the bookshop selling them were raided and charges laid under the Obscene Publications Act (there was speculation that this was all a publicity 'stunt' by Cape). A panel of eminent writers, scientists, doctors, clergymen, and other friends of progress were assembled to defend the book (in spite of the qualms some felt over its literary quality, the principle had to be supported), but the superintending magistrate at the hearing refused to hear their evidence, and his judgement referred to 'horrible', 'vile', 'unnatural', and 'filthy' practices in finding against the book and its publisher. None the less, Hall received thousands of letters of support ('5000 friendly sympathetic letters and 5 abusive ones!'[89]). Bingham indicates that most of the press 'showed no enthusiasm' for extensive reporting or comment on the case, and remained euphemistic in their language.[90]

The whole furore was a shocking revelation to women who, though knowing themselves 'different' and that 'such things were unusual and not generally talked about', did not realize 'just how much they were considered "outside the pale"'.[91] Hall's novel established stereotypes of the lesbian that were to prove enduring (the mannish congenital invert and the more feminine, implicitly or explicitly bisexual partner), but even within *The Well of Loneliness* other models figured. In the same year Virginia Woolf celebrated her liaison with Vita Sackville-West through the playful androgyny of *Orlando*.[92] Many women lived together and formed like-minded communities and networks, particularly if they had a profession and economic independence, without overtly transgressing conventional gender norms in appearance or behaviour. Because of the Great War, many single women were in a position to claim, or to have it assumed, that an actual or potential husband had been lost and, far from being stigmatized, accorded some degree of sympathy for getting on with their lives. However, there was also a developing discourse of older women exercising malign influence over infatuated younger ones.[93]

Alison Oram indicates that women passing as men and being accepted as the husbands of their partners remained one pattern, read as masquerade rather than deviance.[94] However, one case of masquerade became a cause célèbre in 1929 when Major Victor Barker, subjected to a routine medical inspection when sent to Brixton Prison for contempt of court after failing to appear at a bankruptcy hearing, was discovered to be a woman, Valerie Arkell-Smith, and transferred to Holloway Prison. It was also discovered that she had been married and borne children, but had subsequently (in her male persona) married another woman – leading to a charge of perjury for false declaration. The case was largely represented as about 'eccentricity' and imposture for possible economic motives, rather than in terms of sexuality.[95]

*   *   *

In September 1929 the World League for Sexual Reform held an International Congress in London, organized by the ubiquitous Harley Street sex-doctor Norman Haire and Dora Russell. Havelock Ellis, nominally a President, maintained his usual remote attitude towards organizations and meetings. Sheila Jeffreys argued that the Congress demonstrated the strength, influence, and respectability gained by the sex reform movement and the extent to which its ideas had become common parlance in many academic disciplines.[96] In the light of the Hall case and the stigmatization of lesbianism it revealed, as well as the general climate of censorship, the continuing exclusion of birth control advice from maternal welfare centres, and the persisting encoding of 'Double Standards' of sexual morality within the law, these claims for the 'sex reform movement' seem wildly exaggerated. Indeed, Russell in her speech of welcome to the Congress described England as 'the most reactionary country on sex questions'.[97] The WLSR was, at best, a united-front demonstration by a left-liberal 'progressive' vanguard far from happy with things as they were, holding diverse opinions on a range of issues. As with the *Well of Loneliness*, many doubtless felt themselves obliged to support it, if not subscribing personally to every particular, and in spite of the reservations many felt about Haire.[98]

How far from sex-reformed British society was in 1929 is revealed by the case of William Empson, poet and literary critic. Following the discovery of 'birth control mechanisms' in his room by his bedmaker, he was dismissed from his Fellowship at Magdalene College, Cambridge, his name struck from the College records, and given 24 hours to leave town. He went into virtual exile in the Far East.[99] While, by 1929, birth control within marriage was increasingly acceptable, any association with extramarital sexuality (and leaving devices where the lower orders might find them) was still subject to powerful taboos.

7

Population Fears and Progressive Agendas During the Thirties

The 1929 Local Government Act might seem to have little to do with sex, but its tidying up of various anomalies, abolishing the guardians of the poor and transferring their responsibilities, and reorganizing the system of grants in aid had significant implications in at least two areas. Also, the effect of the abolition of the stigmatizing poor law system is hard to calculate (especially as the Depression soon brought the hated Means Test for benefits), but was part of continuing moves towards seeing health and welfare benefits as something to which all members of society were entitled, rather than minimal provision grudgingly doled out to those in extreme need.

Legitimating contraception

Shifts of authority from the centre to localities created a loophole for local authorities to argue that they could make their own decisions about giving birth control advice. Public health doctors had been something of an exception to the general medical refusal to consider contraception and several Medical Officers of Health were open supporters of the birth control movement, if sometimes on eugenic grounds. A number of councils were sympathetic, passing resolutions calling upon the Ministry to desist from interference, and by early 1930 eight had instructed their medical officers to provide advice. Public opinion had changed radically and the tide of support was now running in favour of birth control, at least within marriage, to space and limit families. The leading feminist organization, the National Union of Societies for Equal Citizenship, previously neutral, had declared its support in 1927 and now that the vote was fully won, had energy and resources to spare for this campaign, allying with the Workers' Birth Control Group to lobby Parliamentary candidates and party leaders. The newly enfranchised group of women under 30 were likely to be particularly engaged by an issue so relevant to their interests.

Apart from a few dedicated partisans, the Labour Government which came to power in 1929 was uncommitted, but was targeted by constant representations from campaigners, in and out of Parliament. Arthur Greenwood, the Minister of Health, publicly professed himself against a change of policy, though the Ministry had the issue under secret review. He refused to comment on local authority demands to know if providing contraceptive advice on the rates was legal, but did admit that no statutory authority forbade it. A large meeting on the Giving of Information on Birth Control by Public Authorities in April 1930 represented a wide coalition of interests. Greenwood and Ministry officials, conscious that the topic was still politically sensitive, took a minimalist line, permitting birth control advice for pressing medical cases. What exactly constituted medical justification was devolved to the localities. A Memorandum, 153/MCW, was initially only distributed to Medical Officers of Health who requested guidance. News of its existence leaked out slowly, until Marie Stopes published the text in *Birth Control News*, and it was further disseminated – with an interpretative circular – by the recently formed National Birth Control Council, a coordinating body including the clinics, the Workers' Birth Control Group, and the Birth Control Investigation Committee which conducted research into methods.

The 1930 Lambeth Conference of Anglican bishops conceded that contraception might have a legitimate place within Christian marriage. The Royal Institute of Public Health instituted the first courses of contraceptive instruction to receive the imprimatur of a medical organization.[1] The volte-face of the medical profession was demonstrated in 1933 with another birth control issue of *The Practitioner*, overwhelmingly in favour. Havelock Ellis ('that veteran philosopher') contributed, and the only hostile article was critiqued in Lord Horder's introduction as 'a little inconsistent … certainly opposed to known facts'. According to Horder, the subject 'becomes less and less controversial every year' and concerns were best practice rather than the principle.[2]

These changes made it possible for birth control information to be more widely disseminated and removed some of the stigma, but victory was scarcely won. The NBCC began monitoring whether local authorities were taking advantage of 153/MCW, as well as continuing to lobby for extended grounds. It campaigned on a variety of fronts: policy, education, research, and, from July 1931 when it changed its name and constitution to the National Birth Control Association, enabling new clinics and branches to join, a clinic provider. All were important. Local area organizers trekked cross-country to investigate what was being done in specific localities and to gain allies. By 1935, 66 local authority and 47 voluntary clinics had been established, and some authorities sent patients to clinics or private doctors. There were 28 local NBCA branches. However, 250 maternity and child welfare authorities had done nothing.[3] In 1934 Ministry Circular 1408, discussed in draft with the NBCA, extended the terms of 153/MCW to a more inclusive interpretation of threat to women's health. Conferences were held, and training clinics for doctors began (though students from St Mary's Hospital were shepherded to the North Kensington Clinic under cover of darkness).[4]

The number of women seen in NBCA or local authority clinics was a tiny minority of the potential constituency, and organizational preference for the cap and spermicide method led to neglect of other options, in particular male methods, in spite of significant user resistance. [5] The NBCA, however, also conducted research into standards for rubber and efficacy of chemical spermicides (with funding from the Eugenics Society) and in 1934 produced an Approved List of proprietary products, with cooperation from the industry: this accolade could be used in promotional literature, with sufficient commercial benefit that occasional spurious claims were made.[6] Thus while the majority of couples who employed appliance methods of birth control did so with over-the-counter purchases, the quality and reliability of these was arguably considerably enhanced, particularly given the significant improvement in condoms with the introduction of latex.[7] Given the paucity of clinic provision, the NBCA was unsympathetic to proposals to restrict the sale of contraceptives.[8] Indeed, it was strongly behind initiatives to develop a chemical contraceptive more effective than those already available and obviating the problems associated with female barrier methods. A new chemical pessary, Volpar, was the outcome, but although more efficacious than existing products, it was not the hoped-for 'perfect contraceptive'.[9]

Eugenic resurgence

The Eugenics Society took on a new lease of life in the early 1930s, partly due to a substantial legacy from an Australian sympathizer, and partly due to the efforts of the new, young, General Secretary, C. P. Blacker, to advance a 'reform eugenics' agenda taking account of social as well as hereditary factors, and generate strategic alliances with groups having common interests. The new higher profile of the Society was manifested in lobbying for a Parliamentary Act legalizing sterilization on a voluntary basis (quite early on the English Society dissociated itself from the 'excesses' of the Nazi regime in Germany), primarily directed at what was believed to be a growing amount of mental deficiency.

There was considerable hostility, from both Catholics and the Labour movement, which perceived eugenics as fundamentally anti-working class in spite of the efforts of Blacker and various left-wing intellectuals to suggest that there was no necessary class-bias, as well as widespread shrinking from giving force of law to an operation that even many doctors did not distinguish from castration. Macnicol points out that organized working-class women were more sympathetic, making 'an intuitive but confused connection...[with] broader issues of maternity, birth control, and even the punishment of male sexual offenders'. The Board of Control and the Ministry of Health were cautious in responding to something that seemed to threaten professional interest groups. A Departmental Committee under the chairman of the Board of Control, Sir Laurence Brock, was set up and reported in 1934, recommending voluntary sterilization subject to substantial safeguards. No Act resulted: even men wanting vasectomy for contraceptive purposes within marriage had trouble finding surgeons to undertake the operation.[10]

Blacker also endeavoured to develop alliances with the campaign for Family Allowances (anathema to earlier Society policies) and the birth control movement. The Eugenics Society provided generous funding for contraceptive research and also contributed to the running costs of the National Birth Control Association. Attempts were made to bring about an even closer union (the NBCA was poor but had a large membership via its branches), but the strong grassroots allegiance to the Labour Party in many local branches made the issue tendentious. The NBCA leadership, reluctant to lose a reliable and generous source of funding, continued to keep the Eugenics Society dangling (the thirties concept 'gold-digger' comes to mind), but when the name was changed to the Family Planning Association in 1939, eugenics was conspicuously absent from its new Objects.[11] Publications such as *Life as We Have Known It* (1931) by the Women's Cooperative Guild and Margery Spring-Rice's *Working-Class Wives* (1939) indicated that adverse environmental factors continued to bear heavily upon women's health and their capacity to bear and rear healthy children. Women involved in the birth control movement (like Spring-Rice herself) were acutely aware of these.[12]

Education and sexual health

Whereas the 1929 Local Government Act had been good news for the birth control movement, it was less so for the British Social Hygiene Council. The generous direct block grant from the Ministry of Health was replaced by grants to local authorities, in theory to be returned as a Quota Grant to the BSHC. Many authorities considered this discretionary, and did not pay at all or paid less than the BSHC thought appropriate, or even contributed to the rival Society for the Prevention of Venereal Diseases. This was disastrous given the general economic crisis rendering other sources of funding less available, and also placed the BSHC in a disadvantageous position vis-à-vis an upcoming rival in health education. The Society of Medical Officers of Health was increasingly envisaging health education as essential to a sound public health programme and had set up a Central Council on Health Education in 1927. Emanating from the medical profession, this could present itself as modern, scientific, and up to date. The BSHC was unable to continue the scale of activities of the 1920s, some of which, such as the film programme, were relatively expensive, and was concerned that health professionals employed by local authorities were not receiving necessary education in VD and related issues.[13]

With the obvious success of the clinic system, authorities might have considered that funding these fulfilled their obligations. Some doctors even criticized this provision: H. Wansey Bayly claimed in *The Lancet* that 'persons who can well afford private treatment' were using these clinics, and 'the venereal specialist sees ruin staring him in the face.'[14] Certainly, the vast majority of arsenical preparations for treating syphilis were supplied to public clinics rather than private practitioners.[15] M. W. Browdy claimed that 'all and sundry flock to the clinics' while venereal diseases were rising.[16] (In spite of a slight increase in the early 1930s, the general trend was a decline to the lowest ever recorded figures immediately prior to the outbreak of war.[17]) Francis Louis, however, riposted that 'it is in the interests of the nation that venereal disease be wiped out.'[18] With the advent of sulphonamides in 1937, a reliable antibiotic treatment for gonorrhoea, patients began to return to non-specialist practitioners.[19]

Marriage matters

While cutting back on establishment and office expenses, the BSHC was still undeterred from undertaking new initiatives. In 1931 it turned its attention to preparation for marriage, concerned about troubles that 'could have been prevented with fuller knowledge'. A handbook was prepared by a committee of experts, but it was felt that provision for personal consultations was needed. Mrs Neville-Rolfe, the Secretary-General and prime mover of the BSHC, was asked to establish a Personal Problems Bureau on a self-supporting basis, to advise by interview and correspondence.[20] While the book received glowing recommendations in both the *British Medical Journal* and *The Lancet*,[21] the Bureau project raised medical hackles, threatening competition to the family doctor.[22] Some raised additional objections along the lines that 'the question arises whether people who require this ought to marry at all'.[23] The issue of contraceptive advice proved controversial,[24] and the Bureau project was dropped. Controversy was not all external: some years later the BSHC dissolved its Preparation for Marriage Committee due to irreconcilable internal dissension: Neville-Rolfe informed the Ministry of Health that this was because it dealt with 'controversial subjects on which public opinion is acutely divided',[25] presumably birth control, and possibly divorce.

The idea of sexual pleasure as not only permissible but desirable within marriage was increasingly being accepted, even among religious authorities. Some of the leading voices arguing for a new and higher form of marriage and family life, based on accepting sex rather than dismissing it as 'fallen' and 'dirty', were clergymen of one or other persuasion (Presbyterian A. Herbert Gray, Methodist Leslie Weatherhead), or lay individuals active in religious organizations such as the Student Christian Movement (Edward Fyfe Griffith). The Modern Churchmen's Union issued a pamphlet on 'Marriage' by Helena Wright, medical officer at the North Kensington Women's Welfare (i.e., birth control) Clinic.[26] Gray's introduction to Wright's *The Sex Factor in Marriage* (explicit about the role of the clitoris and its correct stimulation in the arousal and satisfaction of the woman and thus its importance in mutually satisfying conjugal lovemaking) provided a manifesto for this trend:

> Why should you shrink from knowing the truth about your body, or about the body of a member of the opposite sex? Do you not believe that God designed our bodies, and ordained their various functions?[27]

The Archbishop of Canterbury himself had pleaded for sex to take 'its rightful place among the great creative and formative things'.[28]

It was still meant to occur strictly within marriage, however. Pre- or extra-marital sex was not approved of (though members of some vanguards and subcultures were engaging in both). There was some suggestion from contemporary observers that male resort to prostitution was being replaced by more egalitarian relationships with girls from their own social circles, in which sexual favours (of some kind) were exchanged for non-pecuniary treats. Julia Laite, however, is sceptical that commercial sex was in actual decline, even if clients were increasingly marginalized.[29] Recent work by oral historians tends to suggest that for the vast majority of the population, courtship was seriously constrained by the fear of pregnancy and disgrace (affecting men as well as women) and concerns over reputation and respectability. Sex itself was an area of fear and anxiety or at least a site for tensions. The ability of young women to control the progress of intimacy and to keep it within bounds was valued by men and seen as an important element of identity for the women themselves. Relationships developed within a known social context and similar class backgrounds and young people were powerfully motivated by prudential considerations when choosing a lifetime mate.[30] Until 1939, matrimonial agencies were regarded as rather too prudential and unromantic, and barely respectable, though the founding of the exclusive Marriage Bureau by Heather Jenner and Mary Oliver in 1939 aimed at the wealthy and fashionable (and white) did something to lift the stigma. They carefully positioned their premises and the placing of their advertisements, conducted detailed personal vetting interviews, and became a raging success within their carefully set parameters.[31]

Illegitimate births remained at a low level (around 4.5 per cent), barely changed (except for the War years) since the 1890s.[32] However, the Registrar-General commented in his 1938/9 Report that nearly 30 per cent of mothers conceived their first-born out of wedlock (the first time this calculation had been undertaken).[33] It thus seems probable that premarital sex was mostly happening between 'courting couples' who already intended marrying. The implications are obscure. Writers on social purity tended to argue for an increasing equalization of the moral standard, with men no longer gaining experience with prostitutes and then expecting to marry a virgin.[34] Thus, it might represent interwar 'modernity'. Alternatively, it could reflect older patterns of sex within courtship, with the marriage date settled once pregnancy occurred.

Boundary problems

While sex within marriage was becoming more eroticized and increasingly separated from reproduction, the peripheries of sexual identity and permissible conduct continued to be heavily policed. There were various homosexual subcultures (although the 'essential brio' of the Brideshead generation at Oxbridge had evaporated) and the so-called 'Homintern' of left-leaning homosexual (and in some cases bisexual) writers and intelligentsia had a significant influence on cultural life. Matt Houlbrook has delineated in depth the various places and spaces in which homosexual men might find others like themselves in London, a complex network of venues for male same-sex desires, from private clubs to cruising areas in parks. He also points out the extent to which class was intertwined with the 'queer city', not only through the complex interactions between upper- and middle-class men with working-class partners, but in the ways in which those with money and connections could lead lives far less threatened by the law. None the less, stigma persisted and discretion was essential.[35]

The lesbian scene was a good deal less developed, though there are indications that there were some 'lesbian-friendly' if not women-only venues, and certain recognized meeting and pick-up places.[36] However, in spite of the furore around *The Well of Loneliness* and the Colonel Barker case at the end of the 1920s, the generic popular press narratives around gender-crossing women persisted well into the next decade. Both *The Well* and the Barker case emerged from a rather different social milieu to the protagonists of the standard 'female husband' story. They had resonances with discourses of upper-class decadence: this was further elaborated in the (probably fictitious) press accounts of exotic gigolos at French pleasure resorts who turned out to be masquerading women exploiting and robbing their victims. Meanwhile, notions of 'unhealthy' female friendship began to surface in some press accounts. Some popular film stars played with the glamour of androgyny.[37]

From the 1920s local police forces conducted campaigns against (probably) mostly working-class homosexuals, who could not afford privacy, not extensively reported in the national press: only the Sunday paper, *News of the World*, noted for combining moral outrage with reader titillation, routinely scoured local papers for these. The rest of the popular press tended to eschew reporting all but the most high-profile cases, and even then deployed euphemism and evasiveness, for example focusing on gender deviancy as masquerade.[38] Thus it was possible for the realization that 'this could be a criminal offence, in some vague way' to dawn only slowly, even on intelligent and educated men who identified as homosexual.[39] Others thought there was no trouble, even for a male prostitute, 'providing you mind your own business'.[40] There was little consistency in sentencing: in 1935 'savage sentences' were meted out in a Manchester case ('advertising screamers – foolish and repulsive – but that cannot alter one's horror'), whereas an 'evil and repulsive set, crooked in every way … blackmailers, many of them, when they dared' in Birmingham 'were dealt with mercifully … fines only inflicted'.[41] Those who could sometimes still sought 'refuge from the law in flight'.[42] Arrests 'en masse' sometimes resulted in 'vague general conspiracy charges' in court.[43]

A cause célèbre which gained national coverage was that of the 'St Helen's man-woman', Augustine Hull, sentenced at Liverpool Assizes to 18 months' hard labour under the Labouchère Amendment in 1931. Hull was a transvestite of such naturally 'feminine' appearance that when wearing men's clothes, he had been stopped by the police under suspicion of being a woman in drag. In his working-class home he had been treated very much as a daughter, and began cross-dressing in adolescence. In 1931 he was courted by George Burrows, an unemployed labourer who believed him to be a woman, Norma Jackson. The couple lived 'as man and wife' for some months and intended to marry. Following quarrels and a separation Burrows finally discovered that 'she' was a male, and took the story to the police, who traced Hull to Blackpool and arrested him. He was tried for 'gross indecency' with Burrows, who continued to assert that he had never doubted 'Norma' to be a woman and protested continuing devotion. Interesting questions on working-class culture are raised by Hull's family's tolerance of his eccentricity, and what Burrows meant by 'living as man and wife'.[44] McLaren's analysis of this case draws attention to the press's focus on cross-dressing and implications that Hull's offence was 'masquerading' rather than homosexuality (i.e., about gender transgression rather than sexual acts), which they were reluctant to discuss. In most cases involving cross-dressing in men the charges related to homosexuality; transvestism, outside certain approved and circumscribed cultural manifestations of carnivalesque travesty, being little understood as a distinct 'sexual perversion'.[45]

The Hull case precipitated protests from those who felt that they understood the phenomenon much better than the judge or lawyers involved, and that such individuals should be dealt with by medicine rather than the law. John Stevenson of the progressive weekly, *The Weekend Review*, initiated demands for a review of the case. Psychoanalysis was suggested, although Havelock Ellis argued that Hull had a glandular imbalance making him 'naturally intersexual'. Reforming lawyer E. S. P. Haynes pointed out the role played by poverty and low social status in Hull's arrest and conviction. The British Sexology Society held two meetings on the case, and took up a collection for Hull's mother. A petition was got up, arguing that there ought to be provision for sending such cases to a 'State medical home for observation and treatment' (not exactly the liberal toleration for difference suggested by Stella Browne's plea 'to cease persecution of such people'). There was no formal response by the Home Secretary, but Hull was transferred to Wormwood Scrubs prison (in London) and treatment at the Tavistock Clinic (which provided psycho-dynamically orientated, but not strictly Freudian, outpatient therapy) organized. The outcome of the 'treatment' is not known, and as McLaren points out, there is no evidence that Hull himself was unhappy with his 'deviation': it was the community which was discomfited.[46]

Agendas of enlightenment

The Hull incident reveals an increasingly strong and vociferous 'sex reform' lobby. The British Sexology Society took on something of a new lease of life in the early 1930s, while the World League for Sexual Reform, English Branch, mutated into Norman Haire's Sex Education Society, and Janet Chance set up a Sex Education Centre in London. The Federation of Progressive Societies and Individuals, founded in 1932, had a Sex Reform Group, of which Stella Browne was one of the chairs.[47] Other societies and journals with a liberal agenda hosted talks, articles, and discussions on issues concerning sexuality. Many of the individuals and groups involved would have subscribed, in whole or part, to the indictment of the British code of sexual morality and the recommendations for improvement advanced in Janet Chance's *The Cost of English Morals* (1931). With a preface by the ubiquitous Lord Horder, Physician to the Prince of Wales and a progressive with impeccable 'establishment' credentials, the book claimed that 'in England, sexual life is a poor thing.' The standards of conduct adhered to in order 'to be safe, to be acceptable, sometimes even to be sure of one's salary' were based on 'a harmful attitude of mind', and while there was resistance, these standards were still widely accepted or silently tolerated.[48] Chance's agenda for reform took in 'the pathetic and tragic state' of innumerable English married women ignorant of sexual pleasure, the pernicious role of the Church in defining moral standards, the need for birth control and legalization of safe abortion, reform of the divorce laws, and sex education for children. The issue of censorship was not addressed specifically, but was implicit throughout. Alec Craig's *Sex and Revolution* (1934) advanced similar plaints and remedies.[49]

A more mainstream initiative in the wake of the Hull case was the establishment of an Institute for the Scientific Treatment of Delinquency, set up by a group of doctors, psychologists, and psychoanalysts who believed that in many instances (among them homosexuality) existing punitive methods were ineffective and inhumane and counter-productive. While this may at first simply appear to be a manifestation of the replacement of criminalization by medicalization, and certainly the Institute was anxious to appear a reputable and medically-sound organization, Havelock Ellis was a signatory of the initial letters to the press proposing its establishment, and Laurence Housman featured amongst its Vice-Presidents.[50] It is arguable that the British Sexology Society, by providing a space for discussion and meetings between committed reformers and those in the medical professions, had enabled productive interactions with significant influence on the development of more humane attitudes towards the homosexual, and strategies to ameliorate his situation, even if they fell short of actual legal reform. Several names featuring in the Institute's records had varying degrees of association with the Society.[51] Although the Institute apparently repudiated suggestions that it should 'concern itself with questions of penal reform' concerning homosexuality,[52] it worked closely with the judicial system in providing medical reports, organizing seminars for probation officers, and circularizing magistrates, and was invited to be represented on Home Office committees and hold discussions with MPs about relevant clauses in penal reform bills.[53]

On sex education, there was something of an overlap between sex reform and the traditional concerns of social purity, rather than a dichotomy. Organizations in the latter camp continued to deplore the lack of provision of 'adequate sex knowledge' to young people, so that 'inaccurate and perverted ideas are very widespread'.[54] The canard of 'White Slavery' was still prevalent: a schoolteacher who wrote to the National Vigilance Association that 'I am looking forward to the opportunity of answering questions from some of the older girls who are leaving school on the White Slave Traffic' was repressively told to concentrate on 'modesty and decency rather than the questions of brothels and white slave traffic'.[55] While there were recurrent press scares,[56] social purity societies were dismissive of the entire mythology: 'Without exception these tales lead nowhere, as I believe the police could confirm.'[57] Some women's magazines were also promoting the 'need for a proper sex education', though usually in terms of responding to children's spontaneous questions (which 'should never be forced'), and there was concern expressed at the 'distorted and stupid impressions of the sex instinct' many girls were given.[58] The changing perception of masturbation was reflected in popular advice: in an article on child psychology in *Mother: The Home Magazine*, Dr Anne Pedler stated that 'so-called bad habits' were 'not in themselves harmful or dangerous or abnormal. What is harmful is the sense of shame and humiliation.'[59]

Sex education within the school system remained a topic upon which the Board of Education was silent. Although they produced health education guidelines for schools, any mention of the reproductive organs was entirely absent.[60] Some colleges of education provided short courses of lectures, and a few local authorities were developing initiatives in alliance with voluntary bodies. However, given that the main teaching unions were perceived to be opposed, and the Ministry of Education so loathe to give a lead for or against, teachers in favour of sex education were deterred by fears that they would not get backing if trouble blew up, and provision was thus exceedingly sporadic.[61]

[handwritten margin notes: well of loneliness Trial / Orlando publsh]

The limits of knowledge

Research and investigation into sexual questions was gradually becoming somewhat more respectable. The Medical Research Council set up a Sex Hormones Committee in 1930, but its research involved complex chemical compounds tested on laboratory animals. Numerous articles on sex hormones were published in scientific journals, with an unspoken precondition that these dealt with no animals closer to humanity than monkeys, and most discussed ferrets, hamsters, or rats. R. A. McCance undertook a study of periodicity in the human female, 1929–30, using a sample of 200, but had considerable difficulty in getting the research published: twice rejected by the Royal Society, it appeared in *The Journal of Hygiene* in 1937. Undertaking work in reproductive biology to develop improved methods of contraception was also problematic and could adversely affect careers.[62] However, Havelock Ellis achieved widespread recognition: his one-volume synthesis, *The Psychology of Sex* (1933), received extremely favourable reviews.[63] In 1936, nearly 40 years after the publication of *Sexual Inversion*, he was made a Fellow of the Royal College of Physicians, specifically in recognition of his work for sexual science.[64]

However, the arbitrary axe of censorship still continued to fall: in 1935 *The Sexual Impulse* by 'Edward Charles' (Edward C. E. Hemsted), published by Boriswood Press with forewords by Julian Huxley and Janet Chance, and encouragement from Lord Horder, was seized by the police and prosecuted at Westminster Police Court. The publishers entered a plea of 'not guilty', intending to bring 'specialized evidence of witnesses of standing and renown'. While the expert evidence was heard (an advance on *The Well of Loneliness* case), it seems to have made little impression on the presiding magistrate, who remarked that 'not so long ago a book of this kind would be banned altogether', being on a topic 'not considered fit to be discussed in decent society'. While the desirability of having 'such books for sale' was not for him to decide, he found the chapter on sexual union 'indecent…and therefore obscene', but although republication without that chapter had been suggested, 'the whole book must go.' An appeal was filed but did not succeed.[65]

Harry Cocks has indicated that issues of context and promotion played a significant part in whether serious works fell foul of the censor, and that there was continuing conflation of serious would-be scientific studies of sexuality with commercial pornography. The National Vigilance Association condemned as 'Objectionable Literature' materials disseminated by mail-order booksellers or libraries even when, alongside nudist magazines and semi-scientific studies, they distributed works of sexual advice of which, in other contexts, the NVA might have approved. Rather sensationalist layout of promotional leaflets, indiscriminately mailed out by the advertising agents, for Norman Haire's *Encyclopaedia of Sex*, militated in court against his professional status.[66]

In an opinion on a pamphlet the British Sexology Society were considering publishing, the young barrister Gerald Gardiner (later Lord Chancellor in the Labour Government, 1964–70) suggested that prosecution seldom took place unless a book was 'clearly pornographic…something which the sexually unsatisfied will buy because it is "risky"' or if attention had been drawn to it by some non-official source, as with the *Sunday Express* and *The Well of Loneliness* (or by the actions of a local individual or purity group). He thought that 'probably a very large number of books now sold would be condemned if the police chose to prosecute.'[67]

Falling population

The acceptability of birth control increased, clinics spread, and voluntary sterilization was widely debated, but these phenomena occurred against a backdrop of growing concern about absolute (rather than, as with the Eugenics Society, relative and qualitative) population decline. A number of influential texts appeared, most notoriously Dr Enid Charles's *The Twilight of Parenthood* (1934, later known as *The Menace of Underpopulation*). Charles, an economics graduate, took a left-wing angle, blaming the eugenics movement for undue concern over 'imagined eugenic skeletons in [the] closet', causing many in the professional middle classes to have few or no children, and seeing falling population as evidence for the biological sterility of capitalism. Even if the dwindling birth rate stabilized, an unstoppable process of drastic decline was in motion. The 'Depopulation Panic' was given demi-official credence by two articles in *The Times* on 'The Dwindling Family' in September 1936. Visions of an ageing society without an adequate 'steady infusion of youthfulness and vigour' haunted public opinion at a time of economic crisis and political uncertainty. The problem was projected in terms of diminishing numbers of fertile females, rather than 'national virility'.

The Government was resistant to attempts to raise the subject in Parliament, fearing expensive pronatalist measures (such as family allowances, for which Independent MP Eleanor Rathbone, with the support of feminist and women's organizations, had been campaigning for many years) might result. A Population Investigation Committee (an independent body for demographic study with significant overlaps with the Eugenics Society) was established in 1936. In 1937 Conservative MP Ronald Cartland, briefed by the PIC, introduced a motion calling for official investigation. This was thwarted, but a 'modest collaborative enquiry' involving the registrar-general's office and the PIC was set in hand, leading to a Population (Statistics) Bill for improving the gathering of vital statistics to enable more sophisticated demographic analysis. Soon known as the 'Nosey Parker' Bill because of the intrusive nature and intimacy of the questions, it was vigorously opposed by the Labour party, and satirized in a rhyming speech ('And everybody wondered why the population fell') by A. P. Herbert, Independent MP for Oxford University. Though it passed its second reading, vociferous hostility grew. A number of amendments limiting the range of questions, removing controversial penalization implications, and giving stronger confidentiality assurances led to the final passage of the Act in February 1938.[68]

Connected with this anxiety was the continuingly high level of maternal and infant mortality and morbidity. A number of women's organizations addressed these issues from different angles. The National Birthday Trust Fund, set up in 1928 by a group of upper-class women, most with close ties to the Conservative Party, aimed to bring improvements in obstetric care available to better-off women (such as analgesia in childbirth) to the less fortunate. The body was strongly pronatalist, aiming at making childbirth less dangerous, and firmly eschewed birth control.[69] Other bodies were less cautious – though the umbrella organization the National Council of Women found that their approval for birth control led to resignations by Catholic bodies and the Anglican Mother's Union.[70]

A new frontier for reproductive control

Former members of the Workers' Birth Control Group (which had decided that its original intention had been achieved, and so dissolved[71]) took the fight for reproductive control further. Stella Browne had been advocating legalized abortion for decades but was now joined by Janet Chance, Dora Russell, Berthe Lorsignol and others, and newly sympathetic doctors such as Norman Haire, in putting this over in talks to women's organizations, letters in sympathetic journals, and other forums of debate. The topic was given national press prominence by Mr Justice McCardie's strongly-worded criticisms of the state of the law when passing sentence in abortion cases.[72] In 1934 the Women's Cooperative Guild was in the vanguard (as with divorce and birth control), passing a resolution (by an overwhelming majority) in favour of the legalization of surgical abortion and demanding amnesty for women in prison for performing illegal abortions. In the following year, the NCW less radically called for a government investigation and the National Union of Societies for Equal Citizenship adopted a resolution for reform. *Abortion*, a volume of three essays by Stella Browne, Harry Roberts (a doctor supporting limited access under medical control), and A. M. Ludovici (complete opposition), was published and the subject was touched on in other works of the period. In 1936 Joan Malleson, a woman doctor interested in the issue, called a meeting of supporters of legalized abortion and the Abortion Law Reform Association was founded. Stephen Brooke has suggested that while its position could be considered 'a variant of feminist maternalism' in its invocation of the importance of motherhood, the movement none the less had a keen feminist edge and 'comprised a radical challenge to established gender ideologies', as well as being centrally concerned with class.[73]

Although the law embodied in the 1861 Act made no exception for the medical profession, there was something of a traditional perception that clinical judgement respecting the risk to a woman's life ought to be paramount. In practice there was a huge range of individual doctors' approaches, from never to if the price was right. The legal position had been confused by the Infant Life (Preservation) Act of 1929, permitting abortion after the 28th week of pregnancy 'in good faith for the purpose only of preserving the life of the mother', but not entirely clear as to whether it was permissible earlier. The British Medical Association set up a committee on abortion in 1935, which recommended legal abortion as a remedy for the ill-effects of criminal abortion, in certain therapeutically defined circumstances, in cases of rape and incest involving young girls, and also on eugenic grounds.[74] Dugald Baird, the Medical Officer of Aberdeen, took advantage of Scottish law to perform abortions on social grounds, an option not available in other parts of the United Kingdom.[75] The Joint Council on Midwifery (established largely at the initiative of Lady Rhys Williams of the National Birthday Trust Fund) also set up a committee to investigate illegal abortion, which undertook surveys in several areas, and called for restrictions on the sale of abortifacients and the introduction of notification.[76]

In 1937 an Interdepartmental (Home Office/Ministry of Health) Committee – the Birkett Committee – was set up to investigate the question (the classic delaying and defusing official response to controversial sexual issues[77]). It heard extensive evidence from interested groups and individuals, (including Stella Browne, who – an unmarried woman of nearly 60 – informed the Committee, 'if abortion was necessarily fatal or injurious, I should not be here before you'[78]). In its final Majority Report it recommended clarifying the legality of abortions undertaken 'in good faith' by medical practitioners and thus placing the decision in medical hands, and refused to engage with the related issue of birth control, which was strongly recommended in Dorothy Thurtle's (of ALRA and formerly the Workers' Birth Control Group) Minority Report, which also advocated abortion in certain non-medical contingencies such as rape.[79]

Meanwhile a test case occurred. Aleck Bourne, a surgeon at St Mary's Hospital, performed an abortion on a 14-year-old girl who had been gang-raped by soldiers, following approaches from Joan Malleson, in order to clarify and extend common-law assumptions about the lawfulness of doctors' clinical decisions. His argument was that mental as well as physical considerations should be taken into account. He was acquitted by Mr Justice McNaghten, in the famous ruling that operating to prevent the woman becoming 'a physical or mental wreck' was legitimate.[80] This was certainly an advance, but defused the hopes of campaigners by providing a minimal guarantee covering doctors, without engaging with questions of women's rights or wider social factors leading them to seek abortions.

Matrimonial causes

Another legal change which cleared up confusion and anomalies without going as far as radical reformers would have wished was the 1937 Matrimonial Causes Act, introduced as a Private Members' Bill by A. P. Herbert, humorist and writer, whose 1934 novel *Holy Deadlock* satirized the existing state of the divorce law: that to terminate a marriage spouses had to commit either adultery or perjury. The Herbert Act extended the grounds, largely along the lines recommended nearly 30 years previously by the Royal Commission, to include desertion for over three years, cruelty, and prolonged incurable insanity. Women could also divorce husbands guilty of rape (of a woman not their wife), sodomy, or bestiality (crimes assumed specific to the male: a man could not divorce his wife for lesbianism). Numbers of divorces per year (which had less than doubled since the 1923 Act, from 2848 to 4784) went up to 7535 (numbers of petitions increased dramatically, but court backlogs meant delays in decrees granted).[81] The continuing lack of social approval, however, was amply demonstrated by the contemporaneous constitutional crisis concerning King Edward VIII's determination to marry Mrs Wallis Simpson, a twice-divorced American commoner, resulting in his abdication, although the degree of support for the King's wish to marry the woman he loved varied widely across different social groups and in many quarters there was a good deal of sympathy.[82] At a less elevated social level, by 1937 nearly half of all divorce cases were dealt with under the Poor Persons Procedure, but the increased demand for divorces following the extension of grounds severely strained this system, and some solicitors refused to take on these cases.[83]

Herbert presented his Act as being for the 'true support of marriage' and 'the reduction of illicit unions' (i.e., cohabiting partners who could not divorce existing spouses), and restoring due respect for the law. It retained the concepts of 'guilty' and 'innocent' parties and left in place penalties for condonement of matrimonial offences or collusion in seeking divorce, and thus did not even go as far as some recommendations made to the Royal Commission for no-fault divorce by mutual consent. It was still regarded as having 'settled the problem of divorce law reform for a generation'.[84]

The better preservation of marriage was also the concern of the Marriage Guidance Council, formally established, following correspondence and discussions, in February 1938, by a coalition of social purity workers, doctors interested in birth control and sexual hygiene, clergymen, probation officers, magistrates, psychotherapists, eugenicists, and others. The British Social Hygiene Council Marriage Committee had been a precursor, but the new body was committed to a recognition of the potential benefits of birth control to marital harmony, something the BSHC would not contemplate. Its aims were to ensure that couples entered marriage better informed about what it involved, and to provide means of solving postmarital difficulties. Initially it organized conferences and lecture courses to propagate its ideas. As it became known, requests for help from individuals began to arrive, and 'the first fumbling attempts to supply this need' led to the development of counselling (not among the original intentions). The advent of war in 1939, however, 'brought everything to a standstill'.[85]

Pat Thane has suggested that far from marriage being in crisis, the 1930s were the dawn of a brief 'golden age, indeed the only age, of the near universal, stable, long-lasting marriage', establishing this entirely new family pattern, which, however, very soon came to be considered traditional and desirable. Almost everyone married, they had smaller families in which all the children survived, and marriages lasted longer because they were less likely to be prematurely broken by death (maternal mortality, still high at the beginning of the decade, began to fall from around 1935[86]) and at least three generations might be alive at the same time. Although divorce had become easier after 1937, it remained rare and stigmatized.[87]

Studying sex

The founders of the MGC also projected the possibilities of research. The taboos on investigating sexual behaviour were shifting slightly. Issues around population and reproductive health had been studied on several occasions since the first decade of the century, though who could be interrogated and in what terms remained problematic, at least in the minds of researchers. Marie Stopes's questionnaires to doctors and clergymen in 1922 had been answered with a degree of candour also found in the correspondence she received, and McCance's 200 women in his periodicity study recorded intimate physical and emotional changes. But the Birth Control Investigation Committee felt it inappropriate to ask about frequency of intercourse or sexual practices in its questionnaire, addressed exclusively to women.[88]

An entirely new approach to investigating sexual habits within society was that of Mass Observation, founded in 1937 to undertake 'an anthropology of ourselves'. Its founders, Tom Harrisson (recently returned from Melanesia), Charles Madge, a poet, and Humphrey Jennings, a film-maker, were left-wing intelligentsia with an interest in surrealism. It recruited a 'National Panel' of 'ordinary' people who were to observe their own and other peoples' lives, on a 'participant observation' model. It investigated a wide range of social phenomena, but as a by-product of its 'Worktown' survey, an in-depth study of Bolton, observers followed 'Worktowners' to Blackpool during 'Wakes Week' and made extensive endeavours to observe sexual activity in these carnivalesque surroundings. They discovered much flirting, picking-up, and groping, but little actual fornication. Gender and class attitudes of the observers also influenced what they saw, how they understood it, and what they failed to see. Curious exhibitions mentioned were the fairground sideshow of 'Colonel Barker' (Valerie Arkell-Smith) the 'man-woman', and hermaphrodites in the wax museum.[89] Alison Oram has discussed the rise of the 'sex change story' and the invocation of medical science in narratives in the popular press, along with the attempt to stabilize the 'real' gender identity. But there remained an element of the freak-show about such stories, embodied in this display of Barker for the amusement and bafflement of holiday crowds.[90]

* * *

Old and new ways of thinking about sex, of sexual behaviour and attitudes, jostled one another, perhaps typical of this complex decade, overshadowed by the threat of the impending conflict which finally came in September 1939.

8

War and the Welfare State

The Second World War disrupted existing sexual lives and provided, in some cases, new sexual opportunities: men went into the forces, mothers and children were evacuated, women directed according to labour needs. Traditional indicators revealed the effects of social disruption and, doubtless, stress and uncertainty. Illegitimate births among all fertile age groups increased (some, to married women who registered the children as their husbands', presumably occluded from the record),[1] and the number of criminal abortions known to the police quadrupled (probably an underestimate).[2] This did not necessarily signify unrestrained sexual indulgence, many conceptions taking place in circumstances which, in less chaotic times, would have led to marriage. The change was in social context rather than actual activity,[3] and it is perhaps something of an exaggeration to claim that 'sexual restraint had been suspended for the duration, as the traditional licence of the battlefield invaded the home front'.[4]

War always brings it on

There was a massive upsurge in venereal infections, although intensified medical surveillance possibly uncovered previously unknown or unreported cases. There had been little forward planning and facilities were inadequate: information was supposed to be disseminated to all servicemen but ignorance as to risks and prevention was rife across all ranks. Eventually condoms were issued, educational films acquired, lectures given, and poster campaigns initiated. Antibiotics revolutionized treatment, although there was initial resistance to allocating still scarce penicillin to syphilis cases.

The problem was not merely military, given the importance of the Home Front. The Ministry of Health's transfer of responsibility for venereal education and propaganda to the Central Council for Health Education signified commitment to a preventive medical rather than a moral approach. A joint campaign of the Ministry and the CCHE to increase public awareness of the diseases and provisions for their treatment began in 1942.[5] There were still powerful taboos in place: at a 1940 talk to the British Sexology Society the Secretary of the Society for the Prevention of Venereal Disease mentioned that bank managers 'expressly desired that VD should not be mentioned on the cheques, for the sake of the "purity" of the clerks'.[6]

Advertisements in the press and radio broadcasts made some inroads upon breaching this taboo: the *Daily Mirror* had already ventured discussion of the subject, and printed the advertisements in their original form, employing terms in common use such as 'pox' and 'clap', but the 'mistaken sense of delicacy', if not downright prudery, of most other newspaper proprietors weakened this hard-hitting approach, with the *Daily Express* not even printing expurgated versions. Bingham argues that this embodied the *Mirror*'s attempts to position itself as 'an outspoken opponent of prudery and outdated social convention', 'vulgar but honest', and the campaign 'marked an important moment in the public discussion of sex and encouraged the belief that all citizens should be sexually informed'.[7]

A torrent of correspondence from the general public to the Ministry requested further information, and Mass Observation was commissioned to investigate the efficacy of the campaign by approaching members of the public in the street, and asking questions about the advertisements and attitudes more generally towards venereal diseases. Even though some respondents considered the whole subject 'dirty', 'nasty', even 'horrible', Mass Observers found 'great willingness' among the public to know more, and even 'active desire' for greater openness. Responses were enormously diverse. Remedies suggested ranged from traditional recommendations of licensing brothels and inspecting prostitutes, to regular medical examinations for all and punitive measures for the infected, to suggestions for inoculation, and dissemination of information via mass media. The spread of the disease was blamed on 'little cheap loose-living girls', soldiers, and foreigners (especially Americans). Enormous importance was placed – especially by women – on 'keeping clean' and there was a manifest sense of venereal diseases as an almost miasmatic threat detached from actual sexual contacts, though strongly associated with public lavatories (where most individuals would have encountered information prior to the publicity campaign).[8] By 1945 large posters displayed on 'hoardings throughout the country...aroused no criticism' and had 'the approval of the vast majority of the public'.[9]

A more traditional measure was Defence of the Realm Regulation 33B. Mindful of the furore over Regulation 40D in the First World War, 33B was, at least in intention, gender-neutral in requiring notification of contacts. None the less, it bore more heavily upon women – during its first six months 64 women had been informed upon and only two men.[10] While the view persisted that 'the female carrier is the reservoir of infection', male partners in the transaction were becoming increasingly visible, partly due to the rise in contact tracing. Consorting with prostitutes and becoming venereally infected were no longer seen as marks of manhood: however, men were reckless with casually met 'so-called amateurs'. There was concern about the increasing number of infections among 'good' girls. Because professionals were assumed to know 'how to take care of themselves'[11] (as a prostitute respondent to Mass Observation claimed[12]), the 'easy amateur' was seen as the major reservoir of disease, although a 1944 *Lancet* article pointed out that epidemiologically, the prostitute remained a greater risk.[13] By the late 1940s male venereal disease patients were increasingly depicted as irresponsible defaulters from treatment or drunkards incapable of recalling the details of their partner, neurotic or inadequate rather than the finest type of fighting men (although some diehards retained this belief) and it was argued that good morale in a military unit correlated with low incidence of venereal disease. From a manly concomitant of militarism, sexually transmitted diseases had become a mark of failure.[14]

Censoring sex in a nation at war

Active policing against potential contamination of the public mind by inappropriate sexual matters continued, though it might be supposed there were other more pressing issues. The employment of young girls to pack condoms in a London factory (the existing workforce being directed into essential war work) was the subject of agitation by moral reform organizations.[15] In June 1942 *Love without Fear: A plain guide to Sex Technique for every married adult*, by Eustace Chesser, a Harley Street psychiatrist and gynaecologist, was prosecuted under the Obscenity Act, after a policeman had purchased a copy and found it shocking. Chesser remarked, on being served the summons, 'you have left it a long time' (it had sold 5000 copies since being published over a year previously). *Love without Fear* was written in a straightforward style eschewing specialized medical vocabulary, deploying vivid illustrative facts and stories to catch readers' attention, and extensively based on material by other authorities.

The usual procedure in obscenity prosecutions was to plead guilty at summary trial before a magistrate, and pay a small fine. Chesser and his publisher chose to take the case before a jury, risking severer penalties and potentially unpleasant repercussions for Chesser's medical career, gambling on either impressing the jury by their sincerity or appealing to its healthy common sense. The defence gained the important concession that the book should be judged as a whole rather than on passages out of context. Chesser argued in court that much physical ill-health was caused by mental factors arising from sexual difficulties, emphasizing his experience among a wide variety of patients in the northern industrial town of Salford and London. Material about 'deviations', and detailed accounts of sexual techniques for the married couple (including oral sex), he claimed, were intended to help individuals to enjoy marital sex and to encourage consulting doctors about common but little-discussed problems. The book was not cheap – beyond the pockets of young people – with a note, requesting booksellers' cooperation, stating that the book was intended for the married or about to be married only.

The outcome of the case owed much to the Common Serjeant's summing up from the bench. He summarized the defence position as: 'in the year 1942, it is ridiculous and absurd to suggest that the discussion of sex and sex relationship in a book is obscene ... all this hush-hush and secrecy with regard to sex and sex relationship have done a great deal of harm.' He drew the jury's attention to the book's high price and its sale by reputable booksellers. The (rvimind) law amendment act 1923

testimony of three doctors (one a lady) was cited. Finally, he told the jury: 'it is only common sense: the law has left it to you.' After retiring for less than an hour the jury brought in a 'Not Guilty' verdict. In subsequent editions Chesser omitted passages and examples found particularly objectionable, but nevertheless, the July 1942 (post-trial) edition still included accounts of practices in Continental licensed brothels and descriptions of homosexuality, lesbianism, and sadomasochism. The promotion of good sexual relations within marriage was increasingly seen as desirable, but concerns continued about these works finding their way into the wrong hands (the unmarried and, in particular, the young).[16]

The case did not signal anything more than vindication of Chesser's own integrity and professional standing. In the same year (1942) the police raided the Economy Educator Services, a one-man, mostly mail order, lending library. The stock included a number of sexological works: the prosecution argued that circulation had not been to 'members of the medical profession, and students of physiology and psychology', nor was there any means of ascertaining whether declarations that borrowers were over 21 were correct. The defence argued that none of the books in question had themselves been prosecuted for obscenity, and were published by reputable firms. Mr Justice McNaughton, however, connected the 'obscene words' and 'incitements to acts of obscenity' disseminated by the defendant with the 'obscene acts…in most cases…with children of tender years' also before the court during the assizes, and passed a sentence of 12 months. An appeal was unsuccessful: the defendant had also been running a 'confidential advice Bureau', issuing a '"comprehensive letter" dealing with…sexual difficulties'; a sympathizers' campaign did obtain remission of the sentence. Concern was expressed by the Home Secretary (Herbert Morrison) over these proceedings over books which were not themselves prosecuted and continued to be sold elsewhere. Authors and publishers had no opportunity to defend themselves, yet books involved in local prosecutions were added to a secret list circulated to all police forces. Alec Craig, sex reformer and campaigner for censorship reform, considered that arbitrary outbreaks of police activity were usually the outcome of local purity drives generated by current events (e.g. the arrival of US troops) or 'clamour by religious bodies', and often involved serious literary works.[17]

A number of similar businesses circulated volumes not readily available in bookshops or embarrassing to purchase. Their catalogues juxtaposed serious sexological works, reputable sexual manuals, anthropological texts, and banned literary novels, with works on nudism, torture, and flagellation, and volumes which were at least borderline pornography. They also kept in circulation late nineteenth- and early twentieth-century works warning of the dangers of self-abuse. Censorship and shame thus rendered as 'sexual knowledge' a miscellaneous ragbag of texts intended for very diverse purposes.[18]

Adeptly navigating the strictures of the Lord Chamberlain's Office and the licensing requirements of London County Council with static tableaux of nudity among variety acts involving clothed (if scantily and suggestively) dancers deploying a glamourized 'girl-next-door' femininity and male comedians, the Windmill Theatre in London positioned itself as a unique venue providing an acceptable form of sexualized entertainment, situated right on the border of Soho and the more respectable West End theatre district. One of the iconic institutions of the War, it famously boasted 'We never closed' throughout the Blitz.[19]

The state of marriage

Chesser's agenda fitted with general concerns over the state of marriage and its improvement. The Marriage Guidance Council restarted in the autumn of 1942, reflecting a belief that 'the need for marriage guidance had greatly increased', and was likely to become even greater once the War had ended. A distinguished and highly respectable panel of Presidents and Vice- Presidents (including three bishops) was appointed. A London office was opened and an advisory centre offering 'expert, sympathetic, and confidential help' inaugurated. In the first nine months some 250 clients were seen, the 'experiment' moved into a more permanent phase, and plans were in hand for several provincial centres. Lecturers addressed audiences of probation officers, clergy, service units, youth groups, women's organizations, welfare workers, university students, and industrial groups, as well as public meetings. Training courses were organized and in increasing demand. The Council was officially recognized by the Central Council for Health Education as an Affiliated Society, and liaised and collaborated with similar or related organizations. Press interest was largely positive and (paper shortage and printing expenses hindering more active propaganda work) helped make its work known. The Council not only recommended 'the right books on sex and marriage', but decided, since 'so many people have found difficulty in securing these locally' (see above on the arbitrary policing of booksellers, and the very dubious texts that might be procured from suspect sources) that a sales department be set up.[20]

Several investigations concerning marriage and the population question were undertaken, even while the war was in progress. Eliot Slater, a psychiatrist, and Moya Woodside, a psychiatric social worker, undertook an in-depth survey of 200 soldiers and their wives between 1943 and 1946, published as *Patterns of Marriage* in 1951. In spite of the smallness of the sample and the biases in its selection (hospital patients of mostly London origin), Slater and Woodside's account provides vivid insights into working-class courtship and marriage and attitudes toward sex. 'Picking-up' via casual social encounters was an accepted means of meeting, followed by a drift towards marriage within about two years. 'Sexiness' figured very little among the desirable qualities of a mate, being somewhat feared and denigrated by both men and women. Physical attraction played a greater part in male partner selection, but for both, mental and personality traits counted most. In a significant number of cases premarital intercourse had taken place, usually justified on the grounds that marriage was intended. Some individuals claimed that they were unable to remember and there were sometimes differences between spouses in their recollections: possibly 'due to some doubt of what constitutes sex relations'.[21]

Slater and Woodside remarked that throughout, 'the emphasis on sex is a negative one' and it had a 'low value...as a justification for marrying'. 'Sex desires are regarded ambiguously', thought of as 'natural and inevitable, but at the same time not quite respectable, and are usually referred to with evidence of shame'. [22] There was a wide range in the frequency of intercourse once married, exacerbated by the contemporary wartime conditions, averaging around twice a week. There was an assumption that 'there is a standard to which most people conform, and that other people are much the same as themselves', founded, the authors surmised, 'on an almost total ignorance'. Sexual relations were based on male dominance, men taking sex for granted as a regulated indulgence. They hardly expected responsiveness from their wives and sensuality in the woman was regarded with some alarm.

For women sex was seen as a duty to be undertaken with 'passive endurance', from which they did not expect any particular pleasure: many found the act boring, even repulsive or painful. 'A lucky minority' experienced real pleasure, and others achieved some satisfaction, though difficulties in communication between investigators and the women made interpretation problematic: 'it was difficult to word the appropriate question' about orgasm, and 'many who said "yes" sounded unconvincing'. The comment, 'he's very good, he doesn't bother me much', summed up a prevalent attitude.[23] Liz Stanley points out that this was 'the first published survey to show women's unhappiness and dissatis-faction with the sexual aspects of marriage': if, as she remarks, it proceeded from an assumption that 'sex' and 'intercourse' were synonymous, this was largely how the sample surveyed would have conceptualized the question.[24] Szreter and Fisher, however, argue that Slater and Woodside 'failed to look behind women's silences and evasions' or consider what factors might create reluc-tance to talk about sexual pleasure, for example, the lack of a language through which they might articulate positive sexual experience, and thus the impression is unduly negative.[25] Fisher, indeed, has suggested that 'wifely duty' could have been an acceptable way to frame female sexual desires, or at least might not have been antithetical to pleasure.[26]

The problem of parenthood

The phallocentric penetrative model of sex deployed also doubtless owed some-thing to the continuing close connection made between the state of marriage and the population question, still causing anxiety in the early 1940s. Although some women in Slater and Woodside's sample had deliberately become pregnant to avoid conscription, incentive and opportunity to start or increase a family were largely lacking during the war.[27] Reasons given for postponing parenthood usually related to the spouse's unavoidable absence, and the need for secure employment and a stable home as a preliminary.[28] In a small sample of women doctors reporting on their own family planning activities, a couple mentioned the 'political situation' and 'war' as motives for contraception, although another had (spaced) births in 1939, 1941, and 1943, and intended to try for another. A small-scale survey of their patients reported rather similar reasons: 'wartime factors, e.g. accommodation, husband going abroad', 'general insecurity due to war', though one or two also suggested desire to have a child straight away 'in case of anything "happening"'.[29]

None the less, although it might have been anticipated that peace would bring forth a changed attitude, concern about the population led to both a Mass Observation survey, *Britain and Her Birth-Rate* (published in 1945), using an eclectic variety of materials, and the appointment of a Royal Commission. As with Slater and Woodside, MO discovered that children were still perceived as central to marriage, but women were not only having but also wanting smaller families and making deliberate decisions to space births, for reasons as much, if not more, to do with giving the children themselves a 'good start' as with 'selfish' desires.[30] Slater and Woodside found a good deal of cynicism concerning official propaganda about increasing the birth rate ('if they'd make houses for us, we'd make children') and although there was approval for the proposed family allowances, a common response was: '[I'd] like to see them keep a baby on five shillings.'[31] The small survey by medical women also suggested that housing shortages and economic hardships were strong influences against childbearing.[32]

Although MO acquired useful and illuminating information about attitudes to family size and birth control by the simple expedient of asking people, the Royal Commission on Population was rather more cautious. The Royal College of Obstetricians and Gynaecologists was delegated to undertake an 'Enquiry into Family Limitation and its influence on Human Fertility during the Past Fifty Years' in 1944, even though they had not (except for a few individuals) demonstrated themselves particularly friendly towards birth control. Far from taking the straightforward path of Mass Observation, it was decided, after much agonizing, to interview married women in general hospital wards, using specially hired doctors, since 'only members of the medical profession who stood to the women in the relation of doctor to patient' could tactfully elicit answers on such a sensitive subject. While the Committee were pleased to record 'friendly cooperation' and the voluntary provision of 'essential information' by the women interviewed, class bias was created by the reluctance of private hospitals and nursing homes to 'risk incurring unpopularity among their clientele' by participating.[33]

The family planning movement had been seriously affected by the war as well as by this climate of population anxiety. Many Family Planning Association members were involved in other, more prestigious and urgent, wartime activities, and it was keeping services going rather than campaigning for their extension or continuing research. Centres were set up in air-raid shelters, but the War Office reacted in horror to proposals for making contraceptive advice available to married service women. Clinic buildings suffered in air raids. Although rubber was allocated for manufacturing sheaths for VD prevention, female caps were accorded low priority until pressure on government departments through the personal contacts of individual FPA members and supporters finally released supplies for birth control clinics in 1944.[34]

Changing attitudes of women towards the biological events of their lifecycle were clearly apparent as they refused to replicate the experience of earlier generations with large families, a rejection of passive endurance also discernable in attitudes towards childbirth. This was becoming ever safer following the introduction of sulphonamides. None the less, many women regarded it as an ordeal they were no longer obliged to endure. The Medical Women's

Federation Survey noted, not altogether with approval, that one-child families were not uncommonly the result of 'difficult pregnancy or labour with the first child'.[35] Analgesia during childbirth was still by no means a given, and although hospital, as opposed to home, confinements were steadily increasing, many women found the environment and the care given unsympathetic. While some campaigners were fighting for the extension of effective analgesia, Grantly Dick-Read's *Revelation of Childbirth* (later *Childbirth without Fear*), 1942, presented a wholly new vision of childbirth and its potential.

Dick-Read, a general practitioner, had published *Natural Childbirth* in 1933, when women were probably still more concerned about surviving than the quality of the experience. The revised version was far more successful and led to the natural childbirth movement. Dick-Read claimed that women were caught up in a cycle of 'fear-tension-pain', often generated by 'old wives' tales' absorbed at their mother's knee. Through mental and physical preparation, they would find childbirth not merely painless but a positive pleasure. He argued that diminishing fears of parturition would pay off in population terms. While he fits neatly into the model of male expert providing guidance on women's functions (while denigrating traditional women's expertise), numerous women responded to his message with enormous enthusiasm.[36]

Women at war

This emphasis on the rewards of women's traditional sphere, even if managed more efficiently by modern scientific expertise, matched with the general tendency to keep gender roles carefully demarcated in the face of the disruptions and requirements of total war. Although women might be 'heroic' in responding to the demands of the war effort, there was considerable concern lest they lose their essential femininity. Single women were free to serve their country, and were counted as 'mobile' labour, but wives and mothers, although called upon to contribute to the war effort, were not under compulsion; their role in the home being both part of their contribution and what was being fought for. Women who took over 'men's' work usually did so as 'dilutees', or auxiliaries, supporting or supplementing male labour, and what they did was carefully differentiated. They released men for combat, but did not become combatants themselves. Superhuman effort might be required, and even transgress the peacetime conventions of the 'natural', but it was always positioned as temporary, to be relinquished when the war was over.[37]

There were often considerable tensions between women in non-traditional spheres of activity and the men already there, exacerbated since non-combatant men tended to be seen as lacking the heroic masculinity ascribed to the fighting forces. Men in the civil labour force (even if reserved and prevented from joining up) were characterized as too old or too unfit for the active defence of the nation. The tensions were negotiated in a variety of ways according to local contexts and conditions: sometimes the women became 'honorary men', 'one of the boys', whereas in others an emphasis on femininity reduced hostility. Male antagonism sometimes took the form of sexualized teasing or even harassment, but women often responded assertively, giving as good as they got.[38]

Women actually in uniform came in for a good deal of gendered sexual hostility, the ATS (Auxiliary Transport Service) in particular being stigmatized, with parents and husbands refusing to let their daughters or wives become 'some officer's groundsheet'.[39] Uniforms in general aroused 'deep-rooted prejudice', perhaps traceable to long-standing negative images of a 'brutal and licentious soldiery', exacerbated by the gender transgression of women stepping outside a 'natural' role. Women in khaki were the subjects of 'vague and discreditable allegations' of sexual promiscuity and excessive drinking, and a supposed high rate of discharge from the ATS for unmarried pregnancy. This had such an adverse effect upon recruitment that the government undertook an investigation, which found that the unwed pregnancy rate in the ATS was lower than that in the civilian population, and there was 'no justification for the vague and sweeping charges of immorality'.[40]

There was considerable moral panic over the perceived rise in prostitution and the proliferation of venues associated with commercial sex in the metropolis, in particular after the first US troops arrived. There was a persistent rumour that prostitutes were exempt from call-up. In spite of the positioning of prostitutes in debates around VD as responsible professionals who took care over risks of infection, unlike the 'amateur', the idea that they were evading direction of labour aroused enormous hostility, extending to allegations that some women were actually declaring their profession as prostitute to evade call-up. This was urban myth: many prostitutes were ineligible for other reasons, such as a criminal record, non-British nationality (Stefan Slater has illuminated the interwar racket bringing foreign prostitutes to Soho[41]), being over-age. It is also quite likely that many would have been dismissed for health reasons. Some prostitutes might have successfully avoided call-up for which they were eligible but these would have been a minute number with no significant impact on the war effort: furthermore, anxieties were expressed about their potential presence in billets along with 'respectable women' and young girls.[42]

Fears of even more transgressive forms of female sexual behaviour were surprisingly muted. Lesbianism, considered among other issues of social and moral welfare within the ATS, was deemed rare and dealt with discreetly by posting women involved to different locations. Only a 'very few promiscuous lesbians' were actually discharged.[43] While female same-sex activity was frowned upon, though not a crime, it was usually dealt with through petty restrictions and surveillance.[44] Many women experienced close female bonding, but differentiated snuggling up in bed together (a disciplinary charge) for warmth in chilly barracks from 'doing anything wrong', and friends who shared a communal bathroom were distinguished from 'funny women'. The enforced exposure to a range of social types which would not normally have been encountered did open many women's eyes to possibilities they had not previously imagined: 'all sorts…lesbians and things like that'.[45]

Pathologization and transgression

Some historians have suggested that for the male homosexual the war provided unrivalled opportunities, even though in the forces homosexuality had 'horrendous sanctions against it'. The blackout, a curse to many, was 'to people like us…a boon', and Hugh David argues, a more liberatory experience for homosexual men than anything before the 1967 decriminalization. There is some evidence that overt homosexuals (and lesbians) were accepted by their colleagues, who might even be 'protective', although Emma Vickers suggests that toleration or discreet refusals to see might have been based in pragmatism.[46] For some, certainly, 'it was such a lovely war. Oh what went on was no-one's business.'[47] However, broader social attitudes did not change. In 1940 George Ives noted that over 99 per cent of homosexual offences were tried without juries, and commented on the suicide of a homosexual bank manager 'of (they say) the highest character' caught cottaging in Hampstead.[48] In the forces, courts-martial for 'indecency between males' outnumbered those for any other category of offence, and increased massively between 1939 (48) and 1944/5 (324).[49]

The medico-scientific understanding of homosexuality continued to be strongly influenced by the Ellis/Carpenter school of thought, though with growing Freudian inflections.[50] Forensic medical texts began to cite similar views, for example the opinions of Lord Dawson (a leading figure in arranging for Ellis to be elected FRCP) that 'homosexuality was a pathological condition' that 'had one foot in the realm of disease and was not wholly in the realm of crime' and 'Few people were 100 per cent. female or 100 per cent. male'. However, this merely prefaced standard means for detecting evidence of sodomy: said to 'most frequently result from a condition of male inversion or homosexuality', this was not a mitigating circumstance. Further evidence of some acquaintance with sexology was indicated by the inclusion of short descriptions of other 'perversions', some with no legal status (e.g. lesbianism).[51]

Eustace Chesser, discussing ' "She-Men" and "He-Women" ' among 'Byways of Sex' in *Love without Fear*, did not altogether strike a balance between the pathological model and a liberal plea for tolerance. Though praising homosexuals as 'a kindly and tolerant section of the community…gifted, especially in the arts', he still declared that 'the genuine homosexual is suffering from a definitely pathological state' and his accounts of circumstances working on 'innate predisposition' verged on the contagion/corruption model.[52] It is not surprising that a young man, anxious to know whether homosexuality was 'an innate characteristic in man and whether it can be changed back in normal channels by the will', wrote to Julian Huxley in 1942, hoping that scientific expertise would reassure him (two previous authorities had declared homosexuality either 'incurable' or 'incorrigible').[53]

Alison Oram indicates that after the war, there was a distinct change in the tone of press stories involving female same-sex relationships, with increased emphasis on pathology and morbidity and mentions of 'intimacy' and 'perversion'. Women dressing in male clothes or a close approximation had become a common sight during the War rather than a rare and curious masquerade. The pathologization of the lesbian was underscored by the reporting of murders by women of their female lovers, out of jealousy or rejection. However, in spite of this greater awareness of the existence of lesbianism, in 1949 *The Well of Loneliness* was reissued without furore.[54]

Transgressive sexual behaviour during the war years was also associated with non-British 'others'. The Americans, in particular, had a bad reputation ('overpaid, oversexed, and over here') as has been seen in the attribution of the VD epidemic to 'these Yanks'. While their deleterious impact on female sexual morals was the major cause of moral panic, 'American queens' also 'changed a lot of homosexual people's attitudes towards sex'. Not only were they 'much more inventive', they also increased the '[going] rates in the rent boy market'.[55]

Black GIs' attraction, in particular, for young British women was a cause of major anxiety, especially as the girls were said to 'make most of the running' and it was alleged that a growing percentage of the worrying number of illegitimate babies resulted from cross-race liaisons. However, differences in national courtship styles also led to complaints of sexual molestation (at least) by GIs of British women, even though, for an assortment of reasons it was largely the women who were stigmatized for these intercultural and interracial relationships. Fear around female sexuality and the pursuit of pleasure in a nation at war were invoked as well as the transgression of racial boundaries. Leanne McCormick indicates that problems were particularly acute in Northern Ireland, where sexual mores were even more constrained than on the mainland and female chastity and sexual purity regarded as crucial to regional identity. Not only was women's active interest in American troops considered deplorable, the fact that they were pursuing incomers outraged local men.[56]

Sex in the Welfare State

The end of the war brought hopes of a better future, but there were many tensions to be worked out between married couples, between men and women generally, following the disruptions of wartime. Even if there had not been infidelity, husbands and wives might feel that the other failed to understand their experience, while children and fathers, who were almost strangers, had to come to terms with one another. Many women were glad to give up gruelling war work, especially when they also had maternal and domestic responsibilities, but others resented dismissal from employment they enjoyed and were good at, and the lack of respect accorded to their efforts. Housing continued in short supply, so many couples found themselves living with in-laws. Rationing and austerity continued. Support systems for working mothers, such as canteens and nurseries, were run down.[57]

The Welfare State brought into being by the postwar Labour Government rested on strongly gendered notions of the respective contributions of male and female to the nation. Men as workers, women as home-based mothers underpinned social service, health and welfare, and educational provisions. The long-campaigned for Family Allowance scheme was finally introduced, with the money paid directly to the mother, as Eleanor Rathbone had always demanded. Thus women's work as mothers was recognized, even though the sum involved was small and not paid for first children, and the system depended on a normative vision of the family. The rights of particularly able girls to pursue an academic school curriculum and higher education was conceded, though ideas about girls' education were pervaded with the notion that their future lay in the domestic sphere. In the professions, some concessions were achieved: all medical schools were obliged to admit women following the National Health Act, the marriage bar on public and civil service appointments was abolished, but although rights to equal compensation for injuries acquired on war work had been conceded, equal pay took some years to arrive. The arrival of free universal health provision revealed that many women were suffering from preventable or treatable conditions to a degree largely unsuspected (though indicated by various surveys and investigations).[58]

If the new Welfare State failed to interrogate assumptions about appropriate gender roles (while alleviating some injustices), sex was not explicitly part of the brave new world at all, although Stephen Brooke has recently demonstrated that although official Labour Party policy on sexual matters remained evasive at this period, there was strong support among women MPs and Labour women generally for issues such as birth control, marriage guidance, sex education, and divorce law reform.[59]

Birth control was too politically contentious to mention when the National Health Service itself was still a matter for delicate negotiation. The Family Planning Association, though in principle committed to state birth control services, failed to press for contraception under the NHS. Possibly it was felt that given the medical profession's pervasive ignorance of contraception, the time was far from ripe and existing clinics provided a more adequate service. Furthermore, the then President, Lord Horder, was an opponent of socialized medicine. However, the preoccupation of Government bodies, politicians, and the medical profession with other issues, plus continued squeamishness about birth control, must have played a considerable part.[60] Abortion continued marginalized and criminalized, although the Bergmann-Ferguson case of 1948 clarified existing case law, when the judge ruled that abortion was legal if the doctor believed in good faith that continuing pregnancy would be seriously deleterious to a woman's physical or mental health ('irrefutable evidence' was not necessary).[61]

While marriage guidance, similarly, was not incorporated into official social service provision, the Committee on Matrimonial Procedures (the Denning Committee) recommended that a marriage welfare service distinct from divorce provisions was desirable, although – while deserving of State sponsorship – it should not be a state institution.[62] Grants in aid to existing voluntary societies were suggested, a scheme put into effect following the report of a Departmental Committee on Grants for the Development of Marriage Guidance in 1948. Three organizations were specified: the Marriage Guidance Council, the Catholic Marriage Advisory Council, and the Family Welfare Association, which received £5000 a year from the Home Office. Although the Family Planning Association was increasingly advising on marital problems and providing training for doctors, its attempts to gain funding were unsuccessful, 'family spacing and assisting fertility' being deemed 'too specialized' to qualify (and presumably, still anathema to Catholic and some Protestant opinion).[63]

While there were no changes to the terms of the divorce laws during this decade, concerns about the damage to morale in the Armed Forces over the break-up of marriages under wartime conditions led to the extension of the Poor Persons' rules to all service personnel up to NCO rank, the establishment of Forces Legal Advice Bureaux to gather the necessary documentation for the petition, and the Law Society setting up a Services Divorce Division to deal with service divorces and some civilian necessitous cases. By the end of the War, the latter had a staff of over one hundred and processed 4000 cases a year. It was clear by this time that return to the prewar system was not practicable and the Rushcliffe Committee on Legal Aid and Advice, which reported in 1945, led to the establishment of Legal Aid in 1949, administered by the legal profession and removing the stigmatizing concept of 'poor persons'.[64]

Although 1946 was a peak year for venereal infections in Britain, little attention was paid to this service within the NHS: the system created in 1917 continued, although a hasty circular had to be issued reinstating the 'confidentiality' requirement for VD clinic patients. In the age of antibiotics, however, venereal diseases were largely considered 'dying diseases', on their way to becoming extinct or at least rare. The subject had never been congenial: doctors, politicians, and civil servants were happy to ignore it, confident that it was no longer (or would shortly not be) a problem.[65] Sex in general was largely absent from the medical curriculum. Medical students were seldom taught about birth control or common sexual dysfunctions. The Goodenough Committee on Medical Education mentioned the need for instruction in marriage guidance and training in normal psychology, but made no specific recommendations. Doctors had to make up this deficit – if they wished – by their own efforts.[66]

Sex education of the young was said to be desirable, and veteran sex educator Cyril Bibby was appointed a special advisor to the Central Council for Health Education early in the War. The Board of Education finally issued guidelines, although these laid such emphasis on the difficulty and sensitivity of the task and the lack of adequate preparation of most individuals for undertaking it that they hardly constituted an encouragement to teachers to tackle the issue. The National Union of Teachers also issued a generally favourable statement on 'Sex Teaching in Schools'. Under Bibby's active leadership the CCHE was able to report significant degrees of local interest, with well-attended lecture courses and summer schools proliferating. Alas, this turned out a false dawn, partly as the CCHE's priorities altered with the founding of the NHS and partly due to a decline in the sense of crisis over sexual morality and behaviour with the end of the War. The 1944 Education Act paid lip-service to the desirability of sex education in schools, but there was no requirement that it be included in the curriculum and the decision as to whether it should take place, and of what it should consist, rested largely on decisions of individual head teachers or boards of school governors.[67]

Thus, traditional silence was maintained. Although the British Sexology Society expired during the War, a few similar bodies continued its agenda of trying to alleviate repressive attitudes and legislation. Eustace Chesser's Society for Sex Education and Guidance (f.1943) included veteran feminist sex radical Stella Browne as one of its vice-presidents.[68] But, in general, sex remained something to be controlled: a 50-year-old labourer wrote to Julian Huxley in

1949 that his 'powerful though normal sexual impulses' were not 'weakening with time' and wishing 'to be relieved of them', though not too drastically as he hoped to marry eventually.[69]

'Little Kinsey'

Therefore, no British equivalent to the Kinsey report (*Sexual Behaviour in the Human Male* appeared in 1948 and news of Kinsey's work had arrived before then) could have been compiled. None the less, Mass Observation in 1949 undertook a survey known as 'Little Kinsey' to discover 'what people's feelings really are towards sexual morality in this country' (i.e., attitudes rather than behaviour: although a smaller survey of volunteers did report on sexual activities). It was sponsored by the *Sunday Pictorial* in which five substantial articles appeared embodying the results of the research, to an enthusiastic reception. A projected pamphlet version of the entire report was never published: the reasons why a manuscript which had reached an advanced stage of preparation, and about which negotiations with a reputable publisher were in hand, did not appear are obscure, but possibly had something to do with the major changes Mass Observation was concurrently undergoing – rather than issues of censorship, given that so much of the material had already appeared in a popular newspaper.

Standard MO methodology was employed, combining approaches to individuals in the street (the 'street sample') and returns from members of MO's own 'Panel', with 'Leaders of Opinion' (clergymen, doctors, and teachers) specially surveyed, using a carefully designed questionnaire dealing with acquisition of knowledge of sex and desirability of sex education, attitudes towards birth control, views on marriage, children and divorce, extramarital relations (a confused category including premarital and adulterous sex) and opinions on prostitution, also whether the state of morality was improving or deteriorating. A certain amount of miscellaneous and observational material was also acquired. MO were agreeably surprised at the 'friendly and cooperative manner with which our questions were answered' by the 'street sample': only one per cent, it was reported, refused to continue once told what the survey was about.

The expected reticence was not found, and respondents concurred that sex was 'important', indeed insisting that 'sex is natural', although there was also considerable anxiety around 'uncontrolled' sex. There were noticeable gender (and some regional) differences. Sexual information had largely been acquired through 'haphazard, surreptitious passing on'. Premarital sex between couples intending marriage was relatively common, and seldom condemned. Liz Stanley has drawn attention to the preconceptions about sex and gender structuring the survey and the writing of the report, but also to the extensive use of vivid quotations and individual voices from the interviews. While sex was still an area of considerable unease, people were prepared to talk about it (more prepared than 'Leaders of Opinion' and policy-makers perhaps liked to think) and were frequently in favour of more openness and greater enlightenment. Respondents to the articles in the *Sunday Pictorial* were largely in favour of the giving of sex education.[70] The *Sunday Pictorial* (sister paper to the *Daily Mirror*) had already taken the bold step of publishing articles supporting sex education and serializing the pamphlet *How A Baby Is Born*, but their initiative was regarded askance by editors of other papers, who did not consider such topics suitable for 'family newspapers'.[71]

*   *   *

By 1950, therefore, licit sex remained closely allied with marriage. Premarital sex was more likely to occur between engaged or courting couples than between young men and prostitutes (though sex educators warned against 'easy women'). While British sexual reticence persisted, those in power perhaps underestimated the readiness of the public to discuss sexual issues. Sex was less taken for granted, but while represented as (in marriage) a permissible, indeed desirable pleasure, this also implied that this needed working at, was something problematic. On the other hand, individuals were growing less inclined to put up with sexual disharmony and, perhaps, less ashamed of seeking sexual pleasure. One of the great fears overhanging sexuality, that of venereal disease, seemed to have been abolished by modern science.

9

Domestic Ideology and Undercurrents of Change in the Fifties

Austerity persisted as the 1950s began, with many commodities still rationed, and a housing shortage that meant that many married couples commenced wedlock in their parents' houses.[1] There was 'much that remained from the Thirties: ageing celebrities, ancient rituals',[2] and the decade often seen as one of 'right-wing traditionalism and cultural stagnation'.[3] Frank Mort, however, argues that invocation of tradition by elitist 'upper-class revivalism' was heavily inflected by the experiences of the War and involvement with new consumer cultures.[4] On the surface, there seemed to be little that was revolutionary, or even reforming, going on in the area of sexual mores. Rather the converse. However, Geoffrey Gorer's discovery, in *Exploring English Character* (1955), that 'Most English people's views on sexual morality are more rigid than their personal practice' should perhaps be borne in mind.[5]

An age of matrimony

The Legal Aid system and the wider extension of divorce jurisdiction to provincial courts made dissolution of marriage more widely available, but grounds were still limited and the action still adversarial. Numbers of divorces peaked in 1947 (partly due to a backlog), but had halved by 1954.[6] When Mrs Eirene White MP introduced a Private Member's Bill in 1951, well received in the House of Commons, to enable either spouse to dissolve a relationship if the couple had lived apart for seven years without prospect of reconciliation, the Government offered a Royal Commission in exchange for withdrawal of a measure which would have, contentiously, enabled a 'guilty' spouse to divorce an innocent.[7] This was the traditional expedient of appearing to do something, while eschewing action which might actually change things. McGregor describes the Commission as a device for 'obfuscating a socially urgent but politically inconvenient issue',[8] with 'vast and detailed testimony' concerning opinions, and 'endless conjectures', but 'as to matters of fact...scarcely ten pages of evidence'.[9]

The 'abolitionist' argument for removing the concept of matrimonial offence was strongly urged, backed by claims that a substantial proportion of undefended divorces (90 per cent) were collusive actions amounting to divorce by mutual consent. It was also argued (notably by the Women's Cooperative Guild) that 'irretrievable breakdown' could occur in the absence of legally recognizable offence. Under the system as it stood, couples were compelled to remain in unhappy and unedifying unions, extramarital unions between individuals unable to divorce took place, and illegitimacy resulted. Thus divorce by consent was suggested, with discretionary divorce after a period of separation when one spouse did not consent. However, influential individuals and institutions felt that to extend the availability of divorce would lead to its becoming a 'normal feature' of society, undermining social stability. This school of thought took a pessimistic view towards changes in family life, and believed that epidemic 'divorce-mindedness' was corrupting marriage and the nation. Both parties concurred that the private relationships of marriage were of enormous social import.[10] In spite of social changes, there was still a strong feeling against doing anything that would minimize the consequences of sexual transgression. Janet Fink has demonstrated how this played out similarly in debates over the continuing problematic status of the illegitimate child and its parents.[11]

Marriage had hardly ever been more popular. Numbers of marriages noticeably increased and took place at earlier ages. Various reasons for this have been advanced. Increased social welfare provision provided a 'safety net', the spread of contraception meant that beginning a family could be delayed and children spaced, the numerical ratio between men and women improved, council housing became available. Various forms of propaganda during and since the War emphasized the desirability of domesticity. The 1950s was a period of economic growth, full employment, and high incomes. Rising standards of health, it is argued, reduced the age of sexual maturity and thus of readiness for marriage. This was also a period of a relatively drastic decrease in women's wages compared to men's, so for women, the cost-benefit analysis of work versus marriage came down heavily on the side of the latter.[12]

Marriage as a modern, 'companionate' relationship of equality and comradeship was becoming an ever more pervasive ideology: emphasizing 'complementarity' concealed disadvantages to which women were still subject.[13] Marcus Collins has drawn attention to persisting older patterns visible in the Family Welfare Association's marriage counselling case-work, where traditional checks and balances within the still prevalent, at least among the working classes, patriarchal model had broken down.[14] Szreter and Fisher argue that a dynamic of reciprocity and cooperation rather than a strictly companionate view of marriage continued well into the 1960s, among middle-class as well as working-class couples.[15]

Marital sex

None the less, marriage as a relationship was becoming more conscious and thought-about rather than accepted and endured.[16] Works by Helena Wright and Joan Malleson and others sold well and were disseminated through the Family Planning and Marriage Guidance movements, but probably still had a fairly restricted circulation. However, the ideas advanced by gurus of better sex within marriage and women's right to sexual pleasure were becoming more widely known via 'agony columns' and articles in women's magazines, and some popular newspapers. Increasing expert advice to women in books, women's magazines, and radio broadcasts on childbearing and rearing and the maintenance of their own health opposed new and 'scientific' ideas to 'old wives' tales', possibly feeding into a desire for advice necessitated by the break-up of old neighbourhood and kinship networks.[17] Women themselves also found employment within the welfare state advising other women.[18]

A mutually satisfying sex life within marriage was increasingly seen as essential. Geoffrey Gorer's respondents in *Exploring English Character* agreed that sexual love was either 'very' or 'fairly' important in marriage, only 6 per cent thinking it 'not very important', and a tiny percentage denying it any importance or not responding. A majority favoured premarital chastity, and even advocates of premarital experience argued its merits as a learning experience, linking it to subsequent successful marriage.[19] Sex was far from an overriding criterion in actual mate choice. Men valued 'appropriate feminine skills' most highly and deplored 'nagging', whereas women valued 'an agreeable character' and deplored 'selfishness'. Married women respondents in particular gave high marks to 'thoughtfulness' (possibly a sexual subtext).[20]

Both married men and women placed sex relatively low on the list of factors making for happiness within marriage, after 'give and take...understanding, love, mutual trust, equanimity', and incompatibility took a similar place in the list of negative factors (though, expressed in percentage terms, came somewhat higher as a cause of misery).[21] As with Slater and Woodside's couples in the 1940s, wives were more wont than husbands to complain about sexual difficulties ('selfish and demanding', 'takes me for granted').[22] Given the worries about 'divorce-mindedness' expressed to the Morton Commission, Gorer's respondents appeared reluctant to consider divorce, even in a hypothetical case of infidelity: it was often seen as a last resort, and violence was the resort of a small minority. Of the married sample, 40 per cent admitted to 'a real love affair' outside marriage.[23]

Gorer differentiated his sample according to region and class: Eustace Chesser's *The Sexual, Marital, and Family Relationships of the Englishwoman* (1956), though dealing only with women, attempted some generational analysis as well. Liz Stanley has pointed out the methodological murkiness of this survey, based on responses to six different versions of the final questionnaire,[24] but none the less it provides interesting insights. The discussion of specifically marital sexual relationships takes up less than one-quarter of this substantial volume. Chesser emphasized that 'degrees of marital happiness' were 'based entirely on the subjective information of our informants'. A surprisingly high percentage, over two-thirds, felt their marriages to be 'exceptionally happy' or 'very happy'. Only 6 per cent were 'unhappy' or 'very unhappy'. Supporting evidence was supplied through questions relating to feelings towards husbands, and any regrets about marriage.[25]

The analysis of sexual satisfaction within marriage was rendered problematic, as Slater and Woodside's had been, because

> Many women have difficulty in describing their sexual sensations, in defining the nature of their sexual pleasures, and are confused as to the definition of their genital experiences ... coupled with the reticence to admit failure.

Women had some notion that sexual intercourse could be pleasurable; in fact, many 'feel ashamed to admit they do not experience orgasm'. There was, however, a distinction made by many between 'sexual satisfaction in general and orgasm in particular'.[26] The relationship between frequent orgasm and sexual satisfaction, and happiness in marriage more generally, was 'intricate and subtle', suggesting that sexual gratification was not 'an indispensable condition of marital happiness'.[27] In fact, it could have been the product of happiness in marriage rather than its cause; [28] Szreter and Fisher have made a strong argument supporting this.[29] Even women who always or frequently obtained orgasm occasionally refused their husbands, and Chesser concluded that there was a prevalent feeling that 'the sex needs of men exceed those of women'. [30] These responses may have represented 'conventional wisdoms' rather than frank communication of personal experience: respondents were still 'voicing the dominant ideology on male and female sexuality'.[31]

The increased importance given to mutual sexual gratification in marriage brought about its own problems and pressures: the non- or infrequently orgasmic women in Chesser's survey not only had the grudges of a previous generation about sexual demands, but also a feeling that their husbands were depriving them of something coming to be seen as a 'right'.[32] This was a problem which perturbed those who had been working for many years to improve marital sex: Helena Wright confessed, in the sequel to her 1931 *The Sex Factor in Marriage, More About the Sex Factor in Marriage* (1947, reprinted throughout the 1950s, and widely disseminated through marriage guidance and family planning channels) that although 'a certain amount of improvement has resulted ... our earlier optimism', that simply alleviating ignorance would do the trick, 'was ill-founded'.[33]

Rather less sanguine about female sexual satisfaction in marriage than Chesser, Wright claimed that

> fifty out of every hundred wives still go through their years of married life without discovering that physical satisfaction can, and should, be as real and vivid for them as it is for their husbands.[34]

Joan Malleson, another female doctor involved in family planning and marriage guidance, suggested the slightly less sweeping figure of 'perhaps a quarter or a third'.[35] Wright delineated three groups of women whose 'attitude of mind' predetermined sexual failure, women who 'expected nothing' ('Why, doctor? What is there to enjoy?') or 'something, but too little'; other 'women who expect too much' based on misleading ideas from romances, films, and popular music, embittered to discover that real life was rather different. The third group of women experienced 'mild physical pleasure' in lovemaking, but might be unaware that they 'should be capable of reaching a definite climax'.[36]

Wright saw three reasons for even carefully instructed women being unable to overcome 'sexual failure': inability to differentiate 'sexual response in the erogenous zones' from actual orgasm; 'lack of understanding of the unique role played by the clitoris'; and assumptions based on the male response pattern about what a woman was supposed to feel in intercourse. The clitoris was ignored and the vagina imagined to be the 'region of primary female orgasm'.[37] Wright's claim counters prevalent assumptions that the fifties were the heyday of the Freudian myth of the 'vaginal' orgasm. The mind-set she depicts owed less to even the most popularized and bastardized versions of Freudianism than to male-orientated 'commonsense' assumptions of how sex was supposed to 'work'. Wright promoted women's exploration (with their partners) of their own clitoral sensitivity and responses.[38]

Malleson noted frequent inhibition about clitoral touch, and a feeling that orgasm thus obtained was somehow 'wrong', but was of Wright's opinion, that 'the vagina appears to learn best and most quickly after successful experience with the clitoris has been established', creating 'an atmosphere of hope and confidence'.[39] Other advisers suggested that female lack of desire or orgasmic response did not necessarily preclude sexual relations: 'the...tender and precious occasion when she gives herself to her husband simply because he wants her, and she is content that it should be so'.[40] None the less, sex within marriage was coming to be perceived not merely as something which might licitly be a mutual pleasure, but something which ought to be, and needed working at rather than being taken for granted.

There were tentative endeavours to create some form of sex therapy (well over a decade before the more famous work of Masters and Johnson), following perceptions that women were, 'not always verbally or even consciously', seeking help with sexual difficulties 'when coming ostensibly for family planning advice'. Most doctors involved were women, precluded by marriage and motherhood from more orthodox careers, but finding work in family planning which could be fitted around domestic responsibilities. They became dissatisfied with the limitations of their knowledge and techniques (given lack of formal sexual or psychotherapeutic training in the medical curriculum[41]) and a training/research seminar was set up under the guidance of Michael Balint, a psychoanalyst interested in applying psychoanalytic insights to everyday medical practice.[42] Growing recognition that women could be sexually responsive, but did not automatically have orgasms from penetrative sex thus generated conflicting ideas around the 'naturalness' of heterosexual marital sex.

Heterosexuality outside marriage

Much moral panic around sexual issues during the 1950s seems connected to anxieties that sexual pleasure, conceded to be suitable and indeed desirable between husband and wife, might be claimed by other groups, fail to be contained within the socially stabilizing institution of marriage, and manifest as a socially disruptive force. Claire Langhamer has suggested that the prioritization of sexual satisfaction and emotional closeness may even have worked to desta-bilize marriage by making adultery more thinkable. She perceives something of a moral panic about the 'tide of adultery' sweeping over the nation but argues that much reported extra-marital sex was in the context of divorce, where put-up evidence of adultery remained the quickest means of ending a marriage both partners desired to exit. The conditions of the divorce law also led to the establishment of conjugal households by couples unable to marry and the problem of 'illegal wives' who had changed their surnames to that of their partner.[43] The vast majority of illegitimate births took place within these stable unmarried couples.[44] Like most of the unmarried Victorian couples described by Ginger Frost, these couples were not interested in challenging the institution of marriage, but endeavouring to approximate it.

Heterosexual activity among the unmarried was still strongly deplored. The Family Planning Association 1952 Annual General Meeting approved giving contraceptive advice to girls about to be married. How long before the actual wedding they might seek advice, and what evidence they had to present that they were indeed going to be married, varied from clinic to clinic.[45] Anecdotal evidence indicates that to make assurance double sure that the FPA was not encouraging premarital sex, the caps provided for practice at home were perfo-rated.[46] However, in the context of providing birth control for immigrant communities, the FPA recognized West Indian women living in customary common-law unions as eligible for advice.[47]

Not only penetrative sex among the unmarried was cause for concern. There was considerable anxiety about 'petting': a range of non-coital sexual activities. Eustace Chesser hypothesized that some women were using it to fulfil 'a need for affection', but suggested that 'for many women this form of sex behav-iour fulfils natural needs'.[48] He went even further in an article written for the British Medical Association annual booklet, *Getting Married* (1959), asking, 'Is Chastity Outmoded? Outdated? Out?', querying conventional restrictions and suggesting that pre- and extramarital sex ought to be matters of individ-ual choice. The subsequent jamboree in the lay press ('Doctors in Free Love Storm') led the BMA to withdraw the entire booklet, though only after 20,000 copies had already been distributed.[49]

Writers of advice to the young person seldom took the 'fulfils natural needs' line. V. C. Chamberlain in *Adolescence to Maturity* (1952) did suggest, while advising 'matters are best kept well within bounds', reaching 'an agreement on how far to go for the time being' between 'ardent couples...sufficiently sure of themselves to enjoy such intimacies as mutual physical love-play'. This sounds like permission to engage in mutual masturbation: with the proviso to take care 'that it does not finally lead to an originally unintended act of coitus'.[50]

Most took a more cautionary stance. On the one hand there was a 'slippery slope' theory: Gladys Denny Schultz in *Letters to Jane* (1949) argued that 'Any girl who doesn't want to go the limit...had best stay away from petting',[51] which was 'against the interests of the feminine sex'.[52] Kenneth Barnes in *He and She* (1958) warned that 'sex is savage and powerful and may easily take charge of us', leading to illegitimate children or hasty marriages if 'the primitive impulses took charge'.[53] A second line of argument recalls Victorian strictures against masturbation as not merely eroding moral sense and self-discipline, but deleterious in itself. According to Schultz: 'Continual sex excitement without gratification is not good from either a physiological or psychological stand-point.'[54] Barnes stated that petting 'leaves the body nervously strung up and it is sometimes followed by pains in the back and abdomen' and could 'easily upset the relation between the partners and perhaps their future attitude towards sex'.[55] It was also sometimes argued that 'thus far and no further' lovemaking could have a deleterious impact on subsequent marital adjustment, especially for women.[56]

The tradition of the woman being expected to police the boundaries of permissible intimacies against male pressures still endured.[57] Chamberlain, while advising young men to 'respect the integrity of their female friends', cautioned young women to 'keep in mind [their] responsibility to maintain a high moral tone within the relationship'.[58] Barnes advanced similar arguments, also suggesting that, once roused, girls were even more likely than boys to be carried away and 'let anything happen'.[59] This suggests considerable anxiety, even paranoia, about unleashed female sexual desire in an era when premarital sexual experience (petting or penetrational) was almost entirely conceived in terms of young people who could be potential marriage partners rather than young men gaining experience, or an outlet for their desires, with prostitutes.

Fears about the dangerous desires of the young were voiced in more general discussions of the burgeoning 'youth culture'. As a result of the 'baby boom', by the late 1950s there were a million more 15–24-year-olds than a decade previously, and they were more visible as a distinct subculture. Greater disposable income than previous generations was spent on a variety of consumer goods and recreations. Physical maturity occurred at earlier ages, while the period of education increased – the school leaving age was raised and far greater numbers entered further and higher education. Pleasures such as rock music (associated with racial 'others') and jiving, and the male dandyism of 'Teddy Boys' were perceived as profoundly subversive by an older generation or, at least, media commentators. But, however Dionysiac dancing in cinema aisles might have appeared, orgiastic sexual licence was largely in the observers' imagination. As ever, there was anxiety about young unmarried women, especially those of the lower classes: Stephen Brooke has drawn attention to the nostalgic trope of the old-style 'working-class mam', the warm centre of a domestic space, contrasted with 'cheap' and 'trivial' modern young girls relishing the pleasures of a consumer society.[60] This trope failed to register that 'mams' had themselves been the criticized young girls, with their Woolworths finery, their fondness for dancing, and their swooning over film-stars, of an earlier decade.

Mort has drawn attention to an elite cult of the 'man about town' embedded in a sophisticated homosocial (but heterosexual) consumer culture, reflecting a certain degree of social mobility with the incorporation of entertainers and figures from the world of the arts into more traditional networks. The new dandyism, however, was challenged by the adoption of certain styles by afflu-ent members of the lower classes to become associated with the 'teddy boy'.[61] Elements of this culture were also aspirational: Raymond's Revue Bar, offering new forms of 'exotic' erotic entertainment, was positioned as a sophisticated members-only club but police reports emphasized the lax control over membership and the extent to which it was frequented by provincials seeking metropolitan high life (the modern heirs of the readers of nineteenth-century 'sporting guides' and *The Pink 'Un*).[62] Among the working classes, Stephen Brookes suggests, there were developing instabilities in masculine identity with the decline of traditional work patterns and changing gender relations in an era of affluence. This uncertainty occasionally burgeoned into the misogyny of the 'Angry Young Men' writers.[63]

In spite of the climate of anxiety over the burgeoning sexual desires of the adolescent, there was little development in the realm of sex education in schools. The false dawn of the mid-1940s had faded, and when the 1943 Board of Education guidelines for teachers went out of print they were not reissued. In 1955 a *Sunday Pictorial* journalist claimed that 'the majority of our fourteen-year-old schoolgirls are completely in the dark about babies'. However, the 1956 edition of the guidelines on health education finally included a relatively explicit chapter on the reproductive organs, definitely breaching the pre-war silence. Although Parliamentary indifference was absolute – not a single question was asked throughout the decade – at least from the later 1950s the Ministry of Health, as a result of the rise in sexually transmitted infections, became increasingly enthusiastic about sex education as a vital public health intervention, though without having much effect on the Department of Education, whose own civil servants acknowledged that the matter was left up to local education authorities and head teachers with no central direction.[64]

Illegitimacy rates had declined somewhat from the mid-1940s peak, though were higher than the 1930s, and rose further towards the end of the decade. A certain percentage of extramarital conceptions may have been concealed by hasty marriage.[65] Many occurred within the aforementioned stable unmarried couples, but the visibly single mother was increasingly stigmatized during this period. Whereas between the wars there had been significant efforts, supported by the National Council for Unmarried Mothers and their Children and other voluntary bodies, to enable such mothers to keep their children, in the belief that this was beneficial for both, during the 1950s unwed pregnancies were seen as a sign of psychological problems and unfitness for motherhood, and there was a huge rise in adoptions.[66] Holden points out that adoptions by single women, previously seen as potentially beneficial for all concerned, were also now depicted as problematic. [67]

Sexual health matters

Contraception was not easy to obtain; even the married were likely to experience difficulties. Vast areas of the country lacked birth control clinics (though provision was rapidly expanding) and medical education on the subject remained sporadic. The subject was still considered distasteful and there were restrictions on advertising and promoting services. In 1956 the Family Planning Association received an accolade of respectability previously denied, with the well-publicized visit by the Minister of Health, Iain Macleod, for its Silver Jubilee: the media ban against mentioning its work lifted practically

overnight.[68] Given the lack of information about birth control and the difficulty of obtaining it (and few couples engaging in petting would have provided
themselves with this fallback), it seems improbable that many couples were
having contracepted premarital sex.

Nor can it be assumed that more than a minority of unwillingly pregnant
unmarried women had recourse to abortion. Abortion was still criminal, with
some well-defined exceptions. The leeway given by the Bourne judgement and
subsequent cases enabled the evolution of what Alice Jenkins of the Abortion
Law Reform Association defined as *Law for the Rich*, a small industry in semi-
legal 'Harley Street' medical abortions for those who knew the ropes and
had the money. ALRA did endeavour to educate medical professionals and
the public about the legitimate medical grounds for abortion and it seems
that more were being performed on the NHS. The situation was, however,
still unclear and doctors seldom cared to take the risk. For many women the
only recourse was *Back Street Surgery* (the title of another pamphlet issued by
ALRA). The subject was gradually becoming discussed in the media, and there
were two attempts at gaining legislation: Joseph Reeves's Private Member's
Bill of 1952, which sought to give existing case law statutory force; and Lord
Amulree's Bill of 1954, neither of which was successful.[69]

The other sexual nightmare traditionally deployed to discourage premarital
activity, sexually transmitted diseases, must have seemed an outworn bogey-
man in the penicillin era, and there was a general perception that syphilis and
gonorrhoea were 'These Dying Diseases'. Venereologists were concerned about
the decline in training and services, due to 'false confidence' that the diseases
were finished as a public health threat. Cases of non-specific venereal urethritis
(only reported separately from 1951) persistently rose and appeared to have
long-term health consequences, though considered a minor infection. An enormous number of 'worried well' requiring no treatment attended clinics. Syphilis
showed steady decline, with fewer than 1000 cases in 1955, under 5 per cent of
the 1946 peak, although stabilization of the continuing drop gave venereologists some cause for concern. Gonorrhoea, which had not declined to anything
like the same extent, began to increase 'in certain urban areas' in 1956, partially
due to the emergence of penicillin-resistance. VD continued to be located in
dangerous stigmatized bodies: prostitutes were considered 'one of the principal
agents in maintaining the spread of infection', although around only a quarter
to a third of infections appeared to be contracted through bought sex.[70]

The rise in gonorrhoea was also attributed by contemporaries to the growing influx of West Indian and other Commonwealth immigrants since the late
1940s. It was suggested that these came from areas, 'in which the incidence
of venereal disease is very high' (and also the home of rare venereal afflictions
such as granuloma inguinale and lymphogranuloma venereum, which, although
the numbers were still minute, did show an increase).[71] Even liberal reformist
writers on 'race relations' constructed immigrants as a social problem: while
repudiating doctrines of scientific racism, they argued that West Indians, in
particular, manifested distinctive cultural patterns antithetical to British norms.
Chris Waters has pointed out how the language used replicated that about the
dangerous urban underclasses in the nineteenth century.[72] Women who were

in relationships with immigrants tended, according to the well-established stigmatizing tradition in discussing mixed-race marriages,[73] to be classified as prostitutes or at least wayward delinquents (such as the 'Stepney problem' group described by the British Social Biology Council's *Women of the Streets* survey as 'mentally, physically and morally in a lower grade than the ordinary prostitute'[74]), with additional concern expressed about potentially problematic mixed-race offspring.[75]

Women of the streets

In spite of venereologists' concern, it might be supposed that for various reasons – the increasing acceptability of consensual sexual relationships between the unmarried, the advent of the Welfare State – prostitution was no longer a major issue. After many years of campaigning, in 1951 the Association for Moral and Social Hygiene, supported by other reform groups, obtained an Act recognizing certain civil rights for the 'common prostitute' from which she had formerly been excluded; although the British Government failed to subscribe to the United Nations adoption of the Convention for the Suppression of the Traffic in Persons and the Exploitation of the Prostitution of Others of 1949.[76]

None the less, in certain areas of London prostitution was still extremely noticeable, and since these were (understandably) central areas such as Soho and Mayfair, or adjacent to railway stations, this was regarded as a blot on the face of the capital city, in particular with the arrival of significant numbers of foreigners for occasions such as the Festival of Britain in 1951 and the Coronation in 1953. The popular press contributed to this concern with sensational articles, embodying racialized agitation about foreign pimps – Maltese, most notoriously the Messina brothers, Cypriot, and increasingly West Indian – organizing vice in the capital.[77] The police regularly arrested women for soliciting, which most regarded as 'a fundamental fact' of their occupation, though they criticized 'unfairness' on the part of the police.[78] Once in court, prostitutes almost always pleaded guilty and paid their fines.[79] Few were deterred from pursuing their profession. In 1951 there were proposals, not implemented, to 'clean up the streets' by means of very heavy fines and prison sentences.[80]

How fragile the rights gained under the 1951 Act were was demonstrated by this continued concern over street prostitution, manifested in the appointment of the Wolfenden Committee, 1954, to investigate prostitution and male homosexuality, and the subsequent passing of the 1959 Street Offences Act. The insights of moral reform organizations, which had been considering the problems of prostitution since the repeal of the Contagious Diseases Acts, were spurned by Wolfenden, and thus a valuable feminist tradition with decades of experience was excluded from its deliberations.[81] The Act imposed heavy fines and terms of imprisonment for street soliciting in order to – as indeed it did – remove women from the streets and hide prostitution from view, business being conducted by telephone. Although the 1951 Act specifically protected women already engaged in prostitution against procuration, this new system tended to open women to exploitation by the intermediaries necessary to continue their trade.[82] The desire for the appearance of good order in the streets trumped any concern for the prostitute herself. Mort has suggested that while the streets of Soho were 'cleaned up' of their ranks of street prostitutes, new forms of eroti-cized entertainment in the form of 'members-only' striptease clubs proliferated in the same spaces.[83]

The moral reform organizations were in substantial decline by the 1950s, and their agenda was alien to the contemporary mind-set. To 1950s experts, and to journalists, prostitutes, in a welfare state, were no longer unfortunates driven to it by economic necessity or white slavers: they were addicted to sex and glamour, and in revolt against domesticity.[84] The British Social Biology Council report, *Women of the Streets*, however, suggested that a constellation of personal and social factors still rendered women vulnerable. Bad homes, broken marriages, illegitimate children, badly paid and unrewarding work, and the influence of associates were all contributory factors 'likely to weaken the ties holding them into a pattern of social behaviour and discipline'.[85] The press still occasionally drummed up 'white slavery' panics, but these no longer generated legislative action; the focus tended to be on foreign pimps and flagrant urban soliciting.[86]

The Wolfenden moment

The Wolfenden Committee is, of course, best known for its work on homosexu-ality. This was an issue of growing concern. The early 1950s saw a proliferation, after decades of silence and evasion, of newspaper articles and press reports: previously few papers, except *The News of the World*, had even mentioned homosexuality cases. In 1952 *The Sunday Pictorial* published a three-part series on 'Evil Men' (breaking the 'last taboo'). A cluster of cases involving famous or socially elite names in 1953 – the arrest of Sir John Gielgud for importun-ing, the trial of Lord Montagu of Beaulieu – also brought this occluded subject to public prominence. Apart from a few articles in the more progressive peri-odicals calling for decriminalization of private acts between consenting adults, the presentation was almost universally hostile and stigmatizing, although the *Daily Mirror*, uniquely for the popular press, came out in favour of the propos-als of the Wolfenden Report, possibly in line with its general advocacy of a modern, scientific and enlightened approach to matters of sexuality.[87] While the Committee was actually sitting, there was an explosive series of articles about Guy Burgess, the Foreign Office defector to the Soviet Union, by Goronwy Rees, a member of the Committee, associating Burgess's treachery with his homosexuality, but also foregrounding their close friendship. Mort suggests this significantly breached codes of Establishment silence: it had deeply adverse effects for Rees, who lost his academic post and was ostracized in circles where he had previously been welcome.[88]

Police statistics suggested a vast increase in numbers of homosexual offences, in large part due to a change in the calculation of crime statistics, and the prosecution of cases only when a confession was obtained. In London the Metropolitan Police were kept busy policing public manifestations (a pattern also found in other large cities), regularly patrolling men's lavatories ('cottages'), and certain parks and cinemas. They did not collect evidence about homosexual networks or pursue consenting males in private.[89] The provincial situation was different. Local police launched 'provincial pogroms' and viciously prosecuted members of networks discovered through legally dubious searches or extorted confessions. The police and all sectors of the legal profession appear to have felt 'an extraordinary degree of hostility' towards homosexuals. However, prior to 1953 such cases were seldom reported, thus the lifting of the press taboo made homosexuality appear suddenly epidemic.[90] There was also particular hostility to homosexuality at the highest levels: while there may not have been a 'witch-hunt' against British homosexuals orchestrated by the Home Secretary, Patrick Higgins argues that Sir David Maxwell Fyfe, the Director of Public Prosecutions, Sir Theobald Mathew, and the Commissioner of the Metropolitan Police, Sir John Nott-Bower, influential figures in government, the legal system, and the police were significant in creating the homophobic climate. Matt Houlbrook, however, contests both the notion of a 'witch-hunt' and the chronology of more intensive policing of male same-sex activities, arguing that the late forties was the peak period for the latter, and that there were significant disjunctions between the pronouncements and attitudes of senior officials or politicians, and the process of street policing. The rising number of reported incidents was largely due to intensified activity in just three Central London divisions. As with the routine arrest and fining of prostitutes, the quotidian surveillance of homosexuals took place at street level (or below, in public urinals). [91]

Homosexuality was debated in the medical press, the views expressed ranging from 'a cancer at the root of national stability and fitness' to praise for the 'socially useful' work performed by 'adjusted homosexuals of high charac-ter'. The British Medical Association's Gibson Committee prepared evidence for Wolfenden, even while conceding that the problem was 'social rather than medical'. None the less, they had no hesitation in referring to 'outrage against public decency' and 'reprehensible and harmful practices'. They were prepared to take the line that it was a disorder to be treated rather than a crime to be punished, though isolation as well as a range of treatments – psychiatric, drug, and physical – was suggested.[92] Oral history studies by Professor Michael King and his colleagues have illuminated both the experiences of individuals who underwent these treatments and the attitudes of the medical professionals who undertook them.[93] A 1954 report by the Church of England Moral Welfare Council on *The Problem of Homosexuality* was notable for its invocation of a medical model stemming from Havelock Ellis's notions of sexual inversion. The report not only asked for compassion towards the homosexual but advocated decriminalization, although within a theological and moral framework that same-sex acts were, none the less, implicitly sinful.[94]

The Wolfenden Committee heard evidence from a range of bodies and indi-viduals regarded as having a concern with or expertise in the subject; police, magistrates, lawyers, prison officers, doctors, psychologists, representatives of the Church. Only three declared homosexuals gave evidence, all socially elite and distinguished members of the community with a good deal in common, in terms of class, status, and background, with members of the Committee: Peter Wildeblood, who had figured in the Montagu cause célèbre; Carl Winter, a distinguished Cambridge academic and museum curator; and medical consultant

Patrick Trevor-Roper. While revealing extensive circles of homosexuals of which they were part, and acceptance of their sexual orientation, they also emphasized the extent of blackmail and suicide within the homosexual community. Houlbrook points out that their evidence expressed a new sense of a private, discreet, respectable middle-class homosexual identity, eschewing effeminacy, and differentiated from flagrant queans impinging on public spaces.[95]

Given this climate and the intention, when setting up the Committee, that it should recommend more stringent measures, it is extraordinary that the report published in 1957 came to be regarded as a landmark in the liberalization of attitudes towards homosexuality. Limited though the recommendations were – decriminalization of homosexual activity between consenting adults (over 21) in private, a statute of limitations of a year on prosecution of offences, no prosecution on offences revealed in investigating blackmail, entitlement to jury trial in cases of importuning, availability of oestrogen treatment for convicted prisoners, more research into causes and treatment – they ran far too contrary to contemporary opinion to have any chance of becoming law.[96] As with prostitution, the recommendations were largely about removing offence from public view. The suggestion that private sexual relations had some degree of privilege paralleled the recommendations on prostitution, which left the sale of sexual services legal but vigorously prosecuted public soliciting. Sexual offences were generally being defined as a specific class of crimes rather than general 'offences against the person': a Sexual Offences Act, 1956, created a 'new taxonomy' by collating together rape, procurement, underage intercourse, intercourse with those deemed incapable of consent, incest, 'unnatural offences', and indecent assaults.[97]

None the less, the Wolfenden recommendations were sufficiently an improvement on the existing situation – and advanced, moreover, in the context of an official government report – to stimulate the formation of a Homosexual Law Reform Society, founded 12 May 1958. This consisted both of homosexuals, such as A. E. ('Tony') Dyson, the moving force, and sympathizers representing a range of professions and interests, a number of whom had been associated with the sex reform movements of the interwar years. Attempts by the HLRS to lobby MPs prior to the debate on the Wolfenden Report in November, however, rather backfired on them, or at least, failed to shift deeply entrenched prejudices. The Albany Trust was set up at the same time as a research and counselling organization.[98]

Women in the shadows

The Trust also provided counselling for lesbians. As lesbianism was not subject to criminal prosecution, they were not in as discriminatory a position as homosexual men, although women outside the hegemonic regime of matrimony were generally regarded with suspicion and various possibilities available in the interwar period were closed off by revived pathologization of the unmarried woman. M. B. Smith's *The Single Woman of Today* (1951) presented a grim picture of nervous strain, sense of inferiority, loneliness, and despair resulting from subconscious refusal of 'the mature state of married life',[99] and Rebecca

Jennings has drawn attention to the negative depictions of the 'career woman' and the pressures to put on a feminine presentation in the workplace, alongside new and non-traditional career paths providing a certain leeway for gender nonconformity.[100] While some doctors and psychologists continued to argue that adolescent same-sex crushes were transient and harmless, and even a valuable learning experience,[101] Jennings adduces evidence that there were significant anxieties around teenage crushes, with suspicion about the sexual interests of 'spinster teachers' and their influence over their pupils (the abolition of the marriage bar meant that women no longer had to choose between teaching and marriage).[102] Concern over proper development into adult heterosexuality also, arguably, had an impact on the rise of mixed-sexed youth clubs and the marginalization of single-sex ones.[103]

There was still the perhaps old-fashioned view, advanced in a memorandum prepared by the Medical Women's Federation for the Wolfenden Committee, that 'a homosexual relationship between women can be a highly positive and constructive influence': similar arguments were advanced by Malleson in *Any Wife or Any Husband*. The MWF further asserted that the 'promiscuous Lesbian' was rare, and the corruption of young children unknown among lesbians.[104] The image of the woman-woman relationship as one of quasi-matrimonial devotion (though sometimes at risk of jealousy and possessiveness), however, was tending to be replaced by depictions of these menages as unstable and unsustainable, and the lack of available models sometimes caused women difficulties in negotiating joint domesticity.[105] There was a more visible though still small club culture, most notoriously the Gateways in Chelsea: this had a distinctive butch-femme dress code that attracted some but repelled others. A number of other clubs existed and certain pubs became known lesbian meeting places.[106]

However, matters were not all cosy. If a woman's sexual orientation became defined as 'a problem', by herself or others, she might be subjected to medical 'treatment'. The MWF declared that drug treatment was of no use and psychiatry not a 'cure', though it might help women with difficulties of adjustment created by lesbianism,[107] and some practitioners took a similar enlightened attitude. But others promoted psychosurgical solutions likely to have devastating effects, or aversion therapy.[108] In the legal sphere there were suggestions that lesbianism should be made a matrimonial offence,[109] and woman-woman sexual assault was made an offence under the Sexual Offences Act of 1956.[110] The *Sunday Pictorial* included a sensationalist account of lesbian seduction in an article of December 1958.[111]

Destablizing categories

Nevertheless, lesbianism was an area where even the sensationalist press did not have much success in creating a moral panic. There were other topics which achieved temporary prominence and destabilized accepted connections between gender, sex, and reproduction. There had already been a flurry of horrified interest in artificial insemination (practised on a small scale since the 1930s) in the late 1940s, and extended debate in the press in 1958 followed the appointment of the Feversham Committee by the Government. The Eugenics Society 'budded off' an Artificial Insemination by Donor Investigation Council, and several church bodies also engaged with the issue, declared by the Archbishop of Canterbury to be 'evil'. An alleged 10,000 children in Britain were 'test-tube babies', although the Feversham Committee's estimate was around 10 per cent of that figure. Opinions ranged from seeing it as a compassionate solution for childless couples to outrage at unnatural, Frankensteinian, scientific intervention in the reproductive process. It was not available under the National Health Service and a bare handful of doctors were actually performing it.[112] If the increasing acceptability of birth control was detaching sex from reproduction, AID went further and detached reproduction from sex.

Another scientific intervention, rendered possible by the hormone research of the interwar years and advances in plastic surgery facilitated by two world wars, was 'sex change surgery'. A member of the RAF, the father of children, and the son of an eminent surgeon, Roberta Cowell was one of the most publicized of several early UK cases of this operation.[113] There was an unsuspected demand: in 1959 an account of a series of 50 cases (37 males, 13 females) seen at Charing Cross Hospital was published in the *British Medical Journal*.[114] Alison Oram has noted the revival of the 'sex-change' story in the popular press in the 1950s, and the idea was generally becoming more commonplace though still presented as strange and astonishing.[115]

Contesting censorship

While the media brought to a wider public issues such as these, of which they might previously have been unaware, often served up in a titillating and prurient manner, censorship continued severe and arbitrary. An extraordinary case was reported in Norman Haire's *Journal of Sex Education*: a 48-year-old divorced schoolteacher and a married estate agent were prosecuted and fined for (consensually) sending 'obscene communications' (stories and photos) to one another. As Haire pointed out in editorial comment: legally, publication could mean showing to one other person, while 'the conception of "indecency" varies…from class to class, from judge to judge, from magistrate to magistrate.'[116] Haire's papers include 'pornographic literature of a kind which appears to be quite legal in this country', sent to him by a correspondent: flagellant works published through 'The Corpun Educational Organisation' for a body calling itself the National Society for the Retention of Corporal Punishment, which also sold canes and straps and ran an advisory service.[117]

If France had been the source of smut in the early part of the century, by the 1950s it was America, origin of 'cheesecake' photos and magazines such as *Razzle* and *Flirt*, intermittently seized by the police, along with home-grown 'hard-boiled' novels derived from US models. The Home Office issued a secret 'Blue Book' to chief constables listing blacklisted titles of numerous 'trash' works, which were to be forwarded to the Director of Public Prosecutions when found on sale.[118] There was a flurry of local prosecutions of saucy postcards, such as those of Donald McGill, which had formed part of British seaside culture for decades.[119] Apart from the usual confiscations of Rabelais and Maupassant, serious modern novels were taken to court, though in most cases juries failed to be as appalled as the powers-that-be. There was considerable protest from writers and intellectuals when expensive editions of *The Decameron* were condemned alongside titles like *Tricky* and *Wink*. A Select Committee was appointed, there were years of arguing, lobbying, and drafting, but in 1959 a new Obscene Publications Act, sponsored by opposition MP Roy Jenkins, was passed. While it gave the police increased powers of search and seizure, it did concede the defence of 'publication for the public good'. It was soon to be the foundation for a historic test case.[120] Meanwhile, writers continued to push the bounds of acceptability, dealing not only more explicitly with pre- and extramarital heterosexual activity, but also, in the novels of, for example, Angus Wilson, presenting sympathetic portraits of homosexuals (not all, inevitably, doomed to suicide).

* * *

The 1950s therefore look like a period of instability rather than unthinking smug conventionality. The moral pronouncements of the era seem defensive reactions to a sense, whether correct or not, that old constraints were falling away, that erotic energies nurtured by a buoyant economy and the Welfare State were threatening to break out.

10
Swinging? For Whom?
The Sixties and Seventies

The First of January 1960 did not see the sudden dawning of a new age of sexual freedom in Britain. It would be several years before 'the long Victorian' era could be considered over. None the less, premonitory trends already under way in the preceding decade continued and intensified.

Slight shifts of attitude

In May 1960 Labour MP Kenneth Robinson gained parliamentary time for a debate on the Wolfenden recommendations: the Homosexual Law Reform Society (HLRS) arranged its first public meeting, and sent a deputation to the Home Secretary. The meeting, far better attended than anticipated, achieved an overwhelming majority in favour of reform. The Commons debate, though a historic first, was 'interesting, if predictable': there were descriptions of homosexuals as 'a dirty-minded danger to the virile manhood of the country', a slight shift away from punitive solutions among some opponents of reform, and the Home Secretary (R. A. Butler) was sympathetic, without committing himself to positive action. The motion was defeated by 213 votes to 99. In 1962 Leo Abse MP put forward a private member's Sexual Offences Bill embodying the minor (but not the most important) of Wolfenden's recommendations, with no greater success.[1]

The subject was being more generally and more sympathetically discussed. It was becoming possible for sociologists to undertake and publish research, though Michael Schofield's initial studies, even the post-Wolfenden *A Minority: A Report on the Life of the Male Homosexual in Great Britain* (1960), appeared under the pseudonym 'Gordon Westwood'. However, by 1965 Schofield 'came out', publishing *Sociological Aspects of Homosexuality* under his own name. This examined a sample of men in prison for homosexual offences, a group of homosexual men undergoing psychiatric treatment (not all for their orientation), and a 'self-confessed' group, as well as control samples. While in favour of law reform and generally of liberal opinions, Schofield still put the case for reform in terms of 'containing this problem'.[2] Two commercial films about

Oscar Wilde in 1960, and *Victim* (1961), starring Dirk Bogarde, presented sympathetic portrayals of homosexuality. In 1964 a number of prominent women journalists approached the HLRS for assistance in producing press articles 'opening up' the subject, and there was also broadcasting interest.[3]

With rather more ambiguous effect, in 1962 William John Christopher Vassall, a civil servant at the Admiralty, was convicted of spying for the Soviet Union and revealed to be homosexual. This fitted the stereotype of the treacherous homosexual, but also supported arguments that vulnerability to blackmail under the existing law was the real danger.[4] In July 1964 a new Director of Public Prosecutions announced that he had requested chief constables to consult him before prosecuting cases involving private acts between consenting adults, offences over 12 months old, or revealed during blackmail investigations, with a view to achieving greater uniformity. This did not imply any alteration to the law as it stood.[5]

In 1963 the first explicitly lesbian social and political organization in Britain was founded. Known as the Minorities Research Group to avoid undue police interest or salacious male attention, this produced a magazine, *Arena Three*, provided counselling as well as a means of contact for isolated lesbians, informed public opinion, and promoted unprejudiced research into questions of sexual orientation, as well as critiquing the assumptions of existing research. While its activist slant led to the secession of KENRIC, a purely social and contact organization, and others felt it laid too much emphasis on respectability, it succeeded in generating a number of regional groups and providing a forum for those who shunned the club and bar 'scene'.[6]

Prosecutions and progress

During the first year of the Obscene Publications Act 1959 there were 34 prosecutions, largely of traditionally pornographic magazines, films, photos, 'Soho typescripts', and productions from the Olympia Press, Paris. 1960 was the thirtieth anniversary of the death of D. H. Lawrence, who stood extremely high in critical repute. Penguin Books, which already published paperback editions of most of his works, proposed to commemorate the occasion by bringing out *Lady Chatterley's Lover*, never previously issued in the United Kingdom, announcing this in *The Bookseller* in January. The way had been paved by the unsuccessful US prosecution of Grove Press under the Comstock Act, which adjudged the work not obscene and therefore fit to be carried in the US Mail, and was followed by a flurry of cheap paperback editions. There was a general lightening up of censorship: the unexpurgated version of Oscar Wilde's *De Profundis* was released and Nabokov's controversial novel *Lolita* escaped prosecution.

The Director of Public Prosecutions, none the less, took action. Penguin, with a print-run of 200,000 ready for distribution, published the work in a purely technical sense by releasing a dozen copies to the DPP, in a test case for the 1959 Act. Penguin retained as counsel Gerald Gardiner, a lawyer of impeccably liberal credentials (and former member of the British Sexology Society), and assembled a stellar array of witnesses to testify to the literary merits and 'public good' of the novel. It has been supposed that the prosecution proceeded on the (ill-founded) assumption that the beastly obscenity of the work was self-evident and public opinion supportive of continuing the ban, as manifested in Mervyn Griffith-Jones QC's infamous remark in his opening speech to the jury: 'Is it a book that you would even wish your wife or your servants to read?' However, Travis's research in the Director of Public Prosecutions' files indicated that strenuous though fruitless efforts were made to find suitably authoritative prosecution witnesses. Penguin Books were acquitted, the next edition was dedicated to the jury-members, and two million copies were sold within the year.[7]

As a result a number of works previously available only as expensive hardbacks, or not published in the United Kingdom at all, appeared in mass-market paperbacks, including classics such as the *Kama Sutra*, De Sade's *Justine*, and other works which could be considered to have some historical or literary value; also 'hard-boiled best-sellers' as typified by Harold Robbins's *The Carpetbaggers* ('sex and/or sadism every seventeen pages'). Decensorship was, however, far from complete. Cautious publishers restricted works by Henry Miller and William Burroughs to costly hardbacks. In 1963 an unexpurgated paperback reprint of John Cleland's eighteenth-century classic, *Fanny Hill: Memoirs of a Woman of Pleasure*, published by Mayflower, was seized by the police and the retailer (Ralph Gold of the 'Magic Shop', Tottenham Court Road) summonsed; Mayflower, though not charged, assisted the defence. In spite of distinguished witnesses, the defence was unsuccessful – the Golds were concurrently found to be importing copies of the US edition of *Tropic of Capricorn*, society as a whole was gripped by the moral panic surrounding the Profumo case, and the case was heard before a magistrate rather than a jury. Police crackdowns followed around the country and publishers became noticeably more cautious, either issuing expurgated editions or not risking paperback publication. People who could pay 25 shillings for a book were deemed far less likely to be corrupted by the contents than those who could only afford 3s. 6d.

Travis has nuanced the picture of the progress of censorship and decensorship to reveal significant differences between the Home Office (particularly after Roy Jenkins's appointment as Home Secretary), the police (especially following raids on exhibitions in major museums), and Customs, still operating under an 1876 statute and seizing material already on sale in British bookshops. There was increasing official distinction between works which could claim 'literary merit' and pulp novels and magazines which could not.[8]

Reproductive politics

Abortion was in the news as a result of the discovery of the teratogenic effects of thalidomide (withdrawn in late 1961). Cases of women who had gone to extreme lengths to obtain abortion or had murdered their deformed offspring were widely reported. Kenneth Robinson introduced a Private Member's Bill, talked out by Catholic MPs. While the Ministry of Health issued a memorandum in 1962 declaring that 'every possible effort should be taken' to prevent the births of thalidomide babies, the government refused to change the law to cover cases of foetal abnormalities, even following a rubella epidemic that summer. The surreptitious trade in quasi- or completely illegal abortions continued to thrive, some undertaken by idealists who were also fighting for changes in the law, but most as purely commercial operations, while increasingly operations were being performed within the NHS, though with enormous regional variations.[9] Davis and Davidson have shown how difficult it was for women even in Scotland, where the law theoretically prioritized doctors' clinical judgement, to obtain abortions, except in Aberdeen where Dugald Baird, supported by influential local officials, had been performing medico-social abortions since the 1930s.[10] Emma Jones discerns a noticeable shift in how women were talking about abortion in letters to the Abortion Law Reform Association at this period: they were more explicit, reflecting the significant changes in women's lives and expectations since the War. They were also endeavouring to negotiate abortions within the law, an often frustrating process.[11]

Contraception was becoming more discussed and more reliable, and increasingly acceptable, although the British Medical Association's refusal of advertisements for the Family Planning Association in *Family Doctor* was defended in the *British Medical Journal*, claiming 'doubts about the wisdom of publishing in a popular health magazine' something which might 'give the green light to contraceptive practices'. Copious correspondence indicated the divided state of medical opinion.[12] The contraceptive Pill became generally available in the United Kingdom in 1961, and the FPA took a leading role in research and testing.[13] In 1963 the Consumers' Association produced a supplement to its journal *Which?* on contraceptives, leading to the much belated introduction of a British Standard for condoms in 1964.[14]

The FPA itself was undergoing considerable upheaval as a result of new demands and developments. Besides massive expansion in clinic provision, and the introduction of relatively uncontroversial cervical screening facilities and domiciliary work among 'problem families',[15] there was the far more inflammatory issue of birth control for the unmarried. In 1958 Marie Stopes bequeathed her Whitfield Street clinic to the Eugenics Society, out of abiding hostility towards the FPA: the Society promptly called on FPA experts for advice. Under the direction of Helen Brook, this clinic, lacking the constraints affecting the FPA, started sessions for unmarried girls (particularly students of the adjacent University of London). A storm of publicity in October 1963 resulted in the expedient decision to set up an entirely separate centre for the unmarried, and the first Brook Centre was inaugurated.[16]

While unsurprisingly seen as 'official sanction for premarital intercourse', this development recognized rather than stimulated the rise in sexual activity among the young, in particular among women students, who were something of a vanguard, although Carol Dyhouse draws attention to their pervasive fear of unwanted pregnancy, and the significant proportion using no contraception when sexually active.[17] Illegitimate births were increasing, in particular in the teenage group.[18] The single mother was still a stigmatized figure, making women reluctant to seek affiliation orders, which men could evade by alleging the woman's 'bad character', or misrepresenting their income. Even in the mere 12 per cent of cases in which orders were granted (the average amount being a derisory 9s. 6d.), the default rate was high.[19] A number of novels of the decade dealt with the middle-class unmarried mother: Lynn Reid Banks's *The L-Shaped Room* (1960), Margaret Drabble's *The Millstone* (1965), Andrea Newman's *The Cage* (1966).

Sex and the young

While numbers of gonorrhoea cases among the under-twenties age group were relatively low, these were not only increasing but showing a worrying inversion of the usual sex ratio, with more girls than boys affected.[20] Both phenomena were mirrored worldwide, and the rates in the United Kingdom were comparatively low, but this did not prevent an upsurge of moral panic. Part of the anxiety must surely have been due to the perception that the middle-class young were affected as well as the lower classes: an urban legend of the early 1960s, embodying anxieties about the 'loss of moral discipline which was sweeping round the country', invoked the (grammar) school where girls wore yellow golliwog badges to signify lost virginity, mentioned in a House of Commons debate in the summer of 1961 and in a debate on the increase in venereal diseases at the British Medical Association Annual Representative Meeting around the same time. It was still in circulation nearly two years later, and formed the basis for a trashy film, *The Yellow Teddy Bears* (1963).[21]

Michael Schofield, as Research Director to the Central Council for Health Education, undertook a survey, *The Sexual Behaviour of Young People* (investigation into sexual behaviour was finally moving away from the married and heterosexual), originating in concerns about the relationship of this increase in venereal diseases to sexual intercourse among young people.[22] While the survey was in progress, Professor G. M. Carstairs caused a furore with his 1963 Reith Lectures asking 'Is chastity the supreme moral virtue?' and suggesting that charity was more imperative. He also argued that the young regarded sexual experience (with precautions against conception) a 'sensible preliminary to marriage':[23] however, only a minority were engaging in intercourse, though a wide range of 'petting activities' (classified for the first time) were practised.[24] Knowledge about birth control was often rudimentary and the practice rare.[25] There was also very little knowledge about venereal diseases:[26] although, as Schofield pointed out: 'promiscuity...is not a prominent feature of teenage sexual behaviour', and therefore 'the risks of venereal disease are not very great', the level of ignorance meant that those who did become infected might not recognize the symptoms and seek treatment. It was less of a perceived risk than unwanted pregnancy among teenagers.[27] The young were less sexually active than many believed, but also less responsible than others argued.

A rising tide of permissiveness?

It was not just the young whose morals caused anxiety. In 1963 a vice-in-high-places scandal involving the War Minister, John Profumo, broke with wide-ranging repercussions. He had had a transient affair with Christine Keeler, a young part-time prostitute, part of a louche circle around society osteo-path and procurer Stephen Ward, also involved with a Soviet naval attaché. A shooting incident outside Keeler's flat involving two of her Caribbean lovers drew attention to her and she talked about this previous liaison. In spite of Profumo's denials, he resigned in disgrace and the episode seriously damaged the Conservative Government. Revelations about kinky sex parties orchestrated by Ward, although these did not involve Profumo, added to the general sense of corruption, as cheque-book journalists pursued Keeler and Mandy Rice-Davies for inside stories on Ward's circles. Ward himself was tried for living on immoral earnings, Mervyn Griffith-Jones ('... gave the strong impression that he thought that sexual intercourse was shocking') prosecuting: Ward was an habitual associate of prostitutes but the evidence that he was living on immoral earnings was not overwhelming.[28]

Although the 'permissive society' had hardly yet arrived in the United Kingdom, there were those who perceived society as already on the road to perdition. In 1964 Mary Whitehouse set up her Clean-Up TV Campaign, subsequently the National Viewers' and Listeners' Association, to defend 'traditional' values which she saw as menaced in particular by the BBC's commitment to, she claimed, promoting the 'new morality'. This can hardly be described as a backlash, more as a pre-emptive strike against burgeoning tendencies.[29]

Belief that something was rotten in modern society was also encouraged by the 1966 trial of Ian Brady and Myra Hindley, a clerk and a shorthand typist, for the erotic and sadistic 'Moors Murders' of young children. The couple shared a fascination with Nazism and its regalia, engaged in obscene photog-raphy of one another, and Brady notoriously owned the works of the Marquis de Sade. It was one of the first cases to be tried after the abolition of capital punishment (1965). Many worried that it was a sign that permissiveness and liberalism had gone far enough, that there were limits which should not be breached, and among sections of the intelligentsia, decensorship became no longer automatically approved.[30]

However, the term 'permissive society' exaggerates the degree of liberaliza-tion in Britain in the mid-1960s. 'Swinging London' was first identified in the American magazine *Time* in 1966, a collage of 'ephemeral images' apparently indicating that 'Britain had abandoned conventional morality and replaced it with the most frivolous forms of hedonism', symbolized by the miniskirted 'dolly bird'. New male cultural styles such as the 'Mods', however, were 'curi-ously asexual', even if the emphasis on a new decorative display in male attire aroused conventional anxieties about the breakdown of accepted gender mark-ers.[31] How widespread these phenomena were outside certain areas of, and groups within, London is dubious. Certainly there was nothing like a wide-spread sexual revolution according to Geoffrey Gorer's 1969 survey, *Sex and Marriage in England Today: A study of the views and experience of the under-45s*: he claimed that 'Despite...all the emphasis on the "permissive society", "swinging London", and the like in reporting, and the prevalence of erotic themes in much fiction...England still appears to be a very chaste society.' A quarter of male respondents and two-thirds of female were virgins at marriage, while 20 per cent of men and 25 per cent of women married the person with whom they first had intercourse. Few had been in any degree promiscuous. None the less, there was a theoretical feeling in favour of some premarital experience, particularly if it was a 'real' love-affair (possibly lack of opportunities made the difference between theory and practice).[32] There were still constraints on sexual experimentation.

According to Marcus Collins, a new generation of glossy, though still 'straight, soft-core' men's magazines, *King* (1964), *Penthouse* (1965), and *Mayfair* (1966), created a radical hiatus in British pornography. Aiming to transcend the seediness of the existing genre, publishing justifications from noted intellectuals of the day, they presented 'real' women in real rather than fantasized settings, and posited a new reciprocity of sexual desire and pleasure based on recognition of 'healthy female carnality', alongside the trappings of the consumerist 'good life'. That this was more about liberating men from sexual guilt than emancipating women was evidenced by their aggressive backlash against the rise of articulate feminism. They presumably represented male aspiration rather than widespread actuality.[33]

Liberalizing laws

The Labour Government which came to power in 1964 (with Gerald Gardiner as Lord Chancellor) passed several important pieces of liberalizing, if hardly radically permissive, legislation affecting sexual mores, following the election of 1966 which returned them with a substantial majority, including an influx of new younger MPs. It should be noted, however, that nearly all these measures were introduced as Private Member's Bills, although their success was substantially affected by Government support and assistance.[34]

For birth control and abortion, it was 'a good reforming Parliament', with longtime allies of the cause (Kenneth Robinson as Minister of Health, Roy Jenkins at the Home Office) in key positions. Robinson issued a circular to local authorities on family planning early in 1966, while Dr Edwin Brooks, winning a favourable place in the ballot for Private Member's Bills, put forward one to widen local authorities' powers *vis-à-vis* birth control, which he received Ministry assistance in drafting, plus assurance of Government support. The Bill, which enabled, but did not require, local health authorities to give contraceptive advice and supplies under the NHS (i.e., free), at their discretion to persons seeking them (no provisos as to medical necessity, age, or marital status), passed its second reading virtually unopposed in February 1967 and received the Royal Assent in June.[35]

The relative lack of uproar was partially due to the concentration of principled opposition on Liberal MP Dr David Steel's contemporaneous Private Member's Bill to legalize abortion. After a hard-fought struggle – the Society for the Protection of the Unborn Child was founded in January 1967 to resist its passage – the Bill became law in October 1967. It had the support of much of the medical profession, through the British Medical Association, and government assistance and support. However, it left abortion per se illegal, while indicating what constituted 'lawful' abortion, and placed decisions firmly in medical hands. Essentially giving the Bourne judgement statutory force, it included social factors and the threat of abnormality in the foetus as indications.[36]

It has been argued that this Act constituted a 'medicalization' of abortion by placing power in the hands of the medical profession. Davis and Davidson, however, see in the Scottish context a 'reluctant medicalization', with the profession feeling this was being imposed on them from above. The testimonies cited by Emma Jones strongly suggest that far from medicalization of abortion being imposed on women, there was strong demand from women themselves.[37] Davis and Davidson have usefully analysed how the medical profession and institutions in Scotland responded to the new law and the pressures demand was placing on services: the enormous regional variations, the strategies doctors deployed to cope with a procedure which, though legal, many had qualms about performing, such as sending a large number of cases for psychiatric assessment, and how this changed as it became more routine.[38]

Birth control facilitated 'natural' and relatively uncontroversial heterosexual sex. Undergoing perhaps an even stormier passage through Parliament was the Sexual Offences Bill to decriminalize homosexual activity between consenting adults in private. It by no means implemented all the Wolfenden recommendations and the definitions of private ('where more than two persons take part or are present') and age of consent (21) differed from those employed in heterosexual relations, while it did not apply throughout the United Kingdom or in the armed forces. Davidson and Davis have shown that the only way of persuading Scottish MPs not to vote against the Bill was to exclude Scotland entirely. It had long been argued that the relevant legal and policing systems in Scotland were much less problematic yet more effective than those operating in England: however, there was also a huge level of homophobia north of the Border (one of the factors which led David Steel to choose what was, in context, the relatively less controversial measure of abortion law reform as the target of his efforts).[39]

Another liberalizing measure which brought about changes long agitated for was the Theatres Act of 1968. There were a number of notorious cases of the Lord Chamberlain, Baron Cobbold, a city banker, using his powers against serious and experimental drama, even extending to prosecuting the Royal Court Theatre for presenting a club performance (usually immune) of an unlicensed play, Edward Bond's *Saved*, in 1965. This was deplored in Parliament by both Lords and Commons, and George Strauss sponsored a Private Member's Bill to abolish the Lord Chamberlain, with all-party support. The Theatres Act finally became law in September 1968 (and did allow some possibility for prosecution). There was some liberalization of standards by the British Board of Film Censors, but film censorship remained in place.[40] A curious phenomenon was the casting in film adaptations of John Braine's *Room at the Top* (1959) and *The L-Shaped Room* (1962) of French actresses Simone Signoret and Leslie Caron to play the parts of, respectively, the hero's married mistress and an unmarried mother, both English in the originals. In spite of the tackling of more 'sophisticated' themes by British film-makers at this period (e.g. the bisexual triangle in *Sunday Bloody Sunday* [1971]), this was also the heyday of the Carry On films (traditional British innuendo, 1958–1976) and Hammer Horror (sex as allur-ing, dangerous, and probably foreign, 1958–1976).

Also among this large-scale tidying up of anachronisms and anomalies was divorce. There had already been attempts, by Leo Abse with cross-party support, to introduce a Private Members Bill to add separation for seven years to the grounds for divorce, along with various other measures tending to encourage reconciliation procedures such as the abolition of condonation as a bar to divorce, recommended by the Royal Commission Report. However, hardline opposition to separation-divorce (which would permit an unwilling 'innocent party' to be divorced) led to the withdrawal of that clause in order to ensure the other provisions passed. A number of legal decisions, in particu-lar over the extent of the court's discretion in particular cases, modified, rather than challenged, the existing system. The views of the Established Church had hindered reforms for decades, but the Archbishop of Canterbury's Working Party report, *Putting Asunder* (1966), finally acknowledged that the Church should not interfere in the making of laws for secular society or impose stand-ards of behaviour expected of believers on those who were not, and recom-mended divorce for irretrievable breakdown of marriage. In 1965 the remit of the Law Commission, appointed to promote law reform, included marriage and family law, seen as in dire need of extensive overhaul, simplification, and updating. In 1966 its sixth report, *On the Reform of the Grounds of Divorce: The Field of Choice*, recommended abolishing the concept of matrimonial offence, advocated better reconciliation procedures (especially marriage guidance), but for various practical reasons, rejected divorce by consent alone. While recom-mending irretrievable breakdown as the sole ground, this was still conceived in terms of adultery, desertion, or interpretations of cruelty, though divorce by consent after two years' separation, after five years without, was also proposed.

The passage of the Divorce Law Reform Act in 1969, like much of the preceding legislation on matters of morality and sexuality, thus reflected and embodied current opinions rather than making them. The Bill embodying the Law Commission's proposals ran into some controversy. Lady Summerskill coined the expression 'Casanova's' Charter', claiming that it would enable middle-aged men to abandon for younger women ageing wives who could not reasonably be expected either to re-enter the workplace or remarry and would lose many of their rights as wives. The position of vulnerable women was recog-nized in the 1970 Matrimonial Proceedings and Property Act, amending and clarifying existing legislation, following the Law Commission's 1967 working paper, *Matrimonial and Related Proceedings: Financial Relief*. The 1969 Act did not come into effect until this latter measure had passed.[41]

Contraceptive politics

What were the effects of these various pieces of legislation? To a considerable extent they reflected change in social mores and attitudes, while they facili-tated – or led to hopes of – further changes. The least controversial measure was probably the Family Planning Act, probably less momentous than the technological innovation of the contraceptive Pill: a method simple, reliable, and aesthetic, permitting 'completely natural intercourse', with no need for preliminary fumbling with a barrier method. It was vigorously promoted by manufacturers, and extensively covered in the media (scare stories and potential risks were already being discussed by the mid-1960s, and a major scare over thromboembolism in 1969 led to withdrawal of the high-dosage Pill). Unlike earlier methods, the Pill was remote from the genitalia, which doubtless assisted in advertising, promotion, media debates, and medical conversion. It was a prescription drug and doctors, few of whom had ever been interested in fitting caps, were much happier to take a patient's blood pressure and scribble a prescription. However, the general practitioner was in a somewhat ambiguous position as it was far from clear that it could be prescribed on the NHS except in medical cases: eventually standard fees for non-medical contraceptive services were introduced. On the theological rather than medical front, enormous numbers of British Catholic women ignored the Pope's ban on birth control, and even members of the Church hierarchy considered it a matter of individual conscience.[42] Hera Cook makes a persuasive case that the introduction of the Pill was, in spite of later revisionist accounts, fundamentally a 'sexual revolution' and the basis for massive changes in the position of women, even if there had been a small vanguard of precursors.[43]

The effects of the 1967 Act were perhaps most immediately felt by the Family Planning Association itself. The Government was anxious to improve provision, but hospitals were uninterested and few GPs trained. Barely a quarter of the 204 local health authorities were taking full advantage of the Act. A new professionalism and centralization within the FPA took place under the new Director, Caspar Brook. A standardized national family planning agency scheme was devised to offer a menu of options to local authorities.[44]

A number of new players entered the birth control arena. The new wave of feminist militancy – Women's Liberation ('Women's Lib') – included free contraception and abortion on demand among the four demands formulated in 1971: women's right to control their fertility was a central tenet. The Women's Abortion and Contraception Campaign, founded in 1972, added 'safe and reliable' to the demand for contraception: also 'no forced sterilization', sometimes imposed on poor women or those of ethnic minorities as a precondition of abortion. At a very different level, overpopulation was a growing anxiety, both globally and in the British context. This stimulated the development of a number of pressure groups, some directly concerned with overpopulation and others with more general environmental issues. The response to a letter to *The Lancet* by the Doctors and Overpopulation Group revealed a major change in medical attitudes. To some extent population anxieties were strategically mobilized by those more concerned with women's right to reproductive control (as had previously been the case in the deployment of anxieties about maternity and nation between the wars). A new pressure group, the Birth Control Campaign, bringing together many veterans in the field, aimed at an integrated, comprehensive and free birth control service under the NHS, as health service reform was in the air.[45]

Abortion, of course, was already free. In 1971 Phillip Whitehead MP put forward a BCC-drafted amendment to the 1967 Family Planning Act to make vasectomy available at local authority discretion. There had been growing interest in this operation, provided by some FPA and private clinics, and on medical grounds only within the NHS, during the late sixties. It was popular among couples who had completed their families and were reluctant for the wife to take the Pill for several decades (or have an IUD fitted). This radical male choice may have been an indicator of changing masculinity; alternatively it could signal the emergence into visibility (because of the need for resort to surgical intervention) of the longer-standing tradition of male involvement in family limitation, previously achieved by condoms or withdrawal. The Bill had a bumpy ride through Parliament but received the Royal Assent in October 1972.[46]

The free contraception service already operating in London indicated its cost-effectiveness in reducing unwanted pregnancies. However, in December 1972 the Secretary of State for Social Services, Sir Keith Joseph, announced that while family planning advice would be free under new NHS arrangements, supplies would have to be paid for (except by certain exempted groups), though 'medical need' cases would pay only the standard prescription charge. There was heated Parliamentary activity, with the Bill 'ping-ponging' between the Lords, favouring free contraception, and the Commons, in which the issue cut across existing party lines, with a revolt of pro-free contraception Tory back-benchers, but a dangerous degree of apathy among the Opposition leading to defeat of the Lords' amendment. The Lords finally conceded the Commons' privilege of determining expenditure. The NHS Reorganization Act 1973 was passed, with Clause 4 providing free family planning services, and supplies subject to a prescription charge. In 1974 Labour returned to power and Barbara Castle, Secretary of State for Social Services, announced the removal of the charge, regardless of age or marital status.[47]

There might be resistance to 'Love on the NHS', but the old hostility to birth control per se had largely disappeared. Abortion, however, still aroused fervent feelings. The number of legal abortions rose year by year, almost quadrupling from 1968–70, placing pressure on an ill-prepared system. There were considerable regional differences, partly due to resources but also to the attitudes of consultants, many of whom refused to undertake abortions. Inadequacy of NHS provision led to a significant rise in private clinics, many of which were commercial 'rackets' (often catering to women from countries with less liberal laws), but including low-cost non-profit clinics such as those run by the British Pregnancy Advisory Service, initially set up as the Birmingham Pregnancy Advisory Service in an area in which NHS abortions were particularly scarce.[48]

The Abortion Act was the only one of the liberalizing measures of the late sixties which there were persistent attempts to restrict (if not wholly overturn) almost as soon as it had passed into law. In 1969 Norman St John Stevas introduced a Bill under the ten-minute Rule to amend the Act; in 1970 Godman Irvine introduced a Private Member's Bill with the same aim.[49] As a result of continuing pressure, in 1971 the Conservative Government set up a Committee of Enquiry into the Act (known as the Lane Committee after its Chairman the Honourable Mrs Justice Lane, and including, most unusually, a female majority of ten out of 15) to ascertain any problems in its working which ought to be corrected. It was anticipated that this would recommend restrictive amendments. In the event, after deliberating for two and a half years on a wide range of evidence submitted by interested individuals and organizations, the Committee achieved a consensus that the 1967 Act was a humane and necessary measure, and should stand, with recommendations for improved administrative oversight of the private sector, and for the prevention of the need for abortion by better education and contraceptive provision. Sensationalist tales of abuses were demonstrated to be untrue (the notorious *Babies for Burning* appeared in 1974, discredited as a tissue of misrepresentation and fabrication the following year[50]), and the reduction in mortality and morbidity as a result of legally available abortion emphasized.[51] However, in spite of this powerful endorsement, Bills to restrict the Act were put forward almost annually: James White, 1975; Francis Benyon, 1977; Bernard Braine, 1978; and John Corrie, 1979–80, even though a further Select Committee, appointed in 1975, deliberated until 1980.[52] While attempts to limit the terms of Steel's Act were successfully combated, campaigns to extend them in the direction of 'abortion on demand' by increasingly militant feminist organizations, such as the National Abortion Campaign, made no headway.[53]

Gay liberation

What of newly decriminalized homosexuals? Two consecutive chapters of Antony Grey's account of the continuing campaign for reform in the law and attitudes are entitled 'What More do they Want?' and 'No New Deal'. Lord Arran, the Act's sponsor in the Lords, asked those affected 'to show their thanks by comporting themselves quietly and with dignity'. There was a lack of euphoria among the campaigners themselves and a general feeling that they should be grateful, silent, and invisible following a measure which, Jeff Weeks suggests, satisfied only 'the limited aims of adult professional-class homosexuals'. The limitations of the law were demonstrated by the 1970 prosecution of the underground newspaper *IT* (*International Times*) for 'conspiracy to corrupt public decency' by publishing gay contact ads, and moves against the establishment of social clubs and similar facilities.[54]

But things were changing. Apart from the beginnings of a consumerist gay culture of clubs, clothes, and lifestyle magazines,[55] a militant politics arose focusing on the new concept of 'gay' identity, strongly influenced by the US gay liberation movement arising after the Stonewall Riots in July 1969. This led to the founding of the British Gay Liberation Front in October 1970. Influenced by contemporaneous political campaigns, the GLF was 'left-wing in a light-hearted rather than dourly doctrinaire way', with a 'mood of infectious self-confidence'. Unlike the reformist and more bureaucratic Campaign for Homosexual Equality, the GLF did not merely want assimilation into existing society. It was about 'coming out' and confronting society with 'Gay Pride'. As a movement it was effervescent and exciting, but its very energies led to spin-offs, diversions, and splits, including the development of gay Left groups.[56] Hugh David describes the complex emergence of a gay community in what he suggests was 'homosexuality's brief golden age'.[57] However, there was still a great deal of prejudice, and following the Act the numbers of prosecutions of gay men – for behaviour contravening the narrow parameters of legality – actually increased.[58]

Furthermore, solidarity between gay men and lesbians was somewhat fragile. Men massively outnumbered women in most gay organizations, and even if they transgressed conventions of sex and gender (e.g. by wearing 'radical drag'), they often unthinkingly adhered to traditional sexist attitudes. Many lesbians felt more in sympathy with the growing militant Women's Liberation movement: in spite of an early lack of feminist support for lesbianism, by 1971 the issue of sexuality had been raised at the national Women's Liberation Conference, and although controversial, remained centrally significant. There were tensions within both arenas for lesbians, and there were of course many who did not feel any need for identity-based politics – the Gateways Club continued to flourish throughout the seventies.

By the end of the 1970s a specifically lesbian-feminism was being defined as radically dissenting from patriarchy and its systems, with some proponents advocating lesbian separatism. This led to controversies and tensions not only between lesbian-feminists and women who had not wholly given up on heterosexuality, or who felt that this analysis omitted other important factors in the oppression of women, but also over different perceptions of lesbianism – a political choice against men, or an erotic and emotional choice for women?

This previously occluded way of life was becoming more visible in the media.[59] In 1971 a survey, *Love between women* by the elderly psychologist Charlotte Wolff, herself a lesbian, was published to positive press response, as was her later study *Bisexuality* (1977).[60] However, Adrian Bingham notes the emergence of hostile stereotypes in the popular press, drawing on existing tropes of 'ugly feminists' and 'hairy-legged man-haters'. When Labour MP Maureen Colquhoun was 'outed' in 1977, and her local party voted to deselect her, there was vicious mockery from some journalists, although the *Daily Mirror* was supportive of her right to remain in post.[61]

Backlash

As degrees of liberation were occurring, the forces of conventionality – and, as they perceived it, morality – felt increasingly under threat and more inclined to do something about it. In 1970 Kenneth Tynan's light-hearted erotic review, *Oh Calcutta*, opened at the Roundhouse, a London theatre receiving Arts Council subsidy. While the Director of Public Prosecutions considered 'a complaint', no prosecution under the new Theatres Act took place, although there was a good deal of media outcry. Sutherland suggests that this crystallized a 'moral backlash', with 'a remarkable cohesion and purposefulness', producing reports and protests, picketing cinemas, and harassing newsagents, although Mrs Mary Whitehouse's National Viewers' and Listeners' Association had been going since 1963. In March 1971 the Festival of Light was founded, followed in June by The Responsible Society, both arguing that 'we are drowning in a rising tide of filth.' In 1972 the Earl of Longford, a leading figure in the campaign, produced the *Longford Report on Pornography*, proposing a stringent definition of obscenity (in spite of one appendix by a psychologist arguing that there was little hard evidence for the deleterious effects of pornography).

Despite these movements, 'Pornography became industrialized': the demand was met by canny businessmen taking advantage of loopholes in the law established by high-minded sexual progressives (and arrangements with corrupt police officers – a sensational trial in 1977 revealed the systematic 'protection racket' in Soho run by the Obscene Publications Squad of the Metropolitan Police[62]). 'Forbidden topics' emerged in 'above-the-counter magazines'.[63]

Moral campaigners were not deterred: veteran anti-filth campaigner Mary Whitehouse successfully invoked blasphemy laws, long in desuetude, against *Gay News* in 1976, for publishing James Kirkup's poem, 'The Love that Dares to Speak its Name', a homoerotic meditation by a Roman centurion on the crucified Christ. Appeals up to the House of Lords by Denis Lemon, the editor, were rejected, but the case stimulated the formation of the Gay Activist Alliance.[64] Pressured to do something about obscenity, the Labour Government took the traditional method of demonstrating concern, without commitment to politically contentious action, by appointing the Williams Committee in 1977 to investigate 'Obscenity, indecency and violence in publications, entertainments and displays'. Roy Jenkins, the Home Secretary, was a long-standing progressive liberalizer and this was reflected in the composition of this body, which produced a 'tolerant, permissive, unalarmed' report in 1979 (by which time the Conservatives were once more in power).[65]

None the less, while it was sitting, Conservative MP Cyril Townsend put forward a Private Member's Bill embodying Mary Whitehouse's concerns over child pornography. Very little was believed to be in circulation and it was subject to existing legislation, but the Government, unwilling to seem unconcerned, did not oppose the Bill and indeed gave it time, so that it became law in 1978.[66]

Protecting the morals of the young remained a major focus of concern. While 'consenting adults' of either sex might be free to make their own sexual choices in theory, if not in practice, 'the young' remained a target for moral reformers. Two major obscenity trials of the early 1970s centred on fears of the corruption of youth: the anti-authoritarian 'kids' rights' publication, the *Little Red Schoolbook* and the 'Schoolkids' Issue' of *OZ*, 'the market-leader of underground magazines'. This, probably no more obscene than any other issue, was actually edited by under-18s, but the (adult) editorial and managerial staff were charged under the 1959 Obscenity Act for 'conspiracy to corrupt the morals of children and young persons', and under the 1953 Postal Act for sending an indecent article through Her Majesty's mails. They received 'shockingly harsh' sentences – 15 months in prison followed by deportation for Richard Neville, *OZ*'s Australian founder, although some charges were quashed on appeal and a six-month sentence for others suspended.[67]

In a rather different register, though with a similar agenda that children and young people had a right to sexual knowledge and even sexual activity, the Family Planning Association became increasingly involved in sex education. James Hampshire has shown that while, by the 1960s, most major players, including the National Union of Teachers, concurred that sex education was a desirable thing, nobody seemed very enthusiastic about undertaking it: there is a definite sense that all parties hoped someone else would actually do something. Some authorities encouraged teachers to take courses and ran school programmes, but it was 'a matter of geographical chance' whether any particular young person had access to these.

The FPA designated health education as one of its major tasks in 1967, seeing its role as 'educating the educators', working with local authorities to train teachers and health educators. In 1972 Grapevine, an innovative concept involving peer counselling for young people by young people (supported by professionals) was set up on a small scale in North London. Backlash was perhaps inevitable, particularly in the wider context of anxieties over the 'Permissive Society'. Moralists were unable to make much impact on the commercialized proliferation of sexual material and images: publicly funded provision was a politically sensitive soft target. The FPA was accused of promoting promiscuity. The old argument that parents were the best persons to provide sexual information to their children was voiced, even though surveys indicated that this was not happening, and that only a small minority ever encountered formal sex education. Vast local variations continued.[68]

Adrian Bingham has illuminated the response of the popular press to liberalization and the (perceived) rise of 'permissiveness'. No longer able simply to present themselves as modern and progressive in challenging a conspiracy of silence on sexual matters, they had to find new ways of writing about the perennially sales-gleaning topic of sex. Rupert Murdoch's *The Sun* first developed a 'hedonist and consumerist' presentation of (highly heteronormative) sex, the general assumptions of which were embodied in the daily 'Page 3' girl, the culmination of the long tradition of 'cheesecake' pictures of attractive young women. Other papers followed, presenting ever more direct, detailed, and explicit copy. Problem pages and advice columns, which had provided a valuable space for the communication of education and information, were increasingly encouraged to aim for salacious content and to exclude common problems seen as less titillating. However, 'agony aunts' themselves suggest that their real work was still being done in the area of private responses.[69]

Subcultures

Previously little-known sexual subcultures became the subject of studies published for a mainstream audience. In 1967 Gillian Freeman's *The Undergrowth of Literature* revealed a range of 'special interest' pornographic publications, including 'fladge' (flagellation), bondage, transvestite and rubber, and other fetishes. Maurice North's *The Outer Fringe of Sex: A Study in Sexual Fetishism* (1970) took a more detailed look at the world of rubber fetishists. Veteran sex-researcher Michael Schofield turned his attention to *Promiscuity* (1976). Chris Gosselin and Glenn Wilson's study *of Sexual Variations: Fetishism, Sado-Masochism and Transvestism* appeared in 1980. *Forum* magazine provided readers' own accounts of their activities. 'Wife-swapping' or 'swinging' emerged from the shadows. Contact magazines provided a way for individuals and couples to meet those of like desires, as did small ads in the alternative press: although these periodicals existed on a dodgy border of illegality, with the police always ready to clamp down on what they suspected to be prostitutes or homosexuals advertising for trade, using the 'conspiracy to corrupt public morals' charge. However, the prosecution of *Exit* and *Way Out* (1968–1972), where the accused appealed the case all the way up to the House of Lords, preceded lonely hearts classified columns going mainstream and legitimate as 'staple features of ordinary journalism'.[70]

The limits of liberal tolerance, never mind permissiveness, did not extend to infinity. In 1975 there were attempts by paedophiles to represent themselves as a sexual minority along lines already deployed for homosexuality. At first this met with some sympathy, at least as a topic which should be opened for discussion, but the formation of groups such as Paedophile Action for Liberation and Paedophile Information Exchange led to tabloid attacks and moral panic. While there were attempts to position paedophilia as about emotions rather than child abuse, the PIE also campaigned, unsuccessfully, for reforms around the age of consent. Although their campaign appeared to have similarities with contemporary liberal and liberationist activities and areas of common interest, for example, vulnerability to the use of conspiracy charges, other groups found that there was little actual common political ground and that expressing support only led to being smeared with accusations of complicity with child abuse. Feminist groups saw the movement largely as about increasing adult male sexual access to unequal partners.[71]

Liberating the mainstream?

The major area of liberalization was, as always, in the range of possibilities available to the heterosexual majority. Far from the sixties having ushered in an epoch of permissive free love, the percentage of women in the population who married peaked in 1971 at 79.4 per cent, almost a third again as many as at the beginning of the century and slightly more than in 1951.[72] Though this was probably not entirely accounted for by the couples previously unable to marry now freed to do so by the Divorce Act, the decade did see a rise in divorce and remarriage (and the associated creation of new family structures), a considerable rise in cohabitation and delayed marriages, and a decline in marital fertility.[73]

Premarital experimentation grew more common, while within marriage or established monogamous relationships a far wider sexual repertoire was recommended by a proliferating body of advice literature, if perhaps not as extensively put into practice. The implications of this for women, in particular, were complex. They were freer to engage in experimentation without fear of pregnancy, but the belief that this was no longer a valid excuse for refraining could lead to pressures to have coital sex, male-biased penetrative models of sexual practice still predominating. The feminist movement engaged critically with male-defined assumptions of 'sexual liberation', but a range of popular manuals and magazines (many originating from the USA) not only assumed that women would be having non-marital sexual relationships, but exhorted them to acquire a sophisticated armament of techniques for pleasuring men. While the importance of the female orgasm was foregrounded, this sometimes appeared less about the woman's pleasure than about 'doing it right' and servicing male self-esteem.[74] Less has been written about the implications for men and 'performance anxiety': apparently, the most consistent advertiser in the pages of the 'underground' press, with an audience presumably more than averagely sexually liberated, was 'Magnaphall', promising bigger and better erections.[75]

Perhaps the archetypal seventies sex manual was *The Joy of Sex*, edited by veteran sexual liberationist Alex Comfort. While its approach was geared to the bonded (if not married) couple, it represented sex as a recreation, pleasurable and playful, and almost completely dissociated from reproduction, rather than the sacred seal on the conjugal relationship. Illustrated with line drawings of a very 1970s couple, it drew into the marital bedroom techniques and practices previously associated with prostitution or deviant subcultures (bondage, dressing-up, pornography, and fantasy).[76]

Venereal diseases began to rise again, causing growing concern.[77] In 1973 the *British Medical Journal* noted an increasing incidence of venereally transmitted genital herpes. Not serious in itself, though the 'irritant and painful' rash might disrupt 'marital relations', a connection with cervical carcinoma was posited, and there was clear danger in maternal transmission to newborn babies.[78] By 1978: 'Once considered a rare, occupational disease of prostitutes, genital herpes is now recognized as a serious, common infection,' and 'a successful preventive programme' was acutely desirable.[79] Annet Mooij has intriguingly suggested, in the Netherlands context, that the herpes panic (originating in the USA) provided, for those disenchanted with sexual liberation, a basis for sexual caution without retreat into Whitehousian moral orthodoxy.[80] There was also concern over the increased incidence of chlamydia, seen as 'widely prevalent' and responsible for various gynaecological problems, including infertility.[81]

*   *   *

At the end of the seventies, once again the picture is ambiguous. Some degree of 'liberation' had taken place, but for many it was insufficient and did not go far enough, while for others, threatened by what they saw as dangers to society, it was the call to mobilize an influential opposition movement. Commercialized exploitation or privatized, rather than collective, solutions (e.g. the resort to the 'growth movement' instead of 'consciousness-raising' for political struggle) were already beginning to supersede the radical themes of the late sixties and early seventies.

11

Approaching the Millennium

Reversing the permissive moment?

The Tory regime under Margaret Thatcher which came to power in 1979 combined extreme economic libertarianism, aiming at changing a 'culture of dependency' into an energetic 'enterprise culture' (concepts bearing rather gendered overtones), with strong commitment to moral regeneration of a nation perceived as vitiated through the insidious inroads of 'permissiveness' (strongly associated with the Labour Party), by a return to what were specifically designated as 'Victorian values'. While the state was getting 'out of the boardroom' to let business thrive in free-market competitive terms, rather than getting out of the bedroom, it was increasingly regulating areas of 'private' life.[1]

However, 'the legislative and social changes of the sixties proved extremely difficult to reverse.'[2] There were many reasons why government commitment to a new moral 'forward' movement was not embodied in practice. While moral crusading organizations saw the Conservatives as natural allies, their concerns were not necessarily a high political priority. There were strong transatlantic influences on the economic and social philosophies of the 'New Right' but the moralism of the US 'Moral Majority' proved a less resilient import, striking no deep roots in the United Kingdom, possibly because of the relatively lesser importance of fundamentalist Christianity. UK moral organizations, though influenced by developments and initiatives in the United States, largely continued a still vigorous native British tradition of moral disapproval, demands for censorship, and increased policing of those deemed morally deviant. While they hoped for government sympathy, they also undertook action in a variety of other areas: for example, Victoria Gillick's series of highly publicized court-cases to prevent her underage daughters (and by extension all under-16s without parental permission) being given contraceptive advice.[3]

Martin Durham has usefully analysed the nuances of the relationship between conventional and moral politics during the Thatcher years in *Sex and Politics* (1991). However much lip-service might be paid to family values, political considerations were paramount, and there were tensions between (and among) extra-Parliamentary pressure groups and the Government, between back-bench MPs committed to moral crusades and the Government front bench, and different points of view within the Government, between Government and civil servants in relevant departments. A libertarian right wing believed that 'individual freedom and the free market' ought to operate in the private sphere as well as economics. There were significant differences in degrees of success of particular moral campaigns in gaining legislation, and how effective the legislation achieved was.[4]

Fertility politics

Persistent attempts to nibble away at the 1967 Abortion Act – by restricting the time-limit, reducing the grounds, and placing constraints on the operation of clinics – failed. Medical opinion increasingly favoured reducing the legal limit to 24 weeks in the light of developments in neonatology, and in 1985 the Government agreed guidelines with clinics not to undertake abortions beyond this limit (these, always few, could still be performed in hospitals). Ultimately, an overwhelming 'pro-choice' decision was reached concerning the clause on abortion time limits in the Government Bill on embryo research of 1990: 24 weeks and removal of any limit in cases of foetal abnormality or 'grave risk'. Brooke suggests, however, that increasing ambivalence over simplistic slogans among reproductive rights activists, and less than enthusiastic commitment among Labour Party leaders, meant that no radical changes to the existing system occurred.[5]

The 'pro-life' movement was simultaneously conducting a propaganda campaign, although the kind of direct action seen in the United States made little progress in the United Kingdom.[6] Changes in the National Health Service insidiously eroded the availability of abortion: always a 'postcode lottery'. Some authorities, seeing it as a soft target for budgetary cuts, slashed services to all but the most severe medical cases. While low-cost private abortions remained available, for many women £50 was out of the question.[7] Use of RU-486, the 'abortion pill', a medical means of safe termination of early pregnancy, became enmeshed in bureaucratic restrictions under pressure from 'pro-life' organizations.[8]

While the legal right to free birth control continued, its actual availability was more problematic. 'Pill scares' continued: during the 1980s there were recurrent claims of a link with cervical cancer (also associated with 'female promiscuity').[9] With the inclusion of birth control within the NHS, it was assumed that most people would use their general practitioners for contraception and therefore specialized clinics were unnecessary. The Family Planning Association turned its attentions to educating providers and ensuring standards.[10] However, not everyone wanted to use their GP for birth control, and not all GPs were trained: even those who were did not necessarily have the range of expertise available in clinics. Specialized clinics were more cost-effective, with a greater range of consumer choice, extremely important since individuals will not continue with a disliked method, as has been seen in earlier resistance to clinic-promoted methods.[11]

Such services were seen as expendable by health authorities desperate to cut costs, in spite of the short-termism of this view: in areas where family planning sessions were reduced, the numbers of abortions went up, while the long-term costs of unwanted children were not factored in.[12] Obtaining 'morning-after' contraception could be a minefield of deterrent red tape or disapproving doctors.[13] Infertility services were even less readily available under the NHS, with few clinics, long waiting lists, and inadequate facilities, even for physical investigations, apart from any provision for counselling. Private infertility treatment became 'big business', with IVF (in vitro fertilization) costing several thousand pounds and having a success rate of around 10 per cent.[14]

The era of AIDS

The situation of gay men during this period was full of ambiguities. In 1981 (just before AIDS became an issue) Peter Tatchell's candidature in the Bermondsey by-election was characterized by intense homophobia against a gay and left-wing candidate in a context of wider political crisis.[15] There were claims that the Metropolitan Police were using entrapment policies and generally directing activity against the gay community in London.[16] The early eighties saw some gay and lesbian initiatives within local government: several councils, particularly the Greater London Council under Ken Livingstone, took these beyond lip-service to non-discriminatory policies, and were denounced as 'loony lefties', focusing moral-backlash campaigns as well as generating opposition to 'gesture politics' even among the gay Left. However, commitment to gay and lesbian rights in the Labour Party was increasing, especially following gay and lesbian activism in support of the Miners' Strike of 1984–85.[17]

In 1980, Scotland finally attained limited decriminalization of homosexuality by a narrow majority in a much contested amendment to the Criminal Justice (Scotland) Act, a very limited victory in the light of continuing intense Scottish homophobia. Social discrimination continued along with legal harassment: as in England and Wales, new statutory powers probably increased police surveillance and prosecutions by the authorities. Only following appeal to the European Court of Human Rights by an individual, Jeff Dudgeon, was the 1967 Act finally extended to cover Northern Ireland by the Order in Council Homosexual Offences (Northern Ireland) 1982. Common experience of oppression had united Nationalist and Unionist gays and lesbians in the Northern Ireland Gay Rights Association (NIGRA) just as homophobia transcended differences between Catholic and Protestant.[18]

Much has been written about the HIV/AIDs epidemic and its impact. Sexual health anxieties were rising before the advent of this new and lethal disease: concerns around genital herpes were mentioned in the previous chapter.[19] Sexually transmitted hepatitis B was recognized as a particular problem among gay men. Resistant strains of gonorrhoea had appeared.[20] The first reports of an Acquired Immunodeficiency Syndrome among gay men in the United States appeared in major British medical journals and *Gay News* in 1981. 'Don't go with Americans' was one suggestion, although the first UK fatality occurred in 1981. The first British conference, bringing together everyone in the field, took place in May 1983, when there were still very few UK cases – 14 by the end of July 1983. Very little was known about this, apparently, entirely new disease: this did not prevent the outbreak of tabloid press hysteria about the 'Gay Plague'. Media panics and moralists oscillated between fears that AIDS was about to run rife among heterosexuals and assertions that heterosexual AIDS was a 'myth'. Early responses were 'bottom-up' rather than 'top-down', driven by gay community voluntarism, for example the Terrence Higgins Trust, named after one of the earliest UK fatalities, and uncoordinated clinical and scientific interests.[21]

Heterosexual cases began to appear. By the end of October 1985 there were 241 reported cases in Britain, still relatively few, but a worrying rate of increase. The Chief Medical Officer at the Department of Health, Dr Donald Acheson, took a coolheaded line aimed at discouraging hysteria. An experienced epidemiologist, he advocated health education targeting specific high-risk groups, homosexuals, and intravenous drug users, although also education of the general public and inclusion of AIDS in sex education for secondary school pupils. An Expert Advisory Group on AIDS, meeting at the Department of Health, consulted gay activists.[22] The first government debate on the subject, however, did not occur until 1986.[23]

The Government was finally persuaded of the necessity of a general media health education campaign, but, following tradition, the final approved version lacked clarity and specificity, and often created confusion rather than enlightenment. Explicit materials shocked some Government ministers and officials, at least one of whom is recorded as 'deeply ignorant about sexual matters'. Department of Health officials were under pressure to find a 'respectable out', permitting politicians to show concern without having to address intimate sexual matters in too close detail.[24]

A major problem was that, as *The Lancet* commented in a 1988 editorial: 'Medical science knows more about the molecular structure of the human immunodeficiency virus (HIV)…than it knows about human sexual behaviour',[25] but in spite of the need to establish a 'reliable baseline' against which to calibrate attempts to reduce risky behaviour, the Government refused funding to a national survey into sexual attitudes and behaviour (Berridge argues that it was certain ministers, rather than Margaret Thatcher herself, who had qualms about what this might reveal about the heterosexual majority). The survey was ultimately sponsored by the medical charity, the Wellcome Trust.[26]

The demands of public health and the impact of experts within the civil service strongly influenced official agendas on AIDS/HIV, although there were substantial regional differences both in incidence and response.[27] By the beginning of the 1990s the problem was increasingly moving from an acute to a chronic model. Treatments were being tested, there was controversy over the relationship between HIV and AIDS, the rise of an 'AIDS establishment' tended to marginalize gay men, the problem was downgraded in priority for official attention, and with the failure of a widespread heterosexual epidemic to materialize, AIDS/HIV tended to be once more an issue seen as affecting only marginalized groups.[28] There is a convincing argument that permanent health officials had a significant effect on the development and implementation of AIDS policy which ran counter to political agendas of the government in power.[29]

Sexual enterpreneurialism

Commitment to and encouragement of enterprise in the economic sphere also tended to undercut proclaimed moral agendas: in 1979 during the debates of the Select Committee on the Abortion Amendment Act, Ian Mikardo remarked that

> The backstreet abortionists, the Harley Street racketeers and the Heathrow taxi touts, who were their agents and procurers, are in a way...models of enterprise and initiative.[30]

Entrepreneurs realized that there was a demand and that sex would sell. Jacqueline Gold, daughter of the brother and partner of the Ralph Gold prosecuted for selling *Fanny Hill*, went into the family business, Gold Star Publications, as a young girl, but became 'inspired to start a multi-million-pound business empire', selling sex toys and sexy lingerie to women in their own homes via 'Ann Summers' parties.[31]

Sex phone-lines became 'the latest catchpenny craze', charging premium rates for 'a con, the breathtaking scale of it matched only by the breathtaking profits'.[32] Ferris considered that the 'British approach to erotica, sly and under-hand, encouraged commercial exploitation', though with increasing restrictions on selling pornography, while 'an underground porn trade flourished' (as ever), 'the above-ground trade relied on magazines and half-hearted videos.' Men's magazines were vetted by lawyers, and a retailers' code of practice included no penetration, no erections, no flagellation (in spite of its reputation as the archetypal English vice), no necrophilia (Nicholas Whittaker has given an amusing and gruesome account of his 'life in the titillation trade' working on *Fiesta* and *Razzle*[33]). The 1990s saw the development of the new phenomenon of 'porn for women', with 'erotic fiction' imprints such as 'Black Lace' – written textual erotica for private consumption rather than visual representations.[34]

The Video Recordings Act, 1984, conferred defined legal powers on the British Board of Film Censors for the first time, with its certificates bearing the force of law and fines imposed for selling uncertificated videos. Sex videos were either imports so heavily cut as to become meaningless, or produced to conform to the demands of the domestic '18' classification – 'smutty titillation...horseplay and innuendo'. 'Restricted' videos, classified as 'R18' and sold only in licensed sex shops, included simulated but unconvincing sex, 'grubby rather than sensual', while 'sex education' videos presented sexual subjects under the excuse of enabling better sex lives. The BBFC operated a stricter policy over videos than cinematic films, with particular concerns over sexual violence. By the late 1990s, since licensed sex-shops were losing trade to unlicensed blackmarket dealers, it decided to give an R18 certificate to hard-core videos, provided they were non-violent and acts appeared consensual. This met outraged opposition from the new Home Secretary, Jack Straw: the interim licences were withdrawn, and the acting president of the BBFC responsible not confirmed in the post.[35]

Questions of gender

Although the situation in the United Kingdom was very different from that in the United States, by the 1980s there was a strong feminist anti-pornography movement, spreading well beyond the organized women's movement and, indeed, beyond materials traditionally considered 'pornography'. In 1986 Labour MP Clare Short moved a Commons motion to ban newspapers from publishing photographs of topless 'Page 3 Girls', and 'tapped into a bedrock of sexual puritanism'.[36] Feminist anti-porn campaigners dissociated themselves from the 'Mary Whitehouse' tradition of repression (protesting degrading depictions of women rather than upholding old-fashioned moralism).

Representatives of the libertarian tradition within British feminism contested arguments that pornography was a cause (rather than a manifestation) of sexism, and queried the appropriateness of importing US anti-pornography arguments wholesale into the very different, already highly censored, British situation. They cited the very ambiguous results of research into the effects of pornography, and were extremely concerned that laws intended to outlaw violent and degrading images of women would, in fact, be employed to censor educational feminist or gay material.[37] Gay materials were at disproportionate risk of confiscation and prosecution. In 1984 Customs mounted an operation against the London bookshop 'Gay's the Word', raiding both the shop and its directors' homes for imported materials, while individuals bringing in small amounts of gay material for personal use had this seized (contrary to a Customs directive).[38]

Although the death of feminism was often claimed, alongside the rise of 'post-feminist' women allegedly confident of equality and unbothered about sexual politics, feeling free to wear overtly sexual clothes and make-up without moral dilemma (or to be, for example, a 'lipstick lesbian', whose sexual identity was not a political issue), the position of women at the end of the twentieth century was not really so wonderful. Some women were achieving leading positions and a high profile, but if one female icon of the 1980s was the Prime Minister, the other was Diana, Princess of Wales, who gained her place in the public eye through the traditional route of marriage (and whose well-publicized eating disorders and marriage problems revealed the pressures on so apparently privileged a woman). While women entered the workforce in increasing numbers – in particular the percentage of married women rose steeply – the vast majority worked in low-paid, low-status areas. A few highly paid businesswomen became visible, but in many areas even highly qualified professional women still suffered from discrimination in pay and career progression.[39] 'Single mothers' were persistently demonized: many (although a significant percentage of 'illegitimate' births were, as ever, to stable cohabiting couples) being particularly poverty stricken, and dependent on state benefits in a system established on a basis of assumptions about the family, its stability, and the gendering of the division of labour within it, which no longer, in fact, pertained.[40]

During these final decades of the twentieth century there was some recognition of male problems and vulnerability, although the activities of consciously anti-sexist men critical of existing gender arrangements as deleterious to men as well as women, represented in publications such as *Achilles Heel*, were generated by and probably only reached a minority.[41] Male sexual and reproductive health might be presented as neglected, but were gleaning more attention. Occasional articles appeared in the general press about testicular or prostate cancer – common conditions which had not received anything like the concern displayed over analogous disorders in women for which screening was available and information widely disseminated (via, for example, women's magazines)[42] – and about male involvement in infertility investigations.[43] Impotence, once shrouded in secrecy and euphemistically alluded to in discreet small ads, now dared to speak its name. Well before the advent of the potency drug Viagra, advertisements became more prominent and more explicit, displayed in the news sections of papers as well as among small ads: 'Impotence: Impotence can be a worrying experience'; 'Impotence: A Medical Problem Treated Medically. RAPID RECOVERY'.[44] The 'last taboo', acknowledgement that men could be raped, was breached in 1990 with Richie McMullen's book *Male Rape*, and in 1994 became a crime recognizable by law under the Criminal Justice and Public Order Act. The first conviction occurred in 1995. However, it probably remained even more under-reported than rape of women.[45] Books and press articles on the plight of the modern male, suggesting a 'crisis of masculinity' as the millennium approached, appeared with increasing frequency.[46]

Reformulating families

Heterosexual relationships also changed, though deep continuities remained. It was finally conceded in a 1991 judgement by the Court of Appeal that the 'common-law fiction' that men could not rape their wives was 'anachronistic and offensive', and in 1994 amendments to the Criminal Justice and Public Order Act gave Parliamentary force to designating marital rape a crime.[47] Various pieces of legislation affected marriage and the family: while in some cases these largely followed social change, Jane Lewis suggests that the 1984 Matrimonial and Family Proceedings Act was unrealistic in its assumption of women's individual economic status within marriage, and thus the feasibility of a 'clean break' when dissolving it. More rights were conceded to fathers when the Family Law Reform Act 1987 abolished the status of illegitimacy and allowed unmarried fathers to apply for parental rights orders, while the 1989 Children Act allowed them to share parental functions by private agreement with the mother. The 1996 Family Law Act introduced full no-fault divorce on the basis that adversarial actions were bad for the children, expected couples to sort out their affairs prior to applying for a dissolution, and provided for mediation facilities in a surprising revival of the belief that marriages could and ought to be 'saved'. Damage limitation with regard to children became the priority.[48]

Marriage was occurring at later ages, divorce and remarriage were more frequent, and cohabitation common, though for many a prelude to formalizing the relationship, and some legal rights of women in cohabiting relationships were recognized. The dual-career, or at least dual-employment, couple became the norm, although unemployment, particularly in traditional male areas, had a considerable impact on relationships and male identity (Lewis suggests that women's employment should perhaps be disaggregated into women with a definite focus on career and others, primarily focused on family and motherhood, who might be working part-time or with less commitment:[49] both of these positions might of course shift over time). There was greater premarital experimentation with a number of partners. While most still aspired to a stable monogamous relationship, this might consist of several sequential unions rather than a lifelong marriage. Couples engaged in a wider repertoire of sexual practices, but still regarded companionship and affection as equally or more important than sex, and placed a high value on sexual fidelity. Liz Stanley has cautioned against too ready acceptance of the evidence of the National Survey of Sexual Attitudes and Lifestyles on these topics and suggests it may over-represent certain patterns of sexual behaviour.[50] By 1999 half of all pregnancies took place outside wedlock – in some areas nearly two-thirds – and all but a tiny minority of women kept their babies.[51]

With the rise of cohabitation a number of different patterns emerged. The perceived expenses of marriage influenced some, with the ceremony taking place once the couple could afford it, or when they decided to start a family. Many couples just drifted into it. For others it was a deliberate moral choice about an ongoing personal commitment, with the decision to have children based on when the relationship seemed stable and solid enough. In spite of the wish for some kind of recognition of the status of these relationships, research found that there was significant resistance to basing them on explicit contracts. For many women a desire to retain independent identity was significant. However, a substantial group of younger and poorer women with children drifted into sequential, rather than committed long-term, cohabitational relationships. Cohabiting couples were largely accepted by their families as essentially married,[52] but legal recognition of their position has been 'exceptional and unsystematic', with some remedy over the years for the worst injustices, but a persisting reluctance to do anything that might erode the distinctive status of marriage or encourage couples to eschew the formality.[53]

Protecting the children?

Children were as ever central to much moral panic around sex in the 1980s and 1990s. During this period the extent of child sexual abuse became much more widely known. This had complex results: both wide-scale removal of children from their families and widespread denial. Although a number of cases revealed extensive child abuse within care institutions, most of the proven cases involved children abused within the familial setting. Even so, the popular image of the paedophile remained that of a sinister outsider, the traditional 'dirty old man'. The Sexual Offenders Act of 1997 created a national register of individuals convicted of sexual crimes, who are obliged to register with the police.[54] This, however, did not distinguish between child molesters and individuals who had had a consensual, but illegal relationship with someone under the age of consent (which in the case of gay men could mean between 16 and 21).

Anxieties around children and sexuality influenced the continuing concern around obscenity, but the central area in which they were expressed was probably the still-debated territory of sex education, with claims that the breakdown of morals (rising illegitimacy, especially among teenage mothers, a rise in sexually transmitted diseases, instability of families, 'promiscuity', etc.) was contemporary with and caused by the massive spread of sex education since the 1960s. As Carol Lee's account of her experiences as a sex-educator and the 1987 Policy Studies Institute report by Isobel Allen on *Education in Sex and Personal Relationships* revealed, sex education provision within the school system was far from universal and very uneven in quality. Often, it stuck to basic biological facts and cautions about potential dangers. Both children and parents expressed overwhelming support for sex education within the school context, in spite of the persistent rhetoric that educators were usurping the parental role and contravening family values.[55]

The place of sex education in the curriculum and its content continued to be contested. The 1986 Education Act mentioned sex education for the first time in statutory legislation, but only to make it a matter for the governing bodies of schools (rather than Local Education Authorities) to decide. The 1988 Education Reform Act introduced the National Curriculum under which teaching about the biological aspects of sex became compulsory (but sex and relationship education remained marginalized). 'Clause 28' of the Local Government Act, 1988, forbade local councils to 'promote' homosexuality or teach its acceptability as a 'pretended family relationship', though paradoxically generated significant opposition and new campaigning bodies.[56] Medical, pedagogic, and moral values clashed: in 1994 a Health Education Authority guide to sex aimed at teenagers was withdrawn on the basis that its terminology and style, accessible to young people, made it 'smutty and not suitable'.[57] In 1999 the *British Medical Journal* reported that British adolescents had the worst record in Europe for pregnancy, abortions, and sexually transmitted diseases, attributed to inadequate education (general and sex), and also poverty and long parental working hours.[58]

Increasing visibility

The AIDS crisis generated a powerful response among the gay community in undertaking educational work to raise awareness and promote safer sex techniques and in lobbying for the provision of services, although there were claims that AIDS became 'de-gayed', to further alliances with funding bodies and official agencies along with increasing professionalization of workers.[59] AIDS, and the moral backlash embodied in 'Clause 28', paradoxically created a new gay militancy and activism, ranging from relatively 'establishment' bodies such as Stonewall to defiantly 'Queer' protest groups like Act-Up and Outrage.[60] Oscar Wilde received the accolade of a memorial in Westminster Abbey[61] but although the centenary of his trial saw a reduction in the gay age of consent, this went from 21 to 18, still not equivalent to heterosexuals.[62] The return of the Labour Party to power in 1997 saw several 'out' MPs take their seats, and even hold Government appointments (though Minister for the Arts surely adhered to traditional stereotyping), but commitment to equalizing the age of consent fell foul of the prejudices of the House of Lords. Increasing visibility was not entirely a good thing given the continuing strong undercurrent of homophobia, as manifested by the April 1999 nail-bomb attack on a gay pub in Old Compton Street.[63]

Within the lesbian community there were tensions between lesbian feminists and those who argued for a re-emphasis on lesbianism as an erotic choice, promoting the exploration of sexual desires via the creation of lesbian-positive pornography and experimentation with transgressive sexual practices. There were clashes between wider demands for diversity (particularly when projects sought local government funding subject to this condition) and desires for ideological purity, and much in-fighting, revealing some of the problems of founding politics on sexual identity and its definition.[64] Motherhood, as well as sex, was an issue for lesbians. Women who had been married before coming out could find themselves at a serious disadvantage in struggles over child custody, regarded as de facto 'unfit mothers', and experiencing various forms of discrimination. Others, never married and not wanting any relationship with a man, sought artificial insemination in order to have children, something which caused (perhaps predictably) moral panics and press furore.[65]

*   *   *

Limits on the sexually acceptable persisted. Geographical location and economic status significantly affected how free individuals were to choose to be open about their sexual orientation: some orientations continued problematic. Although the police and courts did not pursue non-consensual and violent heterosexual assaults with the rigour that might be considered desirable, in the late 1980s 'Operation Spanner', undertaken by police in the Great Manchester area, resulted in the trial in 1990 of 15 men from a wide social range on charges relating to acts of consensual, though extremely severe, sadomasochism.[66]

While the Blair Government, elected in 1997, emphasized its concern for families and marriage, it also promised significant commitment to issues of gender equality and sexual diversity. As the millennium approached, for some there appeared to be greatly increased choice – for the postmenopausal, fertility treatment; for gays, the 'pink pound' opened many doors – yet access to the appropriate resources was still heavily circumscribed by financial condition or geographical location.

12

Into a New Millennium: Changes and Continuities

Surveying the scene

As we draw closer to the present, it becomes increasingly difficult to write a coherent account of sex, gender, and social change, and more like standing too close to an Impressionist painting. Very little historical work has been done and archival resources may not yet be available. It is hard to assess what will prove most important in the long run: major developments may be occluded by what seems significant in the short term or because of media furore.

A second National Sexual Attitudes and Lifestyles Survey (NATSAL) provides a snapshot of sexual attitudes and behaviour at the turn into the 2000s. This perhaps had less impact than the earlier survey, since its findings were disseminated through a range of journals and reports to the Department of Health.[1] Using a probability sample survey of men and women aged 16–44 years who were resident in Britain, and computer-assisted interviews, it found some significant differences since 1990. Partly this might be attributed to new survey methods reducing individuals' reluctance to report sensitive and risky behaviours, but it also seems accurately to reflect a number of changes in sexual behaviour and attitudes, prompting fuller disclosure, over the previous decade.[2]

For both men and women there were increased reported numbers of heterosexual partners and of homosexual partnerships, concurrent partnerships, oral-genital contact, and heterosexual anal sex, and consistent condom use. A higher rate of cohabitation without marriage was also reported. Particular areas in which increase was noticeable were women reporting both numbers of heterosexual partnerships and homosexual partnerships, and figures for Britain outside London. There was wide variability, but an increase in numbers of partners, particularly among the younger age-group, was discernable, with an increase in risk factors for sexually transmitted infections (STI) in spite of the apparently greater consistent condom use: trends consistent with rises in STIs and attendance at genitourinary medicine clinics over the same period.[3] There was also an attempt to investigate differences in sexual behaviour across ethnic groups. Although there were significant variations in numbers of partners, cases of STIs, and incidence of HIV testing, revealed by a survey specifically on the four largest ethnic minority groups in the United Kingdom (Black Caribbean, Black African, Indian and Pakistani), the investigators suggest that such categorizations assumed homogeneity within these communities and obscured intragroup religious and cultural diversity, not to mention differences of class, economic status, and education.[4]

Sexual health: causes for concern

The sanguine hope of the 1950s that STIs were 'dying diseases' has so far not come to pass. If HIV/AIDS has become, in the United Kingdom, a medically manageable chronic condition, though significant problems remain,[5] the general picture of STI prevalence in the United Kingdom is less than encouraging. The groups most affected are young people under 25 and men who have sex with men (MSM), with significant regional variations, while concern grows about rising numbers of infections among the increasingly sexually active over-45 age-group. There was a worrying increase in the early 2000s of the traditional venereal diseases of syphilis and gonorrhoea, although there has since been some reduction in incidence of gonorrhoea,[6] with cases of syphilis at their highest since the early 1950s. The most significant increase has been among MSM, but heterosexual cases, especially among the young, are also rising and there is concern that congenital syphilis may be making an under-detected comeback.[7]

A number of infections considered negligible if enumerated at all c.1950 have become common and recognized as significant threats to individual and community health.[8] So great is the incidence of chlamydia that free testing for young people was introduced in 2003 and widely publicized.[9] Lymphogranuloma venereum, previously considered rare in the United Kingdom, has presented a significant number of cases since 2003, mostly among MSM.[10] In 2008 concerns over the incidence of Human Papilloma Virus (HPV: genital warts), which can develop into cervical cancer, led to the introduction of a vaccination programme, via schools, for girls aged 12 to 17.[11] There have been demands that this should be extended to boys but so far the cost-benefits are not thought to be compelling.[12] Following the removal of HIV and sexual health from the government priority list in 1997, and given this rise in STIs, genitourinary medicine (GUM) clinics were reported in 2004 as being under heavy stress with extensive waiting times of sometimes up to six weeks,[13] for conditions in which early diagnosis and treatment is critical to prevent further spread of infection.[14]

In another area of sexual health, a wide range of reliable methods suitable for a range of individual and couple preferences is now available for the prevention of conception.[15] However, these still require forethought and planning, leading to the demand for emergency post-coital contraception: this needs to be taken soon after unprotected intercourse, and there can be problems with obtaining a doctors' prescription (free on the NHS) within the time parameters. It was made available on demand from pharmacists in 2007,[16] but women may have to pay unless there is a local arrangement for it to be supplied free. In addition, some pharmacists have refused to supply it on religious grounds,[17] which led the General Pharmaceutical Council to issue guidelines in 2011 on the contractual obligations of pharmacists, meeting with objections from faith organizations.[18]

Abortion has also been under attack: in 2011 Nadine Dorries introduced an amendment to the Health and Social Care Bill under consideration by Parliament to strip abortion providers of their counselling role and to transfer this to 'independent' counselling services: a survey of the counselling provided by these, largely run by faith-based anti-abortion bodies, found them providing factually inaccurate information alongside emotive scaremongering.[19] This was particularly troubling given that the general trend towards earlier abortion (facilitated by the availability of very cheap pregnancy tests) would be adversely affected by such a requirement:[20] the Dorries amendment, however, was not accepted.[21] Almost more worrying than the attempt to force legislative change are reports of anti-abortion campaigners being allowed to present their case in schools.[22]

Sexual violence

One of the reasons for which women may require emergency contraception or abortion is rape. The Fawcett Society estimated that there are c.47,000 rapes per year in the United Kingdom. Conviction rates still remain extremely low in relation to cases reported – 6 per cent, though this reflects the number of cases that do not proceed to court (the attrition rate) as well as those which do, and in actual prosecutions a conviction is achieved in over 50 per cent of cases. However, partly because of this depressing statistic and partly due to still pervasive societal attitudes that mean that women's accusations of rape are either disbelieved, or they are claimed to have somehow brought it upon themselves, an uncounted number of instances are probably never even reported to the police. Provision of rape crisis centres, police responses, and conviction rates are all a postcode lottery, with wide regional variations.[23]

Campaigns still focus on cautioning women to protect themselves from sexual attack by strangers, such as the advice about the 'date-rape' drug rohypnol:

> [T]rust no one. If you are worried, never accept any opened drink, particularly not from a stranger. Tamper-proof bottles or cans are recommended.[24]

Reports of rapes at the Latitude Music Festival in the summer of 2010 led to alerting women to the dangers[25] (rather than improving lighting or providing better security). Similarly, London posters exhorted women to avoid unlicensed minicabs late at night:[26] the implication that licensed black cabs were safe was given a bitterly ironic twist when taxi driver John Worboys was convicted of multiple rapes in 2009 and linked to numerous other attacks on women:

> Worboys continued attacking women because a number of officers did not believe his victims' claims that they had been sexually assaulted by a London cabbie.[27]

The Metropolitan Police were also criticized for failures in the cases of Kirk Reid, who raped and sexually assaulted more than 71 women over eight years and had been identified as a suspect,[28] and of Delroy Grant, who sexually attacked over 200 elderly people in their own homes over 17 years.[29]

In spite of the Sexual Offences Act 2003,[30] judges' attitudes also remain a problem, insisting on their discretion to introduce women's previous sexual history and perpetuating the myth of frequent false accusations (jurors were also found to be influenced by hoary stereotypes).[31] The extent to which women are considered contributors to their own assault was perhaps typified in the 2008 case of rape victims (whose rapists had been successfully prosecuted) who found that their compensation under the Criminal Injuries Compensation Act was being cut on the grounds that they had been drinking prior to the attack.[32] Kenneth Clarke, the Justice Minister, at least aroused a storm of protest in May 2011 when, in outlining plans to increase the maximum sentence discount for rapists entering an early guilty plea, he differentiated 'serious rape' from 'date rape';[33] this was followed by a Tory MEP claiming that date rape victims 'share a part of the responsibility'.[34] While such attitudes may at least cause a furore, myths and prejudices are still prevalent among members of juries sitting on rape cases, as Alison Saunders of the Crown Prosecution Service pointed out in an interview in January 2012.[35] A 2012 review of rape investigations by the Inspectorate of Constabulary and the Crown Prosecution Service reported some progress, especially in support for victims, but still urgent need for improvement in police handling of these cases.[36]

There have recently been disturbing reports of the attitudes towards rape expressed in lads' mags. One study found that participants were unable to distinguish accurately between statements by convicted rapists and descriptions of women in lads' mags.[37] Articles in student magazines trivialize rape and treat it as a joke.[38]

In 2011 the international 'Slutwalk', originating in Canada when a police officer advised women not to dress 'like sluts', in order to avoid rape, leading to mass demonstrations by women asserting their right to dress as they liked without fear of assault, was taken up in the United Kingdom, arousing some controversy.[39] It is, however, also the case that women who cover up too much are also subject to criticism and attack: although the burqa has not been outlawed in the United Kingdom as it has in France[40] the subject has been raised, in particular in the wake of then Justice Minister Jack Straw expressing his discomfort with veils,[41] and acts of hostility towards women wearing the various forms of Islamic veiling are increasingly reported.[42] A private member's Face Coverings (Regulation) Bill 2010–11 is scheduled for debate early in 2012.[43] Women remain disproportionately the victims of policing on the basis of their sartorial choices in one direction or another.

Sex in the marketplace

Particularly at risk of sexual violence, and even murder, are sex-workers. As always, women working on the street are in the most danger and most subject to policing initiatives and vigilante action by local communities. While it remains legal to sell sex in the United Kingdom, this continues constrained by the various laws that surround it, in particular the designation of women who provide sexual services as 'common prostitutes', laying them open to committing a range of offences simply by being in particular places (and the perennial issue of having to go back to work to pay the fines that they have incurred for working). Local policing practices differ wildly, some operating what is in effect a tolerated zone where women may solicit (and punters kerb-crawl) unimpeded, but severely penalizing those who venture beyond that 'beat'. Intermittent crackdowns may result from community or political pressures. Anti-Social Behaviour Orders (ASBOs) have also been deployed to deter individual women from soliciting in particular areas, with the possibility of imprisonment for non-compliance. Technocratic strategies such as higher levels of street lighting, CCTV cameras, and manipulating traffic flow to control or eradicate street prostitution, may just lead to the location shifting. Community Street Watch campaigns and similar initiatives have roused concerns about vigilantism and intimidation. Police and local authorities have worked with such community groups but seldom with individuals actually selling sex, though in some areas outreach initiatives to sex workers aim at reducing harm and addressing health and safety issues.[44]

Indoor working, via escort agencies, premises in which women can work among others (safer but liable to fall foul of brothel-keeping laws), massage parlours or 'outcall' services, is a more substantial but much less visible sector of the sex industry (except via 'tart-cards' in public phone-booths[45]) and harder for researchers to access. It deals largely in ordinary, non-violent, consensual exchanges of sexual services for money and is safer for the women involved, who are also more likely to take care of health and safety issues, insisting on condom use and avoiding drugs. However, a sample of women sex workers followed over 15 years (who moved between various types of work in their careers) demonstrated an above-norm rate of mortality, and significant occupation-related morbidity. The advent of the internet has had a particular impact on this sector, both in promoting services and enabling preliminary negotiation, and allowing sex workers to pass on information including details of problematic customers.[46]

While there has been some attention paid to clients, with the rise of legislation against kerb-crawling and initiatives such as that in Sweden criminalizing the purchase of sex, so far very little is known about the punters, although a number of small-scale localized studies have taken place. A tiny minority are dangerous, murderously targeting sex-workers: most are ordinary law-abiding citizens in regular employment and a majority have other partners. They have various reasons for buying sex, but are predominantly neither sad pathetic outsiders nor seekers of gratification for particularly deviant desires.[47] NATSAL reported a doubling of men paying for sex (or admitting to doing so) between the 1990 and the 2000 surveys, but a lack of information on sexual health and risk behaviours apart from the reported large number of commercial and non-commercial partners. The men in question were mostly single (though might have had a previous marriage), mainly aged 25–34, and there was no association with ethnicity, social class, or education. However, the circumstances in which they paid for sex (apart from sex tourism) were not explored.[48] A survey undertaken by Sandyford Initiative sexual health service in Glasgow found that about half of the men in their sample who paid for sex did so abroad, and approximately a quarter elsewhere in the United Kingdom, and there seemed to be a distinction between those who 'played at home' and those who 'played away' (the latter being less likely to practise safe sex). Men who purchased sex in Glasgow did so in saunas or on the street. There were various sexual health implications including widespread unprotected oral sex.[49]

Over recent years there has been a high degree of concern over the trafficking of women into the United Kingdom, which, although the trade was going in the opposite direction, bears some resemblance to the White Slavery narratives of the early twentieth century in its emphasis on deceit and coercion, and the role of ethnically othered males, emphasizing innocent victimhood in order to garner support.[50] It tends either to conflate women who have migrated illegally to the United Kingdom engaging in sex work with brutalized involuntary conscripts to the trade, or to exclude narratives which do not conform to this particular pattern, for example women who may have been deceived as to the exploitative conditions under which they would be working (this applies similarly to women trafficked for domestic and other labour and in mail-order marriage scenarios), and who may need forms of assistance which are not just about rescue from an abusive situation.[51] A racially-inflected narrative similarly recalling those of the 1900s or 1950s occurred in reports of the 'grooming' of vulnerable young girls for prostitution, in which the role of Asian men was highlighted even though the quality of the data was admittedly 'poor' and local demographics significant.[52]

Other forms of sexual consumption for men have also proliferated, such as 'gentlemen's clubs' with lap-dancing, following the introduction of a new Licensing Act in 2003 which made licences easier to obtain, imposed fewer restrictions on clubs offering eroticized entertainment, and made it more difficult for local protestors to campaign against them.[53] In 2008 the Lap Dancing Association argued against reclassifying their premises as sexual encounter establishments on the grounds that although the entertainment supplied involved nude or semi-nude performers, it was 'not sexually stimulating'. The House of Commons Select Committee was sceptical.[54] It has been argued that besides concerns over the conditions of women working in these clubs, they have a deleterious effect on the safety of women in the neighbourhood; the regulations have now been changed to enable local authorities to license them as sex establishments rather than leisure venues, but this process is not automatic.[55]

Sex and the young

The proliferation of these clubs has been seen as part of a larger phenomenon of 'sexualization' in UK culture in the twenty-first century. This term tends to unhelpfully conflate a number of phenomena. There is a discernable degree of sexual objectification of women in various forms of media and a proliferation of sexual imagery in advertising, on television, in film and fashion, but

some of the concerns expressed recall previous moral panics about the younger generation's wanton and wayward behaviour. Furthermore, the perils of
the impact of sexualization are invoked rather than based on research and the
focus usually on the young. While sex education in schools still remains an
area of contention,[56] and is not a statutory obligation, NATSAL, none the
less, found at the beginning of the decade that the main source of information
on sex for young people was school-based lessons, particularly for young men,
while the extent of parents providing information to daughters had apparently
increased.[57] There appeared to have been some stabilization in the declining
age of first intercourse found during the 1990s survey, along with greater
condom use and employment of contraception, although the numbers of
women reporting sexual activity before age 16 increased. In spite of the positive elements found, early sexual activity continued to be associated, especially
for women, with adverse outcomes, although there was also association with
wider socio-economic factors such as family disruption or low educational
attainment.[58]

With ever-widening access to and use of the internet, this has purportedly
become a major source of sexual knowledge for young people, a somewhat
ambivalent situation. There are frequent media outcries about young people
accessing online porn, often on the basis of simplistic reporting of ill-designed
commercial surveys,[59] but many sites provide sound and useful information for
young people.[60] Panic around the internet, mobile phones and 'sexting'[61] echo
earlier moral panics around 'young people of today' and their engagement with
features of modernity unknown to their forebears. Young people themselves
are usually absent from the debates around sex education and the acquisition
of sexual knowledge, positioned (particularly girls) largely as passive recipients
whether of inappropriate information or healthy understanding about sexuality.[62] Research has demonstrated more active and critical engagement of
young people with the multitude of resources available to them, though also
draws attention to the continuing gender divide and the problems of reaching boys, while the 'savvyness' and scepticism of the young people surveyed
towards media materials does not mean that they are entirely immune to the
messages being conveyed.[63] A report commissioned by Brook, the sexual health
organization for young people, found traditional behind-the-bikeshed myths
about sex and reproduction still circulating, along with pervasive dissatisfaction among young people about school Sex and Relationship Education.[64] In
2011 Nadine Dorries made Parliamentary attempts to introduce abstinence
sex education – for girls only – even though evidence from the United States
suggests that this approach is, if anything, counter-productive, though the bill
was withdrawn before its second reading.[65]

'Problem pages' – in magazines, newspapers, and increasingly as websites –
continue to be a resource for sexual information for those unable or unwilling
to obtain it nearer to hand. This area has so far been understudied, given how
long such columns have existed, although Bingham has some useful observa-
tions relating to the changes affecting in newspaper advice columns in the
1970s, and 'agony aunts' themselves have produced memoirs of their work.[66]
Petra Boynton has noted the supersession of experienced advisors by 'celebrity

advisor' columns ghostwritten by unqualified magazine staff. A particularly noxious instance surfaced in 2010 when 'celebrity agony uncle' Danny Dyer in *Zoo* magazine advised a heartbroken boyfriend to 'cut his ex's face, so no one will want her'. Such advisors are often sexualized figures such as glamour models, young, conventionally attractive, and with some product to promote. The coverage of problems, though superficially a sign of a culture of open sexual discussion, is often conservative and mainstream with a gloss of 'spicy' content, since admitting to sexual problems counters the consumerist lifestyle promoted by these magazines. The emphasis tends to be on performance, pressuring both men and women to be sexually accomplished partners.[67]

New departures

While many issues around sexuality continue to appear intractable or unamenable to legislation, the first decade of the twenty-first century did see a remarkable shift, or perhaps acknowledgement of a shift already underway, in the civil rights of homosexuals, lesbians, and transpeople. In spite of continued opposition from the House of Lords to the government's commitment to equalizing the age of consent, this was finally passed by deploying the Parliament Act, and became law on 1 January 2001 (including Scotland but not Northern Ireland: finally achieved in 2009).[68] The repeal of Section 28 (affecting the extent to which school sex education could positively address homosexuality) was achieved for Scotland in 2000 and England and Wales in 2003[69] (although research by Stonewall indicates that homophobic bullying in schools remains rife[70]). The Employment Equality (Sexual Orientation) Regulations also came into force in 2003.[71] The Sexual Offences Act 2003 made sweeping changes to the existing laws, including consigning specifically homosexual offences to the dustbin of history.[72]

In 2004 gays and lesbians were finally allowed to enter into legally recognized relationships with the passing of the Civil Partnership Act.[73] The 2002 Children and Adoption Act which came into force in 2005 additionally made it possible for same-sex couples to adopt or foster children and lesbian couples were entitled to both be registered as parents of children born through assisted reproduction.[74] While for some people civil partnership does not go far enough in according same-sex couples the status of marriage (but a government consultation on further marriage law reform is promised[75]), for others it normalizes a model of respectable monogamous couple at the expense of more subversive and inclusive possibilities. However, it is also seen as making a significant gesture of commitment, besides conveying various legal protections and benefits to partners. Weeks suggests in a nuanced account of the debates on and the impact of this legislation that civil partnerships add to the range of relationship possibilities, should ultimately be seen more as an important step in the long struggle for recognition, and that the 'very ordinariness of same-sex unions... is surely the most extraordinary achievement of all'.[76]

These developments have not been uncontested. There was a high-profile incident of a registrar refusing to conduct civil partnerships because of religious objections,[77] and some indication that this was not an isolated instance.[78]

Religious objections over same-sex adoptions were invoked by Catholic adoption agencies and in at least one case by a GP who felt himself unable on conscience grounds to provide positive references for same-sex patients of his practice wishing to adopt.[79] Gay couples have also been denied facilities by hoteliers.[80] Although a survey in 2007 found that an overwhelming majority in the United Kingdom supported equal rights and thought that there should be stronger anti-homophobic measures,[81] homophobic attacks, whether purely verbal or involving physical violence, are still widely reported (though victims are still reluctant to inform the police) and may even be increasing.[82] If a massive 'kiss-in' was the response to the ejection of two men for kissing at the John Snow pub in April 2011, at least part of the outrage was because 'You wouldn't think in Soho, this kind of thing would happen'.[83] There are reports of the use of reparative or conversion therapies (with a religious evangelical basis) in the United Kingdom, although professional bodies in the field have issued statements condemning the practice, and a small minority of mental health professionals who would attempt to change clients' sexual orientation if requested.[84]

Transgender people have also been accorded significant rights since 2000 with the passing of the Gender Recognition Act 2004 to give them legal recognition certificates of their acquired gender issued by a Gender Recognition Panel, satisfied that the applicant: has, or has had, gender dysphoria, has lived in the acquired gender throughout the preceding two years, and intends to continue to live in the acquired gender.[85] It may be argued that this reinforces an essentialist and binary view of gender, but at present remains necessary for accessing required medical facilities. However, the very existence of transpeople has opened up a space to think in a more complex fashion about challenging the fixity of gender, and the development of a broader notion of the 'gender queer'.[86] An increasing number of individuals are now seeking gender reassignment, even though issues of prejudice and transphobia continue to present problems.[87] An incident at Gay Pride in 2008 suggested that the acronym LGBT was not as inclusive as it claimed, and there is longstanding hostility among certain radical feminists.[88] A number of support and advocacy groups are in existence for transpeople and their families.[89] The role of the internet in supplying information and support is considerable, and has probably also had a significant impact on the emergence of groups campaigning for or raising awareness of other minority sexualities. There has been growing awareness of intersex conditions and dissemination of information about them.[90] There is also a movement of individuals who self-define as asexual and consider this a valid identity rather than something that needs to be fixed.[91]

Visions of gender

In spite of this increasing attention to the nuanced complexities of gender identity and sexual orientation, popular media and culture tend to promote a narrowly heteronormative vision. A good deal of attention continues to be given to simplistic and populist theories of evolutionary psychology, positing 'common sense' 'just-so stories' concerning binary gender roles and stereotypical views of sexuality.[92] While there may be a greater degree of sexual openness within UK society, much of this is presented within fairly rigid parameters of the acceptable and of what constitutes 'sexy'. This particularly affects women: surveys report that, constantly faced with heavily manipulated images presenting an unrealistic and extremely narrowly defined model of female attractiveness, they are deeply dissatisfied with their bodies even if not seeking surgical remedies, with eating disorders on the rise quite apart from widespread routine dieting.[93] There was a huge furore in 2005 when the 'lads' mag' *Zoo* ran a competition to 'win a boob job for your girlfriend',[94] though a similar prize was also being offered as part of an 'extreme makeover' by a health and beauty magazine.[95] Early in 2012 a coalition of women's groups presented evidence to the Leveson enquiry on the ethics of the press on the objectification and sexualization of women in the media and pervasive sexism in reporting and demanding action.[96]

It is hard to tell how much of the concern over this body dysmorphia is a media construct, but a worrying study was published in the *British Medical Journal* in 2007 about the rise in numbers of women seeking cosmetic genitoplasty ('designer vaginas'), often presenting images from advertisements or pornography (possibly digitally manipulated) of the desired look. It pointed out that many women are not aware of the vast normal variation, and drew attention to the potential negative impact on sexual functioning of operating on sensitive tissues.[97] In a report on related research, comparisons with female genital mutilation were explicitly invoked, suggesting that these elective operations might cause similar problems. An aesthetic plastic surgeon claimed (as a defence of the practice):

> Lads' mags are looked at by girlfriends, and make them think more about the way they look. We live in times where we are much more open about our bodies – and changing them – and labioplasty is simply a part of this.[98]

A 2005 survey purported to reveal that 'A staggering 63% of girls would rather be glamour models than nurses, doctors or teachers' as a result of the impact of celebrity culture',[99] however the composition of the sample and the questions asked were not stated and the poll was conducted by a mobile entertainment company. These figures sit rather incongruously beside repeated claims that women are doing much better than men at school, at gaining university places, and in getting jobs when they graduate, although the narrative in these cases tends to be about male underperformance and perceptions that the educational system favours female strengths.[100] Neither the stereotype of the narcissistic grooming-obsessed 'metrosexual' male, nor his antithesis, the retro-blokish 'lad', are particularly positive or inspiring role models.[101]

While such jeremiads, and the rhetoric of fatherhood rights organizations, seem to posit a society favouring women if not totally dominated by them, alongside a gloomy picture of enfeebled, internet-porn- and violent video-game-addicted manhood,[102] women's situation does not seem entirely positive. Men are still overwhelmingly over-represented in positions of political and economic power, and a recent calculation suggested that it will be nearly a century before women executives attain equal pay.[103] If women get pregnant too young they are stereotyped as feckless and irresponsible, though possibly cunningly qualifying themselves for council housing.[104] Women who delay pregnancy because of career commitments are targeted by repeated warnings that their biological clock is ticking and their ova running out and that all the resources of assisted fertility may not help.[105] If they become mothers they are expected to work on getting their figures back as soon as possible,[106] while if they are looking for clothes and toys for their daughters they discover an explosion of pink sparkly hyperfemininity.[107] Meanwhile there is media agitation about 'ladette' culture of binge-drinking and unfeminine aggressiveness if not actual violence, with fears that this culture is percolating to younger age-groups.[108] A study by Carolyn Jackson and Penny Tinkler, however, draws attention to continuities with previous anxieties about 'modern girls'.[109]

While some of these concerns may relate to anxieties about modern society and the pace of change, others resonate with traditional stigmatization of single mothers or wayward young girls. Also strongly inflected by tradition are issues affecting particular ethnic communities. While, as mentioned above, Muslim women may choose veiling as a gesture of pride in identity, other traditional practices are hard to frame in a positive light and are indeed the focus of campaigning initiatives by women of the communities concerned. There are reports of girls subjected to cultural forms of female genital mutilation either covertly in the United Kingdom or in the country of family origin – FORWARD, an organization established by African Diasporic women in the United Kingdom, campaigns against this practice and provides support.[110] Coerced (as distinct from arranged) marriages are also a problem – Karma Nirvana was set up by Jasvinder Sanghera, herself a survivor of forced marriage, to support victims and survivors of forced marriage and increase reporting of incidence.[111] Karma Nirvana also campaigns against honour-based violence, which may go as far as 'honour killings' by male relatives of women believed to have stained their family's reputation.[112]

It is therefore perhaps not surprising that feminism is undergoing something of a resurgence, facilitated by the internet, although one of the great-grandmother organizations, the Fawcett Society, founded in 1866, descendant of the constitutional suffrage movement, is taking a leading role. This new feminism is inclined to be sceptical about uncritical claims for the 'empowering' nature of lapdancing and stripping and the invocation of 'choice' as a mantra, while eschewing retreat into arguments about decency and indecency.[113]

* * *

The picture early in the second decade of a new millennium is thus extremely ambiguous. The liberation offered by consumerist choice is not that advocated in the late sixties and early seventies – and as Stephen Brooke remarks, 'the major initiatives of the Labour governments of the twenty-first century had little of the utopian flavour' of even earlier reformers[114] – but, none the less, new possibilities have opened up, even if numerous old attitudes and problems persist. It is hard to tell which issues are frothy media-generated spume and which are the token of lasting trends. The current situation in 2012 is troubling: David Cameron's sexist condescension towards female colleagues is at least remarked on and criticized,[115] but his government is presiding over cuts in employment and services disproportionately affecting women,[116] and the National Health Service itself is beleaguered.[117] How all this will play out in the ongoing story of the intricate relationships between sex, gender and social change in the United Kingdom remains to be seen.

Coda: Sex, Gender and Social Change in Britain: What Next for the Historian?

The study of the history of sexuality is becoming increasingly legitimized, and between the publication of the first edition of *Sex, Gender and Social Change* in 2000 and the preparation of a second edition in 2011/12 there was an explosion of relevant historiography. However, significant gaps remain in our knowledge and there are areas still to be fully explored.

Some productive developments are already under way, and I look forward to further studies manifesting the 'spatial' turn, looking at the way certain matters played out in specific localized contexts; in particular, I hope for more studies of local cultures of policing of prostitution and homosexuality and the consequent possibility of comparative analyses. Similarly, work on the particular circumstances leading to the establishment of local birth control clinics from the 1920s is already shedding light on how this contested and controversial issue was dealt with in a range of localities, although relatively few of the hundreds of local clinics have yet been studied.

There are other areas in which attention to local practice would surely prove fruitful. In particular, sex education: it is time to move beyond the caution of Whitehall, and the tentative approaches of professional groups, to investigate where sex education was happening, who was undertaking it, and what it consisted of; and what local opinion on the development was. Emma Jones has already shown what is possible with local press reports and court records in uncovering networks of illegal abortion but this could well be extended. The activities of local morality organizations might also be usefully pursued, for example in matters of censorship.

Going on from these suggestions, I should really like to see nuanced micro-historical studies of localized sexual cultures as manifested through development or non-development of birth control clinics and sex education; the policing of prostitution, homosexuality, and abortion; and how local individuals and organizations were involved in these questions.

There is still a relative lack of attention to issues around male sexuality except in the specific area of homosexuality. Further studies on changing paradigms of heterosexuality would be illuminating, and might indicate different modes of 'normal' masculinity as inflected by class, region, ethnicity, religion, and so on. There has also been relatively little work on heterosexual courtship, and possibly even less on forms of heterosexual interaction which were not framed by marriage or intended marriage. There are pervasive hints of a culture of more casual contacts, not to mention the high-minded, open marriage experiments of intellectuals and bohemians.

Questions of the dissemination of ideas about sexuality remain very much open. Further work on sex education may help with working out what sort of sexual knowledge was being conveyed, though what one would really like to know is what 'knowledge' was being conveyed by 'Johnny Jones' and similar peer educators behind the bikesheds and equivalent venues. Another area so far under-explored except very superficially is the role of women's and other life-style magazines in conveying changing notions of sexuality and how to negotiate changing sexual mores. While it seems unlikely that many publishers in the area will have retained actual letters to the problem pages, the problem pages themselves – what could be published and what answers provided – shed some light on attitudes, as would articles more generally on health and relationship issues.

While it has been proved that there is still more to be got out of looking at the immense complexity of Victorian sexual attitudes and behaviour, there is much room for further work on the twentieth century. Some portions, such as the interwar period, in particular the 1920s, and the 1950s, have been getting a good deal more attention than hitherto but there is still plenty to be done, in particular for more recent decades.

I hope to see productive interactions between people working in the histories of gender and sexuality and those in related fields such as history of the emotions and history of the body, as well as those traditionally connected fields of history of medicine, legal history, and history of demography and the family, and more exciting work emerging in spite of the problems currently facing the historical profession and academia in general.

Notes

Introduction

1. Lucy Bland, *Banishing the Beast: English Feminism and Sexual Morality, 1885–1914* (London: Penguin, 1995); Michael Mason, *The Making of Victorian Sexuality* (Oxford: Oxford University Press, 1994) and *The Making of Victorian Sexual Attitudes* (Oxford: Oxford University Press, 1994); Roy Porter and Lesley A. Hall, *The Facts of Life: The Creation of Sexual Knowledge in Britain, 1650–1950* (New Haven, CT, and London: Yale University Press, 1995); Simon Szreter, *Fertility, Class and Gender in Britain, 1860–1940* (Cambridge: Cambridge University Press, 1996).
2. Jane Lewis, *The End of Marriage: Individualism and Intimate Relations* (Cheltenham: Edward Elgar, 2001).
3. Michel Foucault (trans. Robert Hurley), *The History of Sexuality: An Introduction* (London: Allen Lane, 1978).
4. Robert Proctor and Londa Schiebinger, *Agnotology: The Making and Unmaking of Ignorance* (Palo Alto, CA: Stanford University Press, 2008).
5. Kate Fisher, *Birth Control, Sex, and Marriage in Britain, 1918–1960* (Oxford: Oxford University Press, 2006), 26–75; Simon Szreter and Kate Fisher, *Sex before the Sexual Revolution: Intimate Life in England 1918–1963* (Cambridge: Cambridge University Press, 2010), 63–100.
6. Royal Commission on Venereal Diseases: First Report of the Commissioners [Cd 7474] 1914, Evidence of Dr Helen Wilson, §5647.
7. Lesley A. Hall, *Hidden Anxieties: Male Sexuality, 1900–1950* (Oxford: Polity Press, 1991), 164.
8. Barbara Brookes, *Abortion in England, 1900–1967* (London: Croom Helm, 1988), 14–15.
9. Lesley A. Hall, ' "No Sex, Please, We're Socialists": The Labour Party prefers to close its eyes and think of the electorate', *Socialist History*, 36 (2010), 11–28.
10. Anna Clark, *Desire: A History of European Sexualiy* (London: Routledge, 2008), 6–7.
11. Tanya Evans, 'The Other Woman and her Child: Extra-marital affairs and illegitimacy in twentieth-century Britain', *Women's History Review*, 20 (2011), 67–86; Ginger S. Frost, *Living in Sin: Cohabiting as Husband and Wife in Nineteenth-Century England* (Manchester, Manchester University Press, 2008).
12. David Nash and Anne Marie Kilday, *Cultures of Shame: Exploring Crime and Morality in Britain 1600–1900* (Basingstoke: Palgrave Macmillan, 2010).
13. Lesley A. Hall, 'Venereal Diseases and Society in Britain from the Contagious Diseases Acts to the National Health Service', in Roger Davidson and Lesley Hall (eds), *Sex, Sin, and Suffering: Venereal diseases and European Society since 1870* (London: Routledge, 2001), 120–36.
14. Julia Laite, *Common Prostitutes and Ordinary Citizens: Commercial Sex in London, 1885–1960* (Basingstoke: Palgrave Macmillan, 2011).
15. Sean Brady, *Masculinity and Male Homosexuality in Britain, 1861–1913* (Basingstoke: Palgrave Macmillan, 2005), 101–18.

16. Alan Travis, *Bound and Gagged: A secret history of obscenity in Britain* (London: Profile Books, 2000), 98.
17. Pamela Cox, *Gender, Justice and Welfare: Bad Girls in Britain, 1900–1950* (Basingstoke: Palgrave Macmillan, 2003).
18. David Vincent, *The Culture of Secrecy: Britain 1832–1998* (Oxford: Oxford University Press, 1998), 22–3, 95–106, 158–66.
19. Several versions at http://myweb.tiscali.co.uk/navysong/Data/S0028.htm [Accessed 16 Oct. 2011].
20. Emma L Jones, 'Abortion in England, 1861–1967', PhD thesis, University of London, 2007 and 'Representations of illegal abortionists in England, 1900–1967', in Andrew Mangham and Greta DePledge (eds), *The Female Body in Medicine and Literature* (Liverpool University Press, 2011), 196–215.
21. Adrian Ager and Catherine Lee, 'Prostitution in the Medway Towns, 1860–1885', *Local Population Studies*, 83 (2009), 39–55; Maria Luddy, *Prostitution and Irish Society, 1800–1940* (Cambridge: Cambridge University Press, 2007); Leanne McCormick, *Regulating Sexuality: Women in Twentieth-Century Northern Ireland* (Manchester: Manchester University Press, 2010); Stefan Slater, 'Pimps, Police and Filles de Joie: Foreign Prostitution in Interwar London', *The London Journal*, 3 (2007), 53–74; Laite, *Common Prostitutes and Ordinary Citizens*.
22. *Downward Paths: An Enquiry into the Causes which Contribute to the Making of the Prostitute. With a Foreword by A. Maude Royden* (London: G. Bell & Sons, 1916), 7–9.
23. E. Lewis-Faning, *Papers from the Royal Commission on Population*, Vol. 1: *Report on an Enquiry into Family Limitation and its influence on Human Fertility during the Past Fifty Years Conducted at the Request of the Royal Commission on Population* (London: HMSO, 1949); Eliot Slater and Moya Woodside, *Patterns of Marriage: A study of marriage relationships in the urban working classes* (London: Cassell, 1951), 94–115; Liz Stanley, *Sex Surveyed, 1949–1994: From Mass-Observation's 'Little Kinsey' to the National Survey and the Hite Reports* (London: Taylor & Francis, 1995).
24. Adrian Bingham, *Family Newspapers? Sex, Private Life and the British Popular Press, 1918–1978* (Oxford: Oxford University Press, 2009), 229–61.
25. Roger Davidson, *Dangerous Liaisons: The social history of VD in twentieth-century Scotland* (Amsterdam: Rodopi, 2000).
26. Roger Davidson and Gayle Davis, *The Sexual State: Sexuality and Scottish Governance 1950–80* (Edinburgh: Edinburgh University Press, 2012).
27. Fisher, *Birth Control, Sex, and Marriage*, and '"Teach the Miners Birth Control": The Delivery of Contraceptive Advice in South Wales, 1918–1950', in Pamela Michael and Charles Webster (eds), *Health and Society in Twentieth-Century Wales* (Cardiff: University of Wales Press, 2006), 143–64.
28. Szreter and Fisher, *Sex before the Sexual Revolution*.
29. Russell Davies, *Secret Sins: Sex, Violence and Society in Carmarthenshire, 1870–1920* (Cardiff: University of Wales Press, 1996); Margaret Douglas, 'Women, God and Birth Control: The first hospital birth control clinic', *Llafur*, 6:4 (1995), 110–22; Fisher, '"Teach the Miners Birth Control"; Julie Grier, 'Eugenics and Birth Control: Contraceptive Provision in North Wales, 1918–1939', *Social History of Medicine*, 11 (1998), 443–58.
30. Jeffrey Weeks, *The World We Have Won: The Remaking of Erotic and Intimate Life* (London: Routledge, 2007).
31. Tony Fahey, 'Religion and Sexual Culture in Ireland', in Franz X. Eder, Lesley Hall, and Gert Hekma (eds), *Sexual Cultures in Europe: National Histories*

(Manchester: Manchester University Press, 1999), 53–70; Diarmaid Ferriter, *Occasions of Sin: Sex and society in modern Ireland* (London: Profile Books, 2009); Greta Jones, 'Marie Stopes in Ireland: The Mothers' Clinic in Belfast', *Social History of Medicine*, 5 (1992), 255–77; Luddy, *Prostitution and Irish Society*, McCormick, *Regulating Sexuality*.

32. Szreter, *Fertility, Class and Gender*, 283–432.

33. Harry Cocks, *Nameless Offences: Homosexual desire in the 19th century* (London: I. B. Tauris, 2003), 157–98; Sheila Rowbotham, *Edward Carpenter: A Life of Liberty and Love* (London: Verso, 2008); http: //menmedia.co.uk/manchestere veningnews/news/s/1408659_secrets_out_on_the_hidden_life_of_gay_victorians [accessed 4 Aug. 2011].

34. Jeff Weeks, *Sex, Politics, and Society: The regulation of sexuality in Britain since 1800* (London: Longman, 1981).

35. Brady, *Masculinity and Male Homosexuality*; Cocks, *Nameless Offences*; Charles Upchurch, *Before Wilde: Sex between Men in Britain's Age of Reform* (Berkeley CA: University of California Press, 2009); Matt Cook, *London and the Culture of Homosexuality, 1885–1914* (Cambridge: Cambridge University Press, 2008); Matt Houlbrook, *Queer London: Perils and Pleasures in the Sexual Metropolis, 1918–1957* (Chicago: University of Chicago Press, 2005).

36. Laura Doan, *Fashioning Sapphism: The origins of a modern English lesbian culture* (New York: Columbia University Press, 2001); Sharon Marcus, *Between Women: Friendship, Desire, and Marriage in Victorian England* (Princeton, NJ: Princeton University Press, 2007); Alison Oram, *Her Husband was a Woman!: Women's gender-crossing and twentieth-century British popular culture* (London: Routledge, 2007); Martha Vicinus, *Intimate Friends: Women Who Loved Women, 1778–1928* (Chicago: University of Chicago Press, 2004).

37. Hera Cook, *The Long Sexual Revolution: English Women, Sex, and Contraception 1800–1975* (Oxford: Oxford University Press, 2004); Fisher, *Birth Control, Sex, and Marriage*; Szreter and Fisher, *Sex before the Sexual Revolution*.

38. Paula Bartley, *Prostitution: Prevention and Reform in Britain, 1860–1914* (London: Routledge, 1999); Laite, *Common Prostitutes and Ordinary Citizens*; Catherine Lee, *Policing Prostitution, 1856–1886: Deviance, Surveillance and Morality* (London: Pickering & Chatto, 2012); Luddy, *Prostitution in Ireland*; Helen Self, *Prostitution, Women and Misuse of the Law: The Fallen Daughters of Eve* (London: Cass, 2003).

39. Adrian Bingham, *Gender, Modernity, and the Popular Press in Inter-War Britain* (Oxford: Oxford University Press, 2004), and *Family Newspapers?*; Oram, *Her Husband was a Woman*.

40. Lucy Bland, 'White Women and Men of Colour: Miscegenation Fears in Britain after the Great War', *Gender and History*, 17 (2005), 29–61; Philippa Levine, *Prostitution, Race, and Politics: Policing Venereal Disease in the British Empire* (London: Routledge, 2003); Lisa Z. Sigel, *Governing Pleasures: Pornography and Social Change in England, 1815–1914* (New Brunswick: Rutgers University Press, 2002), 50–80; Laura Tabili, 'Women "of a Very Low Type": Crossing Racial Boundaries in Imperial Britain', in Laura L. Frader and Sonya O. Rose (eds), *Gender and Class in Modern Europe* (Ithaca, NY: Cornell University Press, 1996), 165–90; Wendy Webster, *Imagining Home: Gender, 'Race' and National Identity, 1945–64* (London: UCL Press, 1998).

41. Jenny Birchall, '"The Carnival Revels of Manchester's Vagabonds": Young Working-Class Women and Monkey Parades in the 1870's', *Women's History Review*, 15 (2006), 229–52; Harry Cocks, 'Saucy Stories: Pornography, sex-

ology, and the marketing of sexual knowledge in Britain, c. 1918–70' *Social History*, 29 (2004), 465–84; Matt Houlbrook, 'The Private World of Public Urinals in London, 1918–1957', *The London Journal*, 25 (2000), 52–70; Frank Mort, 'Striptease: The erotic female body and live sexual entertainment in mid-twentieth-century London', *Social History*, 32 (2007), 27–53.

1 The Victorian Background

1. http://www.lesleyahall.net/factoids.htm [accessed 4 Aug. 2011].
2. e.g. Deborah Lutz, *Pleasure Bound: Victorian Sex Rebels and the New Eroticism* (New York: W. W. Norton, 2010).
3. Joanna de Groot, ' "Sex" and "race": The construction of language and image in the nineteenth century', in Catherine Hall (ed.), *Cultures of Empire: A Reader: Colonizers in Britain and the Empire in the nineteenth and twentieth centuries* (Manchester: Manchester University Press, 2000), 37–60; Philippa Levine, *Prostitution, Race, and Politics: Policing Venereal Disease in the British Empire* (London: Routledge, 2003); Anne McClintock, *Imperial Leather: Race, gender and sexuality in the Colonial context* (London: Routledge, 1995).
4. Stephen Cretney, *Family Law in the Twentieth Century: A History* (Oxford: Oxford University Press, 2003), 162–95.
5. A. James Hammerton, *Cruelty and Companionship: Conflict in Nineteenth-Century Married Life* (London: Routledge, 1992); Gail Savage, ' "The Wilful Communication of a Loathsome Disease": Marital Conflict and Venereal Disease in Victorian England', *Victorian Studies*, 34 (1990), 35–54.
6. Gail Savage, 'The Operation of the 1857 Divorce Act, 1860–1910: A Research Note', *Journal of Social History*, 16:4 (1983), 103–10.
7. Gail Savage, 'They Would if They Could: Class, Gender, and Popular Representation of English Divorce Litigation, 1858–1908', *Journal of Family History*, 26 (2011), 173–90.
8. Olive Anderson, 'State, civil society and separation in Victorian marriage', *Past and Present*, 163 (1999), 161–201.
9. Eleanor Gordon and Gwyneth Nair, *Public Lives: Women, Family, and Society in Victorian Britain* (New Haven, CT: Yale University Press, 2003), 72–5.
10. Cretney, *Family Law*, 94–102; Lee Holcombe, *Wives and Property: Reform of the Married Women's Property Law in Nineteenth-Century England* (Toronto: University of Toronto Press, 1983); Mary Lyndon Shanley, *Feminism, Marriage, and the Law in Victorian England,1850–1895* (Princeton, NJ: Princeton University Press, 1989).
11. Ursula Henriques, 'Bastardy and the New Poor Law', *Past and Present*, 37 (1967), 103–29.
12. Shanley, *Feminism, Marriage, and the Law*. Nancy Fix Anderson, ' "Not a Fit or Proper Person": Annie Besant's Struggle for Child Custody, 1878–9', and Ann Sumner Holmes ' "Fallen Mothers": Maternal Adultery and Child Custody in England, 1886–1925', in Claudia Nelson and Ann Sumner Holmes (eds), *Maternal Instincts: Visions of Motherhood and Sexuality in Britain, 1875–1925* (Basingstoke and London: Macmillan Press, 1997), 13–36, 37–57.
13. Anna Clark, 'Humanity or Justice? Wife-beating and the law in the eighteenth and nineteenth centuries', in Carol Smart (ed.), *Regulating Womanhood: Essays on marriage, motherhood and sexuality* (London: Routledge, 1992), 187–206; Maeve E. Doggett, *Marriage, Wife-Beating and the Law in Victorian England* (Columbia, SC: University of South Carolina Press, 1993); Shanley, *Feminism, Marriage, and the Law*, 164–74.

14. J. L. Barton, 'The Story of Marital Rape', *Law Quarterly Review*, 108 (1992), 260–71.
15. Gail Savage, ' "... the instrument of an animal function": Marital Rape and Sexual Cruelty in the Divorce Court, 1858–1908', in Lucy Delap, Ben Griffin and Abigail Wills (eds), *The Politics of Domestic Authority in Britain since 1800* (Basingstoke, Palgrave Macmillan, 2009), 43–57.
16. Martin J. Wiener, 'The Sad Story of George Hall. Adultery, Murder and the Politics of Mercy in Mid-Victorian England', *Social History* 24 (1999), 174–96.
17. David Nash and Anne-Marie Kilday, *Cultures of Shame: Exploring crime and morality in Britain 1600–1900* (Basingstoke: Palgrave Macmillan, 2010), 134–52.
18. Cynthia Fansler Behrman, 'The Annual Blister: A Sidelight on Victorian Social and Parliamentary History', *Victorian Studies*, 11 (1968), 483–502; Philippa Levine, *Victorian Feminism* (London: Hutchison, 1987), 142.
19. J. Miriam Benn, *The Predicaments of Love* (London: Pluto Press, 1992); Sandra Stanley Holton, 'Free Love and Victorian Feminism: The Divers Matrimonials of Elizabeth Wolstenholme and Ben Elmy', *Victorian Studies*, 37 (1994), 199–222.
20. Ginger S. Frost, *Living in Sin: Cohabiting as Husband and Wife in Nineteenth-Century England* (Manchester, Manchester University Press, 2008).
21. Ellen Jordan, *The Women's Movement and Women's Employment in Nineteenth-Century Britain* (London: Routledge, 2000); Levine, *Victorian Feminism*.
22. Gordon and Nair, *Public Lives*.
23. Françoise Barret-Ducrocq, *Love in the Time of Victoria: Sexuality, Class and Gender in Nineteenth-Century London* (London: Verso, 1991).
24. William Acton, 'Unmarried Wet-Nurses', *The Lancet*, I (1859), 175–6.
25. Paula Bartley, *Prostitution: Prevention and Reform in Britain, 1860–1914* (London: Routledge, 1999).
26. Nash and Kilday, *Cultures of Shame*, 153–72.
27. John Tosh, *A Man's Place: Masculinity and the Middle-Class Home in Victorian England* (New Haven, CT: Yale University Press, 1999); Sean Brady, *Masculinity and Male Homosexuality in Britain, 1861–1913* (Basingstoke: Palgrave Macmillan, 2005), 25–49; Megan Doolittle, 'Fatherhood and Family Shame: Masculinity, Welfare and the Workhouse in Late Nineteenth-Century England', in Lucy Delap, Ben Griffin and Abigail Wills (eds), *The Politics of Domestic Authority in Britain since 1800* (Basingstoke: Palgrave Macmillan, 2009), 84–108.
28. Iain McCalman, *Radical Underworld: Prophets, Revolutionaries, and Pornographers in London, 1795–1840* (Oxford: Oxford University Press, 1988); Lisa Z. Sigel, *Governing Pleasures: Pornography and social change in England, 1815–1914* (New Brunswick NJ: Rutgers University Press, 2002), 50–80.
29. Philip Howell, 'Sex and the City of Bachelors. Sporting Guidebooks and Urban Knowledge in Nineteenth-Century Britain and America', *Ecumene* 8 (2001), 20–51.
30. Alfred Swain Taylor, *The Principles and Practice of Medical Jurisprudence* (London: John Churchill and Sons, 1865), 989–1018.
31. Carolyn A. Conley, 'Rape and Justice in Victorian England', *Victorian Studies*, 29 (1986), 519–36; Shani d'Cruze, *Crimes of Outrage: Sex, violence and Victorian working woman* (London: UCL Press, 1998); Kim Stevenson, ' "Ingenuities of the female mind": Legal and public perceptions of sexual violence in Victorian England, 1850–1890', and Joanne Jones ' "She resisted with all her might": Sexual violence against women in late C19th Manchester and the local press', in Shani D'Cruze (ed.), *Everyday Violence in Britain, 1850–1950: Gender and Class* (Harlow: Longman, 2000), 89–103 and 104–18; Nancy Tomes, 'A "Torrent of

Abuse": Crimes of violence between working-class men and women in London, 1840–1875', *Journal of Social History*, 11 (1978), 328–45.

32. Louise Jackson, *Child Sex Abuse and the Law in Victorian England* (London: Routledge, 2000).

33. Ginger Frost, *Promises Broken: Courtship, class and gender in Victorian England* (Charlottesville, VA: University Press of Virginia, 1995).

34. Henriques, 'Bastardy and the New Poor Law'.

35. George K. Behlmer, 'Deadly Motherhood: Infanticide and Medical Opinion in Mid-Victorian England', *Journal of the History of Medicine*, 34 (1979), 403–27; Daniel Grey, *Degrees of Guilt: Infanticide in England 1860–1960* (Liverpool: Liverpool University Press, forthcoming); Ann R. Higginbotham, '"Sin of the Age": Infanticide and Illegitimacy in Victorian London', *Victorian Studies*, 32 (1989), 319–37; Christine L. Krueger, 'Literary Defences and Medical Prosecutions: Representing Infanticide in Nineteenth-Century Britain', *Victorian Studies*, 40 (1997), 271–94.

36. Ginger Frost,. '"I am master here": Illegitimacy, Masculinity and Violence in Victorian England', in Lucy Delap, Ben Griffin and Abigail Wills (eds), *The Politics of Domestic Authority in Britain since 1800* (Basingstoke, Palgrave Macmillan, 2009), 27–42.

37. Offences against the Person Act 1861, 24o and 25o Victoriae, Cap. 100.

38. Taylor, *The Principles and Practice of Medical Jurisprudence* (1865), 1018.

39. Brady, *Masculinity and Male Homosexuality*; H. G. Cocks, *Nameless Offences: Homosexual desire in the 19th century* (London: I. B. Tauris, 2003); Angus McLaren, *Sexual Blackmail: A Modern History* (Cambridge MA: Harvard University Press, 2002), 10–29; Charles Upchurch, *Before Wilde: Sex between Men in Britain's Age of Reform* (Berkeley CA: University of California Press, 2009).

40. Edward Leeves, *Leaves from a Victorian Diary: With an Introduction by John Sparrow* (London: The Alison Press/Secker & Warburg, 1985).

41. Morris B. Kaplan, *Sodom on the Thames: Sex, Love and Scandal in Wilde Times* (Ithaca, NY: Cornell University Press, 2005), 102–65.

42. Ian Anstruther, *Oscar Browning: A biography* (London: John Murray, 1983); Kaplan, *Sodom on the Thames*, 107–9.

43. Brady, *Masculinity and Male Homosexuality*, 162–5.

44. William A. Cohen, *Sex Scandal: The Private Parts of Victorian Fiction* (Durham, NC: Duke University Press, 1996), 73–129; Kaplan, *Sodom on the Thames*, 19–101.

45. Chiara Beccalossi, *Female Sexual Inversion: Same-Sex Desires in Italian and British Sexology, c.1870–1920* (Basingstoke: Palgrave Macmillan, 2012), 79–103.

46. Martha Vicinus, 'Lesbian Perversity and Victorian Marriage: The 1864 Codrington Divorce Trial', *Journal of British Studies*, 26 (1997), 70–98.

47. Martha Vicinus, *Independent Women: Work and community for single women, 1850–1920* (London: Virago, 1985), *Intimate Friends: Women Who Loved Women, 1778–1928* (Chicago: University of Chicago Press, 2004) and 'The Gift of Love. Nineteenth-Century Religion and Lesbian Passion', *Nineteenth-Century Contexts*, 23 (2001), 241–65. Elizabeth Baigent, 'Anne Lister (1791–1840)', *Oxford Dictionary of National Biography*, Oxford University Press, 2004 [http://0-www.oxforddnb.com.libsys.wellcome.ac.uk/view/article/37678 (accessed 8 Aug. 2011)]; Elizabeth Edwards, 'Homoerotic Friendship and College Principals, 1880–1960', *Women's History Review*, 4 (1995), 149–63; Sharon Marcus, *Between Women: Friendship, Desire, and Marriage in Victorian England* (Princeton, NJ: Princeton University Press, 2007); Pauline Phipps, 'Faith, Desire, and Sexual Identity: Constance

Maynard's Atonement for Passion', *Journal of the History of Sexuality*, 18 (2009), 265–86.

48. Bartley, *Prostitution: Prevention and Reform*.

49. Adrian Ager and Catherine Lee, 'Prostitution in the Medway Towns, 1860–1885', *Local Population Studies*, 83 (2009), 39–55; Catherine Lee, *Policing Prostitution, 1856–1886: Deviance, Surveillance and Morality* (London: Pickering and Chatto, 2012); Maria Luddy, *Prostitution and Irish Society, 1800–1940* (Cambridge: Cambridge University Press, 2007).

50. *Report of the Committee Appointed to Enquire into the Pathology and Treatment of Venereal Disease, with the View to Diminish its Injurious Effects on the Men of the Army and Navy*, Cd. 4031, 1868.

51. Philip Howell, 'A Private Contagious Diseases Act. Prostitution and Public Space in Victorian Cambridge', *Journal of Historical Geography*, 26 (2000), 376–402.

52. Levine, *Prostitution, Race, and Politics*, 37–41.

53. Lesley A. Hall, ' "War always brings it on": War, STDs, the military, and the civilian population in Britain, 1850–1950', in Roger Cooter, Mark Harrison and Steve Sturdy (eds), *Medicine and Modern Warfare* (Amsterdam: Rodopi, 1999), 205–23.

54. Paul McHugh, *Prostitution and Victorian Social Reform* (London: Croom Helm, 1980); Frank Mort, *Dangerous Sexualities: Medico-moral politics in Britain since 1830* (London: Routledge & Kegan Paul, 1987), 174–6; Judith R. Walkowitz, *Prostitution and Victorian Society: Women, class and the state* (Cambridge and New York: Cambridge University Press, 1980); F. B. Smith, 'The Contagious Diseases Acts reconsidered', *Social History of Medicine*, 3 (1990), 197–215; Deborah Dunsford, 'Principle versus expediency: A rejoinder to F. B. Smith', *Social History of Medicine*, 5 (1992), pp. 503–13; F. B. Smith, ' "Unprincipled expediency": A comment on Deborah Dunsford's paper', *Social History of Medicine*, 5 (1992), 515–16.

55. Alan Hunt, *Governing Morals: A social history of moral regulation* (Cambridge: Cambridge University Press, 1999), 57–76.

56. 'Social Evil Abstracts' (Scrapbooks of William Acton), The Women's Library, London Metropolitan University.

57. Edward Bristow, *Vice and Vigilance: Purity movements in Britain since 1700* (Dublin: Gee & Macmillan, 1977), 46–9; M. J. D. Roberts, 'Morals, Art, and the Law: The Passing of the Obscene Publications Act, 1857', *Victorian Studies*, 28 (1985), 609–29.

58. Mary Wilson Carpenter, *Imperial Bibles, Domestic Bodies: Women, Sexuality, and Religion in the Victorian Market* (Athens, OH: Ohio University Press, 2003), 33–47.

59. Michael Mason, *The Making of Victorian Sexuality* (Oxford: Oxford University Press, 1994); *The Making of Victorian Sexual Attitudes* (Oxford: Oxford University Press, 1994).

60. Sigel, *Governing Pleasures*.

61. Ivan Crozier, 'Rough Winds do Shake the Darling Buds of May. A Note on William Acton and the Sexuality of the (Male) Child', *Journal of Family History*, 26 (2001), 411–20; Lesley A. Hall, 'Forbidden by God, despised by men: Masturbation, medical warnings, moral panic and manhood in Britain, 1850–1950', *Journal of the History of Sexuality*, 2 (1992), reprinted in John C. Fout (ed.), *Forbidden History: The State, Society, and the Regulation of Sexuality in Modern Europe* (Chicago: University of Chicago Press, 1992), 293–318; Lesley A Hall, ' "It was the doctors who were suffering from it": The history

of masturbatory insanity revisited', *Paedagogica Historica: International Journal of the History of Education*, 39 (2003), 686–99; Alan Hunt, 'The Great Masturbation Panic and the Discourses of Moral Regulation in late Nineteenth and early Twentieth Century Britain', *Journal of the History of Sexuality*, 8 (1998), 575–615.

62. Robert Darby, *A Surgical Temptation: The Demonization of the Foreskin and the Rise of Circumcision in Britain* (Chicago: University of Chicago Press, 2005), 118–214; Roy Porter and Lesley Hall, *The Facts of Life: The Creation of Sexual Knowledge in Britain, 1680–1950*, (New Haven, CT, and London: Yale University Press, 1995), 132–54; Ellen Bayuk Rosenman, *Unauthorized Pleasures: Accounts of Victorian Erotic Experience* (Ithaca, NY: Cornell University Press, 2003), 16–49; Elizabeth Stephens, 'Pathologising Leaky Male Bodies: Spermatorrhoea in C19th British medicine and popular anatomical museums', *Journal of the History of Sexuality*, 17 (2008), 421–38.

63. Laurie Garrison, ' "She read on more eagerly, almost breathlessly": Mary Elizabeth Braddon's challenge to medical depictions of female masturbation in *The Doctor's Wife*', in Andrew Mangham and Greta DePledge (eds), *The Female Body in Medicine and Literature* (Liverpool: Liverpool University Press, 2011), 148–68.

64. Ornella Moscucci, 'Clitoridectomy, circumcision, and the politics of sexual pleasure in Mid-Victorian Britain', in Andrew H. Miller and James Eli Adams (eds), *Sexualities in Victorian Britain* (Bloomington, IN: Indiana University Press, 1997), 60–78; Porter and Hall, *The Facts of Life*, 147–8.

65. M. L. Bush, *What is Love?: Richard Carlile's Philosophy of Sex* (London: Verso, 1998).

66. Lesley A. Hall, 'Malthusian mutations: The changing politics and moral meanings of birth control in Britain', in Brian Dolan and Roy Porter (eds), *Malthus, Medicine and Morality: 'Malthusianism' after 1798* (Amsterdam: Rodopi, 2000), 141–63.

67. Hera Cook, *The Long Sexual Revolution: English Women, Sex, and Contraception 1800–1975* (Oxford: Oxford University Press, 2004); Simon Szreter, *Fertility, Class and Gender in Britain, 1860–1940* (Cambridge: Cambridge University Press, 1996), 310–439.

68. Rachel Maines, *The Technology of Orgasm: "Hysteria," the Vibrator, and Women's Sexual Satisfaction* (Baltimore, MD: Johns Hopkins University Press, 1998).

69. T. Lauder Brunton, *A text-book of pharmacology, therapeutics and materia medica* (London: Macmillan, 1885), 723.

70. Iwan Rhys Morus, *Shocking bodies: Life, death and electricity in Victorian England* (Stroud: History Press, 2011), 136–82.

71. http://www.lesleyahall.net/factoids.htm#hysteria: [Accessed Jul. 2011].

72. Anonymous correspondent to Marie Stopes, Stopes papers in the Wellcome Library, PP/MCS/A.1/25.

2 Social Purity and Evolving Sex in the 1880s

1. Lesley A. Hall 'Hauling down the Double Standard: Feminism, social purity, and sexual science in late nineteenth century Britain', *Gender and History*, 16 (2004), 36–56; Michael Mason, *The Making of Victorian Sexual Attitudes* (Oxford: Oxford University Press, 1994), 49–63.

2. Miss Agnes Cotton to Miss L. M. Hubbard, 16 July 1880 or 1881, Autograph Letters 12B, The Women's Library, London Metropolitan University.

3. 'A Grave Social Problem', *British Medical Journal*, II (1881), 904–5.

4. F. W. Lowndes, 'Venereal and Sexual Hypochondriasis', *British Medical Journal*, II (1883), 564–5.

5. *Tricks and Traps of London: An Exposure of the Frauds, Vices, & c. of Metropolitan London* (London: T. Owen, *c*.1880), in 'Sex, Population and Eugenics', John Johnson Collection at the Bodleian Library, Oxford; *The Sporting Times: Otherwise Known as the 'Pink' 'Un'*, no. 1111 (1885).

6. Edward Bristow, *Vice and Vigilance: Purity Movements in Britain since 1700* (Dublin: Gill & Macmillan, 1977), 203–4.

7. Lee Holcombe, *Wives and Property: Reform of the Married Women's Property Law in Nineteenth-Century England* (Toronto: University of Toronto Press, 1983); Mary Lyndon Shanley, *Feminism, Marriage, and the Law in Victorian England, 1850–1895* (Princeton, NJ: Princeton University Press, 1989).

8. Gail Savage, ' "... the instrument of an animal function": Marital Rape and Sexual Cruelty in the Divorce Court, 1858–1908', in Lucy Delap, Ben Griffin and Abigail Wills (eds), *The Politics of Domestic Authority in Britain since 1800* (Basingstoke, Palgrave Macmillan, 2009), pp 43–57; Shanley, *Feminism, Marriage, and the Law*, 158.

9. Lucy Bland, *Banishing the Beast: English Feminism and Sexual Morality, 1885–1914* (London: Penguin, 1995), 124–30.

10. Jane Jordan, *Josephine Butler* (London: John Murray, 2001); Anne Summers, '*The Constitution Violated*: The Female Body and the Female Subject in the Campaigns of Josephine Butler', *History Workshop Journal* , 48 (1998), 1–15.

11. Deborah Gorham, 'The "Maiden Tribute of Modern Babylon" re-examined: Child prostitution and the idea of childhood in late-Victorian England', *Victorian Studies*, 21 (1978), 353–79; M. J. D. Roberts, 'Feminism and the State in Later Victorian England', *The Historical Journal*, 38 (1995), 85–110.

12. Gorham, 'The "Maiden Tribute ... " re-examined'; W. T. Stead, The Maiden Tribute of Modern Babylon: The Report of the Secret Commission (ed., with annotations and introductory essay, Antony E. Simpson) (Lambertville, N.J.:The True Bill Press: 2007); Judith R. Walkowitz, *City of Dreadful Delight: Narratives of sexual danger in late-Victorian London* (London: Virago, 1992), 81–134.

13. 'Liverpool: A Hideous Superstition', *The Lancet*, I (1884), 963; Frederick W. Lowndes, 'Venereal Diseases in Girls of Tender Age', *The Lancet*, I (1887), 168–9.

14. Julia Laite, *Common Prostitutes and Ordinary Citizens: Commercial Sex in London, 1885–1960* (Basingstoke: Palgrave, 2011), 54–62, 70–7; Stefan Petrow, *Policing Morals: The Metropolitan Police and the Home Office, 1870–1914* (Oxford: Clarendon Press, 1994), 131–6; M. J. D. Roberts, *Making English Morals: Voluntary Association and Moral Reform in England, 1787–1886* (2004), 263–72; Judith Walkowitz: 'Going Public: Shopping, Street Harassment, and Streetwalking in Late Victorian London', *Representations*, 662 (1998), 1–30.

15. Louise Jackson, *Child Sex Abuse and the Law in Victorian England* (London: Routledge, 2000), 105–6.

16. Sean Brady, *Masculinity and Male Homosexuality in Britain, 1861–1913* (Basingstoke: Palgrave Macmillan, 2005), 85–118; H. G. Cocks, *Nameless Offences: Homosexual desire in the 19th century* (London: I. B. Tauris, 2003); F. B. Smith, 'Labouchère's amendment to the Criminal Law Amendment Bill', *Historical Studies*, 17 (1976), 165–73; Alfred Swain Taylor, *The Principles and Practice of Medical Jurisprudence by the late Alfred Swaine Taylor*, 3rd edn, ed. Thomas Stevenson (London: J. and A. Churchill, 1883), 461; Charles Upchurch, *Before Wilde: Sex between Men in Britain's Age of Reform* (2009); Nancy Wilkins,

' "How it Happened": A history of homosexual legislation in England', *Man and Society: Journal of the Albany Trust*, 6 (1963), 8–13.

17. Sean Brady, *Masculinity and Male Homosexuality in Britain, 1861–1913* (Basingstoke: Palgrave Macmillan 2005), 162–94; Ivan Crozier, 'Nineteenth-Century British Psychiatric Writing about Homosexuality before Havelock Ellis: The Missing Story', *Journal of the History of Medicine and Allied Sciences*, 63 (2008), 65–102.

18. Taylor, *The Principles and Practice of Medical Jurisprudence*, 458–61.

19. Wilkins, ' "How it Happened"; Shanley, *Feminism, Marriage and the Law*, 102.

20. Brady, *Masculinity and Male Homosexuality*, 105–6; A D. Harvey, 'Research Notes: Bestiality in Late-Victorian England', *Journal of Legal History*, 21/3 (2000), 85–8.

21. Bland, *Banishing the Beast*, 3–47; Walkowitz, *City of Dreadful Delight*, 135–69.

22. Edward and Eleanor Marx Aveling, *The Woman Question* (London: Swan Sonnenschein, Lowrey, 1886); Karen Hunt, *Equivocal Feminists: The Social Democratic Federation and the woman question, 1884–1911* (Cambridge: Cambridge University Press, 1996).

23. *The Pioneer: A Quarterly Journal issued by the Pioneer Club*, X (April 1887).

24. Hall, 'Hauling down the Double Standard'.

25. National Vigilance Association archives, Executive Committee minutes 1886, The Women's Library, London Metropolitan University.

26. Lisa Z. Sigel, *Governing Pleasures: Pornography and social change in England, 1815–1914* (New Brunswick NJ: Rutgers University Press, 2002), 81–118.

27. Lisa Z. Sigel, 'Name Your Pleasure: The Transformation of Sexual Language in Nineteenth Century British Pornography', *Journal of the History of Sexuality*, 9 (2000), 395–419.

28. 'Sexual Ignorance', *British Medical Journal*, II (1885), 303–4; *The Lancet*, II (1885), 350–1.

29. Lesley A. Hall, *Hidden Anxieties: Male Sexuality, 1900–1950* (Oxford: Polity Press, 1991), 26–9.

30. Anne Jordan, *Love well the hour: The life of Lady Colin Campbell 1857–1911* (Kibworth Beauchamp: Matador, 2010), 55–132.

31. Michael Worboys, 'Unsexing Gonorrhoea: Bacteriologists, Gynaecologists and Suffragists in Britain, 1860–1920', *Social History of Medicine*, 17 (2004), 41–59.

32. Peter Fryer, *The Birth Controllers* (London: Secker & Warburg, 1965), 169–72; 'H. A. Allbutt v. the General Medical Council', *British Medical Journal*, II (1889), 88.

33. Kali Israel, 'French vices and British liberties: Gender, class and narrative competition in a late Victorian sex scandal', *Social History*, 22 (1997), 1–26; National Vigilance Association Executive Committee minutes, 1889, The Women's Library, London Metropolitan University.

34. Mary S. Hartman, *Victorian Murderesses: A True History of Thirteen Respectable French and English Women accused of Unspeakable Crimes* (London: Robson Books, 1985), 174–214; Roy Porter and Lesley Hall, *The Facts of Life: The Creation of Sexual Knowledge in Britain, 1650–1950* (New Haven, CT, and London: Yale University Press, 1995), 140–1, 202–3; George Robb, 'Circe in Crinoline: Domestic Poisonings in Victorian England', *Journal of Family History*, 22 (1997), 176–90.

35. Bristow, *Vice and Vigilance*, 207–8.

36. Laite, *Common Prostitutes and Ordinary Citizens*, 87–93; Walkowitz, *City of Dreadful Delight*, 191–228.

37. Patrick Geddes and J. Arthur Thomson, *The Evolution of Sex* (London: Walter Scott, 1889); Porter and Hall, *The Facts of Life*, 155–8.

3 Scientific Sex, Unspeakable Oscar, and Insurgent Women in the 'Naughty Nineties'

1. Ann Sumner Holmes, ' "Don't Frighten the Horses": The Russell Divorce Case', in George Robb and Nancy Erber (eds), *Disorder in the Court: Trials and Sexual Conflict at the Turn of the Century* (Basingstoke: Palgrave Macmillan, 1999), 140–63.

2. Theo Aronson, *Prince Eddy and the Homosexual Underworld* (London: Murray, 1994); Lewis Chester, David Leitch, and Colin Simpson, *The Cleveland Street Affair* (London: Weidenfeld & Nicolson, 1976); Martin Dockray, 'The Cleveland Street Scandal, 1889–90: The Conduct of the Defence', *Legal History*, 17 (1996), 1–16; Morris B. Kaplan, *Sodom on the Thames: Sex, Love and Scandal in Wilde Times* (Ithaca, NY: Cornell University Press, 2005), 166–223; Timothy d'Arch Smith, *Love in Earnest: Some notes on the lives and writings of English 'Uranian' Poets from 1889–1930* (London: Routledge & Kegan Paul, 1970), 24–9.

3. Peter Fryer, *The Birth Controllers* (London: Secker & Warburg, 1965), 172; 'The Post Office and the Malthusian Propaganda: Important Prosecution for Obscenity', cutting from the *Weekly* [?], 17 October 1891, 'Sex, population and eugenics' Box 1, John Johnson ephemera collection, Bodleian Library, Oxford; Home Office files, 'Indecent Literature: pseudo-medical pamphlets', HO144/238 A52538–9, The National Archives.

4. Fryer, 'The Post Office and the Malthusian Propaganda'; *Shafts: Light comes to those who dare to think*, 14 January, 18 February, July 1893.

5. Roy Porter and Lesley Hall, *The Facts of Life: The Creation of Sexual Knowledge in Britain, 1650–1950* (New Haven, CT, and London: Yale University Press, 1995), 161–2; Carolyn Steedman, *Childhood, Culture and Class in Britain: Margaret Macmillan, 1860–1931* (London: Virago, 1990), 122; 'Our Fabian Circle' Katharine Bruce Glasier papers, Glasier II.3.1, University of Liverpool Library.

6. Chris Nottingham, *The Pursuit of Serenity: Havelock Ellis and the New Politics* (Amsterdam: University of Amsterdam Press, 1999).

7. Paula Bartley, *Prostitution: Prevention and Reform in Britain, 1860–1914* (London: Routledge, 1999), 74–115; Louise Jackson, *Child Sex Abuse and the Law in Victorian England* (London: Routledge, 1999), 132–51; Sue Morgan, *A Passion for Purity: Ellice Hopkins and the Politics of Gender in the Late-Victorian Church* (University of Bristol, Department of Theology & Religious Studies, 1999), 90–112.

8. Angus McLaren, *A Prescription for Murder: The Victorian serial killings of Dr Thomas Neill Cream* (Chicago, IL: University of Chicago Press, 1993), xiii, 63–75.

9. 'Massage Scandal 1894', Presscuttings, archives of the Chartered Society of Physiotherapy, Wellcome Library, SA/CSP/P.1/1–2; Julia Laite, *Common Prostitutes and Ordinary Citizens: Commercial sex in London, 1885–1960* (Basingstoke: Palgrave, 2011), 63–9; Stefan Petrow, *Policing Morals: The Metropolitan Police and the Home Office 1870–1914* (Oxford: Clarendon Press, 1994), 15–45.

10. Peter Bailey, 'Parasexuality and Glamour: The Victorian Barmaid as Cultural Prototype', *Gender and History*, 2 (1990), 148–71.

11. Lucy Bland, *Banishing the Beast: English Feminism and Sexual Morality, 1880–1914* (London: Penguin, 1995), 105–23; E. S. Turner, 'A Flourish of Strumpets', *Roads to Ruin: The shocking history of social reform* (London: Michael Joseph, 1950), 206–31.

12. *The Pelican: A Journal of Today*, 3 May 1890, 537, and 17 May 1890, 601; Judith Walkowitz: 'Going Public: Shopping, Street Harassment, and Streetwalking in Late Victorian London', *Representations* 662 (1998), 1–30.

13. Matt Cook, *London and the Culture of Homosexuality, 1885–1914* (Cambridge: Cambridge University Press, 2008), 50–72.

14. Jenny Birchall, ' "The Carnival Revels of Manchester's Vagabonds": Young Working-Class Women and Monkey Parades in the 1870s', *Women's History Review*, 15 (2006), 229–52.

15. Russell Davies, 'A Broken Dream: Some aspects of sexual behaviour and the dilemma of the unmarried mother in South West Wales, 1887–1914', *Llafur* 3/4 (1984), 24–33.

16. 'Dangerous Quack Literature: The Moral of a Recent Suicide', *British Medical Journal*, II (1982), 753; Lesley A Hall, ' "It was the doctors who were suffering from it": The history of masturbatory insanity revisited', *Paedagogica Historica: International Journal of the History of Education*, 39 (2003), 685–99.

17. Angus McLaren, *The Trials of Manhood: Policing Sexual Boundaries 1870–1930* (Chicago, IL, and London: University of Chicago Press, 1997), 45–51.

18. McLaren, *The Trials of Manhood*, 71–86.

19. Alan Sinfield, *The Wilde Century: Effeminacy, Oscar Wilde, and the Queer Moment* (London: Cassell, 1994), 1–4, 140–1.

20. Kaplan, *Sodom on the Thames*, 224–51.

21. George Ives, *Notes and Various Writings*, no. XCIII 1928[–1929]. O of C [Order of Chaeronea dating] 2266, entry for 21 May 1929, Harry Ransom Humanities Research Center, University of Texas at Austin.

22. D'Arch Smith, *Love in Earnest*.

23. Sean Brady, *Masculinity and Male Homosexuality in Britain, 1861–1913* (Basingstoke: Palgrave Macmillan, 2005), 187–94.

24. Cook, *London and the Culture of Homosexuality*, 138–42; John Stokes, *Oscar Wilde: Myths, Miracles and Imitations* (Cambridge: Cambridge University Press, 1996), 6.

25. Brady, *Masculinity and Male Homosexuality*, 157–61, 194–209; Lesley A. Hall, 'Heroes or Villains? Reconsidering British *fin de siècle* sexology and its impact', in Lynne Segal (ed.), *New Sexual Agendas* (Basingstoke and London: Macmillan, 1997), 3–16; Sheila Rowbotham, *Edward Carpenter: A Life of Liberty and Love* (London: Verso, 2008), 189–94, 213.

26. Laurence Housman to Edward Carpenter, 2 September 1897, Carpenter papers in Sheffield City Archives, MSS 386/75 .

27. H. G. Cocks, *Nameless Offences: Homosexual Desire in the 19th Century* (London: I. B. Tauris, 2003), 157–98.

28. Brady, *Masculinity and Male Homosexuality*, 138–56; Phyllis Grosskurth, *Havelock Ellis: A biography* (London, Allen Lane, 1980), 174–7.

29. Havelock Ellis to Edward Carpenter, 17 December 1892, Carpenter papers in Sheffield City Archives, MSS357/5.

30. Grosskurth, *Havelock Ellis*, 179–83.

31. Hall, 'Heroes or villains?'.

32. Brady, *Masculinity and Male Homosexuality*, 140–7; Grosskurth, *Havelock Ellis*, 191–202; Nottingham, *The Pursuit of Serenity*, 209–11.

33. Lesley A. Hall, ' "The English have hot-water bottles": The morganatic marriage between the British medical profession and sexology since William Acton', in Roy Porter and Mikulas Teich (eds), *Sexual Knowledge, Sexual Science: The History of Attitudes to Sexuality* (Cambridge: Cambridge University Press, 1994), 350–66.

34. Brady, *Masculinity and Male Homosexuality*, 112–15; Petrow, *Policing Morals*, 160–2.

35. Stephen Cretney, *Family Law in the Twentieth Century: A History* (Oxford: Oxford University Press, 2003), 142–7; Maeve E. Doggett, *Marriage, Wife-Beating and the Law in Victorian England* (Columbia, SC: University of South Carolina Press, 1993), 1–4, 134–9; Ginger Frost, 'A Shock to Marriage?: The Clitheroe Case and the Victorians', in George Robb and Nancy Erber (eds.), *Disorder in the Court: Trials and Sexual Conflict at the Turn of the Century* (Basingstoke: Palgrave Macmillan, 1999), 100–18; Mary Lyndon Shanley, *Feminism, Marriage, and the Law in Victorian England, 1850–1895* (London: I. B. Tauris: 1989), 177–83; Bland, *Banishing the Beast*, 135–8.

36. Bland, *Banishing the Beast*, 138–9; Shanley, *Feminism, Marriage, and the Law*, 184–8.

37. Edith Havelock Ellis, 'A Noviciate for Marriage' c.1892, *The New Horizon in Love and Life* (London: A. & C. Black, 1921), 11–22.

38. Karen Hunt, *Equivocal Feminists: The Social Democratic Federation and the woman question, 1884–1911* (Cambridge: Cambridge University Press,1996), 81–115.

39. Bland, *Banishing the Beast*, 156–9, 172; Brady, *Masculinity and Male Homosexuality*, 142–51

40. Bland, *Banishing the Beast*, 205–17; Lesley A. Hall, 'Malthusian mutations: The changing politics and moral meanings of birth control in Britain', in Brian Dolan and Roy Porter (eds), *Malthus, Medicine and Morality: 'Malthusianism' after 1798* (Amsterdam: Rodopi, 2000), 141–63, 'The Next Generation: Stella Browne, the New Woman as Freewoman', in Angelique Richardson and Chris Willis (eds), *The New Woman in Fiction and in Fact: Fin-de-Siècle Feminisms* (Basingstoke: Palgrave Macmillan, 2001), 224–38.

41. Bland, *Banishing the Beast*, 159–61; Karen Hunt, *Equivocal Feminists*, 94–104.

42. Bland, *Banishing the Beast*; Carole Dyhouse, *Feminism and the Family in England*, 1880–1939 (Oxford, 1989); Margaret Jackson, *The Real Facts of Life: Feminism and the Politics of Sexuality, c.1850–1940* (London: Taylor & Francis, 1994); Sheila Jeffreys, *The Spinster and Her Enemies: Feminism and Sexuality 1880–1930* (London: Pandora Press, 1985).

43. Bland, *Banishing the Beast*, 215–17.

44. Richardson and Willis (eds), *The New Woman in Fact and Fiction*; Angelique Richardson, *Love and Eugenics in the Late Nineteenth Century: Rational Reproduction and the New Woman* (Oxford: Oxford University Press, 2003); Elaine Showalter, *A Literature of Their Own: British Women Novelists from Brontë to Lessing* (London: Virago, 1982), 210–14.

45. Simon Szreter, *Fertility, Class and Gender in Britain, 1860–1940* (Cambridge: Cambridge University Press, 1996), 367–439.

46. Hera Cook, *The Long Sexual Revolution: English Women, Sex, and Contraception 1800–1975* (Oxford: Oxford University Press, 2004), 90–121.

47. Porter and Hall, *The Facts of Life*, 201–7.

48. Janet Farrell Brodie, *Contraception and Abortion in 19th-Century America* (Ithaca, NY, and London: Cornell University Press, 1994), 79–86.

49. McLaren, *Prescription for Murder*, 76–87; Opinion of Counsel to the Royal College of Physicians, 1895, cited in *Taylor's Principles and Practice of Medical Jurisprudence*, 6th edn, edited, revised and brought up to date by F. J. Smith, Vol. II (London: J. &.A. Churchill, 1910), 145–6.

50. *Shafts*, June 1897, 193–5; letters from Elizabeth Wolstenholme Elmy to Mrs M'Ilquham, 21 March, 20, 21, 29 May 1897, British Library Department of Manuscripts, Additional Manuscript 47451; June Jordan, *Josephine Butler* (London: John Murray, 2001), 278–81.

51. E. B. Turner, 'The History of the Fight against Venereal Disease', *Science Progress*, 11 (1916/17), 83–8.

52. Lesley A. Hall, *Hidden Anxieties: Male Sexuality, 1900–1950* (Oxford: Polity Press, 1991), 29–30; Alan Hunt, 'The Great Masturbation Panic and the Discourses of Moral Regulation in Nineteenth- and early Twentieth- Century Britain', *Journal of the History of Sexuality*, 8 (1998), 575–615.

53. 'Ellis Ethelemer', *Baby Buds* (Congleton: Mrs Wolstenholme Elmy, 1895), 39–40; Claudia Nelson, '"Under the Guidance of a Wise Mother": British Sex Education at the *fin de siècle*', in Claudia Nelson and Ann Sumner Holmes (eds), *Maternal Instincts: Visions of Motherhood and Sexuality, 1875–1925* (Basingstoke and London: Macmillan Press, 1997), 98–121; Lesley A Hall, 'Birds, Bees and General Embarrassment: Sex education in Britain from social purity to Section 28', in Richard Aldrich (ed.), *Public or Private Education: Lessons from History* (London: Woburn Press, 2004), 98–115.

54. Edith MacDuff to Edward Carpenter, 7 April 1894, Carpenter papers in Sheffield City Archives, MSS271/51; 'ETH of Dawlish' to the Editor, *Shafts*, April 1895.

55. Lisa Z. Sigel, *Governing Pleasures: Pornography and social change in England, 1815–1914* (New Brunswick, NJ: Rutgers University Press, 2002), 119–55.

56. Peter Bailey (ed.), *Music Hall: The Business of Pleasure* (Milton Keynes: Open University Press, 1986), and Peter Bailey, 'Conspiracies of Meaning: Music-Hall and the Knowingness of Popular Culture', *Past and Present*, 142 (1994), 138–70.

57. Richard Anthony Baker, *Marie Lloyd: Queen of the Music-Halls* (London: Robert Hale, 1990), 60, 68–9.

4 Degenerating Nation? Anxieties and Protests in a New Century

1. Samuel Hynes, *The Edwardian Turn of Mind* (London: Pimlico, 1991, 1st publ. 1968), 4–5.

2. Ina Zweiniger-Bargielowska, *Managing the Body: Beauty, Health, and Fitness in Britain, 1880–1939* (Oxford: Oxford University Press, 2010), 17–148.

3. Richard A. Soloway, *Demography and Degeneration: Eugenics and the Declining Birthrate in Twentieth-Century Britain* (Chapel Hill, NC: University of North Carolina Press, 1995), 18–38.

4. George Robb, 'The Way of All Flesh: Degeneration, Eugenics, and the Gospel of Free Love', *Journal of the History of Sexuality*, 6 (1996), 589–603.

5. Carolyn Burdett, 'The Hidden Romance of Sexual Science: Eugenics, the Nation, and the Making of Modern Feminism', in Lucy Bland and Laura Doan (eds), *Sexology in Culture: Labelling Bodies and Desires* (Oxford: Polity Press, 1998), 44–59. Ann Taylor Allen, 'Feminism and Eugenics in Germany and Britain, 1900–1940: A Comparative Perspective', *German Studies Review*, 23 (2000), 477–506.

6. Lucy Bland, *Banishing the Beast: English Feminism and Sexual Morality, 1885–1914* (London: Penguin, 1995), 222–49; Lesley A. Hall, 'Women, Feminism and Eugenics', in Robert A. Peel (ed.), *Essays in the History of Eugenics: Proceedings of a Conference organised by the Galton Institute, London, 1997* (London: The Galton Institute, 1998), 36–51; Greta Jones, 'Women and Eugenics in Britain: The case of Mary Scharlieb, Elizabeth Sloan Chesser, and Stella Browne', *Annals of Science*, 51 (1995), 481–502; Angelique Richardson, *Love and Eugenics in the Late Nineteenth Century: Rational Reproduction and the New Woman* (Oxford: Oxford University Press, 2003); Richard A. Soloway, 'Feminism, Fertility, and Eugenics in Victorian and Edwardian England', in S. Drescher et al. (eds), *Political Symbolism in Modern Europe* (New Brunswick, NJ: Rutgers University Press, 1982), 121–4.

7. Bland, *Banishing the Beast*, 217–21; Lesley A. Hall, 'Suffrage, Sex, and Science', in Maroula Joannou and June Purvis (eds), *The Women's Suffrage Movement: New feminist perspectives* (Manchester: Manchester University Press, 1998), 188–200; Sheila Jeffreys, *The Spinster and her Enemies: Feminism and Sexuality, 1880–1930* (London: Pandora, 1985), 35–9; George Robb, 'Race Motherhood: Moral Eugenics vs Progressive Eugenics, 1880–1920', in Claudia Nelson and Ann Sumner Holmes (eds), *Maternal Instincts: Visions of Motherhood and Sexuality in Britain, 1875–1925* (Basingstoke and London: Macmillan Press, 1997), 58–74.

8. Bland, *Banishing the Beast*, 244–5; Lesley A. Hall, 'Venereal Diseases and Society in Britain from the Contagious Diseases Acts to the National Health Service', in Roger Davidson and Lesley Hall (eds), *Sex, Sin, and Suffering: Venereal diseases and European Society since 1870* (London: Routledge, 2000), 120–36; E. B. Turner, 'The History of the Fight against Venereal Disease', *Science Progress*, 11 (1916/17), 83–8; Papers relating to 1911 Memorial, Venereal Diseases File 1 (Box 311), Association for Moral and Social Hygiene archives, The Women's Library, London Metropolitan University; *Local Government Board, Report as to the Practice of Medicine and Surgery by Unqualified Practitioners in the United Kingdom* [Cd. 5422] (London: HMSO, 1910), 15–16.

9. L. W. Harrison, 'Ehrlich versus Syphilis, as it appeared to L. W. Harrison'; and 'Some Lessons Learnt in Fifty Years Practice in Venereology', *British Journal of Venereal Diseases*, 30 (1954), 2–6, 184–90.

10. Michael Worboys, 'Unsexing Gonorrhoea: Bacteriologists, Gynaecologists and Suffragists in Britain, 1860–1920'. *Social History of Medicine*, 17 (2004), 31–59.

11. Paula Bartley, *Prostitution: Prevention and Reform in Britain, 1860–1914* (London: Routledge, 1999), 119–52; Pamela Cox, *Gender, Justice and Welfare: Bad Girls in Britain, 1900–1950* (Basingstoke: Palgrave Macmillan, 2003), 5–15, 37–50.

12. Ann Sumner Holmes, '"Don't Frighten the Horses": The Russell Divorce Case', in George Robb and Nancy Erber (eds), *Disorder in the Court: Trials and Sexual Conflict at the Turn of the Century* (Basingstoke: Palgrave Macmillan, 1999), 140–63; Gail Savage, '"…Equality from the Masculine Point of View…": The 2nd Earl Russell and Divorce Law Reform in England', *Russell: The journal of the Bertrand Russell Archives*, n.s 16 (summer 1996), 69–84; Stephen Cretney, *Family Law in the Twentieth Century: A History* (Oxford: Oxford University Press, 2003), 203–5.

13. Janice Hubbard Harris, *Edwardian Stories of Divorce* (New Brunswick, NJ: Rutgers University Press, 1996), 7–12.

14. Harris, *Edwardian Stories*, 13, 104–49; Hynes, *The Edwardian Turn of Mind*, 192–5.

15. Cretney, *Family Law*, 206–10; Harris, *Edwardian Stories*, 68–73; Hynes, *The Edwardian Turn of Mind*, 208–9.

16. Jacky Burnett, 'Exposing "the inner life": The Women's Cooperative Guild's attitude to "cruelty"', in Shani D'Cruze (ed.), *Everyday Violence in Britain, 1850–1950: Gender and Class* (Harlow: Longman, 2000), 136–52; Harris, *Edwardian Stories*, 65–103; Gail Savage, '"The Magistrates are Men": Working-Class Marital Conflict and Appeals from the Magistrates' Court to the Divorce Court after 1985', in George Robb and Nancy Erber (eds), *Disorder in the Court: Trials and Sexual Conflict at the Turn of the Century* (Basingstoke: Palgrave Macmillan, 1999), 231–49.

17. Sally Alexander, 'Introduction' to Maud Pember Reeves, *Round About a Pound a Week* (London: Virago, 1979, 1st publ. 1913), ix–xxi; Carol Dyhouse, *Feminism and the Family in England, 1880–1939* (Oxford: Basil Blackwell, 1989), 107–44; Jennifer Haynes, 'Sanitary ladies and friendly visitors: Women public health officers in London, c.1890–1960', University of London Institute of Education PhD thesis 2006; Ellen Ross, *Love and Toil: Motherhood in Outcast London, 1870–1918* (Oxford: Oxford University Press, 1993), 195–221; Simon Szreter, *Fertility, Class and Gender in Britain, 1860–1940* (Cambridge: Cambridge University Press, 1996), 516–20.

18. J. Miriam Benn, *Predicaments of Love* (London: Pluto Press, 1992), 204–6; Ross, *Love and Toil*, 196–8.

19. Szreter, *Fertility, Class and Gender*, 518–19.

20. Victor Bailey and Sheila Blackburn, 'The Punishment of Incest Act 1908: A Case Study of Law Creation', *The Criminal Law Review* (1979), 708–18; Carol Smart, 'Reconsidering the Recent History of Child Sexual Abuse, 1910–1960', *Journal of Social Policy*, 29 (2000), 55–73.

21. *The Lancet*, II (1908), 1373.

22. *The Lancet*, I (1901), 108; Lesley A. Hall, '"The English have hot-water bottles": The morganatic marriage between the British medical profession and sexology since William Acton', in Roy Porter and Mikulas Teich (eds), *Sexual Knowledge, Sexual Science: The History of Attitudes to Sexuality* (Cambridge: Cambridge University Press, 1994), 350–66.

23. Havelock Ellis to Edward Carpenter, 17 May 1907, Carpenter papers in Sheffield City Archives MSS 357/14.

24. 'Professor Freud and Hysteria', *British Medical Journal*, I (1908), 103–4; Theophilius E. M. Boll, 'May Sinclair and the Medico-Psychological Clinic of London', *Proceedings of the American Philosophical Society*, 106 (1962), 310–26; Philippa Martindale, '"Against All Hushing Up And Stamping Down": The Medico-Psychological Clinic of London and the Novelist May Sinclair', *Psychoanalysis and History*, 6 (2004), 177–200; Dean Rapp, 'The early discovery of Freud by the British General Public', *Social History of Medicine*, 3 (1990), 217–43; Suzanne Raitt, 'Early British Psychoanalysis and the Medico-Psychological Clinic', *History Workshop Journal*, 58 (2002): 63–85.

25. Judy Greenway, 'It's What You Do With It That Counts: Interpretations of Otto Weininger', in Bland and Doan (eds), *Sexology in Culture*, 27–43.

26. Chandak Sengoopta, 'Science, sexuality and gender in the "fin de siècle": Otto Weininger as Baedeker', *History of Science*, 30 (1992), 249–79.

27. Frances Swiney, *The Cosmic Procession, or the Feminine Principle in Evolution: Essays of Illumination* (London: Ernest Bell, 1906), 7.

28. Edward Carpenter to Havelock Ellis, 8 October 1906, Harry Ransom Humanities Research Center, University of Texas at Austin.

29. Roy Porter and Lesley Hall, *The Facts of Life: The Creation of Sexual Knowledge in Britain, 1650–1950* (New Haven, CT, and London: Yale University Press, 1995), 164–5.

30. Sheila Rowbotham, *Edward Carpenter: A Life of Liberty and Love* (London: Verso, 2008).

31. 'Reviews: The Uranian', *British Medical Journal*, I (1909), 1546–7.

32. *The Lancet*, I (1901), 108.

33. The Viscountess Rhondda, *This was my World* (London: Macmillan Press, 1933), 126–7.

34. HO/144/1043/183473, The National Archives; Rowbotham, *Edward Carpenter*, 285–7.

35. Sean Brady, *Masculinity and Male Homosexuality in Britain, 1861–1913* (Basingstoke: Palgrave Macmillan, 2005), 101–18.

36. Carol Naylor, '"Commonsense, Manners, Guts": "Manliness" in the English School Story 1887–1917', Deakin University PhD thesis, 2003, particularly Chapter 2 'The Homoemotional/Homoerotic in Public School Fiction', 46–120.

37. Alison Oram, *Her Husband was a Woman!: Women's gender-crossing and twentieth century British popular culture* (London: Routledge, 2007), 17–60.

38. *The Pelican*, 26 May and 3 November 1900; HO/45/10510/129433, TNA; Lisa Z Sigel, *Governing Pleasures: Pornography and social change in England, 1815–1914* (New Brunswick, NJ: Rutgers University Press, 2002), 82–7.

39. Elfreda Buckland, *The World of Donald McGill* (London: Blandford, 1984), 94.

40. Edward Bristow, *Vice and Vigilance: Purity Movements in Britain since 1700* (Dublin: Gill & Macmillan, 1977), 218–21.

41. Hynes, *The Edwardian Turn of Mind*, 212–37; Anthony Aldgate and James C. Robertson, *Censorship in Theatre and Cinema* (Edinburgh: Edinburgh University Press, 2005), 1.

42. Hynes, *The Edwardian Turn of Mind*, 289–302.

43. *The Sporting Times: Otherwise known as the Pink 'Un'*, front page, 1st issue of 1910.

44. Paul Ferris, *Sex and the British: A Twentieth-Century History* (London: Michael Joseph, 1993), 12–13; Sigel, *Governing Pleasures*, 148–52.

45. Annette Kuhn, *Cinema, Censorship, and Sexuality, 1909–1925* (London, Routledge, 1988), 12–18.

46. Harris, *Edwardian Stories*, 32–44; Gail Savage, 'Erotic stories and public decency: Newspaper reporting of divorce proceedings in England', *The Historical Journal*, 41 (1998), 511–28.

47. Hera Cook, *The Long Sexual Revolution: English Women, Sex, and Contraception 1800–1975* (Oxford: Oxford University Press, 2004), 101–5; Jona Schellekens, 'Illegitimate Fertility Decline in England, 1851–1911', *Journal of Family History*, 20 (1995), 365–75; Szreter, *Fertility, Class and Gender*, 393, 460.

48. Lesley A. Hall, *Hidden Anxieties: Male Sexuality, 1900–1950* (Oxford: Polity Press, 1991), 95–6, 163; Szreter, *Fertility, Class and Gender*, 393–7.

49. *The Pelican*, 6 January 1900, 12 January 1910; Ferris, *Sex and the British*, 27–9; Abraham Flexner, *Prostitution in Europe* (abr. edn) (London: Grant Richards, 1919), 233–4; Stefan Petrow, *Policing Morals: The Metropolitan Police and the Home Office, 1870–1914* (Oxford: Clarendon Press, 1994), 137–46, 155.

5 Divorce, Disease, and War

1. *The State and Sexual Morality* (London: George Allen and Unwin, 1920), 7.

2. Havelock Ellis to Edward Carpenter, 16 April 1910, Carpenter papers in Sheffield City Archives MSS357/16.

3. *The Lancet*, I (1910), 1207; Lesley A. Hall, ' "The English have hot water bottles": The morganatic marriage between the British medical profession and sexology since William Acton', in Roy Porter and Mikulas Teich (eds), *Sexual Knowledge, Sexual Science: The History of Attitudes to Sexuality* (Cambridge: Cambridge University Press, 1994), 350–66.

4. Edward Carpenter, *Love's Coming of Age: A Series of Papers on the relations of the sexes* (London: Allen & Unwin, 1906).

5. Roy Porter and Lesley Hall, *The Facts of Life: The Creation of Sexual Knowledge in Britain, 1650–1950* (New Haven, CT, and London: Yale University Press, 1995), 202–8.

6. Gail Savage, 'Erotic stories and public decency: Newspaper reporting of divorce proceedings in England', *The Historical Journal*, 41 (1998), 511–28.

7. Janice Hubbard Harris, *Edwardian Stories of Divorce* (New Brunswick, NJ: Rutgers University Press), 100–1, Appendix 151–5; Samuel Hynes, *The Edwardian Turn of Mind* (London: Pimlico, 1991, 1st publ. 1968), 208–11; Stephen Cretney, *Family Law in the Twentieth Century: A History* (Oxford: Oxford University Press, 2003), 210–14.

8. Rebecca West 'The Divorce Commission: A Report that Will Not Become Law', 1st publ. in *The Clarion*, 29 November 1912, reprinted in Jane Marcus (ed.), *The Young Rebecca: Writings of Rebecca West, 1911–1917* (Basingstoke and London: Macmillan Press, 1982), 124–7.

9. Cretney, *Family Law*, 214–17.

10. Lesley A. Hall, 'No Sex, Please, We're Socialists: The Labour Party prefers to close its eyes and think of the electorate', *Socialist History*, 36 (2010), 11–28; Hynes, *The Edwardian Turn of Mind*, 210–11, 268–9; Stefan Petrow, *Policing Morals: The Metropolitan Police and the Home Office, 1870–1914* (Oxford: Clarendon Press, 1994), 167.

11. Harris, *Edwardian Stories*, 101–3.

12. Gail Savage, 'The Operation of the 1857 Divorce Act, 1860–1910: A Research Note', *Journal of Social History*, 16:4 (1983), 103–10.

13. Julie English Early, 'A New Man for a New Century: Dr Crippen and the Principles of Masculinity', in George Robb and Nancy Erber (eds), *Disorder in the Court: Trials and Sexual Conflict at the Turn of the Century* (Basingstoke: Palgrave Macmillan, 1999), 209–30, and 'Keeping ourselves to ourselves: Violence in the Edwardian suburb', in Shani D'Cruze (ed.), *Everyday Violence in Britain, 1850–1950: Gender and Class* (Harlow: Longman, 2000), 170–84.

14. Rebecca West, 'A Quiet Day with the Constitutionals', 1st publ. in *The Clarion*, 1 Aug 1913, *The Young Rebecca*, 195–8.

15. Petrow, *Policing Morals*, 129–30.

16. Angela V. John and Claire Eustance (eds), *The Men's Share? Masculinities, Male Support and Women's Suffrage in Britain, 1890–1920* (London: Routledge, 1997).

17. Michael Dunnill, *The Plato of Praed Street: The life and times of Almroth Wright* (London: Royal Society of Medicine Press, 2000), 142–60.

18. Christabel Pankhurst, *The Great Scourge and How to End It* (London: E. Pankhurst, 1913).

19. Review of E. M. Corner, *Male Diseases in General Practice*, *The Lancet*, I (1910), 11–48.

20. Local Government Board, *Report as to the Practice of Medicine and Surgery by unqualified persons*, Cd 5422, 1910, 15.

21. Lesley A. Hall, 'Venereal Diseases and Society in Britain, from the Contagious Diseases Acts to the National Health Service', in Roger Davidson and Lesley A. Hall (eds),

Sex, Sin, and Suffering: Venereal Diseases and European Society since 1870 (London: Routledge, 2001), 120–36.

22. Royal Commission on Venereal Diseases, *First Report: Appendix: Minutes of Evidence (1913–1914)* Cd 7475 (London: HMSO, 1914); *Final Report* Cd 8189 (London: HMSO 1916).

23. National Council for Combating Venereal Disease, Provisional Executive Committee minutes 24 Nov 1914, British Social Hygiene Council (BSHC) archives, Wellcome Library, SA/BSH/A.2/1.

24. Paula Bartley, *Prostitution: Prevention and Reform in Britain, 1860–1914* (London: Routledge, 1999), 170–3; Lucy Bland, *Banishing the Beast: English Feminism and Sexual Morality, 1885–1914* (London: Penguin, 1995), 297–9; Paul Ferris, *Sex and the British: A Twentieth-Century History* (London: Michael Joseph, 1993), 34–40; Julia Laite, *Common Prostitutes and Ordinary Citizens: Commercial sex in London, 1885–1960* (Basingstoke: Palgrave Macmillan, 2011), 100–15.

25. Petrow, *Policing Morals*, 168.

26. Bland, *Banishing the Beast*, 299–300; Edward Bristow, *Vice and Vigilance: Purity Movements in Britain since 1700* (Dublin: Gill & Macmillan, 1977) 190–2; Ferris, *Sex and the British*, 40–1; National Vigilance Association, file S127 'Periodical scare stories (hypodermic syringes, drugs, etc.)', The Women's Library, London Metropolitan University

27. Bland, *Banishing the Beast*, 298–303; Petrow, *Policing Morals*, 167–75.

28. Bristow, *Vice and Vigilance*, 144–5; Hynes, *The Edwardian Turn of Mind*, 281–7; Frank Mort, *Dangerous Sexualities: Medico-moral politics in Britain since 1830* (London: Routledge & Kegan Paul, 1987), 174–6.

29. James Marchant to Patrick Geddes, 13 June 1911: Geddes papers T-GED 9/1015, University of Strathclyde.

30. Bristow, *Vice and Vigilance*, 145–6; Havelock Ellis, *The Problem of Race Regeneration* (London: Cassell, 1911), 70–1; Hynes, *The Edwardian Turn of Mind*, 288; Chris Nottingham, *The Pursuit of Serenity: Havelock Ellis and the New Politics* (Amsterdam: University of Amsterdam Press, 1999), 189–90.

31. Marchant to Geddes, 4 December 1912, T-GED 9/1124, 8 February 1914, T-GED 9/1245.

32. Mort, *Dangerous Sexualities*, 153–63.

33. Hilda Kean, *Deeds not Words: The lives of suffragette teachers* (London: Pluto Press, 1990), 60–2.

34. Kean, *Deeds not Words*, 59; Mort, *Dangerous Sexualities*, 156.

35. Alan Hunt, 'The Great Masturbation Panic and the Discourses of Moral Regulation in late Nineteenth and early Twentieth Century Britain', *Journal of the History of Sexuality*, 8 (1998), 575–615.

36. Lord Baden Powell, *Scouting for Boys: A Handbook for Instruction in Good Citizenship* (London: C. Arthur Pearson, 1908), 279.

37. Lesley A. Hall, 'Forbidden by God, despised by men: Masturbation, medical warnings, moral panic and manhood in Great Britain, 1850- 1950', *Journal of the History of Sexuality*, 2 (1992), 365–87, reprinted in John C. Fout (ed.), *Forbidden History: The State, Society, and the Regulation of Sexuality in Modern Europe* (Chicago, IL: University of Chicago Press, 1992), 293–318.

38. Anthony Aldgate and James C. Robertson, *Censorship in Theatre and Cinema* (Edinburgh: Edinburgh University Press, 2005), 2; Bristow, *Vice and Vigilance*, 221; Hynes, *The Edwardian Turn of Mind*, 306; Annette Kuhn, *Cinema, Censorship and Sexuality, 1909–1925* (London: Routledge, 1988), 21–3; James C. Robertson, *Hidden Cinema: British Film Censorship in Action, 1913–1975* (London: Routledge, 1989), 1–2.

39. Hynes, *The Edwardian Turn of Mind*, 304; Bristow, *Vice and Vigilance*, 222.

40. James Marchant (ed.), *The Declining Birth-Rate: Its Causes and Effects, Being the Report of and the Evidence Taken by the National Birth-Rate Commission, Instituted, with Official Recognition, by the National Council of Public Morals—for the Promotion of Race Regeneration—Spiritual, Moral and Physical* (London: Chapman and Hall, 1916), and *Problems of Population and Parenthood, Being the Second Report and the Chief Evidence Taken by the National Birth-Rate Commission, 1918–1920* (London: Chapman & Hall, 1920); Porter and Hall, *The Facts of Life*, 184–7.

41. Rebecca West, "The Freewoman", *Time and Tide*, 16 July 1926, reprinted in Dale Spender, *Time and Tide Wait for No Man* (London: Pandora Press, 1984), 65–6.

42. Les Garner, *A Brave and Beautiful Spirit: Dora Marsden, 1882–1960* (Aldershot: Avebury, 1990), 60.

43. Bland, *Banishing the Beast*, 281–7; Lesley A. Hall, 'The Next Generation: Stella Browne, the New Woman as Freewoman', in Angelique Richardson and Chris Willis (eds), *The New Woman in Fiction and in Fact: Fin-de-Siècle Feminisms* (London: Macmillan, 2001), 224-38; Margaret Jackson, *The Real Facts of Life: Feminism and the Politics of Sexuality, c.1850–1940* (London: Taylor & Francis, 1994), 91–4; Sheila Jeffreys, *The Spinster and Her Enemies: Feminism and Sexuality, 1880–1930* (London: Pandora, 1985), 51–2.

44. Bland, *Banishing the Beast*, 269–70; Porter and Hall, *The Facts of Life*, 181.

45. Laurence Housman to Janet Ashbee, 23 August and 7 December 1913, Ashbee Journals, vol. 25 (1913), Modern Archives Centre, King's College Cambridge.

46. Lesley A. Hall, ' "Disinterested enthusiasm for sexual misconduct": The British Society for the Study of Sex Psychology, 1913–1947', *Journal of Contemporary History*, 30 (1995), 665–86.

47. Stella Browne to Havelock Ellis [1916], Havelock Ellis papers, Department of Manuscripts, British Library, Additional Manuscripts 70539.

48. Stella Browne to Bertrand Russell, 12 September 1917, Bertrand Russell papers: William Ready Division of Archives and Research Collections, Mills Memorial Library, McMaster University, Hamilton, Ontario, Canada.

49. Paul Delany, *The Neo-Pagans: Friendship and Love in the Rupert Brooke Circle* (Basingstoke and London: Macmillan Press, 1987); Samuel Hynes, *A War Imagined: The First World War and English Culture* (London: Bodley Head, 1990), 10–19.

50. Barbara Winslow, *Sylvia Pankhurst: Sexual politics and political activism* (London: UCL Press, 1996), 75–104.

51. Laurence Housman to Janet Ashbee, 17 April 1915, Ashbee Journals, 31, April–May 1915.

52. Angela Woollacott, ' "Khaki Fever" and its Control: Gender, Class, Age and Sexual Morality on the British Homefront in the First World War', *Journal of Contemporary History*, 29 (1994), 325–47.

53. Philippa Levine, ' "Walking the Streets in a Way No Decent Woman Should": Women Police in World War I', *Journal of Modern History*, 66 (1994), 34–78; Woollacott, ' "Khaki Fever" '.

54. Susan R. Grayzel, ' "The Mothers of Our Soldiers' Children": Motherhood, Immorality and the War Baby Scandal, 1914–18', in Claudia Nelson and Ann Sumner Holmes (eds), *Maternal Instincts: Visions of Motherhood and Sexuality in Britain, 1875–1925* (Basingstoke and London: Macmillan Press, 1997), 122–40.

55. Pat Thane, 'Unmarried motherhood in twentieth-century England', *Women's History Review*, 20 (2011), 11–29.

56. Lesley A. Hall, '"War always brings it on": War, STDs, the military, and the civilian population in Britain, 1850–1950', in Roger Cooter, Mark Harrison, and Steve Sturdy (eds), *Medicine and Modern Warfare* (Amsterdam: Rodopi, 1999), 205–23.

57. *History of the Great War Based on Official Documents: Medical Services: Diseases of the War: Volume II* (London: HMSO, 1923), 121.

58. Aldgate and Robertson, *Censorship in Theatre and Cinema*, 6–8; Hall, '"War always brings it on"', and 'Venereal Diseases and Society in Britain'; Robertson, *The Hidden Cinema*, 12–15.

59. Hall, 'Venereal Diseases and Society in Britain'.

60. Philippa Levine, *Prostitution, Race, and Politics: Policing Venereal Disease in the British Empire* (London: Routledge, 2003), 145–75.

61. Lesley A. Hall, 'Impotent ghosts from no-man's land, flappers' boyfriends, or crypto-patriarchs? Men, sex, and social change in 1920s Britain', *Social History*, 21 (1996), 54–70.

62. M. Leonora Eyles, *The Woman in the Little House* (London: Grant Richards, 1922), 132.

63. Edward Carpenter to Havelock Ellis, 24 December 1915, Harry Ransom Humanities Research Center.

64. Stella Browne to Havelock Ellis, 1 February 1916, BL Add Mss 70539.

65. Lucy Bland, 'Trial by Sexology? Maud Allan, Salome, and the Cult of the Clitoris case', in Lucy Bland and Laura Doan (eds), *Sexology in Culture: Labelling Bodies and Desires* (Oxford: Polity Press, 1998), 183–98; Deborah Cohler, *Citizen, Invert, Queer: Lesbianism and War in the Early Twentieth Century Britain* (Minneapolis, MN: University of Minnesota Press, 2010), 128–42; Laura Doan, *Fashioning Sapphism: The origins of a modern English lesbian culture* (New York: Columbia University Press), 31–4; Judith Walkowitz, 'The "Vision of Salome": Cosmopolitanism and Erotic Dancing in Central London, 1908–1918', *The American Historical Review*, 108 (2003), 337–76.

66. Liz Stanley, *The Auto/Biographical Writings I: Theory and Practice of Feminist Autobiography* (Manchester: Manchester University Press, 1992), 227–33.

67. Lesley A. Hall, *The Life and Times of Stella Browne: Feminist and free spirit* (London: I. B. Tauris, 2011), 73–5.

68. Cohler, *Citizen, Invert, Queer*, 116–28; Doan, *Fashioning Sapphism*, 153–5; Hynes, *A War Imagined*, 23–4.

69. Marie Stopes, *Married Love: A New Contribution to the Solution of Sexual Difficulties* (London: A. C. Fifield, 1918, reissued Oxford World Classics, 2004). Lesley A. Hall, 'Uniting Science and Sensibility: Marie Stopes and the Narratives of Marriage in the 1920s', in Angela Ingram and Daphne Patai (eds), *Rediscovering Forgotten Radicals: British Women Writers 1889–1939* (Chapel Hill, NC: University of North Carolina Press, 1993), 118–36, and 'Introduction', *Marie Stopes: Birth Control and Other Writings Vol. 1: Motherhood* (Bristol/Tokyo: Thoemmes Press/Editions Synapse, 2000), vii–xxiii; Porter and Hall, *The Facts of Life*, 220–2.

70. Kate Fisher, '"Teach the Miners Birth Control": The Delivery of Contraceptive Advice in South Wales, 1918–1950', in Pamela Michael and Charles Webster (eds), *Health and Society in Twentieth-Century Wales* (Cardiff: University of Wales Press, 2006), 143–64.

71. Lucy Bland, 'White Women and Men of Colour: Miscegenation Fears in Britain after the Great War' *Gender and History*, 17 (2005), 29–61; Laura Tabili, 'Women "of a Very Low Type": Crossing Racial Boundaries in Imperial Britain', in Laura L. Frader and Sonya O. Rose (eds), *Gender and Class in Modern Europe* (Ithaca, NY: Cornell University Press, 1996), 165–90.

6 Roars of Rebellion, Roars of Reaction: The Ambivalences of the Twenties

1. Douglas Goldring to Jane Burr, 6 November 1949, Jane Burr papers, no. 20, Sophia Smith Collection, Smith College.
2. Douglas Goldring, *The Nineteen-Twenties: A General Survey and some Personal Memories* (London: Nicholson & Watson, 1945), 58–65.
3. Judy Giles, ' "Playing Hard to Get": Working-class women, sexuality and respectability in Britain, 1918–40', *Women's History Review*, 1 (1992), 239–55; Claire Langhamer, 'Love and Courtship in Mid-Twentieth-Century England', *The Historical Journal*, 50 (2007), 173–96; Simon Szreter and Kate Fisher, *Sex before the Sexual Revolution: Intimate Life in England 1918–1963* (Cambridge: Cambridge University Press, 2010); Derek Thompson,'Courtship and marriage in Preston between the wars', *Oral History*, 3/2 (1975), 39–44.
4. H. G. Cocks, *Classified: The secret history of the personal column* (London: Random House, 2009), 43–81.
5. Cheryl Law, 'The old faith living and the old power there: The movement to extend women's suffrage', in Maroula Joannou and June Purvis (eds), *The Women's Suffrage Movement: New feminist perspectives* (Manchester: Manchester University Press, 1998), 201–14.
6. Martin Pugh, *Women and the Women's Movement in Britain, 1914–1959* (Basingstoke and London: Macmillan Press, 1992), 80–3; 'St Mary's: coeducation' 1924–26, 'St Mary's: closure to women students' 1924, 'Co- Education: Proposals by certain London medical schools to exclude women students' 1928–1938, Medical Women's Federation Archives, Wellcome Library, SA/MWF/C.15–16, SA/MWF/ D.9/2–5.
7. Isabel Elmslie Hutton, *Memories of a Doctor in War and Peace* (London: Heinemann, 1960), 207.
8. F. W. Stella Browne, 'Review: The Sexual Crisis: A Critique of our Sex Life. By Grete Meisel-Hess', *The Malthusian*, 1917, 39; Dora Russell, *Hypatia, or Woman and Knowledge* (London: Kegan Paul, Trench, Trubner, 1925), 26–39; Katherine Holden, *The Shadow of Marriage: Singleness in England, 1914–60* (Manchester: Manchester University Press, 2007), 80–139.
9. Marie Stopes, *Radiant Motherhood: A Book for Those Who are Creating the Future* (London: G. P. Putnams' Sons, 1920), 157–9.
10. Margaret Jackson, *The Real Facts of Life: Feminism and the Politics of Sexuality, c.1850–1940* (London: Taylor & Francis, 1994); Sheila Jeffreys, *The Spinster and Her Enemies: Feminism and Sexuality 1880–1930* (London: Pandora, 1985).
11. *The State and Sexual Morality* (London: George Allen & Unwin, 1920), 35.
12. *The State and Sexual Morality*, 40.
13. *The State and Sexual Morality*, 30–2; Julia Ann Laite, 'The Association for Moral and Social Hygiene: Abolitionism and prostitution law in Britain (1915–1959)', *Women's History Review*, 17 (2008), 207–23.
14. Richard Davenport-Hines, *Sex, Death and Punishment: Attitudes to sex and sexuality in Britain since the Renaissance* (London: Collins, 1990), 151.
15. George Ives, 'Notes and Various Writings', 9 July 1914, vol. LX, Harry Ransom Humanities Research Center, University of Texas at Austin.
16. Laura Doan, ' "Acts of Female Indecency": Sexology's Intervention in Legislating Lesbianism', in Lucy Bland and Laura Doan (eds), *Sexology in Culture: Labelling Bodies and Desires* (Oxford: Polity Press, 1998), 198–213; Laura Doan, *Fashioning*

Sapphism: The origins of a modern English lesbian culture, (New York: Columbia University Press, 2001), 35–63; Jeff Weeks, *Coming Out: Homosexual Politics in Britain, from the Nineteenth Century to the Present* (London: Quartet, 1977), 106–7.

17. Alison Oram, *Her Husband was a Woman!: Women's gender-crossing and twentieth century British popular culture* (London: Routledge, 2007), 34–7, 58–9.

18. Carol Smart, 'Reconsidering the Recent History of Child Sexual Abuse, 1910–1960', *Journal of Social Policy*, 29 (2000), 55–73.

19. Pamela Cox, *Gender, Justice and Welfare: Bad Girls in Britain, 1900–1950* (Basingstoke: Palgrave Macmillan, 2003).

20. Angus McLaren, *Sexual Blackmail: A Modern History* (Cambridge, MA: Harvard University Press, 2002), 63–80.

21. *Report of the Street Offences Committee* [Cmd 3231] (London: HMSO, 1928); Laite, 'The Association for Moral and Social Hygiene'.

22. Timothy D'Arch Smith, 'Introduction', *The Quorum: A Magazine of Friendship: facsimile edition* (Asphodel Editions, 2001), 1–15.

23. Cocks, *Classified*, 3–15.

24. Matt Houlbrook, *Queer London: Perils and Pleasures in the Sexual Metropolis, 1918–1957* (Chicago, IL: University of Chicago Press, 2005), 19–37, ' "The Man with the Powder Puff" in interwar London', *The Historical Journal*, 50 (2007) 145–71, and 'The Private World of Public Urinals in London, 1918–1957', *The London Journal*, 25 (2000), 52–70.

25. Norah March [of the SPVD] to Alison Neilans of the Association for Moral and Social Hygiene, 21 December 1921, AMSH 'Venereal Diseases', file 2 (Box 311), AMSH archives, The Women's Library, London Metropolitan University.

26. Stella Browne to Janet Carson, 11 July 1920, British Sexology Society archives, 'Misc', Harry Ransom Center.

27. Davenport-Hines, *Sex, Death and Punishment*, 239–40.

28. Association for Moral and Social Hygiene, 'Venereal Diseases', file 2 (Box 311).

29. Ministry of Health, *Report of the Committee of Enquiry on Venereal Disease* (London: HMSO, 1923).

30. Sir Arthur Newsholme, 'The Decline in Registered Mortality from Syphilis in England. To what is it due?', *Journal of Social Hygiene*, 12 (1926), 514–23.

31. W. Metcalfe Chambers, 'Prostitution and Venereal Disease', *British Journal of Venereal Diseases*, 2 (1926), 68–75.

32. Newsholme, 'The Decline in Registered Mortality from Syphilis'.

33. Pamela Cox, 'Compulsion, Voluntarism, and Venereal Disease: Governing Sexual Health in England after the Contagious Diseases Acts', *Journal of British Studies*, 46 (2007), 91–115.

34. Lesley A. Hall, 'What shall we do with the poxy sailor? Venereal diseases in the British mercantile marine', *Journal of Maritime Research*, 6 (2004), 113–44: http://www.tandfonline.com/doi/abs/10.1080/21533369.2004.9668339 [Accessed 18 Oct. 2011].

35. Tim Boon, 'Films and the contestation of public health in interwar Britain', University of London PhD, 1999, 131–61; Roger Davidson, *Dangerous Liaisons: The social history of VD in twentieth- century Scotland* (Amsterdam: Rodopi, 2000), 135–55; Leanne McCormick, *Regulating Sexuality: Women in Twentieth-Century Northern Ireland* (Manchester: Manchester University Press, 2010), 122–7; Archives of the NCCVD/BSHC in the Wellcome Library, SA/BSH.

36. A. H. Halsey (ed.), *British Social Trends since 1900: A Guide to the Changing Social Structure of Britain* (Basingstoke and London: Macmillan Press 1988), 80.

37. David Butler and Gareth Butler, *British Political Facts, 1900–1994* (Basingstoke and London: Macmillan Press, 1994), 326; Stephen Cretney, *Family Law in the Twentieth Century: A History* (Oxford: Oxford University Press, 2003), 214.

38. Robert Graves and Alan Hodges, *The Long Weekend: A Social History of Great Britain, 1918–1939* (London: Faber & Faber, 1950), 110.

39. 'The Matrimonial Causes Act', *The Shield*, 3rd series, no. 4 (1923–25), 61; Catriona Beaumont, 'Moral Dilemmas and Women's Rights: The attitude of the Mothers' Union and Catholic Women's League to divorce, birth control and abortion in England, 1928–1939', *Women's History Review*, 16 (2007), 463–86; Cretney, *Family Law*, 214–24; Ann Sumner Holmes, 'The Double Standard in the English Divorce Laws, 1857–1923', *Law and Social Enquiry: The Journal of the American Bar Foundation*, 20 (1995), 601–2; Gail Savage, 'Erotic Stories and Public Decency: Newspaper reporting of divorce proceedings in England', *Historical Journal*, 41 (1998), 511– 28.

40. Cretny, *Family Law*, 276–80, 306–10; Graves and Hodges, *The Long Weekend*, 109–10; McGregor, *Divorce in England: A centenary study* (London: Heinemann, 1957) 36; Roderick Phillips, *Untying the Knot: A Short History of Divorce* (Cambridge: Cambridge University Press, 1991), 192–3.

41. Judith Adamson, *Charlotte Haldane: Woman Writer in a Man's World* (Basingstoke and London: Macmillan Press, 1998), 48–9.

42. Hera Cook, *The Long Sexual Revolution: English Women, Sex, and Contraception 1800–1975* (Oxford: Oxford University Press, 2004); Kate Fisher, *Birth Control, Sex, and Marriage in Britain 1918–1960* (Oxford: Oxford University Press, 2006), and 'Contrasting cultures of contraception: Birth control clinics and the working-classes in Britain between the wars', in M Gijswijt-Hofstra, G. M. Van Heteren, and E. M. Tansey (eds), *Biographies of Remedies: Drugs, medicines and contraceptives in Dutch and Anglo-American Healing Cultures* (*Clio Medica* 66, Rodopi, 2002), 141–57; Simon Szreter, *Fertility, Class and Gender in Britain, 1860–1940* (Cambridge: Cambridge University Press, 1996); Simon Szreter and Kate Fisher, *Sex before the Sexual Revolution: Intimate Life in England 1918–1963* (Cambridge: Cambridge University Press, 2010).

43. 'Contraception', *The Practitioner*, July 1923, 1–3.

44. R. A. Soloway, *Birth Control and the Population Question in England, 1877–1930* (Chapel Hill, NC: University of North Carolina Press), 208–32.

45. Deborah A. Cohen, 'Private Lives in Public Spaces: Marie Stopes, the Mothers' Clinics and the Practice of Contraception', *History Workshop Journal*, 35 (1993), 95–116; Pamela Dale and Kate Fisher, 'Contrasting Municipal Responses to the Provision of Birth Control Services in Halifax and Exeter before 1948', *Social History of Medicine*, 23 (2010), 567–85; Clare Debenham, 'Mrs Elsie Plant – Suffragette, socialist, and birth-control activist', *Women's History Review*, 19 (2010), 145–58, and 'Grassroots Feminism: A study of the campaign of the Society for the Provision of Birth Control Clinics, 1924–1938', Manchester University PhD 2010, especially Chapter 3, 82–120; Margaret Douglas, 'Women, God and Birth Control: The first hospital birth control clinic', *Llafur*, 6/4 (1995), 110–22; Fisher, 'Contrasting cultures of contraception, 141–57, and ' "Teach the Miners Birth Control": The Delivery of Contraceptive Advice in South Wales, 1918–1950', in Pamela Michael and Charles Webster (eds), *Health and Society in Twentieth-Century Wales* (Cardiff: University of Wales Press, 2006), 143–64; Julie Grier, 'Eugenics and Birth Control: Contraceptive Provision in North Wales, 1918–1939', *Social History of Medicine*, 11 (1998), 443–58; Emma L. Jones, 'The Establishment of Voluntary Family Planning clinics in Liverpool and Bradford,

1926–1960: A Comparative Study', *Social History of Medicine*, 24 (2011), 352–69; Greta Jones, 'Marie Stopes in Ireland: The Mother's Clinic in Belfast, 1936–1947', *Social History of Medicine*, 5 (1992) 255–77; Tania Macintosh, 'An Abortionist City. Maternal Mortality, Abortion and Birth Control in Sheffield, 1920–1940', *Medical History*, 44 (2000), 75–97.

46. Naomi Mitchison, *Comments on Birth Control* (London: Faber & Faber, 1930), 17–18.

47. Fisher, *Birth Control, Sex and Marriage*, 189–237, Szreter and Fisher, *Sex Before the Sexual Revolution*, 229–67.

48. Bryher to Louise Morgan, *c*.Dec. 1926, Morgan/Theis papers in Beinecke Library, Yale University, GEN MSS 80.

49. Stephen Brooke, 'Bodies, Sexuality and the "Modernization" of the British Working Classes, 1920s to 1960s', *International Labor and Working-Class History*, 60 (2006), 104–22; Lesley Hoggart, 'The campaign for birth control in Britain in the 1920s', in Anne Digby and John Stewart (eds), *Gender, Health and Welfare* (1996), 143–66; Soloway, *Birth Control and the Population Question*, 280–303.

50. 'Contraception', *The Practitioner*, July 1923, 90.

51. Lesley A. Hall, ' "A suitable job for a woman"?: Women doctors and birth control before 1950', in Larry Conrad and Anne Hardy (eds), *Women and Modern Medicine* (Amsterdam: Rodopi, 2001), 127–47.

52. Katherine Holden, 'Imaginary Widows: Spinsters, Marriage, and the "Lost Generation" in Britain after the Great War', *Journal of Family History*, 30 (2005), 388–409.

53. Judy Giles, 'A Home of One's Own: Women and Domesticity in England 1918–1950', *Women's Studies International Forum*, 16 (1993), 239–53; Pugh, *Women and the Women's Movement*, 222–6; Christine Zmorczek, 'Dirty Linen: Women, Class, and Washing Machines, 1920s–1960s', *Women's Studies International Forum*, 15 (1992), 173–85.

54. Marcus Collins, *Modern Love: An Intimate History of Men and Women in Twentieth Century Britain* (London: Atlantic Books, 2003), 39–56; Hera Cook, 'Sex and the Experts. Medicalisation as a Two Way Process, Britain 1920–1950', in Willem de Blécourt and Cornelie Usborne (eds), *Cultural Approaches to the History of Medicine: Mediating Medicine in Early Modern and Modern Europe* (Basingstoke: Palgrave Macmillan, 2003), 192–211.

55. Lesley A. Hall, 'Uniting Science and Sensibility: Marie Stopes and the narratives of marriage in the 1920s', in Angela Ingram and Daphne Patai (eds), *Rediscovering Forgotten Radicals: British Women Writers, 1889–1939* (Chapel Hill, NC: University of North Carolina Press, 1993), 118–36, 'Impotent ghosts from no-man's land, flappers' boyfriends, or crypto- patriarchs? Men, sex and social change in 1920s Britain', *Social History*, 21(1996), 54–70, and 'Marie Stopes and her correspondents: Personalising population decline in an era of demographic change', in Robert A. Peel (ed.), *Marie Stopes, Eugenics and the English Birth Control Movement* (London: The Galton Institute, 1997), 27–48.

56. Naomi Mitchison, *All Change Here: Girlhood and Marriage* (London: Bodley Head, 1975), 157, and *You May Well Ask: A Memoir, 1920–1940* (London: Gollancz, 1979), 69–70.

57. Cook, *The Long Sexual Revolution*; Fisher, *Birth Control, Sex and Marriage*; Steve Humphries, *A Secret World of Sex: Forbidden Fruit, the British Experience, 1900–1950* (London: Sidgwick & Jackson, 1988); Nickie Leap and Billie Hunter, *The Midwife's Tale: An Oral History from Handywoman to Professional Midwife* (London: Scarlet

Press, 1993); Szreter and Fisher, *Sex Before the Sexual Revolution;* Diana Gittins, *Fair Sex: Family size and structure, 1900–39* (London: Hutchinson, 1982).

58. M. Leonora Eyles, *The Woman in the Little House* (London: Grant Richards, 1922), 129–51.

59. Marie Stopes, *Mother England: A Contemporary History self-written by those who have no historian* (London: John Bale and Danielsson, 1928).

60. F. W. Stella Browne, 'Review of Free Thought on Sex (Personal Aspects) ... by ... George Whitehead', *The New Generation*, 2 (1923), 146.

61. Professor Vernon Henry Mottram, unpubl. autobiography, Physiological Society Additional Deposited Papers in the Wellcome Library, GC/151/7.

62. Lesley A. Hall, ' "Disinterested enthusiasm for sexual misconduct": The British Society for the Study of Sex Psychology, 1913–47', *Journal of Contemporary History*, 30 (1995), 665–86.

63. Goldring to Burr, 6 November 1949.

64. R. E. N. to Julian Huxley, 10 June 1920, Sir Julian Huxley Papers at Rice University, Houston, Texas, 6.1.

65. A. S. to Julian Huxley, 19 January 1922, Huxley Papers, 7.1.

66. 'From One Woman to Another: Leonora Eyles invites you to discuss your troubles with her', *Modern Woman*, October 1926.

67. Sue Morgan, ' "The Word made Flesh": Women, religion and sexual cultures', in Sue Morgan and Jacqueline deVries (eds), *Women, Gender and Religious Cultures in Britain, 1800–1940* (London: Routledge, 2010), 157–87.

68. Edward Bristow, *Vice and Vigilance: Purity Movements in Britain since 1700* (Dublin: Gill & Macmillan, 1977), 146–7.

69. Rev. A. Herbert Gray, *Men, Women and God: A Discussion of Sex Questions from the Christian Point of View* (London: Student Christian Movement, 1923), 199–200.

70. Mrs Neville-Rolfe, Secretary-General, British Social Hygiene Council, to Prof. J Arthur Thomson (copied to Professor Huxley), 19 March 1928, Huxley Papers, 9.7.

71. Una Troubridge to Havelock Ellis, 7 November 1928, Havelock Ellis papers in the British Library Department of Manuscripts, Additional Manuscripts 70539.

72. Hall, ' "Disinterested enthusiasm for sexual misconduct" '.

73. Porter and Hall, *The Facts of Life*, 259–60.

74. Paul Ferris, *Sex and the British: A Twentieth-Century History* (London: Michael Joseph, 1993), 99–101; Alan Travis, *Bound and Gagged: A secret history of obscenity in Britain* (London: Profile Books, 2000), 18–44.

75. Hutton, *Memories of a Doctor*, 214–17.

76. Alec Craig, *Above all Liberties* (London: Allen & Unwin, 1942), 103.

77. Hall, 'Marie Stopes and her correspondents'; Porter and Hall, *The Facts of Life*, 217.

78. Adrian Bingham, *Gender, Modernity, and the Popular Press in Inter-War Britain* (Oxford: Oxford University Press, 2004), and *Family Newspapers? Sex, Private Life and the British Popular Press, 1918–1978* (Oxford: Oxford University Press, 2009).

79. Lesley A Hall, *The Life and Times of Stella Browne: Feminist and Free Spirit* (London: I. B. Tauris, 2011).

80. Emma L. Jones, 'Representations of illegal abortionists in England, 1900–1967', in Andrew Mangham and Greta DePledge (eds), *The Female Body in Medicine and Literature* (Liverpool: Liverpool University Press, 2011), 196–215, and 'Abortion in England, 1861–1967' University of London PhD thesis, 2007.

81. René Weis, *Criminal Justice: The True Story of Edith Thompson* (London: Hamish Hamilton, 1988), 70.

82. Annette Kuhn, *Cinema, Censorship and Sexuality, 1909–1925* (London: Routledge, 1988), 49–74. Boon, 'Films and the contestation of public health', 131–61.

83. Stefan Slater, 'Pimps, Police and Filles de Joie: Foreign Prostitution in Interwar London', *The London Journal*, 32 (2007), 53–74.

84. Lucy Bland, 'The Trials and Tribulations of Edith Thompson: The Capital Crime of Sexual Incitement in 1920s England', *Journal of British Studies*, 47 (2008), 624–48, and 'The trial of Madame Fahmy: Orientalism, violence, sexual perversity and the fear of miscegenation', in Shani D'Cruze (ed.), *Everyday Violence in Britain, 1850–1950: Gender and Class* (Harlow: Longman, 2001), 185–97.

85. Angus McLaren, *Sexual Blackmail*, 147–61.

86. Bingham, *Family Newspapers?*, 133–44.

87. Graves and Hodge, *The Long Weekend*, 111–12; Savage, 'Erotic Stories and Public Decency'.

88. Soloway, *Birth Control and the Population Question*, 241–2.

89. George Ives, 'Notes and Various Writings', 17 March 1929, Vol. XCIII, Harry Ransom Center.

90. Bingham, *Family Newspapers?*, 178–9; Doan, *Fashioning Sapphism*, 1–30; Ferris, *Sex and the British*, 107–13; Rebecca O'Rourke, *Reflecting on 'The Well of Loneliness'* (London: Routledge, 1989), 90–4; Travis, *Bound and Gagged*, 45–73; Martha Vicinus, *Intimate Friends: Women Who Loved Women, 1778–1928* (Chicago, IL: University of Chicago Press, 2004), 215–27; Weeks, *Coming Out*, 107–11.

91. Miss E. M. B. to Julian Huxley, 24 May 1929, Huxley papers, 10.1.

92. Cohler, *Citizen, Invert, Queer*, 174–84; Ellen Bayuk Rosenman, 'Sexual Identity and A Room of One's Own: "Secret Economies" in Virginia Woolf 's feminist discourse', *Signs: Journal of Women in Culture and Society*, 14 (1989), 634–50.

93. Emily Hamer, 'Keeping Their Fingers on the Pulse: Lesbian Doctors, 1890–1950', in Franz X. Eder, Lesley A. Hall, and Gert Hekma (eds), *Sexual Cultures in Europe: 2: Themes in Sexuality* (Manchester: Manchester University Press, 1999), 139–55; Holden, 'Imaginary Widows', and *The Shadow of Marriage: singleness in England, 1914–60* (Manchester: Manchester University Press, 2007), 99–104.

94. Oram, *Her Husband was a Woman!*

95. Bingham, *Gender, Modernity, and the Popular Press*, 179; Doan, *Fashioning Sapphism*, 82–94; Oram, *Her Husband Was A Woman!*, 63–7; James Vernon, '"For Some Queer Reason": The Trials and Tribulations of Colonel Barker's Masquerade in Interwar Britain', *Signs: Journal of Women in Culture and Society* 26 (2000), 37–61.

96. Jeffreys, *The Spinster and Her Enemies*, 187.

97. Norman Haire (ed.), *World League for Sexual Reform: Proceedings of the Third Congress* (London: Kegan Paul, Trench, Trubner, 1930), xx.

98. C. P. Blacker to Julian Huxley, 21 February 1929, Norman Haire for the World League of Sexual Reform 3rd International Congress to Julian Huxley, 21 February, 27 June, 2 July 1929, Huxley papers, 10.1; World League for Sexual Reform, 1928–1929, Dora Russell papers, International Institute for Social History, Amsterdam, 407; Ivan Crozier, 'Becoming a Sexologist: Norman Haire, the 1929 London World League for Sexual Reform Congress, and Organizing Medical Knowledge about Sex in Interwar England', *History of Science*, 39 (2001), 299–329, and '"All the World's a Stage": Dora Russell, Norman Haire, and the

1929 London World League for Sexual Reform Congress', *Journal of the History of Sexuality*, 12 (2003), 16–37.

99. Alan Rusbridger, 'French Letters of a Cambridge Don', *The Guardian*, 13 November 1991.

7 Population Fears and Progressive Agendas During the Thirties

1. Audrey Leathard, *The Fight for Family Planning: The Development of Family Planning Services in Britain, 1921–74* (Basingstoke and London: Macmillan Press, 1980), 41–50; R. A. Soloway, *Birth Control and the Population Question in England, 1877–1930* (Chapel Hill, NC: University of North Carolina Press, 1982), 307–16.

2. Lord Horder, 'Birth Control: An Introduction', *The Practitioner*, 131 (1933), 221–7.

3. Leathard, *The Fight for Family Planning*, 51–3.

4. Leathard, *The Fight for Family Planning*, 55–7.

5. Pamela Dale and Kate Fisher. 'Contrasting Municipal Responses to the Provision of Birth Control Services in Halifax and Exeter before 1948', *Social History of Medicine*, 23 (2010), 567–85; Kate Fisher, 'Contrasting cultures of contraception: Birth control clinics and the working-classes in Britain between the wars', in M Gijswijt-Hofstra, G. M. Van Heteren, and E. M. Tansey (eds), *Biographies of Remedies: Drugs, medicines and contraceptives in Dutch and Anglo-American Healing Cultures* (*Clio Medica* 66, Rodopi, 2002), 141–57, and ' "Teach the Miners Birth Control": The Delivery of Contraceptive Advice in South Wales, 1918–1950', in Pamela Michael and Charles Webster (eds), *Health and Society in Twentieth-Century Wales* (Cardiff: University of Wales Press, 2006), 143–64; Julie Grier, 'Eugenics and Birth Control: Contraceptive Provision in North Wales, 1918–1939', *Social History of Medicine*, 11 (1998), 443–58; Emma L. Jones, 'The Establishment of Voluntary Family Planning clinics in Liverpool and Bradford, 1926–1960: A Comparative Study', *Social History of Medicine*, 24 (2011), 352–69; Tania Macintosh, 'An Abortionist City: Maternal Mortality, Abortion and Birth Control in Sheffield, 1920–1940', *Medical History*, 44 (2000), 75–97.

6. Medical Committee of the NBCA Minutes, 13 January 1935, Family Planning Association archives, Wellcome Library, SA/FPA/A.5/88.

7. Jeanette Parisot, *Johnny Come Lately: A short history of the condom* (London: Journeyman Press, 1987), 29–31.

8. Minutes of the NBCA Executive Committee, 23 June 1937, SA/ FPA/A.5/2.

9. Ilana Löwy, ' "Sexual chemistry" before the Pill: Science, industry and chemical contraceptives, 1920–1960', *British Journal of the History of Science*, 44 (2011), 245–74; Richard A. Soloway, 'The "Perfect Contraceptive": Eugenics and Birth Control Research in Britain and America in the Interwar Years', *Journal of Contemporary History*, 30 (1995), 637–64.

10. Lesley A. Hall, *Hidden Anxieties: Male Sexuality, 1900–1950* (Oxford: Polity Press, 1991), 166; John Macnicol, 'Eugenics and the Campaign for Voluntary Sterilization in Britain Between the Wars', *Social History of Medicine*, 2 (1989), 147–69, and 'The Voluntary Sterilization Campaign in Britain', in John C. Fout (ed.), *Forbidden History: The State, Society and the Regulation of Sexuality in Modern Europe* (Chicago, IL: University of Chicago Press, 1992), 417–34.

11. Lesley A. Hall, 'Women, Feminism and Eugenics', in Robert A. Peel (ed.), *Essays in the History of Eugenics: Proceedings of a conference organised by the Galton*

Institute, London, 1997 (London: The Galton Institute, 1998), 36–51; Richard A. Soloway, *Demography and Degeneration: Eugenics and the Declining Birthrate in Twentieth-Century Britain* (Chapel Hill, NC: University of North Carolina Press, 1995), 203–15.

12. Margaret Llewelyn Davies (ed.), *Life As We Have Known It by Cooperative Working Women* (London: Hogarth Press, 1931); Margery Spring-Rice, *Working-Class Wives: Their Health and Conditions* (Harmondsworth: Penguin, 1939).

13. Archives of the British Social Hygiene Council (BSHC), Wellcome Library, SA/BSH/A.2/12–18; Ministry of Health file 'British Social Hygiene Council', MH53/1328, The National Archives.

14. H. Wansey Bayly, 'Free Treatment at Venereal Clinics', *The Lancet*, I (1932), 1229.

15. Paul Langford Adams, 'Health of the State: British and American Public Health Policies in the Depression and World War II', unpubl. thesis for the Doctorate of Social Welfare (University of California at Berkeley,1979), 327.

16. M. W. Browdy, 'Free Treatment at Venereal Clinics', *The Lancet*, I (1932), 1279.

17. L. W. Harrison, discussion of Sir Weldon Dalrymple-Champneys, 'The Epidemiological Control of Venereal Disease', *British Journal of Venereal Diseases*, 23 (1947), 108.

18. Francis Louis, 'Free Treatment at Venereal Clinics', *The Lancet*, I (1932), 1279–80.

19. Dalrymple-Champneys, 'The Epidemiological Control of Venereal Disease', and 'Scotland versus VD', *The Lancet*, 1 (1944), 668.

20. Kenneth Walker and A. H. Harkness, 'Preparation for Marriage', *British Medical Journal*, I (1932), 592.

21. 'Preparation for Marriage', *The Lancet*, I (1932), 1369; 'Preparation for Marriage', *British Medical Journal*, II (1932), 111.

22. C. A. Allan, C. O. Hawthorne, A. Keith Gibson, Arthur Newsholme, and J. Astley Cooper, 'Preparation for Marriage', *British Medical Journal*, I (1932), 687, 727–8, 776, 819, 864.

23. W. J. Logie, 'Preparation for Marriage', *British Medical Journal*, I (1932), 959.

24. Edith Summerskill, 'Preparation for Marriage', *British Medical Journal*, I (1932), 819; Arthur Newsholme, 'Preparation for Marriage', *British Medical Journal*, I (1932), 687.

25. Mrs Neville Rolfe to the Ministry of Health, 21 February 1938, MH53/1328; SA/BSH/F.6.

26. Helena Wright, *Marriage (Faith and Practice, no. 8)* (Orpington: The Orpington Press for the Modern Churchmen's Union, n.d., mid-1930s).

27. Helena Wright, *The Sex Factor in Marriage: A book for those who are or are about to be married, with an introduction by A. Herbert Gray, MA, DD* (London: Williams & Norgate, 1930), 11–12.

28. Wright, *The Sex Factor*, 8.

29. Irene Clephane, *Towards Sex Freedom* (London: John Lane, The Bodley Head, 1935), 220–1; Gladys Hall, *Prostitution: A survey and a challenge* (London: Williams & Norgate, 1933), 301; Julia Laite, *Common Prostitutes and Ordinary Citizens: Commercial sex in London, 1880–1960* (Basingstoke, Palgrave, 2011), 52–3; Alison Neilans, 'Changes in Sex Morality', and Mary Agnes Hamilton, 'Changes in Social Life', in Ray Strachey (ed.), *Our Freedom and its Results by Five Women* (London: The Hogarth Press, 1936), 221–4, 268.

30. Judy Giles, ' "Playing Hard to Get": Working-class women, sexuality and respectability in Britain, 1918–40, *Women's History Review*, 1 (1992), 239–55; Claire

Langhamer, 'Love and Courtship in Mid-Twentieth-Century England', *The Historical Journal*, 50 (2007), 173–96; Simon Szreter and Kate Fisher, *Sex before the Sexual Revolution: Intimate Life in England 1918–1963* (Cambridge: Cambridge University Press, 2010), 113–62, 165–95; Derek Thompson, 'Courtship and marriage in Preston between the wars', *Oral History*, 3/2 (1975), 39–44.

31. Harry Cocks, *Classifed: The secret history of the personal column* (London: Random House, 2009), 119–24.
32. N. L. Tranter, *British Population in the Twentieth Century* (Basingstoke and London: Macmillan Press, 1996), 88–9.
33. Eliot Slater and Moya Woodside, *Patterns of Marriage: A Study of Marriage Relationships in the Urban Working Classes* (London: Cassell, 1951), 111–12.
34. *The Shield: The Journal of the Association of Moral and Social Hygiene*, 5th series, 6 (1938), 125; Douglas White, 'The Basis of a New Moral Appeal', *The Shield*, 5th series, 7 (1939), 1–4.
35. Hugh David, *On Queer Street: A social history of British homosexuality, 1895–1995* (London: HarperCollins, 1997), 99–123); Matt Houlbrook, Queer London; *Perils and Pleasures in the Sexual Metropolis, 1918–1957* (Chicago, IL: University of Chicago Press, 2005), 43–194; Samuel Hynes, *The Auden Generation: Literature and Politics in England in the 1930s* (London: Bodley Head, 1976); Kevin Porter and Jeffrey Weeks (eds), *Between the Acts: Lives of homosexual men 1880–1967* (London: Routledge, 1991).
36. Rebecca Jennings, *A Lesbian History of Britain: Love and Sex Between Women since 1500* (Oxford: Greenwood World Publishing, 2007), 131–5.
37. Alison Oram, *Her Husband was a Woman!: Women's gender-crossing and twentieth century British popular culture* (London: Routledge, 2007), 63–108.
38. Adrian Bingham, *Family Newspapers? Sex, Private Life and the British Popular Press, 1918–1978* (Oxford: Oxford University Press, 2009), 173–80; Patrick Higgins, *Heterosexual Dictatorship: Male Homosexuality in Post-War Britain* (London: Fourth Estate, 1996), 256, 278; Houlbrook, *Queer London*, 43–67, and 'The Private World of Public Urinals in London, 1918–1957', *The London Journal*, 25 (2000), 52–70.
39. Porter and Weeks, *Between the Acts*, 63.
40. Porter and Weeks, *Between the Acts*, 148–9.
41. Cecil French to George Ives, 9 November 1935, Ives papers at the Harry Ransom Humanities Research Center, University of Texas at Austin.
42. C. F. R. Haworth to the British Sexology Society, 23 May 1932, 'Letters received', BSS archives, Harry Ransom Center.
43. Cutting of letter 'The Night Club Trial' from W. J. Wenham, sent by Ives to E. S. P. Haynes, 29 January 1937, Ives papers, Harry Ransom Center.
44. Angus McLaren, *The Trials of Manhood: Policing sexual boundaries, 1870–1930* (Chicago, IL: University of Chicago Press, 1997), 208–13; 'Hull, Augustine Joseph, papers concerning his conviction and imprisonment, 1931–32' BSS archives 'Misc', Harry Ransom Center.
45. McLaren, *The Trials of Manhood*, 214–8; Julie Wheelwright, *Amazons and Military Maids: Women who dressed as men in pursuit of life, liberty and happiness* (London: Pandora, 1989), 1–6.
46. McLaren, *The Trials of Manhood*, 223–6; BSS 'Hull, Augustine Joseph, papers concerning', Harry Ransom Center.
47. Lesley A. Hall, '"Disinterested enthusiasm for sexual misconduct": The British Society for the Study of Sex Psychology, 1913–1947', *Journal of Contemporary History*, 30 (1995), 665–86; Dora Russell's World League for Sexual Reform

files, 408–410, International Institute of Social History, Amsterdam; Progressive League scrapbooks; Executive Committee minutes of the Council of the Federation of Progressive Societies and Individuals [British Isles Section of Cosmopolis], Progressive League archives at the British Library for Political and Economic Science; *Plan: The Journal of the Federation of Progressive Societies and Individuals*; Norman Haire papers, Fisher Library, University of Sydney.

48. Janet Chance *The Cost of English Morals* (London: Noel Douglas, 1931), 15–18.

49. Alec Craig, *Sex and Revolution* (London: George Allen & Unwin, 1934).

50. Institute for the Scientific Treatment of Delinquency (ISTD), volume of newspaper cuttings: Centre for Crime and Justice Studies, Kings College London.

51. ISTD, Scientific Committee minutes, Oct. 1936–Mar. 1939, *passim*, and other records of the Institute.

52. ISTD, Scientific Committee minutes, 17 Mar. 1938.

53. ISTD, Scientific Committee minutes Oct. 1936–Mar. 1939. Director's Minutes Oct. 1936–Mar. 1948, *passim*.

54. 'Summary of Opinions…on The Public Morality Council Social Hygiene Questionnaire', National Vigilance Association, 'Sex Education', file S.10D Box 98, The Women's Library, London Metropolitan University.

55. NVA 'Traffic Cases', S.109 Box 110.

56. Bingham, *Family Newspapers?*, 163–4.

57. NVA 'Periodical scare stories (hypodermic syringes, drugs, etc.)', S.127 Box 110.

58. 'Health Club conducted by Dr Mary Denham', *Modern Woman*, May 1935.

59. *Mother: The Home Magazine*, March 1938, 4; Lesley A. Hall, 'Forbidden by God, despised by men: Masturbation, medical warnings, moral panic and manhood in Britain, 1850–1950', *Journal of the History of Sexuality*, 2 (1992), reprinted in John Fout (ed.), *Forbidden History: The State, Society, and the Regulation of Sexuality in Modern Europe* (Chicago, IL: University of Chicago Press, 1992), 293–315.

60. Jane Pilcher, 'Sex in Health Education: Official Guidance for Schools in England, 1928–1977', *Journal of Historical Sociology*, 17 (2004), 185–208.

61. Lesley A Hall, 'Birds, Bees and General Embarrassment: Sex education in Britain from social purity to Section 28', in Richard Aldrich (ed.), *Public or Private Education: Lessons from History* (London: Woburn Press, 2004), 98–115.

62. Roy Porter and Lesley A. Hall, *The Facts of Life: The Creation of Sexual Knowledge in Britain, 1650–1950* (New Haven, CT, and London: Yale University Press, 1995), 175–6; Soloway, 'The "Perfect Contraceptive"'; Löwy, '"Sexual chemistry" before the Pill'.

63. *British Medical Journal*, I (1933), 1057; *The Lancet*, I (1933), 1348–9.

64. Letters, via Lord Horder, to Ellis concerning his nomination, Ellis papers in the Department of Manuscripts, British Library Additional Manuscripts, 70556; Ellis to Margaret Sanger, 19 May 1936, Sanger papers in the Library of Congress, Washington DC vol. 6 (Reel 5).

65. 'Summary Report of Police Proceedings', and letters from 'Edward Charles', Janet Chance, and Lord Horder about the case to Julian Huxley, Huxley papers, 11.9, Rice University, Houston, Texas; Alec Craig, *The Banned Books of England* (London: George Allen & Unwin, 1937), 61–77.

66. H. G. Cocks, *Classified*, 86–116; Harry Cocks, 'Saucy Stories: Pornography, sexology, and the marketing of sexual knowledge in Britain, *c*.1918–70', *Social History*, 29 (2004), 465–84; NVA 'Objectionable Literature', S88, S885, 88H, Box 107.

67. Gerald Gardiner, Opinion on Rockstro's 'A Plain Talk on Sex Difficulties', 18 Oct. 1933, 'Letters Received', BSS Archives, Harry Ransom Center.

68. Soloway, *Demography and Degeneration*, 226–58.
69. A. Susan Williams, *Women and Childbirth in the Twentieth Century: A History of the National Birthday Trust Fund, 1928–93* (Stroud: Sutton Publishing, 1997), 1–49.
70. Ella Gordon to Cora Hodson, 17 March 1931, 'National Council of Women 1926–33', Eugenics Society archives, Wellcome Library, SA/EUG/D.134.
71. 'FWSB' (Stella Browne), ' Workers' Birth Control Group', *The New Generation*, 10 (1931), 39.
72. Barbara Brookes, *Abortion in England, 1900–1967* (London: Croom Helm, 1988), 37–40.
73. Stephen Brooke, 'A New World for Women? Abortion Law Reform in Britain During the 1930s', *American Historical Review* 106 (2001), 431–59; Brookes, *Abortion in England*, 93–8; ; Lesley A. Hall, *The Life and Times of Stella Browne, feminist and free spirit* (London: I. B. Tauris, 2011), 171–245.
74. Brookes, *Abortion in England*, 67–9.
75. Keith Hindell and Madeleine Simms, *Abortion Law Reformed* (London: Peter Owen, 1971), 53–5.
76. James Thomas and A. Susan Williams, 'Women and abortion in 1930s Britain: A survey and its data', *Social History of Medicine*, 11 (1998), 283–309.
77. Lesley A. Hall, ' "No Sex, Please, We're Socialists": The Labour Party prefers to close its eyes and think of the electorate', *Socialist History*, 36 (2010), 11–28.
78. Stella Browne, evidence to the Birkett Committee, MH71/23, The National Archives; Hall, *The Life and Times of Stella Browne*, 226–32.
79. Brookes, *Abortion in England*, 105–32.
80. Brookes, *Abortion in England*, 69–70; Hindell and Simms, *Abortion Law Reformed*, 69–70.
81. Stephen Cretney, *Family Law in the Twentieth Century: A History* (Oxford: Oxford University Press, 2003), 224–49; O. R . McGregor, *Divorce in England: A centenary study* (London: Heinemann, 1957), 29–30, 36; Roderick Phillips, *Untying the Knot: A Short History of Divorce* (Cambridge: Cambridge University Press, 1991), 193–5.
82. A. Susan Williams, *The People's King: The True Story of the Abdication* (London: Allen Lane, 2003).
83. Cretney, *Family Law*, 310–11.
84. Cretney, *Family Law*, 236–48; McGregor, *Divorce in England*, 29–30.
85. Dr Clara Stewart, 'History of the Movement', Edward Fyfe Griffith papers, Wellcome Library, PP/EFG/A.12, and 'Marriage Guidance: Early days of the movement' correspondence files, PP/EFG/A.8–11.
86. Irvine Loudon, 'Some international features of maternal mortality, 1880–1950', Valerie Fildes, Lara Marks, and Hilary Marland (eds), *Women and children first: International maternal and infant welfare, 1870–1945* (London: Routledge, 1992), 5–28.
87. Pat Thane, 'Family Life and "Normality" in Postwar British Culture', in Richard Bessell and Dirk Schumann (eds), *Life after Death: Approaches to a cultural and social history of Europe during the 1940s and 1950s* (Cambridge: Cambridge University Press, 2003), 193–210.
88. Porter and Hall, *The Facts of Life*, 190–3.
89. Peter Gurney, ' "Intersex" and "Dirty Girls": Mass-observation and working class sexuality in England in the 1930s', *Journal of the History of Sexuality*, 8 (1997), 256–90; Porter and Hall, *The Facts of Life*, 194–5; Liz Stanley, *Sex Surveyed,*

1949–1994: From Mass-Observation's 'Little Kinsey' to the National Survey and the Hite Reports (London: Taylor & Francis, 1995), 11–16, 30–1; James Vernon, '"For Some Queer Reason": The Trials and Tribulations of Colonel Barker's Masquerade in Interwar Britain', Signs: Journal of Women in Culture and Society, 26 (2000), 37–61.

90. Oram, Her Husband was a Woman!, 109–27.

8 War and the Welfare State

1. A. H. Halsey, British Social Trends since 1900: A Guide to the Changing Social Structure of Britain (Basingstoke and London: Macmillan Press, 1988), 64.

2. Barbara Brookes, Abortion in England, 1900–1967 (London: Croom Helm, 1988), 137.

3. Penny Summerfield and Nicole Crockett, '"You weren't taught that with the welding": Lessons in sexuality in the Second World War', Women's History Review, 1 (1992), 435–54.

4. John Costello, Love, Sex and War, 1939–1945 (London: William Collins' Sons, 1985), 23.

5. Lesley A. Hall, 'Venereal diseases and society in Britain, from the Contagious Diseases Acts to the National Health Service', in Roger Davidson and Lesley A. Hall (eds), Sex, Sin, and Suffering: Venereal Diseases and European Society since 1870 (London: Routledge, 2001), 120–36.

6. George Ives, 'Notes and Various Writings', 8 May 1940, vol. CV, Harry Ransom Humanities Research Centre, University of Texas at Austin.

7. Adrian Bingham, 'The British Popular Press And Venereal Disease During The Second World War', Historical Journal, 48 (2005), 1055–76.

8. Hall, 'Venereal Diseases and Society in Britain', and '"War always brings it on": War, STDs, the military, and the civilian population in Britain, 1850–1950', in Roger Cooter, Mark Harrison and Steve Sturdy (eds), Medicine and Modern Warfare (Amsterdam: Rodopi, 1999), 205–23; Mass Observation 'Venereal Disease Survey 1942–1943', Tom Harrisson-Mass Observation Archives, University of Sussex, A.9 Box 1.

9. Ministry of Health Circular 42/45, 'Venereal Diseases: Educational Campaign': papers of J. R. Hutchinson, Wellcome Library PP/JRH/A.338 'Venereal Diseases: Circulars' 1916–46.

10. The Lancet, I (1944), 167.

11. Margaret A. Wailes, 'The Social Aspect of the Venereal Diseases: Contact Tracing and the Prostitute', British Journal of Venereal Diseases, 21 (1945), 15–17.

12. MO VD Survey A.9 1/B.

13. Col. J. E. Gordon, 'The Control of Venereal Disease: An Epidemiological Approach', The Lancet, 2 (1944), 711–15.

14. Hall, 'Venereal Diseases and Society in Britain, and '"War Always Brings It On"'.

15. Heather Creaton, Sources for the History of London, 1939–45: A Guide and Bibliography (London: British Records Association, 1999), 83–4.

16. Eustace Chesser, Love Without Fear: A plain guide to Sex Technique for every married adult (London: Rich & Cowan Medical Publications, 1941, rev. edn 1942); Alec Craig, 'Recent Developments in the Law of Obscene Libel', in A. P. Pillay and A. Ellis (eds), Sex, Society and the Individual (Bombay: International Journal of Sexology, 1952), 302–27; Central Criminal Court: Depositions: Defendant: Ec

lipse Press Services Ltd trading as Rich & Cowan and other Charge: Unlawfully publishing an obscene book, Session June 23 1942, CRIM 1/1416, The National Archives.

17. Craig, 'Recent Developments in the Law of Obscene Libel'.
18. Harry Cocks, 'Saucy Stories: Pornography, sexology, and the marketing of sexual knowledge in Britain, c.1918–70', *Social History*, 29 (2004), 465–84; Porter and Hall, *The Facts of Life: The Creation of Sexual Knowledge in Britain, 1650–1950* (New Haven, CT, and London: Yale University Press, 1995), 262–3.
19. Frank Mort, 'Striptease: The erotic female body and live sexual entertainment in mid-twentieth-century London', *Social History*, 32 (2007), 27–53.
20. Annual Report of the Marriage Guidance Council 1943, papers of Edward Fyfe Griffith in the Wellcome Library, PP/EFG/A.12.
21. Eliot Slater and Moya Woodside, *Patterns of Marriage: A study of marriage relationships in the urban working classes* (London: Cassell, 1951), 94–115; Liz Stanley, *Sex Surveyed, 1949–1994: From Mass Observation's 'Little Kinsey' to the Hite Reports* (London: Taylor & Francis, 1995), 38–40.
22. Slater and Woodside, *Patterns of Marriage*, 119–20.
23. Slater and Woodside, *Patterns of Marriage*, 165–76.
24. Stanley, *Sex Surveyed*, 40.
25. Simon Szreter and Kate Fisher, *Sex before the Sexual Revolution: Intimate Life in England 1918–1963* (Cambridge: Cambridge University Press, 2010), 332.
26. Kate Fisher, ' "Lay back, enjoy it and shout happy England": Sexual Pleasure and Marital Duty in Britain, 1918–60', in Kate Fisher and Sarah Toulalan (eds), *Bodies, sex and desire from the Renaissance to the present* (Basingstoke: Palgrave Macmillan, 2011), 181–200.
27. Slater and Woodside, *Patterns of Marriage*, 178–9.
28. Slater and Woodside, *Patterns of Marriage*, 187.
29. Medical Women's Federation archive in the Wellcome Library, 'Royal Commission on Population 1945', 1944–1945, SA/MWF/J.24/1.
30. Slater and Woodside, *Patterns of Marriage*,177–93: Pat Thane, 'Population Politics in Post-War British Culture', in Becky Conekin, Frank Mort, and Chris Waters (eds), *Moments of Modernity: Reconstructing Britain, 1945–1964* (London: Rivers Oram, 1999), 114–33; Stanley, *Sex Surveyed*, 33–5.
31. Slater and Woodside, *Patterns of Marriage*, 189–90.
32. SA/MWF/J.24/1.
33. E. Lewis-Faning, *Papers from the Royal Commission on Population, Vol. 1: Report on an Enquiry into Family Limitation and its influence on Human Fertility during the Past Fifty Years Conducted at the Request of the Royal Commission on Population* (London: HMSO, 1949).
34. Audrey Leathard, *The Fight for Family Planning: The Development of Family Planning Services in Britain, 1921–74* (Basingstoke and London: Macmillan Press, 1980), 69–72.
35. SA/MWF/J.24/1.
36. Mary Thomas (ed.), *Post-War Mothers: Childbirth letters to Grantly Dick-Read, 1946–1956* (Rochester, NY: University of Rochester Press, 1997), 8–20.
37. Gerald J. De Groot, ' "I Love the Scent of Cordite in Your Hair": Gender Dynamics in Mixed Anti-Aircraft Batteries during the Second World War', *History*, 82 (1997), 73–92; Penny Summerfield, *Reconstructing Women's Wartime Lives: Discourse and subjectivity in oral histories of the Second World War* (Manchester: Manchester University Press, 1998), 78–82.
38. Summerfield, *Reconstructing Women's Wartime Lives*, 116–59.

39. Summerfield and Crockett, '"You Weren't Taught that with the welding"'.

40. *Report of the Committee on Amenities and Welfare Conditions in the Three Women's Services.* Cmd. 6384: Parliamentary Papers, 1941–1942, Vol. 4 (London: HMSO, 1942), cited in Harold L. Smith (ed.), *Britain in the Second World War: A social history* (Manchester: Manchester University Press, 1996), 63–4.

41. Stefan Slater, 'Pimps, Police and Filles de Joie: Foreign Prostitution in Interwar London', *The London Journal*, 32 (2007), 53–74.

42. Lesley A. Hall, '"The Reserved Occupation"? Prostitution in the Second World War', *Women's History Magazine*, 41 (2002), 4–9; Julia Laite, *Common Prostitutes and Ordinary Citizens: Commercial sex in London, 1885–1960* (Basingstoke: Palgrave Macmillan, 2011), 158–63.

43. Emily Hamer, *Britannia's Glory: A History of Twentieth-Century Lesbians* (London: Cassell, 1996), 141.

44. Alkarim Jivani, *It's Not Unusual: A History of Lesbian and Gay Britain in the Twentieth Century* (London: Michael O'Mara Books, 1997), 71–5.

45. Summerfield and Crockett, '"You Weren't Taught That with the Welding"'.

46. Hugh David, *On Queer Street: A social history of British Homosexuality, 1895–1995* (London: HarperCollins, 1997), 140–50; Jivani, *It's Not Unusual*, 55–70; Emma Vickers, '"The Good Fellow": Negotiation, Remembrance, and Recollection – Homosexuality in the British Armed Forces, 1939–1945', in Dagmar Herzog (ed.), *Brutality and desire: War and sexuality in Europe's twentieth century* (Basingstoke: Palgrave Macmillan, 2009), 109–34.

47. Kevin Porter and Jeffrey Weeks (eds), *Between the Acts: Lives of homosexual men 1885–1967* (London: Routledge, 1991), 78.

48. George Ives 'Notes and Various Writings', 28 April, 4 August 1940, vol. CV, Harry Ransom Center.

49. Jivani, *It's Not Unusual*, 70.

50. Chris Waters, 'Havelock Ellis, Sigmund Freud and the State: Discourses of Homosexual Identity in Interwar Britain', in Lucy Bland and Laura Doan (eds), *Sexology in Culture: Labelling Bodies and Desires* (Oxford: Polity Press, 1998), 165–79.

51. John Glaister, *Medical Jurisprudence and Toxicology*, 8th edn (Edinburgh: E. & S. Livingstone, 1945), 405–9.

52. Chesser, *Love without Fear*, 111–14.

53. P. H. S. to Julian Huxley, [1942], Huxley papers at Rice University, Houston, Texas, files 16.5; Hugh Crichton-Miller to Huxley, 9 November 1942, file 16.4.

54. Alison Oram, *Her Husband was a Woman!: Women's gender-crossing and twentieth century British popular culture* (London: Routledge, 2007), 131–46.

55. Porter and Weeks (eds), *Between the Acts*, 141–2.

56. Leanne McCormick, *Regulating Sexuality: Women in twentieth-century Northern Ireland* (Manchester: Manchester University Press, 2010), 148–79; Sonya O. Rose, 'Sex, citizenship and the nation in World War II Britain', in Catherine Hall (ed.), *Cultures of Empire: Colonizers in Britain and the Empire in the nineteenth and twentieth centuries: A reader* (Manchester: Manchester University Press, 2000), 246–77; Smith (ed.), *Britain in the Second World War*, 68–71.

57. Summerfield, *Reconstructing Women's Wartime Lives*, 199–249; Julia Swindells, 'Coming Home to heaven: Manpower and myth in 1944 Britain', *Women's History Review*, 4 (1995), 223–33; Barry Turner and Tony Rennell, *When Daddy Came Home: How Family Life Changed Forever in 1945* (London: Hutchinson, 1995).

58. Colleen Margaret Forrest, 'Familial Poverty, Family Allowances, and the Normative Family Structure in Britain, 1917–1945', *Journal of Family History*,

26 (2001), 508–28; Jane Lewis, *Women in England, 1870–1950: Sexual Divisions and Social Change* (Brighton: Wheatsheaf, 1984), 204–5, and *Women in Britain since 1945: Women, Family, Work and the State in the Post-War Years* (Oxford: Blackwell, 1992), 16–26; Elizabeth Wilson, *Only Half-Way to Paradise: Women in Post-War Britain: 1945–1968* (London: Tavistock Publications, 1980), 15–49.

59. Stephen Brooke, *Sexual Politics: Sexuality, Family Planning, and the British Left from the 1880s to the Present Day* (Oxford: Oxford University Press, 2011), 117–45.
60. Leathard, *The Fight for Family Planning*, 73–4.
61. Brookes, *Abortion in England*, 147.
62. Stephen Cretney, *Family Law in the Twentieth Century: A history* (Oxford: Oxford University Press, 2003), 302–4.
63. National Marriage Guidance Council, 'History of the Movement', December 1967, E. F. Griffith papers, PP/EFG/A.12; Leathard, *The Fight for Family Planning*, 81.
64. Cretney, *Family Law*, 311–17.
65. David Evans, 'Sexually-transmitted diseases in Britain in the second half of the twentieth century', in Roger Davidson and Lesley A. Hall (eds), *Sex, Sin, and Suffering: Venereal Diseases and European Society since 1870* (London: Routledge, 2001), 237–52; Hall, 'Venereal diseases and society in Britain'.
66. Edward F. Griffith, 'Marriage and Parenthood', *British Medical Journal*, I (1944), 540; 'Sex Education for Medical Students', *The Lancet*, I (1949), 744.
67. Lesley A Hall, 'Birds, Bees and General Embarrassment: Sex education in Britain from social purity to Section 28', in Richard Aldrich (ed.), *Public or Private Education: Lessons from History* (London: Woburn Press, 2004), 98–115.
68. 'Society for Sex Education and Guidance', 1945–1952, Family Planning Association archives in the Wellcome Library, SA/FPA/A.13/86.
69. L. H. J. to Julian Huxley, 4 April 1949, Huxley papers, file 18.2.
70. Adrian Bingham, *Family Newspapers? Sex, Private Life and the British Popular Press, 1918–1978* (Oxford: Oxford University Press, 2009), 106–9; Porter and Hall, *The Facts of Life*, 198–199, 255–7; Stanley, *Sex Surveyed*.
71. Bingham, *Family Newspapers?*, 73–5.

9 Domestic Ideology and Undercurrents of Change in the Fifties

1. Paul Ferris, *Sex and the British: A Twentieth-Century History* (London: Michael Joseph, 1993), 154–5.
2. Peter Vansittart, *In the Fifties* (London: John Murray, 1995), 3.
3. Elizabeth Wilson, *Only Half-Way to Paradise: Women in Post-War Britain, 1945–1968* (London: Tavistock Publications, 1980), 7.
4. Frank Mort, *Capital Affairs: London and the Making of the Permissive Society* (New Haven, CT: Yale University Press, 2010), 56–90.
5. Geoffrey Gorer, *Exploring English Character* (New York: Criterion Books, 1955), 94.
6. O. R . McGregor, *Divorce in England: A Centenary Study* (London: Heinemann, 1957), 32–6.
7. McGregor, *Divorce in England*, 127.
8. McGregor, *Divorce in England*, 192–3.
9. McGregor, *Divorce in England*, 176.

10. Stephen Cretney, *Family Law in the Twentieth Century: A History* (Oxford: Oxford University Press, 2003), 324–43; McGregor, *Divorce in England*, 126–76.

11. Janet Fink, 'Natural Mothers, Putative Fathers, and Innocent Children: The Definition and Regulation of Parental Relationships Outside Marriage, in England, 1945–1959', *Journal of Family History*, 25 (2000), 178–95.

12. A. H. Halsey (ed.), *British Social Trends since 1900: A Guide to the Changing Social Structure of Britain* (Basingstoke and London: Macmillan Press 1988), 70–5; Pat Thane, 'Family Life and "Normality" in Postwar British Culture', in Richard Bessell and Dirk Schumann (eds), *Life after Death: Approaches to a cultural and social history of Europe during the 1940s and 1950s* (Cambridge: Cambridge University Press, 2003), 193–210; N. L. Tranter, *British Population in the Twentieth Century* (Basingstoke and London: Macmillan Press, 1996), 94–9.

13. Carol Smart, *The Ties That Bind: Law, marriage, and the reproduction of patriarchal relations* (London: Routledge & Kegan Paul, 1984), 28–32; Thane, 'Family Life and "Normality"'.

14. Marcus Collins, *Modern Love: An Intimate History of Men and Women in Twentieth Century Britain* (London: Atlantic Books, 2003), 91–114.

15. Simon Szreter and Kate Fisher, *Sex before the Sexual Revolution: Intimate Life in England 1918–1963* (Cambridge: Cambridge University Press, 2010), 196–226.

16. Janet Finch and Penny Summerfield, 'Social reconstruction and the emergence of companionate marriage', in David Clark (ed.), *Marriage, Domestic Life and Social Change: Writings for Jacqueline Burgoyne (1944–88)* (London: Routledge, 1991), 7–32.

17. Adrian Bingham, *Family Newspapers? Sex, Private Life and the British Popular Press, 1918–1978* (Oxford: Oxford University Press, 2009), 79; Lesley A. Hall, 'Eyes tightly shut, lying rigidly still and thinking of England? British women and sex from Marie Stopes to Hite', in Michelle Martin and Claudia Nelson (eds), *Sexual Pedagogies: Teaching Sex in America, Britain, and Australia, 1879–2000* (Basingstoke: Palgrave Macmillan, 2003), 53–72.

18. Wendy Webster, *Imagining Home: Gender, 'Race' and National Identity, 1945–64* (London: UCL Press, 1998), 91–127.

19. Gorer, *Exploring English Character*, 94–116.

20. Gorer, *Exploring English Character*, 125–32.

21. Gorer, *Exploring English Character*, 137–40.

22. Gorer, *Exploring English Character*, 133.

23. Gorer, *Exploring English Character*, 144–61.

24. Liz Stanley, *Sex Surveyed, 1949–1994: From Mass Observation's 'Little Kinsey' to the National Survey and the Hite Reports* (London: Taylor & Francis, 1995), 40–4.

25. Eustace Chesser, *The Sexual, Marital and Family Relationships of the English Woman* (London: Hutchinson's Medical Publications, 1956), 397–406.

26. Chesser, *The Sexual...Relationships of the English Woman*, 421–4.

27. Chesser, *The Sexual...Relationships of the English Woman*, 434–6.

28. Chesser, *The Sexual...Relationships of the English Woman*, 452.

29. Szreter and Fisher, *The Long Sexual Revolution*, 317–63.

30. Chesser, *The Sexual...Relationships of the English Woman*, 439, 450.

31. Smart, *The Ties That Bind*, 46.

32. Chesser, *The Sexual...Relationships of the English Woman*, 440, 448.

33. Helena Wright, *More About the Sex Factor in Marriage: A Sequel to the Sex Factor in Marriage* (London: Williams & Norgate, 1947, 2nd edn 1954), 10.

34. Wright, *More About the Sex Factor*, 11.

35. 'Medica' [Joan Malleson], *Any Wife or Any Husband* (London: William Heinemann Medical Books, 1950), 13–14.

36. Wright, *More About the Sex Factor*, 11–19.

37. Wright, *More About the Sex Factor*, 44–9.

38. Wright, *More About the Sex Factor*, 51–68.

39. [Malleson], *Any Wife or Any Husband*, 58–64; Wright, *More About the Sex Factor*, 69–78.

40. Mary Macaulay, *The Art of Marriage* (London: Delisle, 1952; Penguin Handbooks, 1957), 80.

41. Alex Comfort, 'Sex Education in the Medical Curriculum', *International Journal of Sexology*, 3 (1950), 175–7; Bernard Sandler, 'The Student and Sex Education', *The Lancet*, I (1957), 832–3.

42. Prudence Tunnadine, *The Making of Love* (London: Unwin Paperbacks, 1985), 11–14.

43. Claire Langhamer, 'Adultery in post-war England', *History Workshop Journal*, 62 (2006), 86–115.

44. Tanya Evans, 'The Other Woman and her Child: Extra-marital affairs and illegitimacy in twentieth-century Britain', *Women's History Review*, 20 (2011), 67–86; Fink, ' Natural Mothers, Putative Fathers'.

45. Audrey Leathard, *The Fight for Family Planning: The Development of Family Planning Services in Britain, 1921–74* (Basingstoke: Macmillan, 1980), 138.

46. Personal communications.

47. Family Planning Association archive in the Wellcome Library, correspondence on birth control advice to immigrants from the Caribbean, 1950–65, SA/FPA/A21/26–7, and SA/FPA/B10/35.

48. Chesser, *The Sexual...Relationships of the English Woman*, 329–34.

49. Peter Bartrip, *Themselves Writ Large: The British Medical Association, 1832–1966* (London: BMJ Publishing Group, 1996), 318–20.

50. V. C. Chamberlain, *Adolescence to Maturity: A Practical Guide to Personal Development, Fulfilment, and Maturity* (London: John Lane, the Bodley Head, 1952; Penguin Books, 1959), 41–2.

51. Gladys Denny Schultz, *Letters to Jane* (London: The Falcon Press, 1949), 32–4.

52. Gladys Denny Schultz, *It's Time You Knew* (London: Darwen Finlayson, 1956), 167.

53. Kenneth C. Barnes, *He and She* (London: Darwin Finlayson, 1958; Penguin Handbooks, 1962), 136–7.

54. Schultz, *Letters to Jane*, 34–5.

55. Barnes, *He and She*, 137.

56. Macaulay, *The Art of Marriage*, 55.

57. Claire Langhamer, 'Love and Courtship in Mid-Twentieth-Century England', *The Historical Journal*, 50 (2007), 173–96; Schultz, *Letters to Jane*, 31, 37; Szreter and Fisher, *Before the Sexual Revolution*, 113–62.

58. Chamberlain, *Adolescence to Maturity*, 41–2.

59. Barnes, *He and She*, 135–7.

60. Stephen Brooke, 'Gender and Working Class Identity in Britain during the 1950s', *Journal of Social History*, 34 (2001), 773–95; Vansittart, *In the Fifties*, 158; Jeffrey Weeks, *Sex, Politics, and Society: The regulation of sexuality since 1800*, 2nd edn (London: Longman, 1989), 252–5.

61. Mort, *Capital Affairs*, 74–90.

62. Frank Mort, 'Striptease: The erotic female body and live sexual entertainment in mid-twentieth-Century London', *Social History*, 32 (2007), 27–53.

63. Brooke, 'Gender and Working Class Identity'.

64. Lesley A Hall, 'Birds, Bees and General Embarrassment: Sex education in Britain from social purity to Section 28', in Richard Aldrich (ed.) *Public or Private Education: Lessons from History* (London: Woburn Press, 2004), 98–115; James Hampshire, 'The politics of school sex education policy in England and Wales from the 1940s to the 1960s', *Social History of Medicine* 18 (2005), 87–105; Jane Pilcher, 'Sex in Health Education: Official Guidance for Schools in England, 1928–1977', *Journal of Historical Sociology*, 17 (2004), 185–208.

65. Halsey, *British Social Trends*, 62–6; Tranter, *British Population*, 88–93; Thane, 'Family Life and "Normality"'.

66. Katharine Holden, *The Shadow of Marriage: Singleness in England, 1914–1960* (Manchester: Manchester University Press, 2007), 126–9; Pat Thane, 'Unmarried motherhood in twentieth-century England', *Women's History Review*', 20 (2011), 11–29.

67. Holden, *The Shadow of Marriage*, 140–52.

68. Leathard, *The Fight for Family Planning*, 86–94.

69. Barbara Brookes, *Abortion in England, 1900–1967* (London: Croom Helm, 1988), 144–9.

70. Ambrose King, '"These Dying Diseases": Venereology in Decline?', *The Lancet*, I (1958), 651–7.

71. King, '"These Dying Diseases"'; Webster, *Imagining Home*, 51.

72. Chris Waters. '"Dark Strangers in Our Midst": Discourses of race and nation in Britain, 1947–1953', *Journal of British Studies*, 36 (1997), 207–38.

73. Laura Tabili, 'Women "of a Very Low Type": Crossing Racial Boundaries in Imperial Britain', in Laura L. Frader and Sonya O. Rose (eds), *Gender and Class in Modern Europe* (Ithaca, NY: Cornell University Press, 1996), 165–90.

74. C. H. Rolph (ed.), *Women of the Streets: A Sociological Study of the Common Prostitute: For and on behalf of the British Social Biology Council* (London: Secker & Warburg, 1955), 245.

75. Waters, '"Dark Strangers"'.

76. Helen Self, *Prostitution, Women and Misuse of the Law: The Fallen Daughters of Eve* (London: Cass, 2003), 70.

77. Bingham, *Family Newspapers*, 164–70; Julia Laite, *Common Prostitutes and Ordinary Citizens: Commercial sex in London, 1885–1960* (Basingstoke: Palgrave Macmillan, 2011), 171–85; Mort, *Capital Affairs*, 41–8; Self, *Prostitution, Women and Misuse of the Law*, 70–2.

78. Laite, *Common Prostitutes and Ordinary Citizens*, 187–90; Rolph (ed.), *Women of the Streets*, 18–23; Barbara Tate, *West End Girls: The real lives, loves and friendships of 1940s Soho and its working girls* (London: Orion, 2010).

79. Rolph (ed.), *Women of the Streets*, 24–5.

80. Rolph (ed.), *Women of the Streets*, 37.

81. Julia Ann Laite, 'The Association for Moral and Social Hygiene: Abolitionism and prostitution law in Britain (1915–1959)', *Women's History Review*, 17 (2008), 207–23; Laite, *Common Prostitutes and Ordinary Citizens*, 191–202; Mort, *Capital Affairs*, 148–9, 166–72; Self, *Prostitution, Women and Misuse of the Law*, 80–150.

82. Laite, *Common Prostitutes and Ordinary Citizens*, 202–11; Self, *Prostitution, Women and Misuse of the Law*, 163–247.

83. Frank Mort, 'Striptease'.

84. Bingham, *Family Newspapers?*, 168–9; Patrick Higgins, *Heterosexual Dictatorship: Male Homosexuality in Post-War Britain* (London: Fourth Estate, 1996), 32–3.

85. Rolph (ed.), *Women of the Streets*, 245.
86. National Vigilance Association file, 'Periodical scare stories (hypodermic syringes, drugs, etc.)' , NVA archives, Box 110 S109 , The Women's Library, London Metropolitan University; Bingham, *Family Newspapers*, 164–8.
87. Bingham, *Family Newspapers*, 180–90; Higgins, *Heterosexual Dictatorship*, 267–93; Chris Waters, 'Disorders of the Mind, Disorders of the Body Social: Peter Wildeblood and the Making of the Modern Homosexual', in Becky Conekin, Frank Mort, and Chris Waters (eds), *Moments of Modernity: Reconstructing Britain, 1945–1964* (London: Rivers Oram, 1999), 134–51.
88. Mort, *Capital Affairs*, 187–93.
89. Matt Houlbrook, *Queer London: Perils and Pleasures in the Sexual Metropolis, 1918–1957* (Chicago, IL: University of Chicago Press, 2005), 43–67, and 'The Private World of Public Urinals in London, 1918–1957', *The London Journal*, 25 (2000), 52–70.
90. Bingham, *Family Newspapers?*, 180; Higgins, *Heterosexual Dictatorship*, 155–69.
91. Higgins, *Heterosexual Dictatorship*, 249; Houlbrook, *Queer London*, 34–6, and 'The Private World of Public Urinals'.
92. Bartrip, *Themselves Writ Large*, 315–6; Waters, 'Disorders of the Mind'.
93. A. Bartlett, M. King, and P. Phillips, 'Straight talking– an investigation of the attitudes and practice of psychoanalysts and psychotherapists in relation to gays and lesbians', *British Journal of Psychiatry*, 179 (2001), 545–9; M. B. King and A. Bartlett, 'British psychiatry and homosexuality', *British Journal of Psychiatry*, 174 (1999), 106–13; M. King, G. Smith, and A. Bartlett, 'Treatments of homosexuality in Britain since the 1950s – an oral history: The experience of professionals', *British Medical Journal*, 2004; Glenn Smith, Annie Bartlett, and Michael King, 'Treatments of homosexuality in Britain since the 1950s – an oral history: The experience of patients', *British Medical Journal*, 328:427 (2004); http://www.treatmentshomosexuality.org.uk [accessed 18 Aug. 2011].
94. Timothy Jones, 'The Stained Glass Closet: Celibacy and Homosexuality in the Church of England to 1958', *Journal of the History of Sexuality*, 20 (2011), 132–52.
95. Higgins, *Heterosexual Dictatorship*, 15–58. Houlbrook, *Queer London*, 190–218, 254–63; Matt Houlbrook and Chris Waters, 'The Heart in Exile: Detachment and Desire in 1950s London', *History Workshop Journal*, 62 (2006), 142–63; Mort, *Capital Affairs*, 151–86.
96. Higgins, *Heterosexual Dictatorship*, 115–22.
97. Leslie J. Moran, *The Homosexual(ity) of Law* (London: Routledge, 1996), 82–4, 99–100.
98. Ralf Dose, 'The World League for Sexual Reform: Some possible approaches', in Franz X. Eder, Lesley Hall, and Gert Hekma (eds), *Sexual Cultures in Europe: National Histories* (Manchester: Manchester University Press, 1999), 242–59; Antony Grey, *Quest for Justice: Towards Homosexual Emancipation* (London: Sinclair-Stevenson, 1992), 26–33; Stephen Jeffrey-Poulter, *Peers, Queers and Commons: The Struggle for Gay Law Reform from 1950 to the Present* (London: Routledge, 1991), 28–46.
99. M. B. Smith, *The Single Woman of Today: Her Problems and Adjustment* (London: Watts, 1951).
100. Rebecca Jennings, *Tomboys and Bachelor Girls: A Lesbian History of Post-War Britain 1945–1971* (Manchester: Manchester University Press, 2007), 44–75.
101. Doris Odlum, *Journey Through Adolescence* (London: Delisle 1957), 151–2.
102. Jennings, *Tomboys and Bachelor Girls*, 16–43.

103. Collins, *Modern Love*, 59–89.

104. 'Wolfenden Committee on Homosexuality and Prostitution: MWF Evidence for: Memoranda and drafts', Medical Women's Federation Archives, Wellcome Library, SA/MWF/H.9/2; [Malleson], *Any Wife or Any Husband*, 123–34.

105. Jennings, *Tomboys and Bachelor Girls*, 76–106.

106. Jill Gardiner, *From the Closet to the Screen: Women at the Gateways Club, 1945–85* (London: Rivers Oram Press, 2002); Jennings, *Tomboys and Bachelor Girls*), 112–18.

107. SA/MWF/H.9/2.

108. Alkarim Jivani, *It's Not Unusual: A History of Lesbian and Gay Britain in the Twentieth Century* (London: Michael O'Mara Books, 1997), 122–7. Emily Hamer, *Britannia's Glory: A History of Twentieth-Century Lesbians* (London: Cassell, 1996), 147: and see note 93 above.

109. Wilson, *Only Half-Way to Paradise*, 73.

110. Hamer, *Britannia's Glory*, 146–7.

111. Higgins, *Heterosexual Dictatorship*, 297.

112. 'Artificial Insemination' files, Eugenics Society, Wellcome, SA/EUG/D.6–7; 'Presscuttings: AID', SA/EUG/N.65–67; Naomi Pfeffer, *The Stork and the Syringe: A Political History of Reproductive Medicine* (Oxford: Polity Press, 1993), 112–22.

113. *Roberta Cowell's Story By Herself* (London: William Heinemann, 1954).

114. John B. Randell, 'Transvestitism and Trans-Sexualism: A study of 50 cases', *British Medical Journal*, II (1959), 1448–51.

115. Alison Oram, *Her Husband was a Woman!: Women's gender-crossing and twentieth-century British popular culture* (London: Routledge, 2007), 148–51.

116. *Journal of Sex Education*, 3:2 (1950), 84–6.

117. T. Gibson to N. Haire [n.d.] enclosing literature of the National Society for the Retention of Corporal Punishment, Haire Papers, Fisher Library, University of Sydney.

118. Ferris, *Sex and the British*, 167–8; Alan Travis, *Bound and Gagged: A secret history of obscenity in Britain* (London: Profile Books, 2000), 97–100.

119. Travis, *Bound and Gagged*, 95–7; 'The Director of Public Prosecutions' campaign against obscene seaside postcards', http://www.cartoons.ac.uk/dpps-obscene -postcard-index [accessed 18 Aug. 2011].

120. Ferris, *Sex and the British*, 171–4; Travis, *Bound and Gagged*, 100–25; Tim Newburn, *Permission and Regulation: Law and Morals in Post-War Britain* (London: Routledge, 1992), 71–84.

10 Swinging? For Whom? The Sixties and Seventies

1. Antony Grey, *Quest for Justice: Towards Homosexual Emancipation* (London: Sinclair-Stevenson, 1992), 41–4, 52–3; Patrick Higgins, *Heterosexual Dictatorship: Male Homosexuality in Post-War Britain* (London: Fourth Estate, 1996), 123–31; Stephen Jeffrey-Poulter, *Peers, Queers and Commons: The Struggle for Gay Law Reform from 1950 to the Present* (London: Routledge, 1991), 47–54; Alkarim Jivani, *It's Not Unusual: A History of Gay and Lesbian Britain in the Twentieth Century* (London: Michael O'Mara Books, 1997), 146–7.

2. Jivani, *It's Not Unusual*, 115, 127–8; Michael Schofield, *Sociological Aspects of Homosexuality: A Comparative Study of Three Types of Homosexuals* (New York: Little, Brown, 1965).

3. Adrian Bingham, *Family Newspapers? Sex, Private Life and the British Popular Press, 1918–1978* (Oxford: Oxford University Press, 2009), 191–4; Grey, *Quest for Justice*, 82; Jeffrey-Poulter, *Peers, Queers and Commons*, 55–8, 63–7.

4. Hugh David, *On Queer Street: A Social History of British Homosexuality, 1895–1995* (London: HarperCollins, 1997), 197; Jeffrey-Poulter, *Peers, Queers and Commons*, 58–63; Jeffrey Weeks, *Coming Out: Homosexual Politics in Britain, from the Nineteenth Century to the Present* (London: Quartet, 1977), 161–3.

5. Grey, *Quest for Justice*, 85–6.

6. Emily Hamer, *Britannia's Glory: A History of Twentieth-Century Lesbians* (London: Cassell, 1996), 166–90; Rebecca Jennings, *Tomboys and Bachelor Girls: A Lesbian History of Post-War Britain 1945–1971* (Manchester: Manchester University Press, 2007), 134–72; Alison Oram, 'Little by Little? *Arena Three* and Lesbian Politics in the 1960s', in Marcus Collins (ed.), *The Permissive Society and its Enemies: Sixties British Culture* (London; Rivers Oram, 2007), 62–79.

7. Paul Ferris, *Sex and the British: A Twentieth-Century History* (London: Michael Joseph, 1993), 174–82; Tim Newburn, *Permission and Regulation: Law and Morals in Post-War Britain* (London: Routledge, 1992), 84–8; C. H. Rolph (ed.), *The Trial of Lady Chatterley: Regina v. Penguin Books Ltd: The Transcript of the Trial* (Harmondsworth: Penguin, 1961); John Sutherland, *Offensive Literature: Decensorship in Britain, 1960–82* (London: Junction Books, 1982), 10–28; Alan Travis, *Bound and Gagged: A secret history of obscenity in Britain* (London: Profile Books, 2000), 138–65.

8. Newburn, *Permission and Regulation*, 88–102; Sutherland, *Offensive Literature*, 28–40; Travis, *Bound and Gagged*, 166–215.

9. Barbara Brookes, *Abortion in England, 1900–1967* (London: Croom Helm, 1988), 151–4; Paul Ferris, *The Nameless: Abortion in Britain Today*, revised edn (Harmondsworth: Penguin Books, 1967), and Ferris, *Sex and the British*, 190–7.

10. Gayle Davis and Roger Davidson, ' "A Fifth Freedom" or "Hideous Atheistic Expediency"? The Medical Community and Abortion Law Reform in Scotland, *c*.1960–1975', *Medical History*, 50 (2006), 29–48.

11. Emma L. Jones, 'Attitudes to Abortion in the Era of Reform: Evidence from the Abortion Law Reform Association correspondence', *Women's History Review*, 20 (2011), 283–98.

12. Peter Bartrip, *Themselves Writ Large: The British Medical Association, 1832–1966* (London: BMJ Publishing Group, 1996), 320–2.

13. Lara Marks, ' "Public spirited and enterprising volunteers": The Council for the Investigation of Fertility Control and the British clinical trials of the contraceptive pill, 1959–1973', in M. Gijswijt-Hofstra, G. M. Van Heteren, and E. M. Tansey (eds), *Biographies of Remedies: Drugs, Medicines and Contraceptives in Dutch and Anglo-American Healing Cultures* (Amsterdam: Rodopi, 2002), 159–82.

14. Audrey Leathard, *The Fight for Family Planning: The Development of Family Planning Services in Britain, 1921–74* (Basingstoke and London: Macmillan Press, 1980), 104–8.

15. Leathard, *The Fight for Family Planning*, 118–23.

16. Hera Cook, *The Long Sexual Revolution: English Women, Sex, and Contraception 1800–1975* (Oxford: Oxford University Press, 2004), 288–9; Leathard, *The Fight for Family Planning*, 138–41.

17. Carol Dyhouse, *Students: A Gendered History* (London: Routledge, 2006), 103.

18. A. H. Halsey (ed.), *British Social Trends since 1900: A Guide to the Changing Social Structure of Britain* (Basingstoke and London: Macmillan Press, 1988), 62–4.

19. Carol Smart, *The Ties That Bind: Law, marriage and the reproduction of patriarchal relations* (London: Routledge & Kegan Paul, 1984), 71–4.

20. 'Venereal Diseases in England and Wales: Extract from the Annual Report of the Chief Medical Officer for the Year 1964', *British Journal of Venereal Diseases*, 42 (1966), 50–7.

21. Hansard, HC Deb 18 July 1961 vol 644 cc1068–199; *Supplement to the British Medical Journal*, 22 July 1961, 48; 'Sixth Form Views On Chastity', *The Times*, 18 February 1963, 5; Elizabeth Wilson, *Only Half-Way to Paradise: Women in Post-War Britain, 1945–1968* (London: Tavistock Publications, 1980), 105.

22. Michael Schofield, *The Sexual Behaviour of Young People* (New York: Little, Brown, 1965), vii.

23. Ferris, *Sex and the British*, 184–5.

24. Schofield, *The Sexual Behaviour of Young People*, 25–53.

25. Schofield, *The Sexual Behaviour of Young People*, 105–13.

26. Schofield, *The Sexual Behaviour of Young People*, 113–18.

27. Schofield, *The Sexual Behaviour of Young People*, 250–3.

28. Bingham, *Family Newspapers?*, 147–51, 254–7; Frank Mort, *Capital Affairs: London and the Making of the Permissive Society* (New Haven, CT: Yale University Press, 2010), 281–348.

29. Newburn, *Permission and Regulation*, 15–26.

30. Bingham, *Family Newspapers*, 151–4; Jonathan Goodman, *The Moors Murders: The Trial of Myra Hindley and Ian Brady* (Newton Abbott: David & Charles, 1986, 1st publ. 1973); Sutherland, *Offensive Literature*, 72–8.

31. Linda Grant, *Sexing the Millennium: A Political History of the Sexual Revolution* (London: Harper Collins 1994), 84–94; Mort, *Capital Affairs*, 349–52.

32. Geoffrey Gorer, *Sex and Marriage in England Today: A study of the views and experience of the under-45s* (London: Nelson, 1971), 30–7.

33. Marcus Collins, *Modern Love: An Intimate History of Men and Women in Twentieth Century Britain* (London: Atlantic Books, 2003), 134–63.

34. Stephen Brooke, *Sexual Politics: Sexuality, Family Planning, and the British Left from the 1880s to the Present Day* (Oxford: Oxford University Press, 2011), 146–82.

35. Brooke, *Sexual Politics*, 175–6; Leathard, *The Fight for Family Planning*, 132–7.

36. Brooke, *Sexual Politics*, 158–75; Brookes, *Abortion in England*, 154–6; Leathard, *The Fight for Family Planning*, 127–32.

37. Jones, 'Attitudes to Abortion in the Era of Reform'; Davis and Davidson, '"A Fifth Freedom" or "Hideous Atheistic Expediency"?'.

38. Gayle Davis and Roger Davidson, '"Big White Chief", "Pontius Pilate", and the "Plumber": The Impact of the 1967 Abortion Act on the Scottish Medical Community, *c*.1967–1980', *Social History of Medicine*, 18 (2005), 283–306.

39. Roger Davidson and Gayle Davis, '"A Field for Private Members": The Wolfenden Committee and Scottish Homosexual Law reform, 1950–1967', *Twentieth Century British History*, 15 (2004), 174–201; Roger Davidson and Gayle Davis, 'Sexuality and the State: The Campaign for Scottish Homosexual Law Reform, 1967–80', *Contemporary British History*, 20 (2006), 533–58; Grey, *Quest for Justice*, 84–126; Higgins, *Heterosexual Dictatorship*, 132–46; Jeffrey-Poulter, *Peers, Queers and Commons*, 68–89; Brooke, *Sexual Politics*, 176–82.

40. James C. Robertson, *Hidden Cinema: British Film Censorship in Action, 1913–1975* (London: Routledge, 1989), 119–57; Sutherland, *Offensive Literature*, 79–86; Travis, *Bound and Gagged*, 216–30.

41. Stephen Cretney, *Family Law in the Twentieth Century: A History* (Oxford: Oxford University Press, 2003), 345–84; Ferris, *Sex and the British*, 214–7; Smart, *The Ties That Bind*, 59–71.

42. Leathard, *The Fight for Family Planning*, 104–17; Lara Marks, *Sexual Chemistry: A History of the Contraceptive Pill* (New Haven, CT: Yale University Press, 2001), *passim.*

43. Cook, *The Long Sexual Revolution*, 263–337.

44. Leathard, *The Fight for Family Planning*, 157–62.

45. Leathard, *The Fight for Family Planning*, 175–89.

46. Leathard, *The Fight for Family Planning*, 190–1.

47. Leathard, *The Fight for Family Planning*, 190–202.

48. Leathard, *The Fight for Family Planning*, 173–5; Davis and Davidson, ' "Big White Chief","Pontius Pilate", and the "Plumber" '.

49. Abortion Law Reform Association archives in the Wellcome Library, Godman Irvine Abortion Amendment Bill 1960s–1970s, SA/ALR/H.17–20.

50. *Sunday Times*, 30 March 1975; Roger Lewin, 'Abortion: Getting the Facts Right', *New Scientist*, 3 April 1975, 2.

51. Ashley Wivel, 'Abortion Policy and Politics on the Lane Committee of Enquiry, 1971–1974', *Social History of Medicine*, 11 (1998), 109–35.

52. James White Bill, 1975 and Select Committee on Abortion, 1975–80, SA/ALR/B.34; Parliamentary Select Committee on the Abortion Act 1975/76: press-cuttings, SA/ALR/H.61–63; Birth Control Campaign archives in the Wellcome Library, Select Committee on the Working of the Abortion Act 1975–1979, SA/BCC/D.64–79.

53. Brooke, *Sexual Politics*, 185–224.

54. Grey, *Quest for Justice*, 147–74; Jeffrey-Poulter, *Peers, Queers and Commons*, 90–7; Jivani, *It's Not Unusual*, 153; Newburn, *Permission and Regulation*, 61–4; Sutherland, *Offensive Literature*, 104–7; Weeks, *Coming Out*, 176–8.

55. Jeffrey-Poulter, *Peers, Queers and Commons*, 97–8; Jivani, *It's Not Unusual*, 153–4.

56. Brooke, *Sexual Politics*, 225–35; Grey, *Quest for Justice*, 175–84; Jeffrey-Poulter, *Peers, Queers and Commons*, 98–109; Lisa Power, *No Bath But Plenty of Bubbles: An Oral History of the Gay Liberation Front, 1970–73* (London: Cassell, 1995); Weeks, *Coming Out*, 185–206; Lucy Robinson, *Gay men and the Left in post-war Britain: How the personal got political* (Manchester: Manchester University Press, 2007), 65–92.

57. David, *On Queer Street*, 231–40.

58. Richard Davenport-Hines, *Sex, Death and Punishment: Attitudes to Sex and Sexuality in Britain since the Renaissance* (London: Collins, 1990), 327–8; Newburn, *Permission and Regulation*, 62–4; Weeks, *Coming Out*, 176.

59. Jill Gardiner, *From the Closet to the Screen: Women at the Gateways Club, 1945–85* (London: Rivers Oram, 2002), 178–225; Hamer, *Britannia's Glory*, 191–202; Rebecca Jennings, *A Lesbian History of Britain: Love and Sex Between Women Since 1500* (Oxford: Greenwood World Publishing, 2007), 169–77.

60. Charlotte Wolff, *Love Between Women* (London: Gerald Duckworth, 1971), and *Bisexuality* (London: Quarter Books, 1977); Charlotte Wolff papers in the Wellcome Library, *Love Between Women*: Reviews, PSY/WOL/6/7/2, *Bisexuality*: Interviews, Lectures and Reviews PSY/WOL/6/1/1.

61. Bingham, *Family Newspapers?*, 198–9; Jeffrey-Poulter, *Peers, Queers and Commons*, 136–7.

62. Sutherland, *Offensive Literature*, 164–71; Travis, *Bound and Gagged*, 252–4.

63. Ferris, *Sex and the British*, 229–35; Newburn, *Permission and Regulation*, 102–35; Sutherland, *Offensive Literature*, 88–103, 127–31; Travis, *Bound and Gagged*, 231–54; Jeffrey Weeks, *Sex, Politics, and Society: The regulation of sexuality since 1800* (London: Longman, 1989), 277–82.

64. Jeffrey-Poulter, *Peers, Queers and Commons*, 125–6; Newburn, *Permission and Regulation*, 31–4; Robinson, *Gay Men and the Left*, 124–5; Sutherland, *Offensive Literature*, 148–54; Travis, *Bound and Gagged*, 257–62.

65. Newburn, *Permission and Regulation*, 181–3; Sutherland, *Offensive Literature*, 175–8; Travis, *Bound and Gagged*, 261–6.

66. Martin Durham, *Sex and Politics: The Family and Morality in the Thatcher Years* (Basingstoke and London: Macmillan Press, 1991), 13–14.

67. Newburn, *Permission and Regulation*, 115–35; Sutherland, *Offensive Literature*, 111–26; Travis, *Bound and Gagged*, 238–46.

68. Ferris, *Sex and the British*, 239–43; Lesley A Hall, 'Birds, Bees and General Embarrassment: Sex education in Britain from social purity to Section 28', in Richard Aldrich (ed.), *Public or Private Education: Lessons from History* (London: Woburn Press, 2004), 98–115; James Hampshire, 'The politics of school sex education policy in England and Wales from the 1940s to the 1960s', *Social History of Medicine*, 18 (2005), 87–105; Leathard, *The Fight for Family Planning*, 148–56.

69. Bingham, *Family Newspapers?*, 88–95; Virginia Ironside, *Problems! Problems! Confessions of an Agony Aunt* (London: Robson Books, 1991), 129–54; Carol Lee, *The Ostrich Position, sex, schooling and mystification* (London: Writers and Readers, 1983), 80–92.

70. H. G. Cocks, *Classified: The secret history of the personal column* (London: Random House, 2009), 143–73; Ferris, *Sex and the British*, 231, 241, 274–6; Grant, *Sexing the Millennium*, 173–5.

71. Bingham, *Family Newspapers?*, 194–7; Robinson, *Gay Men and the Left*, 129–39.

72. Jane Lewis, *The End of Marriage: Individualism and Intimate Relations* (Cheltenham: Edward Elgar, 2001), 29.

73. Halsey (ed.), *British Social Trends since 1900*, 71–85; N. L. Tranter, *British Population in the Twentieth Century* (Basingstoke and London: Macmillan Press, 1996), 99–101.

74. Rosalind Brunt, '"An Immense Verbosity": Permissive Sexual Advice in the 1970s", in Rosalind Brunt and Caroline Rowan (eds), *Feminism, Culture and Politics* (London: Lawrence & Wishart, 1982), 143–70; Grant, *Sexing the Millennium*, 119–24.

75. Nigel Fountain, *Underground: The London Alternative Press, 1966–1974*, (London: Routledge, 1988), 59.

76. Brunt, '"An Immense Verbosity"'; Alex Comfort (ed.), *The Joy of Sex: A Gourmet Guide to Lovemaking* (London: Quartet, 1972).

77. David Evans, 'Sexually transmitted diseases in Britain since the founding of the National Health Service', in Roger Davidson and Lesley Hall (eds), *Sex, Sin and Suffering: Venereal Diseases in the European Social Context since 1870*, London: Routledge, 2001), 237–52.

78. 'Epidemiology: Herpes Simplex', *British Medical Journal*, III (1974), 636.

79. 'Genital herpes and cervical carcinoma', *British Medical Journal*, I (1978), 807.

80. Annet Mooij, *Out of Otherness: Characters and Narrators in the Dutch Venereal Disease Debates 1850–1990* (Amsterdam: Rodopi, 1998), 198–208.

81. Shirley J. Richmond and J. D. Oriel, 'Recognition and management of genital chlamydial infection', *British Medical Journal*, II (1978), 480–3.

11 Approaching the Millennium

1. Jeff Weeks, *Sex, Politics, and Society: The regulation of sexuality since 1800* (London: Longman, 2nd edition 1989), 292–300.

2. Martin Durham, *Sex and Politics: The Family and Morality in the Thatcher Years* (Basingstoke: Macmillan, 1991), 10.

3. Durham, *Sex and Politics*, 39–56; Carol Lee, *Friday's Child: The threat to moral education* (Wellingborough: Thorson's, 1988), 23–41.

4. Jeffrey Weeks, *The World We Have Won: The Remaking of Erotic and Intimate Life* (London: Routledge, 2007), 94–8.

5. Durham, *Sex and Politics*, 16–31; Stephen Brooke, *Sexual Politics: Sexuality, Family Planning, and the British Left from the 1880s to the Present Day* (Oxford: Oxford University Press, 2011), 215–24.

6. Durham, *Sex and Politics*, 31–6.

7. 'Cutbacks that point to a cause for concern', *Health Services Journal*, 100 (1990), 17–63; 'District cuts NHS-funded abortions', *The Guardian*, 15 November 1991, 24; Jane Roe, 'Abortion on request or quest for abortion? The law in practice', *Breaking Chains*, 57 (1992), 6.

8. Janet Hadley, *Abortion: Between Freedom and Necessity* (London: Virago, 1996), 108–13.

9. Jean Robinson, 'Promiscuity isn't the cause', *New Statesman*, 30 March 1984, 14; 'Pill "has link with cervical cancer', *The Guardian*, 29 March 1985; Aminatta Forna, 'Cervical Cancer – The Smear Campaign', *Chic*, March 1988, 52–3.

10. Audrey Leathard, *The Fight for Family Planning: The Development of Family Planning Services in Britain, 1921–74* (Basingstoke and London: Macmillan Press, 1980), 211–13.

11. See Chapter 6, pp. 92–3.

12. Department of Health Circular to Regional General Managers, EL (90) MB115, 6 June 1990; 'Abortion rate linked to contraceptive cuts', *The Independent*, 27 June 1990; Lynn Hanna, 'Short-term savings, long-term costs', *The Guardian*, 22 November 1990; FPA 'What is Happening to NHS Family Planning Clinics', November 1990.

13. Annabel Ferriman, 'The day after sex', *New Statesman*, 5 June 1998, 28–9.

14. Vivien Seal, *Whose Choice? Working-Class Women and the Control of Fertility* (London: Fortress Books, 1990), 70–3.

15. Stephen Jeffrey-Poulter, *Peers, Queers and Commons: The Struggle for Gay Law Reform from 1950 to the Present* (London: Routledge, 1991), 166; Lucy Robinson, *Gay men and the Left in post-war Britain: How the personal got political* (Manchester: Manchester University Press, 2007), 154–64.

16. Jeffrey-Poulter, *Peers, Queers and Commons*, 167–8.

17. Brooke, *Sexual Politics*, 235-47; Davina Cooper, *Sexing the City: Lesbian and Gay Politics Within the Activist State* (London: Rivers Oram, 1994); Jeffrey-Poulter, *Peers, Queers and Commons*, 202–6.

18. Roger Davidson and Gayle Davis, 'Sexuality and the State: the Campaign for Scottish Homosexual Law Reform, 1967–80', *Contemporary British History*, 20 (2006), 533–58; Jeffrey-Poulter, *Peers, Queers and Commons*, 141–54; Robinson, *Gay men and the Left*, 82.

19. 'The Sex Epidemic', *Cosmopolitan*, July 1982; Alan Burns, 'New Sex Threat for Lovers', *Sunday Mirror*, 1 August 1982.

20. Jennifer Stanton, 'What Shapes Vaccine Policy? The Case of Hepatitis B in the UK', *Social History of Medicine*, 7 (1994), 427-46; NHS Evidence: Clinical Knowledge

Summaries: Evidence on gonococcal resistance to antibiotics http://www.cks
.nhs.uk/gonorrhoea/evidence/supporting_evidence/resistance_to_antibiotics
[Accessed 24 Aug. 2011].

21. Virginia Berridge, *AIDS in the UK: The Making of Policy 1981–1994* (Oxford:
    Oxford University Press, 1996), 13–46; Simon Garfield, *The End of Innocence:
    Britain in the Time of AIDS* (London: Faber & Faber, 1994), 27–47; Jeffrey-
    Poulter, *Peers, Queers and Commons*, 176–83; Jeff Weeks, 'AIDS and the reg-
    ulation of sexuality', in Virginia Berridge and Philip Strong (eds), *AIDS and
    Contemporary History* (Cambridge: Cambridge University Press, 1993), 17–36.
22. Berridge, *AIDS in the UK*, 55–78; Garfield, *The End of Innocence*, 74–9; Jeffrey-
    Poulter, *Peers, Queers and Commons*, 184–93.
23. Weeks, 'AIDS and the regulation of sexuality'.
24. Berridge, *AIDS in the UK*, 123–51.Garfield, *The End of Innocence*, 107–25;
    Jeffrey-Poulter, *Peers, Queers and Commons*, 193–8.
25. 'AIDS and Sex', *The Lancet*, I (1988), 31.
26. Berridge, *AIDS in the UK*, 253; Kaye Wellings et al., *Sexual Behaviour in Britain:
    The National Survey of Sexual Attitudes and Lifestyles* (London: Penguin, 1994),
    vii–viii.
27. Berridge, *AIDS in the UK*, 100–22; Ewan Ferlie, 'The NHS response to HIV/
    AIDS', and John Street, 'A fall in interest? British AIDS Policy, 1986–1990', in
    Berridge and Strong (eds), *AIDS and Contemporary History*, 202–23, 224–39.
28. Berridge, *AIDS in the UK*, 231–79; Jane Lewis, 'Public Health Doctors and AIDS
    as a public health issue', in Berridge and Strong (eds), *AIDS and Contemporary
    History*, 37–54; Weeks, 'AIDS and the regulation of sexuality'.
29. Berridge, *AIDS in the UK*, 100–22; Street, 'A fall in interest?'.
30. *Official Report of the Standing Committee on the Abortion (Amendment) Bill*, 25
    July–18 December 1979, 159.
31. Jacqueline Gold, *Good Vibrations: The true story of Ann Summers* (London:
    Pavilion, 1995).
32. Nicholas Whittaker, *Blue Period: Notes from a Life in the Titillation Trade* (London:
    Victor Gollancz, 1997), 188–9.
33. Paul Ferris, *Sex and the British: A Twentieth-Century History* (London: Michael
    Joseph, 1993), 261–3; Whittaker, *Blue Period*.
34. 'Birthday Lace: Rhalou Allerhand celebrates 15 years of Britain's groundbreaking
    erotic imprint for women', http://www.scribd.com/doc/20474120/Black-Lace
    [Accessed 12 Sep. 2011].
35. Ferris, *Sex and the British*, 251–3; Bill Thompson, *Soft Core: Moral Crusades against
    Pornography in Britain and America* (London: Cassell, 1994), 152–80; James C.
    Robertson, *Hidden Cinema: British Film Censorship in Action, 1913–1975* (London:
    Routledge, 1989), 174–5; Alan Travis, *Bound and Gagged: A secret history of obscen-
    ity in Britain* (London: Profile Books, 2000), 284–9.
36. Adrian Bingham, *Family Newspapers? Sex, Private Life and the British Popular
    Press, 1918–1978* (Oxford: Oxford University Press, 2009), 223–7; Linda Grant,
    Sexing the Millennium: A Political History of the Sexual Revolution (London:
    HarperCollins, 1993), 212–13.
37. Gail Chester and Julienne Dickey (eds), *Feminism and Censorship: The Current
    Debate* (Bridport: Prism Press, 1988).
38. Jeffrey-Poulter, *Peers, Queers and Commons*, 200–1; Laurence O'Toole, *Pornocopia:
    Porn, Sex, Technology and Desire* (London: Serpent's Tail, 1998), 146; Simon
    Watney, *Policing Desire: Pornography, AIDS and the Media* (London: Comedia,
    1987), 58–9.

39. Susan Atkins, 'The Sex Discrimination Act 1975: The End of a Decade', *Feminist Review*, 24 (1986), 57–70; Jane Lewis, *Women in Britain since 1945* (Oxford: Blackwell, 1992), 65–91.

40. Jane Millar, 'State, Family, and Personal Responsibility: The Changing Balance for Lone Mothers in the United Kingdom', *Feminist Review*, 48 (1994), 24–39.

41. Victor J. Seidler, *The Achilles Heel Reader: Men, Sexual Politics and Socialism* (London: Routledge, 1991).

42. 'Medical Briefing: The vital male check', *The Times*, 15 October 1987; John Illman and Rob Stepney, 'Dying from embarrassment', *The Guardian: G2*, 16 March 1993, 15.

43. Lesley A. Hall, *Hidden Anxieties: Male Sexuality, 1900–1950* (Oxford: Polity, 1991), 165; William Peters, 'A tearful test for a much-abused service', *The Guardian*, 27 July 1988, 23; Angela Phillips, 'A handicap in the great egg race', *The Observer*, 15 July 1990, 45.

44. *The Guardian*, 19 June 1993, 16; *The Observer: Life*, 19 March 1995, 62.

45. Jeanne Gregory and Sue Lees, *Policing Sexual Assault* (London: Routledge, 1999), 112–33; Richie J. McMullen, *Male Rape: Breaking the silence on the last taboo* (London: Gay Men's Press, 1990).

46. 'Observer debate: The new sex war', *The Observer*, 22 February 1998, 13; Charlotte Raven, 'Belt up Boys', *The Guardian: G2*, 24 August 1998, 6; Polly Toynbee and Fay Weldon, 'When two scribes go to war', *The Guardian: G2*, 26 May 1998, 4; 'Bringing Up Boys', *The Observer: Life*, 20 June 1999, 14–24.

47. J. L. Barton, 'The Story of Marital Rape', *Law Quarterly Review*, 108 (1992), 260–71; Stephen Cretney, *Family Law in the Twentieth Century: A History* (Oxford: Oxford University Press, 2003), 753; Weeks, *The World We Have Won*, 90.

48. Cretney, *Family Law in the Twentieth Century*, 433–42, 563–5, 722–37, 761–4; Jane Lewis, *The End of Marriage: Individualism and Intimate Relations* (Cheltenham: Edward Elgar, 2001), 114–17.

49. Lewis, *The End of Marriage*, 18, 152.

50. B. Jane Elliott, 'Demographic trends in domestic life, 1945–87', and Janet Finch and David Morgan, 'Marriage in the 1980s: A new sense of realism?', in David Clark (ed.), *Marriage, Domestic Life and Social Change: Writings for Jacqueline Burgoyne (1944–88)* (London: Routledge, 1991), 55–80, 85–108; A. H. Halsey, *British Social Trends since 1900: A Guide to the Changing Social Structure of Britain* (Basingstoke and London: Macmillan Press, 1988), 71–85; Carol Smart, *The Ties That Bind: Law, marriage, and the reproduction of patriarchal relations* (London: Routledge & Kegan Paul, 1984), 108–13; Liz Stanley, *Sex Surveyed, 1949–1994: From Mass Observation's 'Little Kinsey' to the National Survey and the Hite Reports* (London: Taylor & Francis, 1995), 49–53, 59–62; Wellings et al., *Sexual Behaviour in Britain*, 90–177, 262–72.

51. 'Half pregnancies outside wedlock', *The Guardian*, 17 March 1999, 5.

52. Lewis, *The End of Marriage*, 125–45, 181.

53. Cretney, *Family Law in the Twentieth Century*, 516–24.

54. Gregory and Lees, *Policing Sexual Assault*, 17–18.

55. Isobel Allen, *Education in Sex and Personal Relationships* (London: Policy Studies Institute Research Report 665, 1987); Durham, *Sex and Politics*, 99–122; Carol Lee, *The Ostrich Position: Sex, schooling and mystification* (London: Writers and Readers, 1983), and *Friday's Child*; AnnMarie Wolpe, 'Sex in Schools: Back to the Future', *Feminist Review*, 27 (1987), 37–47.

56. Ann Blair and Daniel Monk, 'Sex Education and the Law in England and Wales: The Importance of Legal Narratives', in Roger Davidson and Lutz Sauerteig

(eds), *Shaping Sexual Knowledge: A Cultural History of Sex Education in Twentieth Century Europe* (London: Routledge, 2009), 37–51; Brooke, *Sexual Politics*, 247–54; Durham, *Sex and Politics*, 111–18; Daniel Monk, 'Beyond Section 28: Law, Governance, and Sex Education', in Leslie J. Moran, Daniel Monk, and Sarah Beresford (eds), *Legal Queeries: Lesbian, gay, and transgender legal studies* (London: Cassell, 1998), 96–112; Susan Reinhold, 'Through the Parliamentary Looking Glass: "Real" and "Pretend" Families in Contemporary British Politics', *Feminist Review*, 48 (1994), 61–79.

57. *The Guardian*, 24 March 1994, 2, 25.

58. 'Half pregnancies outside wedlock'; 'British teenagers have worst sexual health in Europe', *The Guardian*, 14 May 1999, 1.

59. Jeffrey Weeks, Peter Aggleton, Chris McKevitt, Kay Parkinson, and Austin Taylor-Laybourn, 'Community Responses to HIV and AIDS: The "De-Gaying" and "Re-Gaying" of AIDS', in Jeffrey Weeks and Janet Holland (eds), *Sexual Cultures: Communities, Values, and Intimacy* (Basingstoke and London: Macmillan Press, 1996), 161–79.

60. Alkarim Jivani, *It's Not Unusual: A History of Lesbian and Gay Britain in the Twentieth Century* (London: Michael O'Mara Books, 1997), 195–8; Jeffrey-Poulter, *Peers, Queers and Commons*, 206–67; Robinson, *Gay Men and the Left*, 170–9.

61. http://www.westminster-abbey.org/our-history/people/oscar-wilde [Accessed 24 Aug. 2011].

62. Leslie J. Moran, *The Homosexual(ity) of Law* (London: Routledge, 1996), 191–6.

63. http://www.guardian.co.uk/uk/1999/apr/30/2 [Accessed 24 Aug. 2011].

64. Susan Ardill and Sue O'Sullivan, 'Sex in the Summer of "88"', *Feminist Review*, 31 (1989), 126–34; Sarah F. Green, *Urban Amazons: Lesbian Feminism and Beyond in the Gender, Sexuality and Identity Battles of London* (Basingstoke: Macmillan, 1997); Emily Hamer, *Britannia's Glory: A History of Twentieth-Century Lesbians* (London: Cassell, 1996), 204–6; Rebecca Jennings, *A Lesbian History of Britain: Love and Sex Between Women Since 1500* (Oxford: Greenwood World Publishing, 2007), 178–89.

65. Sue Allen and Lynne Harne, 'Lesbian Mothers – the fight for child custody', in Bob Cant and Susan Hemmings (eds), *Radical Records: Thirty Years of Lesbian and Gay History* (London: Routledge, 1988), 181–94; Sarah Beresford, 'The Lesbian Mother: Questions of Gender and Sexual Identity', in Moran, Monk, and Beresford (eds*), Legal Queeries*, 57–67.

66. Ferris, *Sex and the British*, 282–8; Moran, *The Homosexual(ity) of Law*, 180–91.

12 Into a New Millennium: Changes and Continuities

1. Natsal Publications: http://www.ucl.ac.uk/sexual-health/research/natsal-publications.html [Accessed 20 Sep. 2011).

2. A. J. Copas, K. Wellings, B. Erens, C. H. Mercer, S. McManus, K. A. Fenton, C. Korovessis, W. Macdowall, K. Nanchahal, and A. M. Johnson, 'The accuracy of reported sensitive sexual behaviour in Britain: Exploring the extent of change 1990–2000', *Sexually Transmitted Infections*, 78 (2002), 26–30.

3. Anne M Johnson, Catherine H Mercer, Bob Erens, Andrew J Copas, Sally McManus, Kaye Wellings, Kevin A Fenton, Christos Korovessis, Wendy Macdowall, Kiran Nanchahal, Susan Purdon, and Julia Field, 'Sexual behaviour in Britain: Partnerships, practices, and HIV risk behaviours', *The Lancet*, 358 (2001), 1835–42.

4. Kevin A. Fenton, Catherine H. Mercer, Sally McManus, Bob Erens, Kaye Wellings, Wendy Macdowall, Christos L. Byron, Andrew J. Copas, Kiran Nanchahal, Julia Field, and Anne M. Johnson, 'Ethnic variations in sexual behaviour in Great Britain and risk of sexually transmitted infections: A probability survey', *The Lancet*, 365 (2005), 1246–55.

5. Johnson et al, 'Sexual behaviour in Britain'; Christine A. McGarrigle, Catherine H. Mercer, Kevin A. Fenton, Andrew J Copas, Kaye Wellings, Bob Erens, and Anne M. Johnson, 'Investigating the relationship between HIV testing and risk behaviour in Britain: National Survey of Sexual Attitudes and Lifestyles 2000', *AIDS*, 19 (2005), 77–84.

6. 'Sexually transmitted infections in England, 2008–2010', *Health Protection Report*, 5/24 (7 June 2011) http://www.hpa.org.uk/hpr/archives/2011 /hpr2411.pdf [Accessed 20 Sep 2011]; http://group.bmj.com/group/media /latest-news/sexually-transmitted-infections-double-in-older-population-in-ten- years [Accessed 20 Feb. 2012].

7. I. Simms and H. Ward, 'Congenital syphilis in the United Kingdom', *Sexually Transmitted Infections*, 82 (2006), 1; I. Simms, G. Bell, and G. Hughes, 'Infectious syphilis in young heterosexuals: Responding to an evolving epidemic', *International Journal of STD and AIDS*, 22 (2011), 481–2.

8. 'Sexually transmitted infections in England, 2008–2010'.

9. Kevin A. Fenton, Christos Korovessis, Anne M. Johnson, Angela McCadden, Sally McManus, Kaye Wellings, Catherine H. Mercer, Caroline Carder, Andrew J. Copas, Kiran Nanchahal, Wendy Macdowall, Geoff Ridgway, Julia Field, and Bob Erens, 'Sexual behaviour in Britain: Reported sexually transmitted infections and prevalent genital Chlamydia trachomatis infection', *The Lancet*, 358 (2001), 1851–4; National Chlamydia Screening Programme, http://www.chlamydias-creening.nhs.uk/index.htm [Accessed 20 Sep. 2011].

10. 'Epidemic of *Lymphogranuloma venereum* (LGV) in men who have sex with men in the UK intensifies', *Health Protection Report*, 5/24 (7 June 2011).

11. HPV Immunisation, http://www.patient.co.uk/health/HPV-Immunisation.htm [Accessed 20 Sep. 2011].

12. http://www.nhs.uk/news/2011/03March/Pages/hpv-vaccination-in-boys. aspx [Accessed 20 Sep. 2011].

13. Terrence Higgins Trust, *Tales from the Clinic: Personal accounts from users and providers of GUM services in England*, http://image.guardian.co.uk/sys-files /Society/documents/2004/11/16/clinic.pdf [Accessed 20 Sep. 2011].

14. Peter J. White, Helen Ward, Jackie A. Cassell, Catherine H. Mercer, and Geoff P. Garnett, 'Vicious and virtuous circles in the dynamics of infectious disease and the provision of health care: Gonorrhoea in Britain as an example', *Journal of Infectious Diseases*, 192 (2005), 824–36.

15. NHS Choices: Guide to Contraception http://www.nhs.uk/Livewell /Contraception/Pages/Guidetocontraception.aspx [Accessed 20 Sep. 2011].

16. http://www.guardian.co.uk/society/2007/dec/13/health [Accessed 20 Sep. 2011].

17. http://www.telegraph.co.uk/news/uknews/3129625/Mother-is-denied-pill- by-Muslim-pharmacist.html, 3 Oct. 2008 [Accessed 20 Sep. 2011].

18. http://www.secularism.org.uk/new-guidelines-make-it-harder-fo.html; http:// www.catholicherald.co.uk/news/2011/08/15/pharmacists-who-object-to- handing-out-pill-could-lose-job/ [Accessed 20 Sep. 2011].

19. http://www.bbc.co.uk/news/uk-politics-14817816 7 Sep 2011; http://www. guardian.co.uk/lifeandstyle/2011/aug/02/abortion-pregnancy-counselling- found-wanting [Accessed 20 Sep. 2011].

20. http://www.guardian.co.uk/commentisfree/2011/aug/31/abortion-advice-poundland-nadine-dorries [Accessed 30 Sep. 2011].
21. http://www.bbc.co.uk/news/uk-politics-14817816 [Accessed 20 Sep. 2011].
22. http://www.guardian.co.uk/education/2008/nov/25/anti-abortion-schools [Accessed 20 Sep. 2011].
23. The Fawcett Society, *Rape: The Facts*, Apr 2007; http://news.bbc.co.uk/1/hi/magazine/6314445.stm 31 Jan 2007. http://www.telegraph.co.uk/news/uknews/law-and-order/5321555/Britain-has-lowest-rape-conviction-rate-in-Europe-study-finds.html 14 May 2009; http://www.telegraph.co.uk/news/uknews/crime/7442785/Rape-conviction-rate-figures-misleading.html 15 Mar 2010; http://www.guardian.co.uk/society/2010/mar/15/rape-conviction-rates-solicitor-general [Accessed 21 Sep. 2011].
24. http://www.bbc.co.uk/health/physical_health/conditions/rohypnol.shtml [Accessed 21 Sep. 2011].
25. http://www.guardian.co.uk/culture/2010/jul/19/latitude-festival-safety-campaign [Accessed 21 Sep. 2011].
26. http://www.thisislondon.co.uk/standard/article-23901468-women-warned-over-minicab-rape-threat.do 26 Nov 2010 [Accessed 21 Sep. 2011].
27. http://www.guardian.co.uk/uk/2009/apr/22/taxi-rapist-jailed [Accessed 21 Sep. 2011].
28. http://www.guardian.co.uk/uk/2009/mar/27/metropolitan-police-rape-inquiry [Accessed 21 Sep. 2011].
29. http://www.guardian.co.uk/uk/2011/mar/25/night-stalker-case-police-sorry [Accessed 21 Sep. 2011].
30. Sexual Offences Act 2003, 2003 c. 42, http://www.legislation.gov.uk/ukpga/2003/42/contents [Accessed 21 Sep. 2011].
31. http://www.guardian.co.uk/uk/2008/oct/25/rape-trials-ruling; http://www.guardian.co.uk/politics/2008/apr/01/justice.gender; http://www.guardian.co.uk/uk/2005/nov/24/ukcrime.claredyer1 [Accessed 21 Sep. 2011].
32. http://www.guardian.co.uk/uk/2008/aug/12/ukcrime.law [Accessed 20 Sep. 2011].
33. http://www.guardian.co.uk/politics/2011/may/18/david-cameron-urged-sack-kenneth-clarke-rape [Accessed 22 Sep. 2011].
34. http://www.labourlist.org/tory-mep-suggests-date-rape-victim-shares-a-part-of-the, 23 May 2011 [Accessed 22 Sep. 2011].
35. http://www.guardian.co.uk/law/2012/jan/30/rapes-murders-criminal-prosecutor [Accessed 21 Feb. 2012].
36. http://www.guardian.co.uk/society/2012/feb/28/review-rape-police-failings [Accessed 1 Mar. 2012].
37. http://www.surrey.ac.uk/mediacentre/press/2011/69535_are_sex_offenders_and_lads_mags_using_the_same_language.htm [Accessed 23 Feb. 2012].
38. http://www.bbc.co.uk/news/uk-england-devon-16852406; http://www.telegraph.co.uk/news/9074819/Cook-up-Rohypnol-to-get-laid-student-paper-jokes.html [Accessed 23 Feb. 2012].
39. http://slutmeansspeakup.org.uk/; http://www.independent.co.uk/news/uk/home-news/women-mobilise-for-first-british-slutwalk-rally-2281611.html,10 May 2011; http://www.thefword.org.uk/blog/2011/04/slutwalk_london; http://www.bbc.co.uk/news/uk-13739876, 11 Jun. 2011 [Accessed 21 Sep. 2011].
40. http://www.guardian.co.uk/uk/2010/jul/18/burqa-ban-unbritish-immigration-minister [Accessed 21 Sep. 2011].
41. http://news.bbc.co.uk/1/hi/uk/5411954.stm, 6 Oct. 2006, [Accessed 21 Sep. 2011].

42. 'Veiled Muslim women are under attack in the UK claims new research', University of Leicester Press Office, 4 April 2011, http://www.24dash.com/news /communities/2011–04-04-Veiled-Muslim-women-are-under-attack-in-the-UK-claims-new-research [Accessed 21 Sep. 2011].

43. Face Coverings (Regulation) Bill 2010–11, http://www.publications.parliament. uk/pa/cm201011/cmbills/020/11020.i-i.html [Accessed 21 Sep. 2011].

44. Rosie Campbell and Maggie O'Neill (eds), *Sex Work Now* (Cullompton: Willan Publishing, 2006), in particular: Phil Hubbard, 'Out of touch and out of time? The contemporary policing of sex work', 1–32; Maggie O'Neill and Rosie Campbell, 'Street sex work and local communities: Creating discursive spaces for *genuine* consultation and inclusion', 33–61; Hilary Kinnell, 'Murder made easy: The final solution to prostitution?', 141–68; Jane Pitcher, 'Support services for women working in the sex industry', 235–62.

45. There is a substantial collection of these in the Wellcome Library: Sex ephemera: Prostitute phonebox cards EPH592–608.

46. Teela Sanders, 'Behind the personal ads: The indoor sex markets in Britain', in Campbell and O'Neill (eds), *Sex Work Now*, 92–115; H. Ward and S. Day, 'What happens to women who sell sex? Report of a unique occupational cohort', *Sexually Transmitted Infections*, 82 (2006), 413–17.

47. Hilary Kinnell, 'Clients of female sex workers: Men or monsters?', in Campbell and O'Neill (eds), *Sex Work Now*, 212–34.

48. H. Ward, C. H. Mercer, K. Wellings, K. Fenton, B. Erens, A. Copas, and A. M. Johnson, 'Who pays for sex? An analysis of the increasing prevalence of female commercial sex contacts among men in Britain', *Sexually Transmitted Infections*, 81 (2005), 467–71.

49. T. M. Groom and R. Nandwani, 'Characteristics of men who pay for sex: A UK sexual health clinic survey', *Sexually Transmitted Infections*, 82 (2006), 364–7.

50. http://www.guardian.co.uk/uk/2007/aug/26/ukcrime.jorevill; http://www. guardian.co.uk/world/2009/jul/07/child-trafficking-ping-lau; http://www. guardian.co.uk/law/2011/apr/19/sex-trafficking-uk-legal-reform [Accessed 22 Sep. 2011].

51. Eaves, *Of Human Bondage: Trafficking in women and contemporary slavery in the UK* (August 2009), http://www.eaves4women.co.uk/Documents /Recent_Reports/Of_Human_Bondage_trafficking_in_women_and_contemporary_slavery_in_the_UK.pdf [Accessed 22 Sep. 2011]; Laura Maria Agustín, 'The conundrum of women's agency: Migration and the sex industry', in Campbell and O'Neill (eds), *Sex Work Now*, 116–40.

52. http://www.guardian.co.uk/society/2011/jun/29/abused-girl-police-grooming-gangs, http://www.guardian.co.uk/society/2011/jun/29 /child-exploitation-survey-26-asian [Accessed 25 Sep. 2011].

53. Isabel Eden, *Inappropriate Behaviour: Adult venues and licensing in London*, The Lilith Project, 2007, http://www.eaves4women.co.uk/Documents /Recent_Reports/Inappropriate_Behaviour_2007.pdf [Accessed 25 Sep. 2011].

54. http://www.guardian.co.uk/politics/2008/nov/26/lap-dancing-association-licensing-commons [Accessed 22 Sep. 2011].

55. http://www.object.org.uk/campaigns/lapdancing-take-action [Accessed 25 Sep. 2011].

56. E. Burtney and M. Duffy (eds), *Young people and sexual health: Individual, social and policy contexts* (Basingstoke: Palgrave Macmillan, 2004); Lesley A. Hall, 'In Ignorance and in Knowledge: Reflections on the history of sex education in Britain', in Roger Davidson and Lutz Sauerteig (eds), *Shaping Sexual Knowledge:*

A Cultural History of Sex Education in Twentieth Century Europe (London: Routledge, 2009), 19–36.

57. Kaye Wellings, Kiran Nanchahal, Wendy Macdowall, Sally McManus, Bob Erens, Catherine H Mercer, Anne M Johnson, Andrew J Copas, Christos Korovessis, Kevin A Fenton, and Julia Field, 'Sexual behaviour in Britain: early heterosexual experience', *The Lancet*, 358 (2001), 1843–50.

58. Wellings et al., 'Sexual behaviour in Britain: Early heterosexual experience'.

59. http://www.drpetra.co.uk/blog/the-bare-all-survey-2006-%E2%80%93-big-doesn%E2%80%99t-mean-best/ 14 Aug. 2006; http://www.drpetra.co.uk/blog/%C2%BC-men-worried-about-the-amount-of-porn-they-watch-online-radio-1-is-the-latest-media-outlet-to-stuff-up-a-sex-survey/ 22 Apr. 2011 [Accessed 20 Sep. 2011].

60. http://www.nhs.uk/Livewell/Sexandyoungpeople/Pages/Sex-and-young-people-hub.aspx [Accessed 20 Sep. 2011].

61. http://news.bbc.co.uk/newsbeat/hi/technology/newsid_8181000/8181443.stm, 4 Aug. 2009 [Accessed 3 Oct. 2011].

62. Clare Bale, 'Sexualised Culture and Young People's Sexual Health: A Cause for Concern?', *Sociology Compass* 4 (2010), 824–40; R. Danielle Egan and Gail L. Hawkes, 'Endangered Girls and Incendiary Objects: Unpacking the Discourse on Sexualization', *Sexuality and Culture*, 12 (2008), 291–311; Gail Hawkes and R. Danielle Egan, 'Landscapes of Erotophobia: The Sexual(ized) Child in the Postmodern Anglophone West', *Sexuality and Culture*, 12 (2008) 193–203.

63. Sara Bragg and David Buckingham, 'Too much too young? Young people, sexual media and learning', in Feona Attwood (ed.), *Mainstreaming Sex: The sexualization of Western Culture* (London: I. B. Tauris, 2009), 129–46.

64. http://www.brook.org.uk/professionals/application/brookpr/index.php?option=com_brookpr&view=article&id=91&Itemid=640 [Accessed 22 Oct. 2011]

65. http://www.guardian.co.uk/politics/2011/may/04/nadine-dorries-teenage-girls; http://www.guardian.co.uk/lifeandstyle/2011/may/28/abstinence-a-question-of-restraint [Accessed 20 Sep. 2011]; http://www.guardian.co.uk/education/2012/jan/20/nadine-dorries-sexual-abstinence-bill-withdrawn {Accessed 21 Feb. 2012].

66. See note 74 to Chapter 10.

67. Petra Boynton, 'Whatever happened to Cathy and Claire?: Sex, advice and the role of the agony aunt', in Attwood (ed.), *Mainstreaming Sex*, 111–25; http://www.guardian.co.uk/media/2010/may/06/danny-dyer-zoo-magazine [Accessed 20 Sep. 2011].

68. http://www.stonewall.org.uk/at_home/hate_crime_domestic_violence_and_criminal_law/2643.asp [Accessed 27 Sep 2011]; Brooke, *Sexual Politics*, 262–3.

69. Ethical Standards in Public Life etc. (Scotland) Act 2000, Section 34, http://www.legislation.gov.uk/asp/2000/7/section/34; Local Government Act 2003 Section 122, http://www.legislation.gov.uk/ukpga/2003/26/section/122 [Accessed 27 Sep. 2011]; Brooke, *Sexual Politics*, 263–5.

70. http://www.stonewall.org.uk/at_school/4883.asp [Accessed 27 Sep. 2011].

71. http://www.legislation.gov.uk/uksi/2003/1661/contents/made [Accessed 27 Sep. 2011].

72. http://www.legislation.gov.uk/ukpga/2003/42/contents [Accessed 27 Sep. 2011].

73. http://www.legislation.gov.uk/ukpga/2004/33/contents [Accessed 27 Sep. 2011].

74. New Family Social: Strong and happy LGBT adoptive and foster families throughout the UK https://www.newfamilysocial.co.uk/about-us/; http://news.bbc.co.uk/1/hi/uk/8225158.stm, 31 Aug. 2009 [Accessed 27 Sep. 1011].

75. http://www.guardian.co.uk/lifeandstyle/2011/feb/17/civil-partnerships-marriage [Accessed 27 Sep. 2011].

76. Jeffrey Weeks, *The World We Have Won: The Remaking of Erotic and Intimate Life* (London: Routledge, 2007), 183–98.

77. http://www.islington.gov.uk/Council/CouncilNews/PressOffice/2009/03/PR3759.asp [Accessed 27 Sep. 2011].

78. http://www.telegraph.co.uk/news/religion/7949179/Registrars-refused-to-run-gay-ceremonies.html, 17 Aug. 2010 [Accessed 27 Sep. 2011].

79. http://www.timesonline.co.uk/tol/news/politics/article1295482.ece, 23 Jan 2007; http://www.telegraph.co.uk/news/uknews/1541707/GP-seeks-opt-out-in-gay-adoption-cases.html, 6 Feb. 2007 [Accessed 27 Sep. 2011].

80. http://www.bbc.co.uk/news/uk-england-bristol-12214368, 18 Jan. 2011 [Accessed 4 Oct. 2011].

81. *Living together: British attitudes to lesbian and gay people*, 2007, http://www.stonewall.org.uk/documents/living_together.pdf [Accessed 27 Sep. 2011].

82. http://news.bbc.co.uk/1/hi/magazine/8337446.stm, 3 Nov. 2009; Sam Dick (Stonewall), *Homophobic hate crimes and hate incidents*, 2009, http://www.stonewall.org.uk/documents/sexual_orientation_hate_crimes_paper.pdf [Accessed 27 Sep. 2011].

83. http://www.bbc.co.uk/news/uk-england-london-13096519, 15 Apr. 2011 [Accessed 27 Sep. 2011].

84. Annie Bartlett, Glenn Smith, and Michael King, 'The response of mental health professionals to clients seeking help to change or redirect same-sex sexual orientation', 2009, http://www.biomedcentral.com/1471–244X/9/11; http://www.independent.co.uk/news/uk/this-britain/the-exgay-files-the-bizarre-world-of-gaytostraight-conversion-1884947.html, 1 Feb. 2010; *UKCP statement on the 'reparative' therapy of members of sexual minorities – Feb 2010*, http://www.psychotherapy.org.uk/article1260.html; Royal College of Psychiatrists, *Psychiatry and LGB People*, http://www.rcpsych.ac.uk/rollofhonour/specialinterestgroups/gaylesbian/submissiontothecofe/psychiatryandlgbpeople.aspx; Michael King, Joanna Semlyen, Helen Killaspy, Irvin Nazareth, and David Osborn, *A systematic review of research on counselling and psychotherapy for lesbian, gay, bisexual & transgender people* (BACP, 2007), http://www.bacp.co.uk/research/Systematic_Reviews_and_Publications/LGBT.php [Accessed 27 Sep. 2011].

85. Gender Recognition Act 2004, http://www.legislation.gov.uk/ukpga/2004/7/contents; Gender Recognition Panel http://www.justice.gov.uk/guidance/courts-and-tribunals/tribunals/gender-recognition-panel/index.htm [Accessed 27 Sep. 2011].

86. Weeks, *The World We Have Won*, 144–5.

87. *Gender Variance in the UK: Prevalence, Incidence, Growth and Geographic Distribution* (GIRES, 2009), http://www.gires.org.uk/assets/Medpro-Assets/GenderVarianceUK-report.pdf [Accessed 27 Sep. 2011].

88. http://www.pinknews.co.uk/2010/07/06/review-trans-at-london-pride/; http://www.thefword.org.uk/features/2011/09/radical_feminism_transphobia [Accessed 27 Sep. 2011].

89. http://www.depend.org.uk/; http://www.mermaidsuk.org.uk/; http://gendertrust.org.uk/; http://www.gires.org.uk/about.php; http://transequality.co.uk/default.aspx [Accessed 27 Sep. 2011].

90. http://www.aissg.org/12_HISTORY.HTM; http://www.ukia.co.uk/about.htm; http://intersexuk.org/vison-mission-statement/[Accessed 27 Sep. 2011].

91. http://www.asexualexplorations.net/home/about.html; http://www.asexuality.org/home/overview.html [Accessed 27 Sep. 2011].

92. Angela Cassidy, 'The (Sexual) Politics of Evolution. Popular Controversy in the Late 20th-Century United Kingdom', *History of Psychology*, 10 (2007), 199–226.

93. http://www.guardian.co.uk/society/2010/oct/08/new-anorexics-women-over-30; http://www.guardian.co.uk/commentisfree/2011/jul/29/loreal-adverts-pulled-by-asa-beauty-tanya-gold; http://www.guardian.co.uk/commentisfree/2011/feb/27/fashion-women-cosmetic-surgery-debate [Accessed 30 Sep. 2011].

94. http://www.drpetra.co.uk/blog/buy-me-some-boobs/, 12 Jul. 2005; http://news.bbc.co.uk/1/hi/uk/4377968.stm, 26 Oct. 2005 [Accessed 29 Sep. 2011].

95. http://www.independent.co.uk/life-style/health-and-families/health-news/magazines-criticised-for-offering-boob-jobs-as-competition-prizes-505570.html, 5 Sep. 2005 [Accessed 29 Sep. 2011].

96. http://www.guardian.co.uk/media/2012/jan/24/leveson-inquiry-sexualised-images-ban [Accessed 23 Feb. 2012].

97. Lih Mei Liao and Sarah M Creighton, 'Requests for cosmetic genitoplasty: How should healthcare providers respond?', *British Medical Journal*, 334 (2007), http://www.ncbi.nlm.nih.gov/pmc/articles/PMC1877941/ [Accessed 27 Sep. 2011].

98. http://news.bbc.co.uk/1/hi/8352711.stm, 11 Nov. 2009 [Accessed 27 Sep. 2011].

99. http://news.sky.com/home/sky-news-archive/article/13365755, 6 Jun. 2005 [Accessed 29 Sep. 2011].

100. http://www.guardian.co.uk/education/2009/may/03/boys-under-achievement-school-education; http://www.guardian.co.uk/commentisfree/2010/jul/04/boys-men-education-work; http://www.guardian.co.uk/education/2010/jul/04/unemployment-male-graduates [Accessed 29 Sep. 2011].

101. http://fashion.telegraph.co.uk/beauty/news-features/TMG3341168/Male-order-the-rise-of-the-metrosexual.html, 7 Jun. 2005; http://www.guardian.co.uk/theobserver/2005/jan/23/features.review7; http://www.newstatesman.com/society/2007/08/lad-culture-cochrane-loaded [Accessed 4 Oct. 2011].

102. http://www.independent.co.uk/life-style/love-sex/sex-industry/filth-and-fury-the-porn-addicts-struggling-to-shake-off-their-online-sex-habit-1231560.html, 11 Jan. 2009; http://www.mirror.co.uk/life-style/real-life/2010/07/14/porn-britain-s-fastest-growing-addiction-115875–22410875/; http://news.bbc.co.uk/panorama/hi/front_page/newsid_9251000/9251687.stm 6 Dec 2010; http://www.telegraph.co.uk/culture/tvandradio/8184386/Is-video-game-addiction-really-so-dangerous.html, 6 Dec. 2010 [Accessed 4 Oct. 2011].

103. http://www.guardian.co.uk/society/2011/aug/31/cmi-equal-pay-report [Accessed 29 Sep. 2011].

104. http://www2.lse.ac.uk/newsAndMedia/news/archives/2010/02/teenpreg.aspx [Accessed 30 Sep. 2011].

105. http://curezone.com/art/read.asp?ID=140&db=1&C0=1, 30 Apr. 2002; http://www.dailymail.co.uk/femail/article-1246375/Why-biological-clock-ticking-women-aged-30.html, 30 Jan. 2010; http://news.bbc.co.uk/1/hi/health/8497719.stm, 10 Feb. 2010; http://www.telegraph.co.uk/health/healthnews/8687975

/Test-to-tell-how-fast-biological-clock-is-ticking.html, 8 Aug. 2011 [Accessed 30 Sep. 2011].

106. http://www.mirror.co.uk/life-style/dieting/2009/08/10/how-to-get-amazing-post-pregnancy-figures-like-victoria-beckham-and-gwen-stefani-115875-21585390/ [Accessed 30 Sep. 2011].
107. http://www.pinkstinks.co.uk/ / [Accessed 30 Sep. 2011].
108. http://www.guardian.co.uk/society/2003/oct/17/drugsandalcohol.medicine-andhealth; http://www.timesonline.co.uk/tol/news/uk/crime/article3941772. ece, 16 May. 2008; http://www.telegraph.co.uk/news/uknews/law-and-order/5251042/Rise-of-ladette-culture-as-241-women-arrested-each-day-for-violence.html, 1 May 2009 [Accessed 4 Oct. 2011].
109. Carolyn Jackson and Penny Tinkler, '"Ladettes" and "Modern Girls": "Troublesome" young femininities', *The Sociological Review*, 55 (2007), 251–72.
110. http://www.guardian.co.uk/society/2010/jul/25/female-circumcision-children-british-law; http://www.forwarduk.org.uk/about [Accessed 2 Oct. 2011].
111. http://www.fco.gov.uk/en/travel-and-living-abroad/when-things-go-wrong/forced-marriage/information-for-victims; http://www.karmanirvana.org.uk [Accessed 2 Oct. 2011].
112. http://www.guardian.co.uk/society/2009/oct/25/honour-killings-victims-domestic-violence [Accessed 2 Oct. 2011].
113. http://www.fawcettsociety.org.uk/; http://www.object.org.uk/; http://www.thefword.org.uk/ [Accessed 4 Oct. 2011].
114. Brooke, *Sexual Politics*, 267.
115. http://www.telegraph.co.uk/news/politics/david-cameron/8803017/Conservative-Party-Conference-2011-David-Cameron-should-calm-down.html [Accessed 7 Oct. 2011].
116. http://www.fawcettsociety.org.uk/index.asp?PageID=1195 [Accessed 7 Oct. 2011].
117. http://www.keepournhspublic.com/index.php [Accessed 7 Oct. 2011].

Recommended Further Reading

Adrian Ager and Catherine Lee, 'Prostitution in the Medway Towns, 1860–1885', *Local Population Studies*, 83 (2009), 39–55

Anthony Aldgate and James C. Robertson, *Censorship in Theatre and Cinema* (Edinburgh: Edinburgh University Press, 2005)

Feona Attwood (ed.), *Mainstreaming Sex: The Sexualization of Western Culture* (London: I. B. Tauris, 2009)

Françoise Barret-Ducrocq, *Love in the Time of Victoria: Sexuality, Class and Gender in Nineteenth-Century London* (London: Verso, 1991)

Paula Bartley, *Prostitution: Prevention and Reform in Britain, 1860–1914* (London: Routledge, 1999)

J. L. Barton, 'The Story of Marital Rape', *Law Quarterly Review*, 108 (1992), 260–71

Chiara Beccalossi, *Female Sexual Inversion: Same-Sex Desires in Italian and British Sexology, c. 1870–1920* (Basingstoke: Palgrave Macmillan, 2012)

J. Miriam Benn, *The Predicaments of Love* (London: Pluto Press, 1992)

Virginia Berridge, *AIDS in the UK: The Making of Policy 1981–1994* (Oxford: Oxford University Press, 1996)

Virginia Berridge and Philip Strong (eds), *AIDS and Contemporary History* (Cambridge: Cambridge University Press, 1993)

Adrian Bingham, *Gender, Modernity, and the Popular Press in Inter-War Britain* (Oxford: Oxford University Press, 2004)

Adrian Bingham, *Family Newspapers? Sex, Private Life and the British Popular Press, 1918–1978* (Oxford: Oxford University Press, 2009)

Adrian Bingham, 'The British Popular Press and Venereal Disease During The Second World War', *Historical Journal*, 48 (2005), 1055–76

Lucy Bland, *Banishing the Beast: English Feminism and Sexual Morality, 1885–1914* (London: Penguin, 1995)

Lucy Bland and Laura Doan (eds), *Sexology in Culture: Labelling Bodies and Desires* (Oxford: Polity Press, 1998)

Lucy Bland, 'The trial of Madame Fahmy: Orientalism, violence, sexual perversity and the fear of miscegenation', in Shani D'Cruze (ed.), *Everyday Violence in Britain, 1850–1950: Gender and Class* (Harlow: Longman, 2001), 185–97

Lucy Bland, 'White Women and Men of Colour: Miscegenation Fears in Britain after the Great War', *Gender & History*, 17 (2005), 29–61

Lucy Bland, 'The Trials and Tribulations of Edith Thompson: The Capital Crime of Sexual Incitement in 1920s England', *Journal of British Studies*, 47 (2008), 624–48

Sean Brady, *Masculinity and Male Homosexuality in Britain, 1861–1913* (Basingstoke: Palgrave Macmillan, 2005)

Edward Bristow, *Vice and Vigilance: Purity movements in Britain since 1700* (Dublin: Gee & Macmillan, 1977)

Stephen Brooke, *Sexual Politics: Sexuality, Family Planning, and the British Left from the 1880s to the Present Day* (Oxford: Oxford University Press, 2011)

Barbara Brookes, *Abortion in England, 1900–1967* (London: Croom Helm, 1988)

Rosie Campbell and Maggie O'Neill (eds), *Sex Work Now* (Cullompton: Willan Publishing, 2006)

Bob Cant and Susan Hemmings (eds), *Radical Records: Thirty Years of Lesbian and Gay History* (London: Routledge, 1988)

H. G. Cocks, *Nameless Offences: Homosexual desire in the 19th century* (London: I. B. Tauris, 2003)

H. G. Cocks, *Classified: The secret history of the personal column* (London: Random House, 2009)

Harry Cocks, 'Saucy Stories: Pornography, sexology, and the marketing of sexual knowledge in Britain, c.1918–70', *Social History*, 29 (2004), 465–84

Deborah A. Cohen, 'Private Lives in Public Spaces: Marie Stopes, the Mothers' Clinics and the Practice of Contraception', *History Workshop Journal*, 35 (1993), 95–115

Deborah Cohler, *Citizen, Invert, Queer: Lesbianism and War in the Early Twentieth Century Britain* (Minneapolis, MN: University of Minnesota Press, 2010)

Marcus Collins, *Modern Love: An Intimate History of Men and Women in Twentieth Century Britain* (London: Atlantic Books, 2003)

Hera Cook, *The Long Sexual Revolution: English Women, Sex, and Contraception 1800–1975* (Oxford: Oxford University Press, 2004)

Matt Cook, *London and the Culture of Homosexuality, 1885–1914* (Cambridge: Cambridge University Press, 2008)

Pamela Cox, *Gender, Justice and Welfare: Bad Girls in Britain, 1900–1950* (Basingstoke: Palgrave Macmillan, 2003)

Pamela Cox, 'Compulsion, Voluntarism, and Venereal Disease: Governing Sexual Health in England after the Contagious Diseases Acts', *Journal of British Studies*, 46 (2007), 91–115

Stephen Cretney, *Family Law in the Twentieth Century: A History* (Oxford: Oxford University Press, 2003)

Pamela Dale and Kate Fisher. 'Contrasting Municipal Responses to the Provision of Birth Control Services in Halifax and Exeter before 1948', *Social History of Medicine*, 23 (2010), 567–85

Roger Davidson, *Dangerous Liaisons: The social history of VD in twentieth-century Scotland* (Amsterdam: Rodopi, 2000)

Roger Davidson and Gayle Davis, *The Sexual State: Sexuality and Scottish Governance 1950–80* (Edinburgh: Edinburgh University Press, 2012)

Shani d'Cruze, *Crimes of Outrage: Sex, violence and Victorian working woman* (London: UCL Press, 1998)

Shani D'Cruze (ed.), *Everyday Violence in Britain, 1850–1950: Gender and Class* (Harlow: Longman, 2000)

Lucy Delap, Ben Griffin, and Abigail Wills (eds), *The Politics of Domestic Authority in Britain since 1800* (Basingstoke, Palgrave Macmillan, 2009)

Joanna de Groot, '"Sex" and "race": The construction of language and image in the nineteenth century', in Catherine Hall (ed.), *Cultures of Empire: A Reader: Colonizers in Britain and the Empire in the nineteenth and twentieth centuries* (Manchester: Manchester University Press, 2000), 37–60

Laura Doan, *Fashioning Sapphism: The origins of a modern English lesbian culture,* (New York: Columbia University Press, 2001)

Maeve E. Doggett, *Marriage, Wife-Beating and the Law in Victorian England* (Columbia, SC: University of South Carolina Press, 1993)

Margaret Douglas, 'Women, God and Birth Control: The first hospital birth control clinic' *Llafur*, 6:4 (1995), 110–22

Martin Durham, *Sex and Politics: The Family and Morality in the Thatcher Years* (Basingstoke: Macmillan, 1991)

David Evans, 'Sexually transmitted diseases in Britain since the founding of the National Health Service', in Roger Davidson and Lesley Hall (eds), *Sex, Sin and Suffering: Venereal Diseases in the European Social Context since 1870* (London: Routledge, 2001), 237–52

Tanya Evans, 'The Other Woman and her Child: Extra-marital affairs and illegitimacy in twentieth-century Britain', *Women's History Review*, 20 (2011), 67–86

Paul Ferris, *Sex and the British: A Twentieth-Century History* (London: Michael Joseph, 1993)

Diarmaid Ferriter, *Occasions of Sin: Sex and society in modern Ireland* (London: Profile Books, 2009)

Janet Fink, 'Natural Mothers, Putative Fathers, and Innocent Children: The Definition and Regulation of Parental Relationships Outside Marriage, in England, 1945–1959', *Journal of Family History*, 25 (2000), 178–95

Frances Finnegan, *Poverty and Prostitution: A Study of Victorian Prostitutes in York* (Cambridge: Cambridge University Press, 1979)

Kate Fisher, *Birth Control, Sex, and Marriage in Britain 1918–1960* (Oxford: Oxford University Press, 2006)

Kate Fisher, 'Contrasting cultures of contraception: Birth control clinics and the working-classes in Britain between the wars', in M. Gijswijt-Hofstra, G. M. Van Heteren, and E. M. Tansey (eds), *Biographies of Remedies: Drugs, medicines and contraceptives in Dutch and Anglo-American Healing Cultures* (*Clio Medica* 66, Rodopi, 2002), 141–57

Kate Fisher, ' "Teach the Miners Birth Control": The Delivery of Contraceptive Advice in South Wales, 1918–1950', in Pamela Michael and Charles Webster (eds), *Health and Society in Twentieth-Century Wales* (Cardiff: University of Wales Press, 2006), 143–64

Ginger Frost, *Promises Broken: Courtship, class and gender in Victorian England* (Charlottesville, VA: University Press of Virginia, 1995)

Ginger S. Frost, *Living in Sin: Cohabiting as Husband and Wife in Nineteenth-Century England* (Manchester: Manchester University Press, 2008)

Peter Fryer, *The Birth Controllers* (London: Secker & Warburg, 1965)

Jill Gardiner, *From the Closet to the Screen: Women at the Gateways Club, 1945–85* (London: Rivers Oram, 2002)

Simon Garfield, *The End of Innocence: Britain in the Time of AIDS* (London: Faber & Faber, 1994)

Eleanor Gordon and Gwyneth Nair, *Public Lives: Women, Family, and Society in Victorian Britain* (New Haven, CT: Yale University Press, 2003)

Daniel Grey, *Degrees of Guilt: Infanticide in England 1860–1960* (Liverpool: Liverpool University Press, forthcoming)

Julie Grier, 'Eugenics and Birth Control: Contraceptive Provision in North Wales, 1918–1939', *Social History of Medicine*, 11 (1998), 443–58

Lesley A. Hall, *Hidden Anxieties: Male Sexuality, 1900–1950* (Oxford: Polity Press, 1991)

Lesley A. Hall, *Outspoken Women: Women writing about sex, 1870–1969* (London: Routledge, 2005)

Lesley A. Hall, *The Life and Times of Stella Browne: Feminist and free spirit* (London: I. B. Tauris, 2011)

Lesley A. Hall, 'Forbidden by God, despised by men: Masturbation, medical warnings, moral panic and manhood in Britain, 1850–1950', *Journal of the History of Sexuality*,

2 (1992), reprinted in John C. Fout (ed.), *Forbidden History: The State, Society, and the Regulation of Sexuality in Modern Europe* (Chicago, IL: University of Chicago Press, 1992), 293–318

Lesley A. Hall, ' "The English have hot-water bottles": The morganatic marriage between the British medical profession and sexology since William Acton', in Roy Porter and Mikulas Teich (eds), *Sexual Knowledge, Sexual Science: The History of Attitudes to Sexuality* (Cambridge: Cambridge University Press, 1994), 350–66

Lesley A. Hall, ' "Disinterested enthusiasm for sexual misconduct": The British Society for the Study of Sex Psychology, 1913–1947', *Journal of Contemporary History*, 30 (1995), 665–86

Lesley A. Hall, ' "War always brings it on": War, STDs, the military, and the civilian population in Britain, 1850–1950', in Roger Cooter, Mark Harrison, and Steve Sturdy (eds), *Medicine and Modern Warfare* (Amsterdam: Rodopi, 1999), 205–23

Lesley A. Hall, 'Malthusian mutations: The changing politics and moral meanings of birth control in Britain', in Brian Dolan and Roy Porter (eds), *Malthus, Medicine and Morality: 'Malthusianism' after 1798* (Amsterdam: Rodopi, 2000), 141–63

Lesley A. Hall, 'Venereal Diseases and Society in Britain from the Contagious Diseases Acts to the National Health Service', in Roger Davidson and Lesley Hall (eds), *Sex, Sin and Suffering: Venereal Diseases in the European Social Context since 1870*, London: Routledge, 2001), 120–36

Lesley A. Hall, ' "A suitable job for a woman"?: Women doctors and birth control before 1950', in Larry Conrad and Anne Hardy (eds), *Women and Modern Medicine* (Amsterdam: Rodopi, 2001), 127–47

Lesley A. Hall, ' "The Reserved Occupation"? Prostitution in the Second World War', *Women's History Magazine*, 41 (Jun 2002), 4–9

Lesley A Hall, ' "It was the doctors who were suffering from it": The history of masturbatory insanity revisited', *Paedagogica Historica: International Journal of the History of Education*, 39 (2003), 685–99

Lesley A. Hall, 'Eyes tightly shut, lying rigidly still and thinking of England? British women and sex from Marie Stopes to Hite', in Michelle Martin and Claudia Nelson (eds), *Sexual Pedagogies: Teaching Sex in America, Britain, and Australia, 1879–2000* (Basingstoke: Palgrave Macmillan, 2003), 53–72

Lesley A. Hall, 'Hauling down the Double Standard: Feminism, social purity, and sexual science in late nineteenth-century Britain', *Gender and History*, 16 (2004), 36–56.

Lesley A. Hall, 'What shall we do with the poxy sailor? Venereal diseases in the British mercantile marine', *Journal of Maritime Research*, 6 (2004), 113–44: http://www.tandfonline.com/doi/abs/10.1080/21533369.2004.9668339

Lesley A Hall, 'Birds, Bees and General Embarrassment: Sex education in Britain from social purity to Section 28', in Richard Aldrich (ed.), *Public or Private Education: Lessons from History* (London: Woburn Press, 2004), 98–115

Lesley A. Hall, ' "No Sex, Please, We're Socialists": The Labour Party prefers to close its eyes and think of the electorate', *Socialist History*, 36 (2010), 11–28

Emily Hamer, *Britannia's Glory: A History of Twentieth-Century Lesbians* (London: Cassell, 1996)

A. James Hammerton, *Cruelty and Companionship: Conflict in Nineteenth-Century Married Life* (London: Routledge, 1992)

James Hampshire, 'The politics of school sex education policy in England and Wales from the 1940s to the 1960s', *Social History of Medicine*, 18 (2005), 87–105

Patrick Higgins, *Heterosexual Dictatorship: Male Homosexuality in Post-War Britain* (London: Fourth Estate, 1996)

Lesley Hoggart, 'The campaign for birth control in Britain in the 1920s', in Anne Digby and John Stewart (eds), *Gender, Health and Welfare* (London: Routledge, 1996), 143–66

Lee Holcombe, *Wives and Property: Reform of the Married Women's Property Law in Nineteenth-Century England* (Toronto: University of Toronto Press, 1983)

Katharine Holden, *The Shadow of Marriage: Singleness in England, 1914–1960* (Manchester: Manchester University Press, 2007)

Ann Sumner Holmes, 'The Double Standard in the English Divorce Laws, 1857–1923', *Law and Social Enquiry: The Journal of the American Bar Foundation*, 20 (1995), 601–20

Matt Houlbrook, *Queer London: Perils and Pleasures in the Sexual Metropolis, 1918–1957* (Chicago, IL: University of Chicago Press, 2005)

Matt Houlbrook, 'The Private World of Public Urinals in London, 1918–1957', *The London Journal*, 25 (2000), 52–70

Matt Houlbrook, ' "The Man with the Powder Puff" ' in interwar London', *The Historical Journal*, 50 (2007) 145–71

Matt Houlbrook and Chris Waters, 'The Heart in Exile: Detachment and Desire in 1950s London', *History Workshop Journal*, 62 (2006), 142–63

Philip Howell, *Geographies of Regulation: Policing Prostitution in Nineteenth-Century Britain and the Empire* (Cambridge: Cambridge University Press, 2009)

Janice Hubbard Harris, *Edwardian Stories of Divorce* (New Brunswick, NJ: Rutgers University Press, 1996)

Alan Hunt, *Governing Morals: A social history of moral regulation* (Cambridge: Cambridge University Press, 1999)

Samuel Hynes, *The Edwardian Turn of Mind* (London: Pimlico, 1991, 1st publ. 1968)

Louise Jackson, *Child Sex Abuse and the Law in Victorian England* (London: Routledge, 1999)

Stephen Jeffrey-Poulter, *Peers, Queers and Commons: The Struggle for Gay Law Reform from 1950 to the Present* (London: Routledge, 1991)

Rebecca Jennings, *A Lesbian History of Britain: Love and Sex Between Women Since 1500* (Oxford: Greenwood World Publishing, 2007)

Rebecca Jennings, *Tomboys and Bachelor Girls: A Lesbian History of Post-War Britain 1945–1971* (Manchester: Manchester University Press, 2007)

Alkarim Jivani, *It's Not Unusual: A History of Lesbian and Gay Britain in the Twentieth Century* (London: Michael O'Mara Books, 1997)

Emma L Jones, 'The Establishment of Voluntary Family Planning Clinics in Liverpool and Bradford,1926–1960: A Comparative Study', *Social History of Medicine*, 24 (2011), 352–69

Greta Jones, 'Marie Stopes in Ireland: The Mother's Clinic in Belfast, 1936–1947', *Social History of Medicine*, 5 (1992) 255–77

Jane Jordan, *Josephine Butler* (London: John Murray, 2001)

Morris B Kaplan, *Sodom on the Thames: Sex, Love and Scandal in Wilde Times* (Ithaca, NY: Cornell University Press, 2005)

Annette Kuhn, *Cinema, Censorship, and Sexuality, 1909–1925* (London: Routledge, 1988)

Julia Ann Laite, 'The Association for Moral and Social Hygiene: Abolitionism and prostitution law in Britain (1915–1959)', *Women's History Review*, 17 (2008), 207–23

Julia Laite, *Common Prostitutes and Ordinary Citizens: Commercial Sex in London, 1885–1960* (Basingstoke: Palgrave Macmillan, 2011).

Claire Langhamer, 'Adultery in post-war England', *History Workshop Journal*, 62 (2006), 86–115

Claire Langhamer, 'Love and Courtship in Mid-Twentieth-Century England', *The Historical Journal*, 50 (2007), 173–96

Audrey Leathard, *The Fight for Family Planning: The Development of Family Planning Services in Britain, 1921–74* (Basingstoke: Macmillan, 1980)

Catherine Lee, *Policing Prostitution, 1856–1886: Deviance, Surveillance and Morality* (London: Pickering & Chatto, 2012)

Philippa Levine, *Prostitution, Race, and Politics: Policing Venereal Disease in the British Empire* (London: Routledge, 2003)

Philippa Levine, ' "Walking the Streets in a Way No Decent Woman Should": Women Police in World War I', *Journal of Modern History*, 66 (1994), 34–78

Jane Lewis, *The End of Marriage: Individualism and Intimate Relations* (Cheltenham: Edward Elgar, 2001)

Maria Luddy, *Prostitution and Irish Society, 1800–1940* (Cambridge: Cambridge University Press, 2007)

Anne McClintock, *Imperial Leather: Race, gender and sexuality in the colonial context* (London: Routledge, 1995)

Leanne McCormick, *Regulating Sexuality: Women in Twentieth-Century Northern Ireland* (Manchester: Manchester University Press, 2010)

O. R. McGregor, *Divorce in England: A centenary study* (London: Heinemann, 1957)

Paul McHugh, *Prostitution and Victorian Social Reform* (London: Croom Helm, 1980)

Tania Macintosh, 'An Abortionist City. Maternal Mortality, Abortion and Birth Control in Sheffield, 1920–1940', *Medical History*, 44 (2000), 75–97

Angus McLaren, *A Prescription for Murder: The Victorian serial killings of Dr Thomas Neill Cream* (Chicago, IL: University of Chicago Press, 1993)

Angus McLaren, *The Trials of Manhood: Policing Sexual Boundaries 1870–1930* (Chicago, IL: University of Chicago Press, 1997)

Angus McLaren, *Sexual Blackmail: A Modern History* (Cambridge, MA: Harvard University Press, 2002)

John Macnicol, 'Eugenics and the Campaign for Voluntary Sterilization in Britain Between the Wars', *Social History of Medicine*, 2 (1989), 147–69

John Macnicol, 'The Voluntary Sterilization Campaign in Britain', in John C. Fout (ed.), *Forbidden History: The State, Society and the Regulation of Sexuality in Modern Europe* (Chicago, IL: University of Chicago Press, 1992), 417–34

Andrew Mangham and Greta DePledge (eds), *The Female Body in Medicine and Literature* (Liverpool: Liverpool University Press, 2011)

Sharon Marcus, *Between Women: Friendship, Desire, and Marriage in Victorian England* (Princeton, NJ: Princeton University Press, 2007)

Lara Marks, *Sexual Chemistry: The Story of the Contraceptive Pill* (New Haven, CT: Yale University Press, 2001)

Michael Mason, *The Making of Victorian Sexuality* (Oxford: Oxford University Press, 1994)

Michael Mason, *The Making of Victorian Sexual Attitudes* (Oxford: Oxford University Press, 1994)

Leslie J. Moran, *The Homosexual(ity) of Law* (London: Routledge, 1996)

Leslie J. Moran, Daniel Monk, and Sarah Beresford (eds), *Legal Queeries: Lesbian, gay, and transgender legal studies* (London: Cassell, 1998)

Sue Morgan, *A Passion for Purity: Ellice Hopkins and the Politics of Gender in the Late-Victorian Church* (University of Bristol, Department of Theology & Religious Studies, 1999)

Frank Mort, *Dangerous Sexualities: Medico-moral politics in Britain since 1830* (London: Routledge & Kegan Paul, 1987)

Frank Mort, *Capital Affairs: London and the Making of the Permissive Society* (New Haven, CT: Yale University Press, 2010)

Frank Mort, 'Striptease: The erotic female body and live sexual entertainment in mid-twentieth-century London', *Social History*, 32 (2007), 27–53

David Nash and Anne Marie Kilday, *Cultures of Shame: Exploring Crime and Morality in Britain 1600–1900* (Basingstoke: Palgrave Macmillan, 2010)

Claudia Nelson and Ann Sumner Holmes (eds), *Maternal Instincts: Visions of Motherhood and Sexuality in Britain, 1875–1925* (Basingstoke: Macmillan, 1997)

Tim Newburn, *Permission and Regulation: Law and Morals in Post-War Britain* (London: Routledge, 1992)

Chris Nottingham, *The Pursuit of Serenity: Havelock Ellis and the New Politics* (Amsterdam: University of Amsterdam Press, 1999)

Alison Oram, *Her Husband was a Woman!: Women's gender-crossing and twentieth-century British popular culture* (London: Routledge, 2007)

Stefan Petrow, *Policing Morals: The Metropolitan Police and the Home Office, 1870–1914* (Oxford: Clarendon Press, 1994)

Naomi Pfeffer, *The Stork and the Syringe: A Political History of Reproductive Medicine* (Oxford: Polity Press, 1993)

Jane Pilcher, 'Sex in Health Education: Official Guidance for Schools in England, 1928–1977', *Journal of Historical Sociology*, 17 (2004), 185–208

Roy Porter and Lesley A. Hall, *The Facts of Life: The Creation of Sexual Knowledge in Britain, 1650–1950* (New Haven, CT, and London: Yale University Press, 1995)

Lisa Power, *No Bath But Plenty of Bubbles: An Oral History of the Gay Liberation Front, 1970–73* (London: Cassell, 1995)

Carmel Quinlan, *Genteel Revolutionaries: Anna and Thomas Haslam, Pioneers of Irish Feminism* (Cork: Cork University Press, 2002)

George Robb, 'The Way of All Flesh: Degeneration, Eugenics, and the Gospel of Free Love', *Journal of the History of Sexuality*, 6 (1996), 589–603

George Robb, 'Race Motherhood: Moral Eugenics vs Progressive Eugenics, 1880–1920', in Claudia Nelson and Ann Sumner Holmes (eds), *Maternal Instincts: Visions of Motherhood and Sexuality in Britain, 1875–1925* (Basingstoke: Macmillan, 1997), 58–74

George Robb and Nancy Erber (eds.), *Disorder in the Court: Trials and Sexual Conflict at the Turn of the Century* (Basingstoke: Palgrave Macmillan, 1999)

M. J. D. Roberts, *Making English Morals: Voluntary Association and Moral Reform in England, 1787–1886* (Cambridge: Cambridge University Press, 2004)

James C. Robertson, *Hidden Cinema: British Film Censorship in Action, 1913–1975* (London: Routledge, 1989)

Lucy Robinson, *Gay men and the Left in post-war Britain: How the personal got political* (Manchester: Manchester University Press, 2007)

June Rose, *Marie Stopes and the Sexual Revolution* (London, Faber & Faber, 1992)

Sonya O. Rose, 'Sex, citizenship and the nation in World War II Britain', in Catherine Hall (ed.), *Cultures of Empire: Colonizers in Britain and the Empire in the nineteenth and twentieth centuries: A reader* (Manchester: Manchester University Press, 2000), 246–77

Ellen Ross, *Love and Toil: Motherhood in Outcast London, 1870–1918* (Oxford: Oxford University Press, 1993)

Sheila Rowbotham, *Edward Carpenter: A Life of Liberty and Love* (London: Verso, 2008)

Lutz D. H. Sauerteig and Roger Davidson (eds), *Shaping Sexual Knowledge: A Cultural History of Sex Education in C20th Europe* (London: Routledge, 2009)

Gail Savage, 'The Operation of the 1857 Divorce Act, 1860–1910: A Research Note', *Journal of Social History*, 16 (1983), 103–10

Gail Savage, '"The Wilful Communication of a Loathsome Disease": Marital Conflict and Venereal Disease in Victorian England', *Victorian Studies*, 34 (1990), 35–54

Gail Savage, '"...Equality from the Masculine Point of View...": The 2nd Earl Russell and Divorce Law Reform in England', *Russell: The journal of the Bertrand Russell Archives*, n.s 16 (1996), 69–84

Gail Savage, 'Erotic stories and public decency: Newspaper reporting of divorce proceedings in England', *The Historical Journal*, 41 (1998), 511–28

Gail Savage, '"... the instrument of an animal function": Marital Rape and Sexual Cruelty in the Divorce Court, 1858–1908', in Lucy Delap, Ben Griffin, and Abigail Wills (eds), *The Politics of Domestic Authority in Britain since 1800* (Basingstoke, Palgrave Macmillan, 2009), 43–57

Gail Savage, ' They Would if They Could: Class, Gender, and Popular Representation of English Divorce Litigation, 1858–1908', *Journal of Family History*, 36 (2011), 173–90

Helen Self, *Prostitution, Women and Misuse of the Law: The Fallen Daughters of Eve* (London: Cass, 2003)

Mary Lyndon Shanley, *Feminism, Marriage, and the Law in Victorian England, 1850–1895* (Princeton, NJ: Princeton University Press, 1989)

Lisa Z. Sigel, *Governing Pleasures: Pornography and social change in England, 1815–1914* (New Brunswick, NJ: Rutgers University Press, 2002)

Lisa Z. Sigel, 'Name Your Pleasure: The Transformation of Sexual Language in Nineteenth Century British Pornography', *Journal of the History of Sexuality*, 9 (2000), 395–419

Stefan Slater, 'Pimps, Police and Filles de Joie: Foreign Prostitution in Interwar London', *The London Journal*, 32 (2007), 53–74

Carol Smart, *The Ties That Bind: Law, marriage, and the reproduction of patriarchal relations* (London: Routledge & Kegan Paul, 1984)

Carol Smart (ed.), *Regulating Womanhood: Essays on marriage, motherhood and sexuality* (London: Routledge, 1992)

Carol Smart, 'Reconsidering the Recent History of Child Sexual Abuse, 1910–1960', *Journal of Social Policy*, 29 (2000), 55–73

Timothy d'Arch Smith, *Love in Earnest: Some notes on the lives and writings of English 'Uranian' Poets from 1889–1930* (London: Routledge & Kegan Paul, 1970)

Richard A. Soloway, *Birth Control and the Population Question in England, 1870–1930* (Chapel Hill, NC: University of North Carolina Press, 1982)

Richard A. Soloway, *Demography and Degeneration: Eugenics and the Declining Birthrate in Twentieth-Century Britain* (Chapel Hill, NC: University of North Carolina Press, 1995)

Liz Stanley, *Sex Surveyed, 1949–1994: From Mass-Observation's 'Little Kinsey' to the National Survey and the Hite Reports* (London: Taylor & Francis, 1995)

Penny Summerfield, *Reconstructing Women's Wartime Lives: Discourse and subjectivity in oral histories of the Second World War* (Manchester: Manchester University Press, 1998)

Penny Summerfield and Nicole Crockett, ' "You weren't taught that with the welding": Lessons in sexuality in the Second World War', *Women's History Review*, 1 (1992), 435–54

John Sutherland, *Offensive Literature: Decensorship in Britain, 1960–82* (London: Junction Books, 1982)

Simon Szreter, *Fertility, Class and Gender in Britain 1860–1940* (Cambridge: Cambridge University Press, 1996)

Simon Szreter and Kate Fisher, *Sex before the Sexual Revolution: Intimate Life in England 1918–1963* (Cambridge: Cambridge University Press, 2010)

Laura Tabili, 'Women "of a Very Low Type": Crossing Racial Boundaries in Imperial Britain', in Laura L. Frader and Sonya O. Rose (eds), *Gender and Class in Modern Europe* (Ithaca, NY: Cornell University Press, 1996), 165–90

Pat Thane, 'Population Politics in Post-War British Culture', in Becky Conekin, Frank Mort, and Chris Waters (eds), *Moments of Modernity: Reconstructing Britain, 1945–1964* (London: Rivers Oram, 1999), 114–33

Pat Thane, 'Family Life and "Normality" in Postwar British Culture', in Richard Bessell and Dirk Schumann (eds), *Life after Death: Approaches to a cultural and social history of Europe during the 1940s and 1950s* (Cambridge: Cambridge University Press, 2003), 193–210

Pat Thane, 'Unmarried motherhood in twentieth-century England', *Women's History Review*, 20 (2011), 11–29

John Tosh, *A Man's Place: Masculinity and the Middle-Class Home in Victorian England* (New Haven, CT: Yale University Press, 1999)

N. L. Tranter, *British Population in the Twentieth Century* (Basingstoke: Macmillan, 1996)

Alan Travis, *Bound and Gagged: A secret history of obscenity in Britain* (London: Profile Books, 2000)

Charles Upchurch, *Before Wilde: Sex between Men in Britain's Age of Reform* (Berkeley, CA: University of California Press, 2009)

James Vernon, ' "For Some Queer Reason": The Trials and Tribulations of Colonel Barker's Masquerade in Interwar Britain', *Signs: Journal of Women in Culture and Society*, 26 (2000), 37–61

Martha Vicinus, *Intimate Friends: Women Who Loved Women, 1778–1928* (Chicago, IL: University of Chicago Press, 2004)

Martha Vicinus, 'The Gift of Love: Nineteenth-Century Religion and Lesbian Passion', *Nineteenth-Century Contexts*, 23 (2001), 241–65

Judith R. Walkowitz, *Prostitution and Victorian Society: Women, class and the state* (Cambridge: Cambridge University Press, 1980)

Judith R. Walkowitz, *City of Dreadful Delight: Narratives of sexual danger in late-Victorian London* (London: Virago, 1992)

Judith Walkowitz, 'Going Public: Shopping, Street Harassment, and Streetwalking in Late Victorian London', *Representations*, 662, (1998), 1–30

Chris Waters, *Queer Treatments: Homosexual Selfhood and the Therapeutic Ideal in Twentieth-Century Britain* (forthcoming)

Chris Waters, 'Disorders of the Mind, Disorders of the Body Social: Peter Wildeblood and the Making of the Modern Homosexual', in Becky Conekin, Frank Mort, and Chris Waters (eds), *Moments of Modernity: Reconstructing Britain, 1945–1964* (London: Rivers Oram, 1999), 134–51

Wendy Webster, *Imagining Home: Gender, 'Race' and National Identity, 1945–64* (London: UCL Press, 1998)

Jeffrey Weeks, *Coming Out: Homosexual Politics in Britain, from the Nineteenth Century to the Present* (London: Quartet, 1977)

Jeff Weeks, *Sex, Politics, and Society: The regulation of sexuality in Britain since 1800* (London: Longman, 1981)

Jeffrey Weeks, *The World We Have Won: The Remaking of Erotic and Intimate Life* (London: Routledge, 2007)

Jeffrey Weeks, Peter Aggleton, Chris McKevitt, Kay Parkinson, and Austin Taylor-Laybourn, 'Community Responses to HIV and AIDS: The "De-Gaying" and

"Re-Gaying" of AIDS', in Jeffrey Weeks and Janet Holland (eds), *Sexual Cultures: Communities, Values, and Intimacy* (Basingstoke: Macmillan, 1996), 161–79

Elizabeth Wilson, *Only Half-Way to Paradise: Women in Post-War Britain: 1945–1968* (London: Tavistock, 1980)

Angela Woollacott, ' "Khaki Fever" and its Control: Gender, Class, Age and Sexual Morality on the British Homefront in the First World War', *Journal of Contemporary History*, 29 (1994), 325–47

Michael Worboys, 'Unsexing Gonorrhoea: Bacteriologists, Gynaecologists and Suffragists in Britain, 1860–1920', *Social History of Medicine*, 17 (2004), 41–59

Index

religion, and sexual attitudes and
behaviour, 3
*Report as to the Practice of Medicine
and Surgery by Unqualified Persons*
(1910), 73
Report of the Royal Commission on the
Poor Law (1909), 60
reproduction, and separation from sex, 1
reproductive biology, 111
respectability, 4, 6, 16, 69, 74, 85, 86,
107, 149
The Responsible Society, 160
Reynold's Weekly, 46
Rice-Davies, Mandy, 153
Ricord, Philippe, 23
Robb, George, 58, 59
Robbins, Harold, 150
Roberts, Harry, 113
Robinson, Kenneth, 148, 150, 154
rohypnol, 177
Roman Catholic Church, and birth
control, 157
Rosebery, Lord, 49
Routh, C H F, 27–8
Rowbotham, Sheila, 8
Royal College of Obstetricians and
Gynaecologists, 6, 123
Royal College of Physicians, 111
Royal Commission on Marriage and
Divorce, 62–3, 70–1
Royal Commission on
Population (1944), 123
Royal Commission on the
Poor Laws (1911), 73
Royal Court Theatre, 155
Royal Institute of Public Health, 103
Royal Medical and Chirurgical Society, 23
Royden, Maude, 95
Rushcliffe Committee on Legal Aid and
Advice (1945), 129
Russell, Bertrand, 78
Russell, Dora, 86, 100, 113
Russell, 2nd Earl (John Francis
Stanley), 61–2

Sackville-West, Vita, 100
Salisbury, Lord, 55
Salvation Army, 34
Sandyford Initiative, 180
Sanger, Margaret, 92
Sanghera, Jasvinder, 185
Saunders, Alison, 178

Savage, Gail, 12, 13, 32, 71
Scharlieb, Mary, 74, 95
Schofield, Michael, 148, 152, 162
Schreiner, Olive, 34, 37
Schultz, Gladys Denny, 137
science, and sex research, 111
Scotland
and abortion, 114, 151, 155
and decriminalization of
homosexuality, 167
and divorce, 12
Scott, Edith Mabel, 61–2
Second World War
and Americans, 127
and birth control, 122–3
and birth rate, 122–3
and censorship, 119–21
and divorce, 128–9
and family planning, 122–3
and gender roles, 124
and homosexuality, 125–6
and impact of, 117
and lesbianism, 125, 126
and marriage, 121–2
and prostitution, 125
and sex education, 129
and transgressive sexual
behaviour, 125–7
and venereal disease, 117–19
and women in, 124–5
secrecy, 6–7
Section 28, 173, 182
Sengoopta, Chandak, 65
separate spheres, 15
Sex Disqualification (Removal) Act
(1919), 83
sex education
in Victorian period, 30–1, 38–9, 55–6
in pre-First World War period, 75–6
in 1930s, 105, 110–11
in Second World War, 129
in 1950s, 139
in 1960s, 161–2
in 1970s, 162
in 1980s, 173
in 1990s, 173
in 2000s, 181
and the internet, 181
and problem pages, 181–2
and venereal disease, 90, 117–18
Sex Education Society, 109
sex offenders register, 172–3

World League for Sexual Reform, 100, 109
World's Great Marriage Association, 48
Wright, Sir Almroth, 73
Wright, Helena, 106, 133–4, 135

yellow golliwogs, 152

Yellow Teddy Bears (film, 1963), 152
Young, Henry, 44–5
young people, and sexual behaviour
    among, 152, 181–2
youth clubs, 145
youth culture, 138